The Essential Gandhi

VINTAGE SPIRITUAL CLASSICS

General Editors
John F. Thornton
Susan B. Varenne

ALSO AVAILABLE

The Bhagavad Gita
The Book of Job
Buddhist Wisdom: The Diamond Sutra and The Heart Sutra
The Confessions of Saint Augustine
The Desert Fathers
Devotions Upon Emergent Occasions
Faith and Freedom: An Invitation to the Writings of Martin Luther
The Five Scrolls
The Imitation of Christ
Introduction to the Devout Life
The Little Flowers of St. Francis of Assisi
The Rule of St. Benedict
John Henry Newman: Selected Sermons, Prayers, and Devotions
A Serious Call to a Devout and Holy Life
The Spiritual Exercises of St. Ignatius
The Wisdom of John Paul II

The Essential Gandhi

AN ANTHOLOGY OF HIS WRITINGS
ON HIS LIFE, WORK, AND IDEAS

EDITED BY

Louis Fischer

PREFACE BY

Eknath Easwaran

VINTAGE SPIRITUAL CLASSICS

VINTAGE BOOKS
A DIVISION OF RANDOM HOUSE, INC.
NEW YORK

A VINTAGE SPIRITUAL CLASSICS EDITION, NOVEMBER 2002
SECOND EDITION

The research for this book was done by Deirdre Randall.

The editor is grateful to the Navajivan Trust of India for permission to use extracts from
the writings of Mahatma Gandhi. The editor also wishes to thank: Asia Publishing House,
for permission to reproduce excerpts from *A Bunch of Old Letters,* by Jawaharlal Nehru;
Narayan Desai, for permission to reproduce excerpts from *The Diary of Mahadev Desai;*
Harper & Brothers, for permission to quote from *The Life of Mahatma Gandhi,* by Louis
Fischer; and New American Library, for permission to quote from *Gandhi: His Life and
Message for the World,* by Louis Fischer.

Library of Congress Cataloging-in-Publication Data
Gandhi, Mahatma, 1869–1948.
The essential Gandhi.
Includes index.
Reprint. Originally published: New York: Random House, [1962]
1. Gandhi, Mahatma, 1869–1948.   2. Statesmen—India—Biography.
I. Fischer, Louis, 1896–1970.   II. Title.
[DS481.G3A28 1983] 954.03'5'0924 [B] 82-48890

ISBN 1-4000-3050-1 [pbk.]

Book design by Fritz Metsch

www.vintagebooks.com

Printed in the United States of America
20 19 18 17 16 15 14 13

CONTENTS

ABOUT THE VINTAGE SPIRITUAL CLASSICS

    by John F. Thornton and Susan B. Varenne, General Editors   vii

PREFACE TO THE VINTAGE SPIRITUAL CLASSICS

    EDITION *by Eknath Easwaran*   ix

FOREWORD *by Louis Fischer*   xxvii

PART ONE: THE MAN

1. Beginnings of a Great Man   3
2. Gandhi in England   21
3. Gandhi Fails   27
4. The Method Is Born   31
5. The Struggle   58
6. Victory in South Africa   75

PART TWO: THE MAHATMA

7. Facing the British in India   101
8. Segregation in India   116
9. Civil Disobedience Succeeds   121
10. Murder in an Indian Garden   128
11. Non-Violence   133
12. Gandhi's Road to Jail   142
13. The Power of the Mind   156
14. National Independence Is Not Enough   164
15. Gandhi's Message to All Men   173
16. Gandhi's Political Principles   182
17. Belief and Human Welfare   198

18. Sex, Sanitation, and Segregation   207

19. The Liberty March   224

20. How to Enjoy Jail   236

21. Fast Against Indian Prejudice   241

22. Blueprint for a Better Life   246

23. Gandhi on Socialism and Communism   264

24. Gandhi About Himself   268

25. Gandhi's Advice to Negroes   280

26. Love Versus War and Dictators   284

27. "Quit India"   295

28. Independence and Sorrow   307

29. Last Victory   322

Suggestions for Further Reading   325

Index   329

by John F. Thornton and Susan B. Varenne, General Editors

A turn or shift of sorts is becoming evident in the reflections of men and women today on their life experiences. Not quite as adamantly secular, and perhaps a little less insistent on material satisfactions, the reading public has recently developed a certain attraction to testimonies that human life is leavened by a Presence that blesses and sanctifies. Recovery, whether from addictions or personal traumas, illness, or even painful misalignments in human affairs, is evolving from the standard therapeutic goal of enhanced self-esteem. Many now seek a deeper healing that embraces the whole person, including the soul. Contemporary books provide accounts of the invisible assistance of angels. The laying on of hands in prayer has made an appearance at the hospital bedside. Guides for the spiritually perplexed have risen to the tops of bestseller lists. The darkest shadows of skepticism and unbelief, which have eclipsed the presence of the Divine in our materialistic age, are beginning to lighten and part.

If the power and presence of God are real and effective, what do they mean for human experience? What does God offer to men and women, and what does He ask in return? How do we recognize Him? Know Him? Respond to Him? God has a reputation for being both benevolent and wrathful. Which will He be for me, and when? Can these aspects of the Divine somehow be reconciled? Where is God when I suffer? Can I lose Him? Is God truthful, and are His promises to be trusted?

Are we really as precious to God as we are to ourselves and to our loved ones? Do His providence and amazing grace guide our faltering steps toward Him, even in spite of ourselves? Will God abandon us if the sin is serious enough, or if we have episodes of resistance and forgetfulness? These are fundamental questions any person might address to God during a lifetime. They are pressing and difficult, often becoming wounds in the soul of the person who yearns for the power and courage of hope, especially in stressful times.

The Vintage Spiritual Classics present the testimony of writers across the centuries who have considered all these difficulties and who have pondered the mysterious ways, unfathomable mercies and deep consolations afforded by God to those who call upon Him from out of the depths of their lives. These writers, then, are our companions, even our champions, in a common effort to discern the meaning of God in personal experience. For God is personal to us. To whom does He speak if not to us, provided we have the desire to hear Him deep within our hearts?

Each volume opens with a specially commissioned essay by a well-known contemporary writer that offers the reader an appreciation of its intrinsic value. A chronology of the general historical context of each author and his work often is provided, as are suggestions for further reading.

We offer a final word about the act of reading these spiritual classics. From the very earliest accounts of monastic practice—dating back to the fourth century—it is evident that a form of reading called *lectio divina* (divine, or spiritual, reading) was essential to any deliberate spiritual life. This kind of reading is quite different from scanning a text for useful facts and bits of information, or advancing along an exciting plot line to a climax in the action. It is, rather, a meditative approach by which the reader seeks to savor and taste the beauty and truth of every phrase and passage. This process of contemplative reading has the effect of enkindling in the reader compunction for past behavior that has been less than beautiful and true. At the same time, it increases the desire to seek a realm where all that is lovely and unspoiled may be found. There are four steps in *lectio divina:* first, to read; next to meditate; then to rest in the sense of God's nearness; and ultimately, to resolve to govern one's actions in the light of new understanding. This kind of reading is itself an act of prayer. And indeed, it is in prayer that God manifests His Presence to us.

PREFACE TO THE
VINTAGE SPIRITUAL CLASSICS
EDITION

by Eknath Easwaran

In India, Mahatma Gandhi is officially Father of the Nation. Under his leadership India attained freedom from the British Empire through a thirty-year campaign based on complete nonviolence that ended with both sides allied in respect and friendship. That alone would secure his place in the history books, but not necessarily his place in a series of the world's spiritual classics. For that we need to understand why he belongs not so much to twentieth-century history as to the timeless lineage of the world's great mystics, kith and kin with Francis of Assisi and other luminous figures whose writing appears in this series. More than that, we need to understand what his special contribution to this lineage is. The mystics, though they teach universals, are also each unique. Each has an intuition or insight, so to speak, a particular message that arises as a deep response to the needs of the times. And here Gandhi shines like a beacon. He showed us the way out of the greatest problem of our age, that of the downward spiral of violence in every sphere of life that threatens to drag civilization back into barbarism if we do not learn to master it.

Most precious of all—like every great spiritual figure, but belonging to our own times—he gives us a glimpse of our evolutionary potential as human beings. He shows us that the spiritual life, far from being otherworldly, means living to one's highest ideals and giving full expression to every facet of personality in a life of selfless service.

Even before he began his work in India, Gandhi was charged with being "a saint dabbling in politics." Rather, he insisted, it was the other way around: he was an ordinary man with ordinary human frailties trying his best to apply basic ideals in whatever

field his passion for service led him. We need to think of him as an
explorer, or perhaps a compulsive tinkerer like Thomas Edison,
constantly experimenting with his character and conduct in search
of what he called Truth in the midst of the messy details of real life.
As he did so, he was constantly trying to explain it all to himself
and to others. At any point in this volume we are dropping in on a
lifelong conversation between the seeker after Truth and an endless train of critics, not the least of whom was he himself: "What
did you mean by this? Why did you do that?" When he says he is
"not a visionary" but a "practical idealist," he means that he knows
precisely where he is going but is constantly testing his next step.

Most of us who have survived a college education probably think
of a book as some kind of edifice, or at least as a series of snapshots.
But Gandhi's words are a river. His collected works fill one hundred volumes, but only one of these, *Satyagraha in South Africa,* was
written as a book. Virtually all the rest comprise speeches, letters,
recorded conversations, and the brief columns in the weekly papers
in which he opened his heart to an eager nation. Speaking mostly
to Indians, he takes a good deal for granted. I must have read him
weekly from college on, and it was like watching him think aloud.
It makes an extraordinarily rich story, one of the twentieth century's greatest dramas; but it is also, for all that, a flood of details.

We need a way to navigate through all this, and I think our best
guide is Gandhi himself—but not Gandhi the writer or leader; we
need a sense of Gandhi the man. And that requires first a little
stage-setting.

Gandhi's India

When Gandhi was born in 1869, India had already been under foreign domination for centuries. Remarkably, for the last hundred-
odd years of this period, it lay in the grip not of an ordinary
conqueror but of a mercantile operation, the British East India
Company. Licensed by the Crown to pursue its fortunes by virtually any means it liked, including raising its own armies and wag-
ing war, the Company got a foothold on the subcontinent early in
the eighteenth century and by 1757 had managed to secure control
of the whole of north India. Sometimes in visible authority, often
content to rule behind puppet regimes, it set about systematically

draining the wealth of India into private hands. The fortunes made were staggering even to contemporary eyes; historians have observed that Great Britain's place in the Industrial Revolution was essentially financed by the loot of India.

The economic burden of this on Indians was equally staggering, though in those days no one was really looking. Within a generation cities became nightmarish extremes of wealth and poverty, with Calcutta, built by the Company, the most notorious example. But most Indians lived in villages and there, consequences were worse. Forced to grow crops for export instead of local use and then taxed heavily for the privilege of doing so, hundreds of thousands of villages under Company control lost all capacity to sustain themselves. By British figures, approximately four hundred thousand Indians died of starvation in the second quarter of the nineteenth century, but five million in the third quarter, and an appalling fifteen million between 1875 and 1900, the years in which Gandhi would come of age.

In 1857, after a century of this kind of exploitation, the spontaneous mutiny of some native troops exploded into open rebellion all over north India. That the fury spread so rapidly and erupted into such violence is a measure of how deep India's anger ran. But the Mutiny was a collection of local explosions, without unity or coordination. The Company put it down like a series of brush fires, and a bloodbath of reprisals followed.

The tragedy haunted the rest of British rule. Fear just short of panic ran to the marrow on both sides. For the British, it was clear that survival depended on keeping India divided and on putting down even a hint of insubordination immediately and ruthlessly enough to "teach a lesson." To Indians, it seemed equally clear that with a little more violence next time they might succeed. Fear and mistrust smoldered just under the surface on both sides, ready to burst into flame.

The near success of an accidental rebellion also made it obvious in London that so precious a possession as India could not remain solely in commercial hands. A few months later, with the wounds of the Mutiny still raw and open, India became an imperial colony, "the jewel in the Crown," and the British government stepped in "to do things right."

The long-term effects of this kind of domination on consciousness may not be obvious to those who have not lived under such conditions. After two or three generations, beyond the political deprivation and economic exploitation, a people begins to lose confidence in itself. Indians now grew up in the belief that they were inferior, born to be ruled over, not fit to be masters in their own home. To survive they learned to "ape the Englishman." The best and brightest went to London for their education and returned to careers in the bureaucracies of British India or, occasionally, to terrorism or revolution. In any case it was axiomatic that any road to success, personal or national, had to be by imitation of Western ways.

Into this world, just twelve years after India became a Crown colony, a boy named Mohandas Karamchand Gandhi was born. He appears to have been, as he says, a very average youth, timid, inarticulate, painfully shy. Like everyone else whose family could afford it, he was sent off to London as a teenager to learn to become an English gentleman and to study law. Depressed by failure on his return, he decided to "try his luck" in a temporary job in South Africa, where a handful of Indian traders had made a niche for themselves in a community of a hundred thousand indentured Indian laborers working in mines and fields. A decidedly unpromising nobody, he left India in 1893 and dropped out of sight completely.

By the time he returned in 1915, this "nobody" was hailed as *mahatma*, or "great soul." Those twenty years in South Africa hold the secret of the "essential Gandhi." We will return to look there more closely, for it is that transformation—not just an extraordinary success story, but the utter remaking of personality—that holds Gandhi's ultimate significance for us today.

I like to say I grew up not in British India but in Gandhi's India, because I was born just a few years before his return and he dominated my world like a Colossus. I was too young (and my little village too isolated) to have much awareness of the tragedies that impelled him into national leadership in those early years. Only when I went to college, at the age of sixteen, did I discover his weekly "viewspaper," *Young India*. Gandhi was pouring his heart out in those pages, and despite the country's widespread illiteracy, I daresay his words reached into every one of India's villages as copies of the paper were passed from hand to hand and read out to audiences everywhere along the way.

Today Gandhi is associated with marches and demonstrations. I look back and realize with some surprise that in the currency of the time each of these grand events seemed to fizzle and that most of those years Gandhi spent not in marching but in rebuilding foundations, healing divisions, unifying the country by urging us to take responsibility for our own problems. If we got our house in order, he told us, independence would fall like a ripe fruit as a natural consequence.

He enlisted everyone in this task, not only the underdogs but the upper dogs too; some of India's wealthiest industrialists were not only benefactors but personal friends. By his example, he led India's leaders and elite to focus the work of independence on the seven hundred thousand villages that everyone had forgotten but that make up the heart of India. It was a completely characteristic approach: begin at home, begin with yourself, correct the underlying conditions, and suffer the consequences. The rest will fall into place.

One of the first lessons Gandhi had learned in South Africa was to begin by bringing people together onto higher ground. India was exploitable because it exploited our own people. We were weak because we were divided into innumerable factions, each seeking its own gain, making it simple to play us against each other—an old Roman Empire tactic practiced by the East India Company and made official imperial policy after the Mutiny. His analysis made perfect sense, once grasped, but it wasn't a matter of politics to Gandhi. It was an obvious corollary of the unity of life, in which the welfare of all of us together was bound up with those whom the poet Rabindranath Tagore (1861–1941) called "the lowest, the lowliest, and the lost."

These ideas sound conventional enough today, but to put them into practice is always a shock. In India they caused an earthquake. By linking independence with the way we treated one another, Gandhi shook the country from top to bottom. For centuries, millions of Indians who were considered below any caste had been cruelly exploited by caste Hindus. Gandhi made a cornerstone of his campaign for national freedom the freedom of those whom the rest of India called "untouchable." He campaigned for them from the Himalayas to India's southernmost tip.

Everywhere he told us that all of us were one and that we would never have the unity to throw off foreign rule, or even be worthy of self-government, until we ceased exploiting our own people. He gave outcaste Hindus a new name—Harijans, "children of God"—and called on temples to open their doors to them and on caste Hindus to bring them into their homes. It was an impossible appeal because it attacked ways of thinking ground deep into unconscious conditioning for countless generations. Yet people all over India responded. Over and over I would think of the words of Jesus when he comes and tells the paralytic, "Arise, take up your bed and walk." The man *had* to walk! And with equal joy and amazement, India arose too.

My college years were turbulent ones in Indian affairs. I must have been a junior on the night of December 31, 1929, when at the stroke of midnight the Indian Congress declared independence and unfurled the flag of a free India. Its motto, pure Gandhi, came from our most ancient scriptures: *Satyam eva jayate,* "Truth ever conquers." Jawaharlal Nehru said later that on that night "we made a tryst with destiny." Those were thrilling times for a village boy away at college, but they were only the beginning. Like the Americans with their Declaration of Independence, we had also made a tryst with war.

But this was to be a war without weapons. In March 1930, Gandhi wrote the British Viceroy that he intended to launch nonviolent resistance by marching to the sea to break a statute that made the sale and manufacture of salt a government monopoly, adding that he would accept the consequences cheerfully and that he was inviting the rest of India to do the same. That letter, Louis Fischer observes with pleasure, "was surely the strangest ever received by the head of a government." But the Salt March provided brilliant theater. Gandhi and his small band of volunteers took fourteen days to reach the sea, stopping at every village along the way and making headlines around the world. By the time he reached the ocean the procession was several thousand strong. When he picked up a handful of sea salt from the beach and raised it as a signal to the rest of India, millions of people around the world must have watched him on the newsreels. But in India nobody needed the media. The country simply exploded in utterly nonviolent disobedience of British law.

What no one dared to expect was that in the face of police charges, beatings, arrests, and worse, the nonviolence held. Everyone knew Gandhi would drop the campaign if there was any violence on our part, no matter what the provocation. We "kept the pledge" day after day, filling the jails literally to overflowing. Many veterans of those days recall their terms in prison as the high point of their lives; Gandhi had made "suffering for Truth" a badge of honor.

I can't describe the effect this had on me, on all of India. Obviously it was high drama, but most significant for me was the human alchemy being wrought. These were ordinary people, family, friends, school chums, acquaintances, men and women we saw daily in the marketplace or at temple, at work or school; all ages, high caste and low, educated and ignorant, cultured and crude, rich beyond calculation and unbelievably poor. How had they suddenly become heroes and heroines, cheerfully stepping forward to be beaten with steel-tipped batons, hauled off to jail, stripped of their livelihoods, sometimes even shot? Called to be more than human, we looked around and saw that we were capable of it. Gandhi was right: the body might be frail but the spirit was boundless. We were much, much stronger than we had thought, capable of great things, not because we were great but because there was divinity in us all—even in those who swung the clubs and wielded the guns.

For me, the burning question became: what was the secret of this alchemy? Everyone in India knew that Gandhi had transformed himself in South Africa, but most of these millions of followers had scarcely even laid eyes on him. How was it that ordinary people became heroes and heroines simply through his example?

Gandhi's Secret

Graduate studies took me to a university in central India very near Gandhi's ashram, the little community he called Sevagram, "village of service." For the first time for me he was actually within reach. One weekend I decided to visit him and perhaps find answers to my questions.

I had to walk the last few miles from the train station, and the sun was low on the horizon when we arrived. A crowd had gathered outside a little thatched cottage where Gandhi had been closeted in urgent national negotiations since early morning. My heart sank. He would be tired after all that, tense and irritable, with little time for guests like me.

But when the cottage door opened, out popped a lithe brown figure of about seventy with the springy step and mischievous eyes of a teenager, laughing and joking with those around him. He might as well have been playing Bingo all day. Later I read that a journalist once asked Gandhi if he didn't think he should take a vacation. Gandhi had laughed and replied, "I'm always on vacation." That's just what I saw.

He was striding off for his evening walk and motioned us to come along. But after a while most of the crowd fell away. He didn't simply walk fast; he seemed to fly. With his white shawl flapping and his gawky bare legs he looked like a crane about to take off. I have always been a walker, but I had to keep breaking into a jog to keep up with him.

My list of questions was growing. This was a man in his seventies—the twilight of life by Indian standards of those days—burdened daily with responsibility for four hundred million people. He must have lived under intense pressure fifteen hours a day, every day, for probably fifty years. Why didn't he get burned out? How was he able to maintain this freshness? What was the source of this apparently endless vitality and good humor?

After the walk and a meal it was time for Gandhi's prayer meeting. By this time it was dark, and hurricane lanterns had been lit all around. Gandhi sat straight with his back against a tree, and I managed to get a seat close by, where I could fix my whole heart on him. A Japanese monk opened with a Buddhist chant and then a British lady began one of Gandhi's favorite hymns, John Henry Newman's "Lead, Kindly Light." Gandhi had closed his eyes in deep concentration, as if absorbed in the words.

Then his secretary, Mahadev Desai, began to recite from the Bhagavad Gita, India's best-known scripture, which is set on a battlefield that Gandhi said represents the human heart. In the verses being recited, a warrior prince named Arjuna, who represents you and me, asks Sri Krishna, the Lord within, how one can recognize a person who is aware of God every moment of his life. And Sri Krishna replies in eighteen magnificent verses unparalleled in the spiritual literature of the world:

He lives in wisdom who sees himself in all and all in him, who has renounced every selfish desire and sense craving tormenting the heart. Neither agitated by grief nor hankering after pleasure, he lives free from lust, fear, and anger. Established in meditation, he is truly wise. . . . As rivers flow into the ocean but cannot make the vast ocean overflow, so flow the streams of the sense world into the sea of peace that is the sage.

Sanskrit is a sonorous language, perfect for recitation. As Arjuna's opening question reverberated through the night air, Gandhi became absolutely motionless. His absorption was so profound that he scarcely seemed to breathe, as if he had been lifted out of time. Suddenly the Gita's question—"Tell me of the man established in wisdom"—became a living dialogue. I wasn't just hearing the answer, I was seeing it, looking at a man who to the best of my knowledge fulfilled every condition the Gita lays down:

That one I love who is incapable of ill will, who is friendly and compassionate. Living beyond the reach of "I" and "mine," and of pleasure and pain, patient, contented, self-controlled, firm in faith, with all his heart and all his mind given to me—with such a one I am in love.

Not agitating the world nor by it agitated, he stands above the sway of elation, competition, and fear. . . . Who looks upon friend and foe with equal regard, not buoyed up by praise or cast down by blame, alike in heat and cold, pleasure and pain, free from selfish attachments, the same in honor and dishonor, quiet, ever full, in harmony everywhere, firm in faith—such a one is dear to me.

I had always loved the Gita for its literary beauty, and I must have read it and listened to commentaries on it many times. But seeing it illustrated by Gandhi opened its inner meaning. Not just "illustrated": he had *become* those words, become a living embodiment of what they meant. "Free from selfish desires" didn't mean indifference; it meant not trying to get anything for yourself, giving your best whatever comes without depending on anything except the Lord within. And the goal clearly wasn't the extinction of personality. Gandhi practically defined personality. He was truly original; the rest of us seemed bland by comparison, as if living in our sleep. He spoke of making himself zero but seemed to have become instead a kind of cosmic conduit, a channel for some tremendous universal power, an "instrument of peace."

These verses are the key to Gandhi's life. They describe not a political leader but a man of God, in words that show this is the very height of human expression. They tell us not what to do with our lives but what to be. And they are universal. We see essentially the same portrait in all scriptures, reflected in the lives of spiritual aspirants everywhere.

The reason is that the experience itself is universal. The Bhagavad Gita is a comprehensive presentation of what Leibniz called the Perennial Philosophy because it crops up in every culture and every age. The Perennial Philosophy is characterized by three deep convictions born of direct experience. First, underlying everything in the phenomenal world is a changeless reality, which most religions call God. Second, this changeless reality is present in every living creature and can be personally discovered by following certain strenuous disciplines that remove the layers of conditioning that cover it. And third, this discovery is the real goal of life. Whatever else we may accomplish, nothing will satisfy us until we realize God in our own consciousness.

Gandhi himself expresses all this in famous words as carefully chosen as if he were drafting a legal brief:

I do dimly perceive that whilst everything around me is ever changing, ever dying, there is underlying all that change a Living Power that is changeless, that holds all together, that creates, dissolves, and re-creates. That informing Power or Spirit is God. And since nothing else I see merely through the senses can or will persist, He alone is.

And is this power benevolent or malevolent? I see it as purely benevolent, for I can see that in the midst of death life persists, in the midst of untruth truth persists, in the midst of darkness light persists. Hence I gather that God is Life, Truth, Light. He is love. He is the supreme Good.

But He is no God who merely satisfies the intellect, if He ever can. God to be God must rule the heart and transform it. . . . This can only be done through a definite realization, more real than the five senses can ever produce. . . . It is proved not by extraneous evidence but in the transformed conduct and character of those who have felt the presence of God within.

The Transformation

But I have to confess that this insight, though inspiring, did not convey to me the significance it does today. I wasn't really a religious person, and while I respected those who were, at that time in my life I had never given a thought to leading the spiritual life. I had seen that Gandhi was really a mystic and the living embodiment of the Bhagavad Gita, but how had he managed to translate the Gita into his very consciousness? Not until I took to meditation myself did the rest of the puzzle fall into place.

There are really two chapters in the story of Gandhi in South Africa. The second covers the eight years after 1906 in which Gandhi developed and tested his new method of nonviolent resistance. But the first chapter to me is even more important, because it holds the chrysalis of his transformation.

The crucial event came soon after his arrival in South Africa, when Gandhi was thrown off a train at Maritzburg station because of the color of his skin (p. 31). Something similar must have happened to every non-European in South Africa. But there are times in human affairs—sometimes in a profound external crisis, sometimes for no apparent reason at all—when superficial awareness is torn open and a channel into deeper consciousness is laid bare. That is what happened to Gandhi that night. It was bitter cold, and his coat and luggage were with the stationmaster, but he would not go and beg for them. He sat up all night thinking furiously about what had happened and what to do. He felt a strong impulse to turn around and go back to India rather than live in a place where he would be expected to put up with this kind of indignity.

By dawn he had made a curious resolve that came right from the depths of his heart: he would stay and he would fight, but against racial prejudice and on behalf of all, and in that fight he would not resort to any tactic that would diminish the humanity he was fighting for. He would cling to the truth and suffer the consequences in trying to "root out this disease" that was infecting all parties involved.

The following day he proceeded on the next leg of his journey by carriage. There again he met with prejudice; though there was room in the carriage, he was forced by the driver to sit in a degrading place outside. When he refused, the driver tried to drag him off, alternately beating him and pulling at him; Gandhi refused to yield but refused also to defend himself and clung to the carriage rail until the white passengers were moved to pity and begged the driver to let him join them at their side. It was a curiously symbolic moment. No philosophy was involved; it would take years for him to make the "matchless weapon" of nonviolence out of this dogged determination never to retaliate but never to yield. But he had become a different man. The Sanskrit scriptures would say that on that night in Maritzburg "faith entered his heart." In practice this means that in the very depths of his consciousness he had glimpsed a new image of himself. He was not just a separate, physical crea- ture; he saw that he—and, crucially, every other human being— was essentially spiritual, with "strength [that] does not come from physical capacity [but] from an indomitable will."

After this first instinctive "holding on to Truth," Gandhi turned inward. He had met injustice; it degraded everyone, but everyone accepted it: How could he change *himself* to help everyone involved see more clearly? Somehow, dimly at first, but with increasing sureness, he had already grasped that a person can be an "instru- ment of peace," a catalyst of understanding, by getting himself out of the way. This marks the beginning of his life as a spiritual aspi- rant, and in the years that follow, hidden under the affairs of a ter- ribly busy life, we can see him working tirelessly on the business of mystics everywhere: training his mind, transforming personal pas- sions, "reducing himself to zero."

It is this spiritual aspirant who is the "essential Gandhi." With- out understanding this we cannot really understand what he was trying to do and how he was trying to do it, nor, more important, can we understand what his life offers for the modern world. It makes him blood brother to other, more clearly mystical figures like Francis of Assisi or Teresa of Avila. From this family relation- ship we can see that his transformation follows the traditional pat- tern of mystics everywhere.

Gandhi gives himself away at the very outset of this volume when, surprisingly, he says, "What I want to achieve—what I have been striving and pining to achieve these thirty years—is self- realization, to see God face to face" (p. 3). Writing for Indians, he uses the word *mokṣa,* a Hindu term for a state of being that is not at all Hindu but universal. The dictionary definition, which

Louis Fischer understandably gives here, misses the point. *Moksha,* like the similarly misunderstood *nirvana,* refers to the state of being empty of oneself but full of God. One of the hallmarks of the Perennial Philosophy is the recognition that nothing separates us from God but self-will, the deep clinging to oneself as something separate from the rest of creation. The whole of the spiritual life is a systematic attempt to remove this illusion of separateness once and for all. The task sounds bleak until we see, through a living example, that this "zero" is what allows the infinitude of God to burst forth through the human personality. Meister Eckhart says inimitably, "God expects but one thing of you: that you should come out of yourself in so far as you are a created being and let God be God in you." And again: "God is *bound* to act, to pour himself into you, as soon as he finds you ready."

St. Francis took the Gospels as his model; Gandhi took the Gita. For both it was a systematic daily practice. Translating the Gita into character, conduct, and consciousness was precisely what Gandhi was doing in South Africa. He knew it by heart, knew it *in* his heart, studied it over and over every day, used it in prayer until it became a living presence. It was, he says, his "dictionary of daily reference." Whenever he had a question about what to do or how to act, he took it to the Gita. Then, with the willpower that was his surest gift, he set about bringing his life into conformity with its teachings, no matter how unpleasant or inconvenient that might have been. Those years in South Africa were a studio in which Gandhi worked every day like an artist, studying his model and chipping away at the block of stone that hid the vision he was striving to set free, painstakingly removing everything that is not Gita.

In many ways, allowing for differences in personal style, Gandhi goes about this very much like every other mystic. The crucial difference is that he does not withdraw from public life to do it. All his training is in the midst of around-the-clock public service. In most mystics we see personal passions being consumed in the love of God. Gandhi was transformed by his deep-running, passionate love of other people, wherein he found God, and an increasing desire to lose himself in salving their wounds and sorrows. Many mystics abrade their selfishness away; Gandhi dissolved his in love and service.

He made astonishing personal discoveries in those years, and perhaps the most significant for us today is that anger can be transformed. It is raw energy that can be transformed and fed back into a positive channel. Anger transformed becomes compassion. In South Africa, beginning in his own home, Gandhi learned to transform his anger and then harness it in service. All the furious indignation of that night at Maritzburg station gets channeled first into transforming his bursts of temper with his wife.

In every tradition, by whatever name it is called—"training the mind," "guarding the heart," "transforming the passions"—this is the essence of the spiritual life. Gandhi was a terribly passionate young man with a hot, imperious temper. All that passion transformed is what fueled a passionate life of selfless service. "I have learnt through bitter experience," he says later, "the one supreme lesson to conserve my anger, and as heat conserved is transmuted into energy, even so our anger controlled can be transmuted into a power which can move the world." That one sentence is enough to place him among the world's greatest teachers. He is telling us this is a skill; it can be learned. And as it is learned, it changes everything in its field.

His "staff of life" through these transformations, Gandhi tells us, was prayer, but not petitionary prayer in the usual sense. Though he writes about prayer in the language of a Protestant Christian, "there is nothing in it analogous to the Christian prayers in which people ask for definite things." When he describes his prayer as "inward communion," he seems more to be talking about what the Spanish mystics call "the prayer of quiet" or contemplation. In any case he makes it clear over and over that for him "prayer is nothing else but an intense longing of the heart." Such prayer could be wordless, and sometimes was, but most often his prayer seems to be absorption in the words of the Gita ("the constant reading of the Gita has filled my life with prayer") or a most important practice that is easy to miss in his writings: *Ramanama,* the repetition of the name of God, a kind of rosary that Gandhi learned in childhood from his nurse.

This technique of purifying the heart by repetition of the Holy Name is found in all major spiritual traditions. In the West today, it is probably most familiar from the little book known as *The Way of a Pilgrim,* which describes the use of the Jesus Prayer. We do not know when Gandhi began this practice regularly, but it is clearly part of his life in South Africa from the earliest years.

The Way of a Pilgrim describes vividly the state in which this kind of prayer becomes "self-acting": begins to repeat itself, so to speak, which is the traditional understanding of St. Paul's injunction to "pray without ceasing." There are signs by which this can be recognized, and I have very little doubt that Gandhi was established in unbroken prayer when he launched his first *satyagraha* campaign in South Africa in 1906. To my knowledge, when the "heartfelt yearning" that Gandhi described is poured into the repetition of the name of God—precisely as in the mystical traditions of Christianity, Judaism, Islam, and Buddhism—nothing is more effective in transforming anger into compassion, ill will into good will, hatred into love.

It is important for us in the modern world that there is absolutely nothing in this of conventional religion. Gandhi observed no rituals, didn't go to temple, read all scriptures, found Truth in all religions and "some error" in all as well. His God, though a living presence, is an impersonal force—Law rather than Lawgiver; Truth, Love, Goodness, the unity of life. When he repeated the name of God in Ramanama, he was calling not on the Rama of traditional Hindu devotion but on "an indefinable mysterious Power that pervades everything," "the eternal, the unborn, the one without a second," and that sustaining Power, present in the heart of every creature, is within; there is no appeal to an external power. I do not know at what point in his life he began to say "I am not only a Hindu; I am a Moslem, a Christian, a Jew," but I think it would be true at any point once he "crossed the Sahara of atheism" as a youth.

For Gandhi, as for almost all mystics, the last personal passion to be transformed was sexual desire. Characteristically, the point of decision came not in seclusion but during the long days and nights of bearing stretchers as a medic during the brutal suppression of a Zulu rebellion against the British in South Africa. Gandhi's agony over the suffering released a desire to serve that swept every personal desire into its path. It is no coincidence that just weeks after he took his vow of celibacy—for the third but last time, he tells us with dry humor—came the great scene in Johannesburg's Imperial Theatre when he rose to address a crowd of angry Indians protesting a new piece of anti-Indian legislation and hit on the idea of offering nonviolent resistance. From that day (September 11, 1906) he stepped out onto the world stage.

Nonviolence

"It was only when I had learned to reduce myself to zero," Gandhi says, "that I was able to evolve the power of *satyagraha* in South Africa." *Satyagraha*—literally "holding on to Truth"—is the name he coined for this method of fighting without violence or retaliation.

Gandhi had a genius for making abstruse ideas practical, and one of the best examples comes when he explains the basis of *satyagraha*. In Sanskrit the word *satya*, "truth," is derived from *sat*, "that which is." Truth *is;* untruth merely appears to be. Gandhi brought this out of the realm of Ph.D. dissertations and into the middle of politics. It means, he said, that evil is real only insofar as we support it. The essence of holding on to Truth is to withdraw support of what is wrong. If enough people do this—if, he maintained, even one person does it from a great enough depth—evil has to collapse from lack of support.

Gandhi was never theoretical. He learned by doing. *Satyagraha* continued to be refined in action all his life; he was experimenting up to the day he was assassinated. But the essentials are present from the very beginning in South Africa.

First is the heartfelt conviction that a wrong situation wrongs both sides. Europeans and Indians alike were degraded by race prejudice; a lasting solution, therefore, had to relieve this burden for all involved. In spiritual terms this follows from the unity of life, which is what Gandhi's Truth means in practice. But it is also profoundly practical, because only a solution for everyone can actually resolve the problem and move the situation forward. More than just both sides "winning," everyone is a little nobler, a little more human, for the outcome.

Equally essential but hardest to grasp intellectually, nonviolent action means voluntary suffering. That in fact is how it works. Gandhi discovered in South Africa that reason is ultimately impotent to change the heart. Race prejudice was already causing suffering; the task of *satyagraha* was to make that suffering visible. Then, sooner or later, opposition had to turn to sympathy, because deep in everyone, however hidden, is embedded an awareness of our common humanity.

Clearly there is nothing passive about this kind of resistance. "The nonviolence of my conception," Gandhi says, "is a more

active and a more real fighting than retaliation, whose very nature
is to increase wickedness." That is the point: violence only makes a
situation worse. It cannot help but provoke a violent response.

Strictly speaking, *satyagraha* is not "nonviolence." It is a means, a
method. The word we translate as "nonviolence" is a Sanskrit
word central in Buddhism as well: *ahimsa,* the complete absence of
violence in word and even thought as well as action. This sounds
negative, just as "nonviolence" sounds passive. But like the English
word "flawless," *ahimsa* denotes perfection. *Ahimsa* is uncondi-
tional love; *satyagraha* is love in action.

I said at the outset that every mystic seems to have a unique mission. Gandhi's was not really the liberation of India. That was a
tremendous achievement, but India was essentially a showcase, a
stage for the world to see what nonviolence can accomplish in the
highly imperfect world of real life. I haven't even touched the surface of those achievements; there are miracles enough in Gandhi's
story to show that human nature is much loftier than we imagine.
Our future depends on making that discovery.

"There is nothing new about *ahimsa,*" Gandhi insisted. "It is as
old as the hills." Throughout history all lasting relationships, all
communities and societies, even civilization itself, have been built
on the renunciation of violence for the sake of some greater good.
Every conflict large or small is an opportunity to advance a little in
evolution or move backwards. In this sense I believe civilization
has reached a crossroads. A handful of angry people today, perhaps
even one angry person, can wreak destruction on the other side of
the globe. Violence has ceased to surprise us even in our homes and
schools. We have made a culture of violence, and unless we change
direction, it can destroy a great deal of progress that has been
painstakingly built up over centuries of human evolution.

In today's language, Gandhi gave us the basis for a technology of
peace. He gave us tools for resolving conflicts of all kinds, which
anyone can learn to use. But it is urgent to understand his message
that nonviolence is a way of thinking, a way of life—not a tactic, but
a way of putting love to work in resolving problems, healing relationships, and generally raising the quality of our lives. We don't
begin on the grand stage he acted on; he did not begin that way himself. He began with his personal relationships, aware that he could
not expect to put out the fires of anger and hatred elsewhere if the

same fires smoldered in his own home and heart. His nonviolence is not a political weapon or a technique for social change so much as it is an essential art—perhaps *the* essential art—of civilization.

In other words, nonviolence is a skill, just like learning to read. Love is a skill. Forgiveness is a skill. The transformation of anger is a skill. All these can be learned. We cannot say we aren't capable of nonviolence; all we can say is we are not willing to do what is necessary to learn.

Finally, for spiritual seekers of all persuasions, Gandhi showed us that the spiritual life need not mean retiring to a monastery or cave. It can be pursued in the midst of family, community, and a career of selfless service. Even without reference to spirituality, if we look upon the overriding purpose of life as making a lasting contribution to our family and society, Gandhi gave us a higher image for ourselves, a glorification of the innate goodness in the human being, whose joy lies in living for the welfare of all.

It has been said that the world's great mystics must come from the same country because they all speak the same language. Gandhi and St. Francis, Teresa of Avila and the Compassionate Buddha are brothers and sisters. They seem so lofty that we sometimes feel they belong to another race or come from a different realm of being. But this does them a great disservice, for their message is just the contrary. They are our kinsfolk as well, and the country they come from is our own. They are like a relative who has disappeared for years and then returns to tell of a fabulous land. They give us maps, fill our ears with tips about which roads are safe and where the hostels are, tell us stories, show us their slides: anything to convince us that this country they have discovered is our real home and that, until we find our way there, as Augustine says, nothing else can fill the homesickness in our hearts.

This is Gandhi's ultimate message for us, and no sentence of his is more significant than where he says—and remember, this fussy old man never let so much as a single word stand if he did not know it to be true from his own experience—"I have not the shadow of a doubt that any man or woman can achieve what I have, if he or she would make the same effort and cultivate the same hope and faith."

FOREWORD

No man knows himself or can describe himself with fidelity. But he can reveal himself. This is especially true of Gandhi. He believed in revealing himself. He regarded secrecy as the enemy of freedom—not only the freedom of India but the freedom of man. He exposed even the innermost personal thoughts which individuals usually regard as private. In nearly a half-century of prolific writing, speaking, and subjecting his ideas to the test of actions, he painted a detailed self-portrait of his mind, heart, and soul.

Gandhi was a unique person, a great person, perhaps the greatest figure of the last nineteen hundred years. And his words have been preserved as they came from his mouth and pen.

Then let the Mahatma speak. What he said has an intimate relevance to many of our problems today.

Louis Fischer
Princeton, New Jersey
March 16, 1961

PART ONE

The Man

[1]

BEGINNINGS OF A GREAT MAN

[To the end of his days, Gandhi attempted to master and remake himself. He called his autobiography *The Story of My Experiments with Truth,* an "experiment" being an operation within and upon oneself. The following excerpts are taken from the book.]

. . . [It] is not my purpose to attempt a real autobiography. I simply want to tell the story of my numerous experiments with truth, and as my life consists of nothing but those experiments, it is true that the story will take the shape of an autobiography. But I shall not mind if every page of it speaks only of my experiments. I believe, or at any rate flatter myself with the belief, that a connected account of all these experiments will not be without benefit to the reader. My experiments in the political field are now known, not only in India but to a certain extent to the "civilized" world. For me, they have not much value and the title of Mahatma [Great Soul] that they have won for me, has, therefore, even less. Often the title has deeply pained me and there is not a moment I can recall when it may be said to have tickled me. But I should certainly like to narrate my experiments in the spiritual field which are known only to myself and from which I have derived such power as I possess for working in the political field. If the experiments are really spiritual, then there can be no room for self-praise. They can only add to my humility. The more I reflect and look back on the past, the more vividly do I feel my limitations.

What I want to achieve—what I have been striving and pining to achieve these thirty years—is self-realization, to see God face to face, to attain Moksha [Salvation—oneness with God and freedom from later incarnations]. I live and move and have my being in pursuit of this goal. All that I do by way of speaking and writing, and all my ventures in the political field are directed to this same end. . . .[1]

To see the universal and all-pervading Spirit of Truth face to face one must be able to love the meanest of creation as oneself. And a man who aspires after that cannot afford to keep out of any field of life. That is why my devotion to Truth has drawn me into the field of politics and I can say without the slightest hesitation and yet in all humility, that those who say that religion has nothing to do with politics do not know what religion means.[2]

. . . In the march towards Truth, anger, selfishness, hatred, etc., naturally give way, for otherwise Truth would be impossible to attain. . . . A successful search for Truth means complete deliverance from the dual throng, such as of love and hate, happiness and misery. . . .[3]

[As] I have all along believed that what is possible for one is possible for all, my experiments have not been conducted in the closet but in the open. . . .[4]

The Gandhis belong to the Bania [Businessman] caste and seem to have been originally grocers. ["Gandhi" means grocer.] But for three generations, from my grandfather, they have been Prime Ministers in several Kathiawad [Western India] States. Uttamchand Gandhi, alias Ota Gandhi, my grandfather, must have been a man of principle. State intrigues compelled him to leave Porbandar, where he was Diwan [Prime Minister] and to seek refuge in Junagadh [the nearby little state]. There he saluted the Nawab [Ruler] with his left hand. Someone noticing the apparent discourtesy asked for an explanation, which was thus given: "The right hand is already pledged to Porbandar."

Ota Gandhi married a second time, having lost his first wife. He had four sons by his first wife and two by his second wife. I do not think that in my childhood I ever felt or knew that these sons . . . were not all of the same mother. The fifth of these six brothers was Karamchand Gandhi, alias Kaba Gandhi, and the sixth was Tulsi-

---

[1] M. K. Gandhi, *The Story of My Experiments with Truth* (London: Phoenix Press, 1949), Introduction, pp. xi–xii.

[2] *Ibid.*, "Farewell," p. 420.

[3] *Ibid.*, Part IV, Chapter 37, p. 288.

[4] *Ibid.*, Introduction, p. xii.

das Gandhi. Both these brothers were Prime Ministers in Porbandar, one after the other. Kaba Gandhi was my father. He was a member of the Rajasthanik Court. It is now extinct but in those days it was a very influential body for settling disputes between the chiefs and their fellow clansmen. He was for some time Prime Minister in Rajkot and then in Vankaner. He was a pensioner of the Rajkot State when he died.

Kaba Gandhi married four times in succession, having lost his wife each time by death. He had two daughters by his first and second marriages. His last wife, Putlibai, bore him a daughter and three sons, I being the youngest.

My father was a lover of his clan, truthful, brave and generous but short-tempered. To a certain extent he might have been given even to carnal pleasures. For he married for the fourth time when he was over forty. But he was incorruptible and had earned a name for strict impartiality in his family as well as outside. His loyalty to the state was well-known. [A British] Assistant Political Agent [once] spoke insultingly of the Rajkot Thakore Saheb, his chief, and he stood up to the insult. The agent was angry and asked Kaba Gandhi to apologize. This he refused to do and was therefore kept under detention for a few hours. But when the Agent saw that Kaba Gandhi was adamant he ordered him to be released.

My father never had any ambition to accumulate riches and left us very little property.

The outstanding impression my mother has left on my memory is that of saintliness. She was deeply religious. She would not think of taking her meals without her daily prayers. Going to Haveli—the Vaishnava [Orthodox Hindu] temple—was one of her daily duties. As far as my memory can go back I do not remember her having ever missed the Chaturmas [a fasting period similar to Lent]. She would take the hardest vows and keep them without flinching. Illness was no excuse for relaxing them. . . . To keep two or three consecutive fasts was nothing to her. Living on one meal a day during Chaturmas was a habit with her. Not content with that she fasted every alternate day during one Chaturmas. During another Chaturmas she vowed not to have food without seeing the sun. We children on those days would stand, staring at the sky, waiting to announce the appearance of the sun to our mother. Everyone knows that at the height of the rainy season the sun often does not condescend to show his face. And I remember days when, at his sudden appearance, we would rush and announce it to her. She would run out to see with her own eyes, but by that time the fugitive sun would be gone, thus depriving her of her meal. "That does not matter," she would say cheerfully, "God did not want me to eat today." And she would return to her round of duties.

Of these parents I was born at Porbandar, otherwise known as Sudamapuri, on the second October, 1869. I passed my childhood in Porbandar. I recollect having been put to school. It was with some difficulty that I got through the multiplication tables. The fact that I recollect nothing more of those days than having learnt, in company with other boys, to call our teacher all kinds of names would strongly suggest that my intellect must have been sluggish and my memory raw.[5]

I must have been about seven when my father left Porbandar for Rajkot to become a member of the Rajasthanik Court. There I was put into a primary school . . . I could have been only a mediocre student. From this school I went to the suburban school and thence to the high school, having already reached my twelfth year. I do not remember having ever told a lie during this short period either to my teachers or to my schoolmates. I used to be very shy and avoided all company. My books and my lessons were my sole companions. To be at school at the stroke of the hour and to run back home as soon as the school closed—that was my daily habit. I literally ran back because I could not bear to talk to anybody. I was afraid even lest anyone should poke fun at me.

[When he grew older, however, he found some congenial mates and played in the streets. He also played by the sea.]

[An] incident which occurred at the examination during my first year at the high school . . . is worth recording. Mr. Giles, the [British] Education Inspector, had come on a visit of inspection. He had set us five words to write as a spelling exercise. One of the words was "kettle." I had misspelt it. The teacher tried to prompt me with the point of his boot but I would not be prompted. It was

[5] *Ibid.,* Part I, Chapter 1, pp. 3–5.

beyond me to see that he wanted me to copy the spelling from my neighbor's slate for I had thought the teacher was there to supervise us against copying. The result was that all the boys except myself were found to have spelt every word correctly. Only I had been stupid. The teacher tried later to bring this stupidity home to me but without effect. I never could learn the art of "copying."

Yet the incident did not in the least diminish my respect for my teacher. I was by nature blind to the faults of elders. Later I came to know many other failings of this teacher but my regard for him remained the same. For I had learnt to carry out the orders of elders, not to scan their actions.[6]

[But compliance at school did not preclude revolt outside it.]

A [young] relative and I became fond of smoking . . . we began to steal pennies from the servant's pocket money . . . to purchase Indian cigarettes. . . .

But we were far from satisfied. . . . Our want of independence began to smart. It was unbearable that we should be unable to do anything without the elders' permission. At last, in sheer disgust, we decided to commit suicide!

. . . But our courage failed us. Supposing we were not instantly killed? And what was the good of killing ourselves? . . .

I realized it was not as easy to commit suicide as to contemplate it. And since then, whenever I have heard of someone threatening to commit suicide it has little or no effect on me.

The thought of suicide ultimately resulted in both of us bidding goodbye to the habit of smoking . . . and of stealing the servant's pennies. . . .[7]

[Presently, adult matters claimed the child's attention.]

. . . It is my painful duty to have to record here my marriage at the age of thirteen. As I see the youngsters of the same age about me who are under my care, and think of my own marriage, I am inclined to pity myself and to congratulate them on having escaped my lot. I can see no moral argument in support of such a preposterously early marriage.

[6] *Ibid.,* Part I, Chapter 6, pp. 5–6.
[7] *Ibid.,* Part I, Chapter 8, p. 22.

Let the reader make no mistake. I was married, not betrothed. . . . It appears that I was betrothed thrice, though without my knowledge. I was told that two girls chosen for me had died. . . .

Marriage among Hindus is no simple matter. The parents of the bride and the bridegroom often bring themselves to ruin over it. They waste their substance, they waste their time. Months are taken up over the preparations—in making clothes and ornaments and in preparing [menus] for dinners. Each tries to outdo the other in the number and variety of courses to be prepared. Women, whether they have a voice or no, sing themselves hoarse, even get ill, and disturb the peace of their neighbors. These in their turn quietly put up with all the turmoil and bustle, all the dirt and filth, representing the remains of the feast, because they know a time will come when they also will be behaving in the same manner.

. . . I do not think [my marriage] meant to me anything more than the prospect of good clothes to wear, drum beating, marriage processions, rich dinners and a strange girl to play with. The carnal desire came later. . . . Everything on that day seemed to me right and proper and pleasing. There was also my own eagerness to get married. And as everything my father did then struck me as beyond reproach, the recollection of those things is fresh in my memory. . . .

[The bride was Kasturbai, the daughter of a Porbandar merchant named Gokuldas Makanji. The marriage lasted sixty-two years.]

. . . I can picture to myself, even today, how we sat on our wedding dais, how we performed the Seven Steps, how we, the newly wedded husband and wife, put the sweet Wheat Cake into each other's mouths, and how we began to live together. And oh! That first night! Two innocent children all unwittingly hurled themselves into the ocean of life. My brother's wife had thoroughly coached me about my behavior on the first night. I do not know who had coached my wife. I have never asked her about it. . . . The reader may be sure that we were too nervous to face each other. We were certainly too shy. How was I to talk to her, and what was I to say? The coaching did not carry me far. But no coaching is really necessary in such matters. The impressions of the former birth are potent enough to make all coaching superfluous. We gradually began to know each other and to speak freely together. We were the same age. But I took no time in assuming the authority of a husband.[8]

. . . I had absolutely no reason to suspect my wife's fidelity but jealousy does not wait for reasons. I must needs be forever on the look-out regarding her movements and therefore she could not go anywhere without my permission. This sowed the seeds of a bitter quarrel between us. The restraint was virtually a sort of imprisonment. And Kasturbai was not the girl to brook any such thing. She made it a point to go out whenever and wherever she liked. More restraint on my part resulted in more liberty being taken by her and in my getting more and more cross. Refusal to speak to one another thus became the order of the day with us, married children. I think it was quite innocent of Kasturbai to have taken those liberties with my restrictions. How could a guileless girl brook any restraints on going to the temple or on going on visits to friends? If I had the right to impose restrictions on her, had not she also similar right? All this is clear to me today. But at the time I had to make good my authority as a husband!

I must say I was passionately fond of her. Even at school I used to think of her and the thought of nightfall and our subsequent meeting was ever haunting me. Separation was unbearable. I used to keep her awake till late in the night with my idle talk. . . .

. . . Along with the cruel custom of child marriages, Hindu society has another custom which to a certain extent diminishes the evils of the former. Parents do not allow young couples to stay long together. The child-wife spends more than half her time at her father's place. Such was the case with us. That is to say, during the first five years of our married life (from the age of thirteen to eighteen), we could not have lived together longer than an aggregate period of three years. We would hardly have spent six months together when there would be a call to my wife from her parents. Such calls were very unwelcome in those days but they saved us both. . . .[9]

[8] *Ibid.,* Part I, Chapter 3, pp. 7–9.
[9] *Ibid.,* Part I, Chapter 4, pp. 10–12.

[Gandhi himself lost a year at high school through getting married.]

. . . I had not any high regard for my ability. I used to be astonished whenever I won prizes and scholarships. But I very jealously guarded my character. The least little blemish drew tears from my eyes. When I merited, or seemed to the teacher to merit, a rebuke, it was unbearable for me. I remember having once received corporal punishment. I did not so much mind the punishment as the fact that it was considered my desert. I wept piteously. . . .[10]

[The] teacher wanted me to make good the [grade] loss by skipping [one]—a privilege usually allowed to industrious boys. . . . English became the medium of instruction in most subjects . . . I found myself completely at sea. Geometry was a new subject in which I was not particularly strong and the English medium made it still more difficult for me. The teacher taught the subject very well but I could not follow him. Often I would lose heart and think of going back. . . . But this would discredit not only me but also the teacher, because, counting on my industry, he had recommended my promotion. So fear of the double discredit kept me at my post. When, however, with much effort I reached the thirteenth proposition of Euclid, the utter simplicity of the subject was suddenly revealed to me. A subject which required only a pure and simple use of one's reasoning powers could not be difficult. Ever since that time geometry has been both easy and interesting for me.[11]

[Gandhi likewise had trouble with Sanskrit but after the teacher, Mr. Krishnashanker, reminded him that it was the language of Hinduism's sacred scriptures, the future Mahatma persevered and succeeded.]

. . . I never took part in any exercise, cricket or football, before they were made compulsory. My shyness was one of the reasons for this aloofness, which I now see was wrong. I then had the false notion that gymnastics had nothing to do with education. Today I know that physical training should have as much place in the curriculum as mental training.

. . . I was none the worse for abstaining from exercise. . . . I had read in books about the benefits of long walks in the open air, and

[10] *Ibid.,* Part I, Chapter 5, p. 13.
[11] *Ibid.,* p. 14.

having liked the advice I had formed a habit of taking walks which has still remained with me. These walks gave me a fairly hardy constitution.[12]

[Mohandas envied the bigger, stronger boys. He was frail compared with his older brother, and especially compared with a Moslem friend named Sheik Mehtab, who could run great distances with remarkable speed. Sheik Mehtab was spectacular in the long and high jump as well. These exploits dazzled Gandhi.]

. . . This [admiration] was followed by a strong desire to be like him. I could hardly jump or run. Why should not I also be as strong as he?

Moreover, I was a coward. I used to be haunted by the fear of thieves, ghosts and serpents. I did not dare to stir out of doors at night. Darkness was a terror to me. It was almost impossible for me to sleep in the dark. . . . How could I disclose my fears to my wife, no child but already at the threshold of youth, sleeping by my side? I knew she had more courage than I and I felt ashamed of myself. . . . My friend knew all these weaknesses of mine. He would tell me that he could hold in his hand live serpents, could defy thieves and did not believe in ghosts. And all this was, of course, the result of eating meat.

[The boys at school used to recite this poem.]

> *Behold the mighty Englishman,*
> *He rules the Indian small,*
> *Because being a meat-eater*
> *He is five cubits tall.*

. . . "We are a weak people because we do not eat meat" [argued Sheik Mehtab]. "The English are able to rule over us because they are meat-eaters. You know how hardy I am and how great a runner too. It is because I am a meat-eater. Meat-eaters do not have boils or tumors and even if they sometimes happen to have any, these heal quickly. Our teacher and other distinguished people who eat meat are no fools. They know its virtues. You should do likewise. There is nothing like trying. Try, and see what strength it gives."

[12] *Ibid.,* p. 13.

All these pleas . . . were not advanced at a single sitting. They
represent the substance of a long and elaborate argument. . . .

. . . I was beaten. . . .

A day was thereupon fixed for beginning the experiment. It had
to be conducted in secret. [The family was strictly vegetarian by
religious conviction, and so were almost all inhabitants of the
district.] . . . I was extremely devoted to my parents. I knew that
the moment they came to know of my having eaten meat they
would be shocked to death. Moreover, my love of truth made me
extra cautious. . . . And having insured secrecy, I persuaded myself
that mere hiding the deed from parents was no departure from
truth.[13]

So the day came. . . . We went in search of a lonely spot by the
river and there I saw, for the first time in my life—meat. There was
baker's bread [with yeast] also. I relished neither. The goat's meat
was as tough as leather. I simply could not eat it. I was sick and had
to leave off eating.

I had a very bad night afterwards. A horrible nightmare
haunted me. Every time I dropped off to sleep it would seem as
though a live goat were bleating inside me and I would jump up
full of remorse. But then I would remind myself that meat-eating
was a duty and so become more cheerful.

My friend was not a man to give in easily. He now began to cook
various delicacies with meat and dress them neatly. . . .

The bait had its effect. I got over my dislike for bread, forswore
my compassion for the goats and became a relisher of meat dishes,
if not of meat itself. This went on for about a year. . . .

[I] knew that if my mother and father came to know of my having become a meat-eater they would be deeply shocked. This
knowledge was gnawing at my heart.

Therefore I said to myself: "Though it is essential to eat meat . . .
yet deceiving and lying to one's father and mother is worse than not
eating meat. In their lifetime, therefore, meat-eating must be out of
the question. When they are no more and I have found my freedom, I will eat meat openly but until that moment I will abstain
from it."

[13] *Ibid.,* Part I, Chapter 6, pp. 17–18.

[By now Gandhi developed an urge to reform Sheik Mehtab. This prolonged the relationship. But the naïve and younger Gandhi was no match for the shrewd, monied wastrel who offered revolt and adventure.]

. . . My zeal for reforming him . . . proved disastrous for me, and all the time I was completely unconscious of the fact.

The same company would have led me into faithlessness to my wife. . . . [He] once took me to a brothel. He sent me in with the necessary instructions. It was all pre-arranged. The bill had already been paid. . . . I was almost struck blind and dumb in this den of vice. I sat near the woman on her bed but I was tongue-tied. She naturally lost patience with me and showed me the door with abuses and insults. I then felt as though my manhood had been injured and wished to sink into the ground for shame. But I have ever since given thanks to God for having saved me. . . .[14]

[About that time—Mohandas must have been fifteen—he pilfered a bit of gold from his older brother. This produced a moral crisis. He had gnawing pangs of conscience and resolved never to steal again.]

. . . I also made up my mind to confess it to my father. But I did not dare to speak. Not that I was afraid of my father beating me. No, I do not recall his ever having beaten any of us. I was afraid of the pain that I should cause him. But I felt the risk should be taken, that there could not be a cleansing without a confession.

I decided at last to write out the confession, to submit it to my father and ask his forgiveness. I wrote it on a slip of paper and handed it to him myself. In this note not only did I confess my guilt but I asked adequate punishment for it and closed with a request to him not to punish himself for my offense. I also pledged myself never to steal in the future.

I was trembling as I handed the confession to my father. [He sat up in his sick bed to read it.]

He read it through and pearl-drops trickled down his cheeks, wetting the paper. For a moment he closed his eyes in thought and then tore up the note. . . . He again lay down. I also cried. I could see my father's agony. . . .

[14] *Ibid.*, Part I, Chapter 7, pp. 19–20.

Those pearl-drops of love cleansed my heart and washed my sin away. Only he who has experienced such love can know what it is. . . .

This was for me an object lesson in Ahimsa [Love and Non-Violence]. Then I could read in it nothing more than a father's love but today I know that it was pure Ahimsa. When such Ahimsa becomes all-embracing it transforms everything it touches. There is no limit to its power.

This sort of sublime forgiveness was not natural to my father. I had thought he would be angry, say hard things and strike his forehead. But he was so wonderfully peaceful and I believe this was due to my clean confession. A clean confession, combined with a promise never to commit the sin again, when offered before one who has the right to receive it, is the purest type of repentance. I know my confession made my father feel absolutely safe about me and increased his affection for me beyond measure.[15]

[Lest he give pain to his father and especially his mother, Mohandas did not tell them that he absented himself from temple.]

[The temple] never appealed to me. I did not like its glitter and pomp. . . .

. . . I happened about this time to come across Manusmriti [Laws of Manu—Hindu religious laws] which was amongst my father's collection. The story of creation and similar things in it did not impress me very much but on the contrary made me incline somewhat towards atheism.

There was a cousin of mine . . . for whose intellect I had great regard. To him I turned with my doubts. But he could not resolve them. . . .

[Contrary to the Hindu precept of non-killing] I also felt it was quite moral to kill serpents, bugs and the like. . . .

But one thing took deep root in me—the conviction that morality is the basis of things and that truth is the substance of all morality. Truth became my sole objective . . . and my definition of it also has been ever widening.

A Gujarati [Gandhi's native language] stanza likewise gripped

[15] *Ibid.,* Part I, Chapter 8, pp. 23–24.

my mind and heart. Its precept—return good for evil—became my guiding principle. . . .[16]

[Gandhi's anti-religious sentiments quickened his interest in religion and he listened attentively to his father's frequent discussions with Moslem and Parsi friends on the differences between their faiths and Hinduism.]

[The "shackles of lust" tormented Gandhi. They gave him a feeling of guilt. The feeling grew when sex seemed to clash with the keen sense of duty which developed in him at an early age. One instance of such a conflict impressed itself indelibly.]

The time of which I am now speaking is my sixteenth year. My father . . . was bed-ridden [with a fistula]. . . . My mother, an old servant of the house and I were his principal attendants. I had the duties of a nurse, which mainly consisted of dressing the wound, giving my father his medicine and compounding drugs whenever they had to be made up at home. Every night I massaged his legs and retired only when he asked me to do so or after he had fallen asleep. I loved to do this service. I do not remember ever having neglected it. All the time at my disposal after the performance of the daily duties was divided between school and attending on my father. I would go out only for an evening walk either when he permitted me or when he was feeling well.

This was also the time when my wife was expecting a baby—a circumstance which . . . meant a double shame for me. For one thing I did not restrain myself, as I should have done, whilst I was yet a student. And secondly, this carnal lust got the better of what I regarded as my duty to study and of what was even a greater duty, my devotion to my parents. . . . Every night whilst my hands were busy massaging my father's legs my mind was hovering about the bedroom—and that too at a time when religion, medical science and common sense alike forbade sexual intercourse. I was always glad to be relieved from my duty and went straight to the bedroom after doing obeisance to my father.

At the same time my father was getting worse every day. . . . He

[16] *Ibid.*, Part I, Chapter 10, pp. 27–30.

despaired of living any longer. He was getting weaker and weaker until at last he had to be asked to perform the necessary functions in bed. But up to the last he refused to do anything of the kind, always insisting on going through the strain of leaving his bed. The Vaishnavite [Orthodox Hindu] rules about external cleanliness are so inexorable.

The dreadful night came. . . .

It was ten-thirty or eleven P.M. I was giving the massage. My uncle offered to relieve me. I was glad and went straight to the bed-room. My wife, poor thing, was fast asleep. But how could she sleep when I was there? I woke her up. In five or six minutes, however, the servant knocked at the door. I started with alarm. "Get up," he said. "Father is very ill." I knew of course that he was very ill and so I guessed what "very ill" meant at that moment. I sprang out of bed.

"What is the matter? Do tell me!"

"Father is no more."

So all was over! I had but to wring my hands. I felt deeply ashamed and miserable. I ran to my father's room. I saw that if ani-mal passion had not blinded me I should have been spared the tor-ture of separation from my father during his last moments. I should have been massaging him and he would have died in my arms. But now it was my uncle who had this privilege. . . .

[The] poor mite that was born to my wife scarcely breathed for more than three or four days. Nothing else could be expected. . . .[17]

[Kasturbai was illiterate. Her husband had every intention of teaching her but she disliked studies and he preferred love-making.]

. . . By nature she was simple, independent, persevering and, with me at least, reticent. . . .

[Kasturbai never learned to read or write anything but elemen-tary Gujarati, her native language.]

. . . I am sure that had my love for her been absolutely untainted with lust she would be a learned lady today, for I could then have conquered her dislike for studies. I know that nothing is impossi-ble for pure love.[18]

[17] *Ibid.,* Part I, Chapter 9, pp. 24–26.
[18] *Ibid.,* Part I, Chapter 4, p. 11.

*   *   *

[When his father died in 1885, Mohandas' mother took advice on family matters from a Jain monk named Becharji Swami. Jainism prohibits the killing of any living creature, even insects. Jain priests wear white masks over their mouths lest they breathe in and thus kill an insect. They are not supposed to walk out at night lest they unwittingly step on a worm.

The Jain monk, Becharji Swami, helped Gandhi go to England.]

I passed the [high school] matriculation examination in 1887. . . .

My elders wanted me to pursue my studies at college after the matriculation. There was a college in Bhavnagar [a town on the inland side of the Kathiawar peninsula] as well as in Bombay and, as [it] was cheaper, I decided to go there . . . I went but found myself entirely at sea. Everything was difficult . . . I was so raw. At the end of the first term I returned home.

We had, in Mavji Dave, who was a shrewd and learned Brahman, an old friend and adviser of the family. He had kept up his connection with the family even after my father's death. . . . In conversation with my mother and elder brother, he inquired about my studies. . . .

Joshiji—that is how we used to call old Mavji Dave—turned to me with complete assurance and asked: "Would you not rather go to England than study here?" Nothing could have been more welcome to me. I was fighting shy of my difficult studies. So I jumped at the proposal and said that the sooner I was sent the better. It was no easy business to pass examinations quickly. Could I not be sent to qualify for the medical profession?

My brother interrupted me: "Father never liked it. He had you in mind when he said that we Vaishnavas should have nothing to do with the dissection of dead bodies. Father intended you for the bar."

My mother was sorely perplexed. She did not like the idea of parting with me. . . .

. . . She had begun making minute inquiries. Someone had told her young men got lost in England. Someone else had said they took to meat, and yet another that they could not live there without liquor. "How about all this?" she asked me. I said: "Will you not trust me? I shall not lie to you. I swear I shall not touch any of those things. . . ."

"I can trust you," she said. "But how can I trust you in a distant land? I am dazed and know not what to do. I will ask Becharji Swami."

. . . He came to my help and said: "I shall get the boy solemnly to take the three vows and then he can be allowed to go." He administered the oath and I vowed not to touch wine, women and meat. This done, my mother gave her permission.[19]

With my mother's permission and blessings, I set off exultantly for Bombay, leaving my wife with a baby of a few months. . . .

Time hung heavily on my hands in Bombay. I dreamt continually of going to England.

Meanwhile my caste-people were agitated over my going abroad. . . . A general meeting of the caste was called and I was summoned to appear before it. I went. How I suddenly managed to muster up courage I do not know. Nothing daunted, and without the slightest hesitation, I came before the meeting. The Sheth—the headman of the community—who was distantly related to me and had been on very good terms with my father, thus accosted me:

"In the opinion of the caste your proposal to go to England is not proper. Our religion forbids voyages abroad. We have also heard that it is not possible to live there without compromising our religion. One is obliged to eat and drink with Europeans!"

To which I replied: "I do not think it is at all against our religion to go to England. I intend going there for further studies. And I have solemnly promised to my mother to abstain from the three things you fear most. I am sure the vow will keep me safe."

"But we tell you," rejoined the Sheth, "that it is *not* possible to keep our religion there. You know my relations with your father and you ought to listen to my advice."

"I know these relations," said I. "And you are as an elder to me. But I am helpless in this matter. I cannot alter my resolve to go to England. My father's friend and adviser, who is a learned Brahman, sees no objection to my going to England and my mother and brother have also given me their permission."

[19] *Ibid.,* Part I, Chapter 11, pp. 30–33.

"But will you disregard the orders of the caste?"

"I am really helpless. I think the caste should not interfere in the matter."

This incensed the Sheth. He swore at me. I sat unmoved. So the Sheth pronounced his order: "This boy shall be treated as an out-caste from today. Whoever helps him or goes to see him off at the dock shall be punishable with a fine of one rupee four annas" [about fifty cents].

The order had no effect on me and I took my leave of the Sheth. But I wondered how my brother would take it. Fortunately he remained firm and wrote to assure me that I had his permission to go, the Sheth's order notwithstanding.[20]

[Gandhi bought a steamer ticket, a necktie, a short jacket and enough food, chiefly sweets and fruit, for the three weeks to Southampton. On September 4, 1888, he sailed. He was not yet nineteen. Several months earlier, Kasturbai had borne him a male child and they called it Harilal. Now the voyage to England gave Gandhi "a long and healthy separation" from his wife.]

The storm in my caste over my foreign voyage was still brewing [on Gandhi's return three years later]. It had divided the caste into two camps, one of which immediately re-admitted me, while the other was bent on keeping me out. . . .

I never tried to seek admission to the section that had refused it. Nor did I feel even mental resentment against any of the head-men. . . . Some of these regarded me with dislike but I scrupu-lously avoided hurting their feelings. I fully respected the caste regulations about excommunication. According to these, none of my relations, including my father-in-law and mother-in-law and even my sister and brother-in-law, could entertain me and I would not so much as drink water at their houses. They were prepared secretly to evade the prohibition but it went against the grain with me to do a thing in secret that I would not do in public.

The result of my scrupulous conduct was that I never had the occasion to be troubled by the caste. . . . I have experienced nothing but affection and generosity from the general body of the section that still regards me as excommunicated. They have even helped

[20] *Ibid.,* Part I, Chapter 12, pp. 34–35.

me in my work without ever expecting me to do anything for the
caste. It is my conviction that all these good things are due to my
non-resistance. Had I agitated for being admitted to the caste, had
I attempted to divide it into more camps, had I provoked the caste-
men, they would surely have retaliated and, instead of steering
clear of the storm, I should . . . have found myself in a whirlpool of
agitation. . . .[21]

[21] *Ibid.,* Part II, Chapter 2, pp. 75–76.

[2]

GANDHI IN ENGLAND

[After arrival in London] I was very uneasy . . . I would continually think of my home and country. My mother's love always haunted me. At night the tears would stream down my cheeks and home memories of all sorts made sleep out of the question. It was impossible to share my misery with anyone. And even if I could have done so, where was the use? I knew of nothing that would soothe me. Everything was strange—the people, their ways and even their dwellings. I was a complete novice in the matter of English etiquette and had to be on my guard. There was the additional inconvenience of the vegetarian vow. Even the dishes I could eat were tasteless and insipid. . . .[1]

[An English friend] had not ceased to worry about me. His love for me led him to think that if I persisted in my objections to meat-eating I should not only develop a weak constitution but should remain a duffer because I should never feel at home in English society. . . .

. . . I could see and appreciate the love by which all my friend's efforts were actuated and my respect for him was all the greater on account of our differences in thought and action.

But I decided that I should . . . assure him I would be clumsy no more but try to become polished and [cultivate] other accomplishments which fitted one for polite society. And for this purpose I undertook the all too impossible task of becoming an English gentleman.

The clothes after the Bombay cut that I was wearing were, I thought, unsuitable . . . and I got new ones . . . I also went in for a chimney-pot hat costing nineteen shillings [three dollars]—an

---

[1] M. K. Gandhi, *The Story of My Experiments with Truth*, Part I, Chapter 13, p. 38.

excessive price in those days. . . . I wasted ten pounds [about forty dollars] on an evening suit made in Bond Street, the center of fashionable life in London, and got my good and noble-hearted brother to send me a double watch-chain of gold. It was not correct to wear a ready-made tie and I learnt the art of tying one for myself. While in India the mirror had been a luxury permitted on the days when the family barber gave me a shave; here I wasted ten minutes every day before a huge mirror watching myself arranging my tie and parting my hair in the correct fashion. My hair was by no means soft and every day it meant a regular struggle with the brush to keep it in position. . . .[2]

[Dr. Sachchidananda Sinha, an Indian then a student in London, recalls meeting Gandhi in February, 1890, in Piccadilly Circus. Gandhi, he says, "was wearing at the time a high silk top hat 'burnished bright,' a stiff and starched collar [known as a Gladstonian], a rather flashy tie displaying all the colors of the rainbow, under which there was a fine striped silk shirt. He wore as his outer clothes a morning coat, a double-breasted waistcoat and dark striped trousers to match, and not only patent-leather shoes but spats over them. He also carried leather gloves and a silver-mounted stick but wore no spectacles. His clothes were regarded as the very acme of fashion for young men about town at that time and were largely in vogue among the Indian youth prosecuting their studies in law at one of the four institutions called the Inns of Court." The Inner Temple, the one in which Gandhi enrolled, was considered by Indians "the most aristocratic," says Dr. Sinha.[3]]

. . . I directed my attention to other details that were supposed to go towards the making of an English gentleman. I was told it was necessary for me to take lessons in dancing, French and elocution. . . . I decided to take dancing lessons at a class and paid down three pounds as fees for a term. I must have taken about six lessons in three weeks. But it was beyond me to achieve anything like rhythmic motion. I could not follow the piano and hence found it impossible to keep time. . . . I thought I should learn to play the

[2] *Ibid.,* Part I, Chapter 15, p. 43.
[3] Louis Fischer, *The Life of Mahatma Gandhi* (New York: Harper & Brothers, 1951), Part I, Chapter 3, p. 24.

violin in order to cultivate an ear for Western music. So I invested three pounds in a violin and something more in fees. I sought a third teacher to give me lessons in elocution and paid him a preliminary fee. . . . He recommended Bell's *Standard Elocutionist* as the textbook, which I purchased. . . .

But Mr. Bell rang the bell of alarm in my ear and I awoke.

I had not to spend a lifetime in England, I said to myself. What then was the use of learning elocution? And how could dancing make a gentleman of me? The violin I could learn even in India. I was a student and ought to go on with my studies. I should qualify myself to join the Inns of Court. If my character made a gentleman of me, so much the better. Otherwise I should forego the ambition.

This infatuation must have lasted about three months. The punctiliousness in dress persisted for years. . . .[4]

. . . In India I had never read a newspaper. But here I succeeded in cultivating a liking for them by regular reading. I always glanced over the *Daily News, The Daily Telegraph* and *The Pall Mall Gazette*. This took me hardly an hour. I therefore began to wander about. I launched out in search of a vegetarian restaurant. The landlady had told me there were no such places in the city. I would trot ten or twelve miles each day, go into a cheap restaurant and eat my fill of bread but would never be satisfied. During these wanderings I once hit on a vegetarian restaurant. . . .

The sight of it filled me with the same joy that a child feels on getting a thing after its own heart. . . . I noticed books for sale exhibited under a glass window near the door. I saw among them Salt's *Plea for Vegetarianism*. This I purchased . . . and went straight to the dining room. This was my first hearty meal since my arrival in England. . . .

I read Salt's book . . . and was very much impressed by it. . . . I blessed the day on which I had taken the vow before my mother. I had all along abstained from meat in the interests of truth and of the vow I had taken, but had wished at the same time that every Indian should be a meat-eater, and had looked forward to being one myself freely and openly some day and to enlisting

[4] M. K. Gandhi, *Experiments,* Part I, Chapter 15, pp. 43–45.

others in the cause. The choice was now made in favor of vegetarianism. . . . [5]

A convert's enthusiasm for his new religion is greater than that of a person who is born in it. . . . Full of the neophyte's zeal for vegetarianism I decided to start a vegetarian club in my locality. . . . The club went well for a while but came to an end in the course of a few months. For I left the locality according to my custom of moving from place to place periodically. But this brief and modest experience gave me some little training in organizing and conducting institutions.[6]

I was elected to the Executive Committee of the Vegetarian Society and made it a point to attend every one of its meetings but I always felt tongue-tied. . . .

This shyness I retained throughout my stay in England. Even when I paid a social call the presence of half a dozen or more people would strike me dumb.

It was only in South Africa that I got over this shyness though I never completely overcame it. It was impossible for me to speak impromptu. I hesitated whenever I had to face strange audiences and avoided making a speech whenever I could. Even today I do not think I could or would even be inclined to keep a meeting of friends engaged in idle talk.

I must say that beyond occasionally exposing me to laughter, my constitutional shyness has been no disadvantage whatever. In fact . . . it has been all to my advantage. My hesitancy in speech, which was once an annoyance, is now a pleasure. Its greatest benefit has been that it has taught me the economy of words. I have naturally formed the habit of restraining my thoughts. And I can now give myself the certificate that a thoughtless word hardly ever escapes my tongue or pen. I do not recollect ever having had to regret anything in my speech or writing. I have thus been spared many a mishap and waste of time. . . . Proneness to exaggerate, to suppress or modify the truth, wittingly or unwittingly, is a natural weakness of man and silence is necessary in order to surmount it. A

[5] *Ibid.,* Part I, Chapter 14, p. 41.
[6] *Ibid.,* Part I, Chapter 17, p. 50.

man of few words will rarely be thoughtless in his speech, he will measure every word. We find so many people impatient to talk. . . . All this talking can hardly be . . . of any benefit to the world. It is so much waste of time. My shyness has been in reality my shield and buckler. It has allowed me to grow. It has helped me in my discernment of truth.[7]

Let no one imagine that my experiments in dancing and the like marked a stage of indulgence in my life . . . even then I had my wits about me. That period . . . was . . . relieved by a certain amount of self-introspection on my part. I kept account of every farthing I spent and my expenses were carefully calculated. Every little item, such as [bus] fares or postage or a couple of [pennies] spent on newspapers would be entered and the balance struck every evening before going to bed. The habit has stayed with me ever since and I know that as a result, though I have had to handle public funds amounting to thousands I have succeeded in exercising strict economy in their disbursement and instead of outstanding debts have had invariably a surplus balance in respect to all the movements I have led. . . .

As I kept strict watch over my way of living I could see it was necessary to economize. . . .[8]

. . . The thought of my struggling brother who nobly responded to my regular calls for monetary help deeply pained me. . . .[9]

So I decided to take rooms on my own . . . and also to [move] from place to place according to the work I had to do. . . . The new arrangement combined walks and economy as it meant a saving of fare and gave me walks of eight or ten miles a day. It was mainly this habit of long walks that kept me practically free from illness throughout my stay in England and gave me a fairly strong body.[10]

. . . This was also a period of intensive study. Plain living saved me plenty of time and I passed my examination.

Let not the reader think this manner of living made my life by any means a dreary affair. . . . The change harmonized with my

[7] *Ibid.,* Part I, Chapter 18, pp. 50–53.
[8] *Ibid.,* Part I, Chapter 15, pp. 44–45.
[9] *Ibid.,* Part I, Chapter 15, p. 47.
[10] *Ibid.,* p. 45.

inward and outer life. It was also more in keeping with the means of my family. My life was certainly more truthful and my soul knew no bounds of joy.[11]

[The purpose for which Gandhi came to England receives only a few lines in his reminiscences, far fewer than his dietetic adventures. He was admitted as a student at the Inner Temple on November 6th, 1888. In addition to law, he learned French and Latin, and physics.]

The curriculum of study was easy. . . . Everyone knew the examinations had practically no value. . . . There were regular textbooks prescribed for these examinations . . . but scarcely anyone read them. . . . Question papers were easy and examiners were generous. . . . [The examinations] could not be felt as a difficulty.

But I succeeded in turning them into one. I felt I should read all the textbooks. It was a fraud, I thought, not to read these books. I invested much money in them. I decided to read Roman Law in Latin. . . . And all this reading was not without its value later on in South Africa where Roman Dutch is the common law. The reading of Justinian, therefore, helped me a great deal in understanding the South African law.

It took me nine months of fairly hard labor to read through the Common Law of England. . . .

I passed my examinations, was called to the bar on the 10th of June, 1891, and enrolled in the High Court on the 11th. On the 12th I sailed for home.[12]

[Gandhi does not seem to have been happy in England. It was a necessary interim period: he had to be there to get professional status. In *Young India* of September 4, 1924, he said his college days were before the time "when . . . I began life."[13] Gandhi was not the student type, he did not learn essential things by studying. He was the doer, and he grew and gained knowledge through action. The Gita, Hinduism's holy scripture, therefore became Gandhi's gospel, for it glorifies action.]

[11] *Ibid.,* p. 47.
[12] *Ibid.,* Part I, Chapter 24, pp. 66–68.
[13] Louis Fischer, *Life of Gandhi,* Part I, Chapter 3, p. 28.

[3]

GANDHI FAILS

[At Bombay] my elder brother had come to meet me at the dock. . . .

I was pining to see my mother. I did not know that she was no more in the flesh to receive me. . . . The sad news was now given me. . . . My brother had kept me ignorant of her death, which took place whilst I was still in England. He wanted to spare me the blow in a foreign land. The news, however, was none the less a severe shock to me. . . . My grief was even greater than over my father's death. . . . But I remember that I did not give myself up to any wild expression of grief. I could even check the tears and took to life just as though nothing had happened.[1]

My relations with my wife were still not as I desired. Even my stay in England had not cured me of jealousy. I continued my squeamishness and suspiciousness in respect to every little thing. . . . I had decided that my wife should learn reading and writing and that I should help her in her studies but my lust came in the way and she had to suffer for my own short-coming. . . .

. . . My brother had children and my own child [Harilal] was now a boy of nearly four. It was my desire to teach these little ones physical exercise and make them hardy and also to give them the benefit of my personal guidance. In this I had my brother's support and I succeeded in my efforts more or less. I very much liked the company of children and the habit of playing and joking with them has stayed with me till today. I have ever since thought that I should make a good teacher of children.[2]

[Gandhi performed all the duties of a husband except to support his wife and child; he had no money.

Laxmidas Gandhi, a lawyer in Rajkot, had built high hopes on

---

[1] M. K. Gandhi, *The Story of My Experiments with Truth,* Part II, Chapter 1, p. 73.
[2] *Ibid.,* Part II, Chapter 2, pp. 76–77.

his younger brother. But Mohandas was a complete failure as a
lawyer in Rajkot as well as in Bombay.]

[It] was difficult to practice at the bar. I had read the laws but not
learned how to practice law. . . .

Besides, I had learned nothing at all of Indian law. . . . I had serious misgivings as to whether I should be able to earn even a living
by the profession.[3]

About this time I took up the case of one Mamibai. It was a
"small cause." . . .

This was my debut in the Small Causes [Small Claims] Court. I
appeared for the defendant and had thus to cross-examine the
plaintiff's witnesses. I stood up but my heart sank into my boots.
My head was reeling and I felt as though the whole court was
doing likewise. I could think of no question to ask. The judge must
have laughed and the other lawyers no doubt enjoyed the spectacle.
But I was past seeing anything. I sat down and told the agent I
could not conduct the case, that he had better engage [another
lawyer] and have the fee back from me. [The other lawyer] was
duly engaged. . . .

I hastened from the Court not knowing whether my client won
or lost her case but was ashamed of myself and decided not to take
up any more cases until I had courage enough to conduct them.
Indeed I did not go to court again until I went to South Africa. . . .[4]

Disappointed, I left Bombay and went to Rajkot where I set up
my own office. Here I got along moderately well. . . .[5]

[Laxmidas, who had financed Gandhi's studies in England, was
even more disappointed at his brother's failure to carry out a delicate mission for him.]

My brother had been secretary and adviser to the late [heir to the
throne of Porbandar] and hanging over his head at this time was
the charge of having given wrong advice when in that office. The
matter had gone to the [British] Political Agent, who was preju-
diced against my brother. Now I had known this officer when in
England and he may be said to have been fairly friendly to me. My
brother thought I should avail myself of the friendship and, put-

---

[3] *Ibid.,* Part I, Chapter 25, p. 68.
[4] *Ibid.,* Part II, Chapter 3, p. 79.
[5] *Ibid.,* Part II, Chapter 4, p. 81.

ting in a good word on his behalf, try to disabuse the Political Agent of the prejudice. I did not at all like this idea. I should not, I thought, try to take advantage of a trifling acquaintance in England. If my brother was really at fault, what use was my recommendation? If he was innocent he should submit a petition in the proper course and, confident of his innocence, face the result. My brother did not relish this advice. ". . . Only influence counts here. It is not proper for you, a brother, to shirk your duty when you can clearly put in a good word about me to an officer you know."

I could not refuse him so I went to the officer much against my will. I knew I had no right to approach him and was full conscious that I was compromising my self-respect. But I sought an appointment and got it. I reminded him of the old acquaintance but I immediately saw that . . . an officer on leave was not the same as an officer on duty. The Political Agent owned the acquaintance but the reminder seemed to stiffen him. "Surely you have not come here to abuse that acquaintance, have you?" appeared to be the meaning of his stiffness and seemed to be written on his brow. Nevertheless I opened my case. . . . "Your brother is an intriguer. I want to hear nothing more from you. I have no time. If your brother has anything to say let him apply through the proper channel." The answer was enough, was perhaps deserved. But selfishness is blind. I went on with my story. The [Agent] got up and said "You must go now."

"But please hear me out," said I. That made him more angry. He called his peon and ordered him to show me the door. I was still hesitating when the peon came in, placed his hands on my shoulders and put me out of the room.

. . . I pocketed the insult but also profited by it. "Never again shall I place myself in such a false position, never again shall I try to exploit friendship in this way," said I to myself and since then I have never been guilty of a breach of that determination. This shock changed the course of my life.[6]

[At this juncture a business firm of Porbandar Moslems offered to send Gandhi to South Africa for a year as their lawyer. He seized the opportunity to see a new country and have new experiences.]

[6] *Ibid.,* pp. 81–83.

. . . I wanted somehow to leave India. . . .[7]

This time I felt only the pang of parting with my wife. Another baby [a second son named Manilal] had been born to us since my return from England. Our love could not yet be called free from lust but it was getting gradually purer. Since my return from Europe we had lived together very little and . . . I had now become her teacher, however indifferent. . . . But the attraction of South Africa rendered the separation bearable. "We are bound to meet again in a year," I said to her, by way of consolation. . . .[8]

[Gandhi was a self-remade man and the transformation began in South Africa. It is not that he turned failure into success. Using the clay that was there he turned himself into another person. His was a remarkable case of second birth in one lifetime.]

[7] Ibid., Part II, Chapter 5, p. 85.
[8] Ibid., Part II, Chapter 6, pp. 85–86.

4

THE METHOD IS BORN

[When Gandhi landed at Durban, Natal, in May, 1893, his mission was simply to win a lawsuit, earn some money and, perhaps, at long last start his career. As he left the boat to meet his employer, a Moslem businessman named Dada Abdulla Sheth, Gandhi wore a fashionable frock coat, pressed trousers, shining shoes and a turban.

The lawsuit required Gandhi's presence in Pretoria, the capital of Transvaal. First-class accommodations were purchased for him at Durban, where he boarded the train for the overnight journey.]

The train reached Maritzburg, the capital of Natal, at about 9 P.M. [A white man entered the compartment] and looked me up and down. He saw that I was a "colored" man. This disturbed him. Out he went and came in with one or two officials. They all kept quiet, when another official came to me and said, "Come along, you must go to the van [third class] compartment."

"But I have a first-class ticket," said I.

"That doesn't matter," rejoined the other. "I tell you, you must go to the van compartment."

"I tell you, I was permitted to travel in this compartment at Durban and I insist on going on in it."

"No you won't," said the official. "You must leave this compartment or else I shall have to call a police constable to push you out."

"Yes you may. I refuse to get out voluntarily."

The constable came. He took me by the hand and pushed me out. My luggage also was taken out . . . and the train steamed away. I went and sat in the waiting room. . . .

It was winter, and winter in the higher regions of South Africa is severely cold. Maritzburg being at a high altitude, the cold was extremely bitter. My overcoat was in my luggage but I did not dare

to ask for it . . .[1] lest I might be insulted and assaulted once again.[2]
[So] I sat and shivered. There was no light in the room. . . .[3]

. . . Sleep was out of the question. . . .[4]

I began to think of my duty. Should I fight for my rights or go
back to India or should I go on to Pretoria without minding the
insults and return to India after finishing the case? It would be
cowardice to run back to India without fulfilling my obligation.
The hardship to which I was subjected was superficial—only a
symptom of the deep disease of color prejudice. I should try, if possible, to root out the disease and suffer hardships in the process.
Redress for wrongs I should seek only to the extent that would be
necessary for the removal of the color prejudice.[5]

. . . This resolution somewhat pacified and strengthened me but
I did not get any sleep.

. . . I suffered further insults and received more beatings on my
way to Pretoria. But all this only confirmed me in my determination.

Thus . . . I obtained full experience of the condition of Indians
in South Africa. . . .[6]

[Many years later in India, Dr. John R. Mott, a Christian missionary, asked Gandhi, "What have been the most creative experiences in your life?" In reply, Gandhi told the story of the night in
the Maritzburg Station.[7]]

I will not describe my bitter experience in the courts within a
fortnight of my arrival, the hardships I encountered . . . and the
difficulty in, and the practical impossibility of, securing accommodation in hotels. Suffice it to say that all these experiences sank into
me. . . .[8]

[1] M. K. Gandhi, *The Story of My Experiments with Truth,* Part II, Chapter 8, pp.
93–94.
[2] M. K. Gandhi, *Satyagraha in South Africa* (Triplicane, Madras: S. Ganesane,
1928), Chapter 6, p. 69.
[3] M. K. Gandhi, *Experiments,* p. 94.
[4] M. K. Gandhi, *Satyagraha in South Africa,* p. 69.
[5] M. K. Gandhi, *Experiments,* p. 94.
[6] M. K. Gandhi, *Satyagraha in South Africa,* pp. 70–71.
[7] Louis Fischer, *The Life of Mahatma Gandhi,* Part I, Chapter 6, p. 41.
[8] M. K. Gandhi, *Satyagraha in South Africa,* p. 68.

[Within a week of his arrival in Pretoria, Gandhi summoned all the Indians of the city to a meeting. He wanted "to present to them a picture of their condition." He was twenty-four. This was his first public speech. The audience consisted of Moslem merchants interspersed with a few Hindus.]

. . . I had always heard the merchants say truth was not possible in business. I did not think so then nor do I now. . . . I strongly contested this position in my speech and awakened the merchants to a sense of their duty. . . .

I had found our peoples' habits to be insanitary as compared with those of the Englishmen around them and drew their attention to it. I laid stress on the necessity of forgetting all distinctions such as Hindus, Mussalmans [Moslems], Parsis, Christians . . . and so on.

. . . As I felt knowledge of English would be useful in that country I advised those who had leisure to learn English. I told them it was possible to learn a language even at an advanced age and cited cases of people who had done so. I undertook, besides, to teach a class if one was started or to instruct individuals personally. . . .

. . . I had no misgivings regarding my capacity to teach. My pupils might become tired but not I. . . .[9]

[A barber, a clerk and a shopkeeper accepted his offer. Gandhi dogged them for months and would not let them be lazy or lax in their studies.]

I was satisfied with the result of the meeting. It was decided to hold such meetings . . . once a week or, maybe, once a month. These were held more or less regularly and . . . there was a free exchange of ideas. The result was that there was now in Pretoria no Indian I did not know or whose condition I was not acquainted with. . . .[10]

[I] felt it would be well if a permanent organization was formed to watch Indian interests. But where was I to live and how? [The Indian community] offered me a regular salary but I expressly declined. One may not receive a large salary for public work. Besides, I was a pioneer. According to my notions at the time I

[9] M. K. Gandhi, *Experiments,* Part II, Chapter 12, p. 105.
[10] *Ibid.,* pp. 105–106.

thought I should live in a style usual for barristers [attorneys] and reflecting credit on the community, and that would mean great expense. It would be improper to depend for my maintenance upon a body whose activities would necessitate a public appeal for funds, and my power of work would be thereby crippled. For this and similar reasons I flatly refused to accept remuneration for public work. But I suggested I was prepared to stay if the principal traders among them could see their way to give me legal work and give me retainers for it beforehand. . . . We might deal with each other for [a year], examine the results and then continue . . . if both parties were agreeable. This suggestion was cordially accepted by all.

I applied for admission as an advocate of the Supreme Court of Natal. The Natal Law Society opposed my application on the sole ground that the law did not contemplate that colored barristers should be placed on the roll. . . . The Senior Court over-ruled the Law Society's objection and granted my application. . . . The newspapers of South Africa ridiculed the Law Society and some of them even congratulated me.

. . . I had never attended a session of the Indian National Congress [Party of India] but had read about it. . . . I was . . . a Congress devotee and wished to popularize the name. Inexperienced as I was, I did not try to find out a new name. I was also afraid of committing a mistake. So I advised the Indians to call their organization the Natal Indian Congress. . . . [It] worked throughout the year and those who paid an annual subscription of at least three pounds [about fifteen dollars] were admitted to membership. . . . About three hundred members were enrolled in a month. They included Hindus, Moslems, Parsis and Christians. . . . The well-to-do traders went about far-off villages in their own conveyances enrolling new members and collecting subscriptions. . . . Some [potential members had] to be persuaded. This persuasion was a sort of political training and made people acquainted with the facts of the situation. . . . [A] meeting of the Congress was held at least once a month, when detailed accounts were presented and adopted. Current events were explained and recorded in the minute-book. Members asked various questions. Fresh subjects were considered. The advantage of all this was that those who never spoke at such meetings got accustomed to do so.... All this was a novel experience. The community was deeply interested....[11]

[Another] feature of the Congress was propaganda. This consisted in acquainting the English in South Africa and England and people in India with the real state of things in Natal....[12]

Side by side with external agitation the question of internal improvement was also taken up. The Europeans throughout South Africa had been agitating against Indians on the ground of their ways of life. They always argued that the Indians were very dirty and close-fisted. They lived in the same place where they traded.... How could clean open-handed Europeans with their multifarious wants compete in trade with such parsimonious and dirty people? Lectures were therefore delivered, debates held, and suggestions made at Congress meetings on subjects such as domestic sanitation, personal hygiene, the necessity of having separate buildings for houses and shops and for well-to-do traders, of living in a style befitting their position....

... Steps were taken to save the community from the habit of exaggeration. Attempts were always made to draw their attention to their own shortcomings. Whatever force there was in the arguments of the Europeans was duly acknowledged. Every occasion when it was possible to coöperate with the Europeans on terms of equality and consistent with self-respect, was heartily availed of. The newspapers were supplied with as much information about the Indian movement as they could publish, and whenever Indians were unfairly attacked in the press, replies were sent to the newspapers concerned.[13]

All this activity resulted in winning the Indians numerous friends in South Africa and in obtaining the active sympathy of all parties in India. It also opened out and placed before the South African Indians a definite line of action.[14]

*   *   *

[11] M. K. Gandhi, *Satyagraha in South Africa,* pp. 73–76.
[12] M. K. Gandhi, *Experiments,* Part II, Chapter 16, p. 126.
[13] M. K. Gandhi, *Satyagraha in South Africa,* p. 78.
[14] M. K. Gandhi, *Experiments,* p. 127.

[The lawsuit for which Gandhi came to South Africa brought him into contact with Roman Catholics, Quakers and Protestants. Some of them tried to convert him to Christianity. Gandhi did not discourage their efforts. He read the books they gave him and tried to answer their searching questions about Indian religions. None of the books made much of an impression on him, however— except one.]

Tolstoy's *The Kingdom of God Is Within You* overwhelmed me. It left an abiding impression on me. Before the independent thinking, profound morality and the truthfulness of this book, all the books given me . . . seemed to pale into insignificance.[15]

[Gandhi's Christian friends taught him the essence of Christianity. They said if he believed in Jesus he would find redemption.]

"If this be the Christianity acknowledged by all Christians, I cannot accept it," [Gandhi told them]. "I do not seek redemption from the consequences of my sin. I seek to be redeemed from sin itself. . . . Until I have attained that end, I shall be content to be restless."[16]

[Gandhi liked the sweet Christian hymns and many of the Christians he met. But he could not regard Christianity as the perfect religion or the greatest religion.]

. . . It was impossible for me to believe that I could go to heaven or attain salvation only by becoming a Christian. . . .

. . . I could accept Jesus as a martyr, an embodiment of sacrifice and a divine teacher, but not as the most perfect man ever born. . . . The pious lives of Christians did not give me anything that the lives of men of other faiths had failed to give. I had seen in other lives just the same reformation that I had heard of among Christians. Philosophically there was nothing extraordinary in Christian principles. . . .

Thus, if I could not accept Christianity either as a perfect or the greatest religion, neither was I then convinced of Hinduism's being such. Hindu defects were pressingly visible to me. If untouchability could be a part of Hinduism, it could be but a rotten part or an excrescence. I could not understand the [reason for] a multitude of

[15] *Ibid.,* Part II, Chapter 15, pp. 114–115.
[16] *Ibid.,* Part II, Chapter 11, p. 104.

sects and castes. What was the meaning of saying that the Vedas [Hindu scripture] were the inspired Word of God? If they were inspired, why not also the Bible and the Koran?[17]

[Gandhi recoiled from the competitiveness of religions. He also disliked the competitiveness of lawyers. His client and the opposing party were relatives, and the cost of the litigation, dragging out for more than a year, was ruining both. Gandhi suggested a compromise out of court. An arbitrator who heard the case decided in favor of Gandhi's client, Dada Abdulla Sheth. Now a new problem confronted Gandhi. The opposing party, Tyeb Sheth, was called upon to pay thirty-seven thousand pounds—i.e., about eight hundred and fifty thousand dollars—and costs. This threatened him with bankruptcy. Gandhi induced Dada Abdulla to permit the loser to pay in installments stretched over a very extended period.

In preparing the case, Gandhi learned the secrets of bookkeeping and some of the fine points of law. Above all, it reinforced his opinion that settlements out of court were preferable to trials.]

. . . My joy was boundless. I had learnt the true practice of law. I had learnt to find out the better side of human nature and to enter men's hearts. I realized that the true function of a lawyer was to unite parties riven asunder. The lesson was so indelibly burnt into me that a large part of my time during the twenty years of my practice as a lawyer was occupied in bringing about private compromises of hundreds of cases. I lost nothing thereby—not even money, certainly not my soul.[18]

[The lawsuit settled, Gandhi returned to Durban and prepared to sail for India. He had been in South Africa almost twelve months. Before his departure his associates gave him a farewell party. During the festivities someone handed him the day's *Natal Mercury* and in it he found a brief item regarding the Natal government's proposed bill to deprive Indians of their right to elect members of the legislature. Gandhi stressed the necessity of resisting this move. His friends were ready but they were "unlettered, lame"[19] men, they said, and powerless without him. He consented to stay a

---

[17] *Ibid.,* Part II, Chapter 15, pp. 113–114.
[18] *Ibid.,* Part II, Chapter 14, p. 112.
[19] Louis Fischer, *Life of Gandhi,* Part I, Chapter 6, p. 45.

month. He remained twenty years fighting the battle for Indian rights. He won.]

[Natal in 1896 had 400,000 Negro inhabitants, 50,000 whites and 51,000 Indians. The Cape of Good Hope Colony had 900,000 Negroes, 400,000 Europeans and 10,000 Indians. The Transvaal Republic had 650,000 Negroes, 120,000 whites and about 5,000 Indians. Similar proportions were to be found in other areas.

Indians or no Indians, the whites were a permanent minority in South Africa. But the Indians were thrifty, able and ambitious and they worked hard. Given normal opportunities, they became rivals of the whites in business, agriculture, law and the other professions.

Is that why the Indians were persecuted?

The Dutch, who first settled South Africa in the sixteenth century, brought their slaves from Malaya, Java and other Pacific islands. They were concentrated in the Transvaal and the Orange Free State. The British arrived much later. In Natal they found they could grow sugar cane, tea and coffee. But the Negroes were reluctant to work for them. Arrangements were accordingly made for the shipment of indentured laborers from India.

The first Indian contract workers landed in Natal in 1860. They came from India voluntarily or, frequently, involuntarily and not knowing where they were going. Many were untouchables snatched from semi-starvation. The system tied them to private farms for five years. They were given free board and lodgings for themselves and their families, and ten shillings, or about three dollars, a month in the first year, and an additional shilling, or twenty-five cents, a month each year thereafter. At the end of the five years the contractor paid their passage back to India. He did the same if they remained another five years as free laborers. In numerous cases, the indentured laborers chose to become permanent residents.

When Gandhi had been in South Africa just over a year—on August 18, 1894—these conditions were altered. At the end of the first five-year period, the indentured laborer had to return to India or agree to be a serf in South Africa forever. But if he wished to stay as a free workingman, he had to pay an annual tax of three pounds for himself and for each of his dependents. Three pounds was the equivalent of six months' pay.

THE METHOD IS BORN

This aroused a storm, at the center of which stood Gandhi.]

We organized a fierce campaign against this tax. . . .

. . . It ever remained the determination [of the Natal Indian Congress] to get the tax remitted but it was twenty years before the determination was realized. . . .

But truth triumphed in the end. The sufferings of the Indians were the expression of that truth. Yet it would not have triumphed except for unflinching faith, great patience and incessant effort. Had the community given up the struggle, had the Congress abandoned the campaign and submitted to the tax as inevitable, the hated impost would have continued to be levied from the indentured Indians until this day, to the eternal shame of the Indians in South Africa and of the whole of India.[20]

[In three years in South Africa, Gandhi had become a prosperous lawyer and the outstanding Indian political figure. He was widely known as the champion of indentured laborers. He addressed conferences, drafted memorandums to government ministers, wrote letters to newspapers, circulated petitions (one was signed by ten thousand Indians), and made many friends among whites, Indians and Negroes. He published two pamphlets: *An Appeal to Every Briton in South Africa* and *The Indian Franchise, An Appeal.*

"Appeal" was the key to Gandhi's politics. He appealed to the common sense and morality of his adversary.]

It has always been a mystery to me how men can feel themselves honored by the humiliation of their fellow-beings.[21]

[Gandhi's struggle in South Africa did not aim to achieve "equality" for the Indians there, as he wrote to the Editor of the *Natal Mercury*.]

. . . You have said that the Indians want social equality with the Europeans. I confess I do not quite understand the phrase but I know that the Indians have never asked [British Colonial Secretary Joseph Chamberlain] to regulate the social relations between the two communities, and so long as the manners, customs, habits and religions of the two communities differ there will, naturally, be a social distinction. What the Indians fail to understand is why that

[20] M. K. Gandhi, *Experiments,* Part II, Chapter 21, p. 131.
[21] *Ibid.,* Part II, Chapter 20, p. 129.

difference should come in the way of the two living cordially and harmoniously in any part of the world without the Indians having to accept a degradation of their status in the eyes of the law. If the sanitary habits of the Indians are not quite what they ought to be, the Sanitary Department can, by strict vigilance, effect the needed improvement. If Indians have not got decent-looking stores, licensing authorities can soon turn them into decent-looking ones. These things can be done only when European Colonists, as Christians, look upon the Indians as brethren or as British subjects, look upon them as fellow-subjects [of the British Empire]. Then, instead of cursing and swearing at the Indians as now, they would help them to remove any defects that there may be in them and thus raise them and themselves also in the estimation of the world.[22]

[Though there was only slight visible evidence, as yet, of the great Gandhi of history, he had proved himself an effective leader and an excellent organizer. His Indian co-workers felt acutely, and he could not fail to see, that without him the struggle for Indian rights would collapse, or at least lag.

Gandhi, accordingly, took six months' leave and went to India to fetch his family.

Arrived in the homeland in the middle of 1896, the twenty-seven-year-old man with a mission engaged in furious activity. In Rajkot, he spent a month in the bosom of his family writing a pamphlet on Indian grievances in South Africa.]

. . . It had a green cover and came to be known afterwards as the Green Pamphlet. In it I drew a purposely subdued picture of the conditions of Indians in South Africa. The language I used was more moderate than that of the two pamphlets which I have referred to before [An Appeal to Every Briton in South Africa and The Indian Franchise, An Appeal—both written in South Africa], as I knew that things heard of from a distance appear bigger than they are.

---

[22] Letter to the Editor of the Natal, South Africa, Mercury, April 16, 1897, in M. K. Gandhi, The Collected Works of Mahatma Gandhi (The Publications Division, Ministry of Information and Broadcasting, Government of India. Ahmedabad: Navajivan Trust, 1958), pp. 309–310.

Ten thousand copies were printed and sent to all the papers and leaders of every party in India. . . .

To get these pamphlets ready for posting was no small matter. It would have been expensive too, if I had employed paid help for preparing wrappers, etc. But I hit upon a much simpler plan. I gathered together all the children in my locality and asked them to volunteer two or three hours' labor of a morning when they had no school. This they willingly agreed to do. I promised to bless them and give them, as a reward, used postage stamps which I had collected. They got through the work in no time. That was my first experiment of having little children as volunteers. Two of those little friends are my co-workers today.

Plague broke out in Bombay about this time and there was panic all around. There was fear of an outbreak in Rajkot. . . . I offered my services to the State . . . and I was put on the committee which was appointed to look into the question. I laid especial emphasis on the cleanliness of latrines and the committee decided to inspect these in every street. The poor people had no objection . . . and what is more, they carried out the improvements suggested to them. But when we went to inspect the houses of the [rich], some of them even refused us admission, not to talk of listening to our suggestions. It was our common experience that the latrines of the rich were more unclean. . . .

The Committee had to inspect the untouchables' quarters also. Only one member of the Committee was ready to accompany me there. . . . That was the first visit in my life to such a locality. The men and women there were surprised to see us. . . .

"[You] won't mind if we inspect your houses?" I asked.

"You are perfectly welcome, sir. You may see every nook and corner of our houses. Ours are no houses, they are holes."

I went in and was delighted to see that the insides were as clean as the outsides. The entrances were well-swept . . . and the few pots and pans were clean and shining. There was no fear of an outbreak in those quarters.[23]

*   *   *

[23] M. K. Gandhi, *Experiments,* Part II, Chapter 25, pp. 140–142.

[From Rajkot Gandhi went to Bombay to arrange a public meeting on South Africa. Meanwhile he nursed his sister's husband, who was ill, and later moved the dying patient into his own room.]

My aptitude for nursing gradually developed into a passion, so much so that it often led me to neglect my work, and on occasions I engaged not only my wife but the whole household in such service.

Such service can have no meaning unless one takes pleasure in it. When it is done for show or for fear of public opinion it stunts the man and crushes his spirit. Service which is rendered without joy helps neither the servant nor the served. But all other pleasures and possessions pale into nothingness before service which is rendered in a spirit of joy.[24]

[The Bombay meeting was a tremendous success. Gandhi continued his mission, traveling to Poona and Madras.]

The affection showered on me by most of the friends I met and their enthusiasm for the cause were so great that, in spite of my having to communicate with them in English, I felt myself entirely at home. What barrier is there that love cannot break?[25]

[In Calcutta, Gandhi attempted to enlist the support of newspapers for his campaign. But often the editors kept him waiting or refused to see him.]

However serious a grievance may be in the eyes of the man who suffers from it, he will be but one of the numerous people invading the editor's office. . . . How is the editor to meet them all? Moreover, the aggrieved party imagines that the editor is a power in the land. Only he knows that his powers can hardly travel beyond the threshold of his office. But I was not discouraged. I kept on seeing editors of other papers. . . .

Mr. Saunders, editor of *The Englishman,* claimed me as his own. . . .

. . . What Mr. Saunders liked in me was my freedom from exaggeration and my devotion to truth. He subjected me to a searching cross-examination before he began to sympathize with my cause,

[24] *Ibid.,* Part II, Chapter 26, p. 145.
[25] *Ibid.,* Part II, Chapter 28, p. 149.

and he saw that I had spared neither will nor pains to place before him an impartial statement of the case even of the white man in South Africa, and also to appreciate it.

My experience has shown me that we win justice quickest by rendering justice to the other party.[26]

[A cable from Natal, South Africa, recalled Gandhi to cope with an emergency—the opening of a hostile parliament. He rushed back to Bombay where, with his wife, two sons and the widowed sister's only son, he boarded the S.S. *Courland*. The S.S. *Naderi* sailed for Natal at the same time. The two ships carried about eight hundred passengers.

Gandhi's efforts to arouse Indian public opinion on the South African issue had been reported, with exaggeration, in the South African press. Now he was arriving with eight hundred free Indians. This provoked fierce resentment among the whites, who charged him with flooding Natal and the Transvaal with unwanted, unindentured colored people. Gandhi was, of course, innocent of recruiting or encouraging the travelers.]

[The] two ships cast anchor in the port of Durban on or about the 18th of December [1896]. . . . As there had been plague in Bombay when we set sail . . . our ship was . . . ordered to be put in quarantine. . . . But this quarantine order had more than health reasons behind it.

The white residents of Durban had been agitating for [the Indians'] repatriation and the agitation was one of the reasons for the order. . . .

The real object of the quarantine was thus to coerce the passengers into returning to India by somehow intimidating them. . . .

. . . On Christmas Day the captain invited the saloon passengers to dinner. . . . I knew this was not an occasion for a serious speech. But mine could not be otherwise. I took part in the merriment but my heart was in the combat that was going on in Durban. . . .

I therefore deplored the civilization of which the Natal whites were the fruit and which they represented and championed. . . . The captain and other friends gave me a patient hearing . . . afterward I had long talks with the captain and other officers regarding

<hr />

[26] *Ibid.*, Part II, Chapter 29, p. 151.

the civilization of the west. . . . The questioners pinned me to my faith, and one of them—the captain, so far as I can recollect—said to me:

"Supposing the whites carry out their threats, how will you stand by your principle of non-violence?" To which I replied: "I hope God will give me the courage and the sense to forgive them and to refrain from bringing them to law. I have no anger against them. I am only sorry for their ignorance and their narrowness. I know that they sincerely believe that what they are doing today is right and proper. I have no reason therefore to be angry with them."

At the end of twenty-three days the ships were permitted to enter the harbor and orders permitting the passengers to land were passed.[27]

But Mr. [Harry] Escombe [the Attorney-General of the Natal Government who had openly participated in the anti-Gandhi agitation] had sent word to the captain that as the whites were highly enraged against me and my life was in danger, my family and I should be advised to land at dusk. . . . I agreed to act accordingly. But scarcely half an hour after this, Mr. Laughton [an Englishman and legal counsellor of the steamship company] came to me and said somewhat to this effect: "If you are not afraid, I suggest that Mrs. Gandhi [who was pregnant] and the children should drive to Mr. Rustomji's [an Indian friend's] house, whilst you and I follow them on foot. I do not at all like the idea of your entering the city like a thief in the night. . . . Everything is quiet now. The whites have all dispersed." . . . I readily agreed. My wife and children drove safely to Mr. Rustomji's place. . . . I went ashore with Mr. Laughton. Mr. Rustomji's house was about two miles from the dock.

As soon as we landed, some youngsters recognized me and shouted "Gandhi, Gandhi." About half a dozen men rushed to the spot and joined in the shouting. Mr. Laughton feared the crowd might swell and hailed a rickshaw. . . . But the youngsters would not let me get into it. They frightened the rickshaw boy out of his life and he took to his heels. As we went ahead, the crowd continued to swell until it became impossible to proceed further. They

[27] *Ibid.,* Part III, Chapter 2, pp. 157–59.

first caught hold of Mr. Laughton and separated us. Then they pelted me with stones, brickbats and rotten eggs. Someone snatched away my turban, whilst others began to batter and kick me. I fainted and caught hold of the front railings of a house and stood there to get my breath. But it was impossible. They came upon me boxing and battering. The wife of the police superintendent, who knew me, happened to be passing by. The brave lady came up, opened her parasol . . . and stood between the crowd and me. This checked the fury of the mob, as it was difficult for them to deliver blows on me without harming Mrs. Alexander.

Meanwhile, an Indian youth who witnessed the incident had run to the police station. The police superintendent, Mr. Alexander, sent a posse of men to ring me round and escort me safely to my destination. They arrived in time. . . . Escorted by the police, I arrived without further harm at Mr. Rustomji's place. I had bruises all over but no abrasions except in one place. . . .

There was quiet inside, but outside the whites surrounded the house. Night was coming on, and the yelling crowd was shouting "We must have Gandhi." The quick-sighted police superintendent was already there trying to keep the crowds under control, not by threats but by humoring them. But he was not entirely free from anxiety. He sent me a message to this effect: "If you would save your friend's house and property and also your family, you should escape the house in disguise, as I suggest."

It is idle to adjudicate upon the right and wrong of incidents that have already happened. It is useful to understand them and, if possible, to learn a lesson from them for the future. . . .

[The] preparations for escape made me forget my injuries. As suggested by the superintendent, I put on an Indian constable's uniform and wore on my head a Madrasi scarf wrapped round a plate to serve as a helmet. Two detectives accompanied me, one of them disguised as an Indian merchant and with his face painted to resemble an Indian. I forget the disguise of the other. We . . . threaded our way through the crowd to a carriage that had been kept for me at the end of the street. In this we drove off to the police station where Mr. Alexander had offered me refuge a short time before, and I thanked him and the detective officers.

. . . Mr. Escombe sent for me, expressed his regret for the

injuries I had sustained and said, "Believe me, I cannot feel happy over the least little injury done to your person. If you can identify the assailants I am prepared to arrest and prosecute them. . . ."

"I do not want to prosecute anyone. It is possible that I may be able to identify one or two of them, but what is the use of getting them punished? Besides, I do not hold the assailants to blame. They were given to understand that I had made exaggerated statements in India about the whites in Natal and calumniated them. If they believed these reports, it is no wonder they were enraged. The leaders and, if you will permit me to say so, you are to blame. You could have guided the people properly . . . I do not want to bring anyone to book. I am sure that when the truth becomes known, they will be sorry for their conduct."[28]

[Gandhi had been interviewed by the *Natal Advertiser* the day he landed. This] interview and my refusal to prosecute the assailants produced such a profound impression that the Europeans of Durban were ashamed of their conduct. The press declared me to be innocent and condemned the mob. Thus the lynching ultimately proved to be a blessing for me, that is, for the cause. It enhanced the prestige of the Indian community in South Africa and made my work easier.[29]

[A photograph of Mrs. Gandhi on her first arrival in South Africa in 1897—at twenty-eight—shows her a beautiful woman, elegant in a rich silk sari, the dress of Indian women. It is a long piece of cloth wrapped around the waist and gracefully draped over a short blouse, with the end often pulled Madonna-like over the head. Kasturbai's fine oval face with eyes wide apart, well-formed nose, delicately curved lips and perfectly shaped chin must have made her very attractive indeed. She was not as tall as Gandhi.

Harilal and Manilal, their two sons who came with them to South Africa, were dressed in knee-length coats and long, Western trousers.]

. . . Some of the recollections of those days are amusing to look back upon.

[28] *Ibid.,* Part III, Chapter 3, pp. 159–163.
[29] *Ibid.,* Part III, Chapter 4, pp. 163–164.

*   *   *

I believed . . . that in order to look civilized, our dress and manners had, as far as possible, to approximate the European standard. Because, I thought, only thus could we have some influence, and without influence it would not be possible to serve the community.

. . . Of course no one could be without shoes and stockings. It was long before my wife and children could get used to them. The shoes cramped their feet and the stockings stank with perspiration. The toes often got sore. . . . They agreed to the changes in dress as there was no alternative. In the same spirit and with even more reluctance they adopted the use of knives and forks. When my infatuation for these signs of civilization wore away, they gave up the knives and forks. . . . I can see today that we feel all the freer and lighter for having cast off the tinsel of "civilization."[30]

[Gandhi was not only his family's authority and teacher, but nurse—and midwife to Kasturbai—as well. He helped care for his infant sons: Ramdas, his third son, born in 1897, and Devadas, born in 1900. He had studied a popular work on childbirth, which constituted a full course in obstetrics and infant care, and when labor came too swiftly for professional help to be fetched, Gandhi himself delivered his fourth son.]

I had started on a life of ease and comfort, but the experiment was short-lived. Although I had furnished the house with care . . . it failed to have any hold on me . . . I began to cut down expenses. The washerman's bill was heavy and, as he was besides by no means noted for his punctuality, even two to three dozen shirts and collars proved [an insufficient supply] for me. . . . I bought a book on washing, studied the art and taught it also to my wife. This no doubt added to my work, but its novelty made it a pleasure.

I shall never forget the first collar that I washed myself. I had used more starch than necessary, the iron had not been made hot enough, and for fear of burning the collar, I had not pressed it sufficiently. The result was that though the collar was fairly stiff, the superfluous starch continually dropped off it. I went to court with the collar on, thus inviting the ridicule of brother barristers, but even in those days I could be impervious to ridicule.

[30] *Ibid.,* Part III, Chapter 1, pp. 155–156.

"Well," said I, "this is my first experiment at washing my own collars. . . . But it does not trouble me and then there is the advantage of providing you with so much fun."

"But surely there is no lack of laundries here?" asked a friend.

"The laundry bill is very heavy," said I. "The charge for washing a collar is almost as much as its price, and even then there is the eternal dependence on the washerman. I prefer by far to wash my things myself."

But I could not make my friends appreciate the beauty of self-help. In the course of time I became an expert washerman so far as my own work went . . . My collars were no less stiff or shiny than others'.

In the same way . . . I threw off dependence on the barber. All people who go to England learn there at least the art of shaving, but none, to my knowledge, learn to cut their own hair. I had to learn that too. I once went to an English hair-cutter in Pretoria. He contemptuously refused to cut my hair. I certainly felt hurt, but immediately purchased a pair of clippers and cut my hair before the mirror. I succeeded more or less in cutting the front hair but I spoiled the back. The friends in the court shook with laughter.

"What's wrong with your hair, Gandhi? Rats have been at it?"

"No. The white barber would not condescend to touch my black hair," said I, "so I preferred to cut it myself, no matter how badly."

The reply did not surprise the friends.

The barber was not at fault in having refused to cut my hair. There was every chance of his losing his [customers] if he should serve black men. We do not allow our barbers to serve our untouchable brethren. I got the reward of this in South Africa not once but many times, and the conviction that it was the punishment for our own sins saved me from becoming angry.[31]

[In the Boer War, which was waged in South Africa from 1899 to 1902 between Dutch settlers and the British, Gandhi's personal sympathies "were all with the Boers."[32]]

[31] *Ibid.,* Part III, Chapter 9, pp. 177–179.
[32] *Ibid.,* Part III, Chapter 10, p. 179.

[But] I believed then that I had yet no right, in such cases, to enforce my individual convictions. . . . Suffice it to say that my loyalty to the British rule drove me to participation with the British in that war. . . .[33]

Hardly ever have I known anybody to cherish such loyalty as I did to the British Constitution. . . . The National Anthem used to be sung at every meeting that I attended in Natal. I then felt I must also join in the singing. Not that I was unaware of the defects in British rule, but . . . I believed British rule was, on the whole, beneficial to the ruled.[34]

I . . . taught the National Anthem to the children of my family. . . . Later on, the text began to jar on me. . . . The lines . . .

> *Scatter her enemies,*
> *And make them fall;*
> *Confound their politics,*
> *Frustrate their knavish tricks,*

particularly jarred upon my sentiment of Ahimsa [Love and Non-Violence]. . . . How could we assume that the so-called "enemies" were "knavish"? And because they were enemies, were they bound to be in the wrong?[35]

Never in my life did I exploit this loyalty, never did I seek to gain a selfish end by its means. It was for me more in the nature of an obligation, and I rendered it without expecting a reward.[36]

. . . I felt that if I demanded rights as a British citizen, it was also my duty as such to participate in the defense of the British Empire. I held then that India could achieve her complete emancipation only within and through the British Empire. So I collected together as many comrades as possible, and with very great difficulty got their services accepted as an ambulance corps.[37]

[Gandhi led the corps. Three hundred free Indians volunteered

[33] *Ibid.,* p. 179.
[34] *Ibid.,* Part II, Chapter 26, p. 142.
[35] *Ibid.,* pp. 143–144.
[36] *Ibid.,* p. 143.
[37] *Ibid.,* Part III, Chapter 10, p. 179.

together with eight hundred indentured laborers furloughed by their masters. For days they worked under the fire of enemy guns and carried wounded soldiers back to base hospital. The Indians sometimes walked as much as twenty-five miles a day. England and South Africa were impressed. Gandhi and several comrades received the War Medal and the corps was mentioned in dispatches.

Gandhi hoped that the fortitude of the Indians in the war would appeal to South Africa's sense of fair play and help to moderate white hostility. But further repressive measures were passed.]

"It was at your instance that the community helped in the war, and you see the result now," were the words with which some people taunted me. But the taunt had no effect. "I do not regret my advice," said I. "I maintain we did well in taking part in the war. In doing so we simply did our duty. We may not look forward to any reward for our labors, but it is my firm conviction that all good action is bound to bear fruit in the end. Let us forget the past and think of the task before us." . . .[38]

[Gandhi had no unspent belligerence and no further plans or ambitions in South Africa—nothing foreshadowed the epic opportunity for leadership and realization that came later. He yearned to go home to India, and did, at the end of 1901.]

. . . I felt my work was no longer in South Africa but in India. Not that there was nothing to be done in South Africa, but I was afraid that my main business might become merely money-making.

Friends at home were also pressing me to return and I felt that I should be of more service in India . . . so I requested my co-workers to relieve me. After very great difficulty my request was conditionally accepted . . . that I should be ready to go back to South Africa if, within a year, the community should need me. I thought it was a difficult condition but the love that bound me to the community made me accept it.

Gifts [from the Indian community] had been bestowed on me before when I returned to India in 1899, but this time the farewell

[38] *Ibid.*, p. 143.

was over-whelming. The gifts, of course, included things in gold and silver but there were articles of costly diamond as well.

What right had I to accept all these gifts? Accepting them, how could I persuade myself that I was serving the community without remuneration?

I knew that I should have some difficulty in persuading my wife. . . .

"You may not need them," said my wife. "Your children may not need them. Cajoled, they will dance to your tune. . . ."

". . . You deprived me of my ornaments, you would not leave me in peace with them. . . . And pray what right have you to my neck-lace?"

"But," I rejoined, "is the necklace given you for your service or for my service?"

"I agree. But service rendered by you is as good as rendered by me. I have toiled and moiled for you day and night. Is that no ser-vice? You forced all and sundry on me, making me weep bitter tears, and I slaved for them!"

These were pointed thrusts and some of them went home. But I was determined to return the ornaments. I somehow succeeded in extorting a consent from her. The gifts . . . were all returned. A trust-deed was prepared and they were deposited with a bank, to be used for the service of the community, according to my wishes or to those of the trustees.

. . . The fund is still there, being operated upon in times of need, and it has regularly accumulated.

I have never since regretted the step, and as the years have gone by, my wife also has seen its wisdom. It has saved us from many temptations.

I am definitely of the opinion that a public worker should accept no costly gifts.[39]

[Back in India, Gandhi again traveled around the country. In Cal-cutta, he was invited to attend a darbar—a state function—given by Lord Hardinge, Viceroy of India.]

[39] *Ibid.,* Part III, Chapter 12, pp. 183–185.

I was distressed to see the Maharajas [Princes] bedecked like women—silk pyjamas . . . pearl necklaces round their necks, bracelets on their wrists, pearl and diamond tassels on their turbans, and, besides all this, swords with golden hilts hanging from their waistbands.

I discovered these were insignia not of their royalty, but of their slavery. I had thought they must be wearing these badges of impotence of their own free will, but I was told that it was obligatory for these Rajas to wear all their costly jewels at such functions. I also gathered that some of them had a positive dislike for wearing these jewels and that they never wore them except on occasions like the darbar.

How heavy is the toll of sins and wrongs that wealth, power and prestige exact from man![40]

During these days I walked up and down the streets of Calcutta. . . .

[An Indian friend] had spoken to me about the Kali [Hindu goddess of death and destruction] temple, which I was eager to see. . . . On the way I saw a stream of sheep going to be sacrificed to Kali. . . . [At the temple, Gandhi and some beggars "were greeted by rivers of blood."] I could not bear to stand there. I was exasperated and restless. I have never forgotten that sight.

. . . I felt the cruel custom ought to be stopped. I thought of the story of Buddha, but I also saw the task was beyond my capacity.

. . . I hold that the more helpless a creature, the more entitled it is to protection by man from the cruelty of man. . . . It is my constant prayer that there may be born on earth some great spirit, man or woman, fired with divine pity, who will deliver us from this heinous sin. . . .[41]

Just when I seemed to be settling down [in Bombay] as I had intended, I received an unexpected cable from South Africa: "Chamberlain expected here. Please return immediately." . . . I gave up the [law office] chambers and started for South Africa.

[40] *Ibid.,* Part III, Chapter 16, pp. 192–193.
[41] *Ibid.,* Part III, Chapter 18, pp. 196–197.

[Joseph Chamberlain, the British Colonial Secretary, was making a trip to South Africa, one which the Indian community regarded as fateful; they wanted Gandhi to present their grievances to him.

Kasturbai and the boys remained in Bombay.]

The separation from wife and children, the breaking up of a settled establishment, and the going from the certain to the uncertain—all this was for a moment painful but I had inured myself to an uncertain life. I think it is wrong to expect certainties in this world where all else but God that is Truth is an uncertainty. . . .[42]

[Chamberlain, Gandhi assumed, had come to get a gift of thirty-five million pounds from South Africa and to cement the post-war bonds between the Boers and the British. Britain was ministering to Boer wounds and therefore did not intend to wound Boer sensibilities by redressing Indian grievances.]

Mr. Chamberlain . . . gave a cold shoulder to the Indian deputation.

"You know," he said, "that the Imperial Government has little control over self-governing colonies. Your grievances seem to be genuine. I shall do what I can but you must try your best to placate the Europeans if you wish to live in their midst."

The reply cast a chill over the members of the deputation. I was also disappointed. It was an eye-opener for us all. . . .

. . . It was well that he did not mince matters. He had brought home to us in a rather gentle way the rule of might being right or the law of the sword.

But sword we had none. We scarcely had the nerve and the muscle even to receive sword-cuts.[43]

[The Gandhi who worsted the South African government in prolonged combat first conquered himself and transformed his living habits and inner essence.]

While I was working with the [Indian ambulance corps during the Boer War], two ideas which had been floating in my mind became firmly fixed. First, an aspirant after a life devoted exclusively to service must lead a life of celibacy. Secondly, he must

---

[42] *Ibid.,* Part III, Chapter 23, p. 209.
[43] *Ibid.,* Part IV, Chapter 1, pp. 213–214.

accept poverty as a constant companion through life. He may not take up any occupation which would prevent him or make him shrink from undertaking the lowliest of duties or largest risks.[44]

About the time I took up chambers in Bombay [a year later], an American insurance agent had come there—a man with a pleasing countenance and a sweet tongue. As though we were old friends, he discussed my future welfare. . . .

Up to this time I had given the cold shoulder to all the agents I had met in South Africa and India, for I had thought life assurance implied fear and want of faith in God. . . . As he proceeded with his argument I had before my mind's eye a picture of my wife and children. "Man, you have sold almost all the ornaments of your wife," I said to myself. "If something were to happen to you, the burden of supporting her and the children would fall on your poor brother. . . ."

But when my mode of life changed in South Africa, my outlook changed too. . . . What happened to the families of the numberless poor in the world? Why should I not count myself as one of them?[45]

. . . I already had faith in the Gita, which had a fascination for me. Now I realized the necessity of diving deeper into it. . . .

[Gita or "Song" is short for Bhagavad-Gita, the "Song of God" or "Song of Heaven." It is an exquisite poem of seven hundred stanzas, as sacred to Hinduism as the Koran is to Islam, the Old Testament to Judaism and the New Testament to Christianity.]

[To] me the Gita became an infallible guide of conduct. . . . Just as I turned to the English dictionary for the meanings of English words that I did not understand, I turned to this dictionary of conduct for a ready solution of all my troubles and trials. Words like Aparigraha [Non-Possession] and Samabhava [Equability] gripped me. . . . How was one to treat alike insulting, insolent and corrupt officials, co-workers of yesterday raising meaningless opposition, and men who had always been good to one? How was one to divest oneself of all possessions? . . . Were not wife and children possessions? Was I to destroy all the cupboards of books I had? Was I to give up all I had and follow Him? Straight came the answer: I

[44] M. K. Gandhi, *Satyagraha in South Africa,* Chapter 11, p. 155.
[45] M. K. Gandhi, *Experiments,* Part IV, Chapter 4, p. 219.

could not follow Him unless I gave up all I had. My study of English law came to my help.

. . . I understood the Gita teaching of non-possession to mean that those who desired Salvation [union with God, the attainment of freedom from birth and death] should act like the trustee who, though having control over great possessions, regards not an iota of them as his own. . . . I then wrote to . . . allow the insurance policy to lapse . . . for I had become convinced that God, who created my wife and children as well as myself, would take care of them. To my brother . . . I wrote explaining that I had given him all that I had saved up to that moment, but that henceforth he should expect nothing from me, for future savings, if any, would be utilized for the benefit of the community.[46]

I cannot tell you with truth that when this belief came to me I discarded everything immediately. I must confess to you that progress at first was slow. . . . It was also painful in the beginning. But as days went by I saw I had to throw overboard many other things which I used to consider as mine, and a time came when it became a matter of positive joy to give up those things. One after another, then by almost geometric progression, things slipped away from me. [A] great burden fell off my shoulders, and I felt I could now walk with ease and do my work also in the service of my fellow men with great comfort and still greater joy. The possession of anything then became a troublesome thing and a burden.

Exploring the cause of that joy, I found that if I kept anything as my own, I had to defend it against the whole world. . . . And I said to myself: if [other people] want it and would take it, they do so not from any malicious motive but . . . because theirs was a greater need than mine.

And I said to myself: possession seems to me to be a crime, I can only possess certain things when I know that others who also want to possess similar things are able to do so. But we know . . . such a thing is an impossibility. Therefore, the only thing that can be possessed by all is non-possession, not to have anything whatsoever. Or . . . a willing surrender. . . .[47]

[46] *Ibid.,* Part IV, Chapter 5, pp. 221–222.
[47] From an address at the Guild Hall, London, September 27, 1931, in D. G.

From the standpoint of pure Truth, the body too is a possession. It has been truly said that desire for enjoyment creates bodies for the soul. When this desire vanishes, there remains no further need for the body and man is free from the vicious cycle of births and deaths. . . . We thus arrive at the ideal of total renunciation and learn to use the body for the purposes of service so long as it exists, so much so that service, and not bread, becomes with us the staff of life. We eat and drink, sleep and awake, for service alone. Such an attitude of mind brings us real happiness. . . .

. . . Therefore . . . such must be my constant desire that this body also may be surrendered . . . and while it is at my disposal, must be used not for dissipation, not for self-indulgence, not for pleasure, but merely for service. . . . And if this is true with reference to the body, how much more with reference to clothing and other things that we use?

And those who have followed out this vow of voluntary poverty to the fullest extent possible . . . testify that when you dispossess yourself of everything you have, you really possess all the treasures of the world.[48]

My brother gave me up, and practically stopped all communication. I was deeply distressed, but it would have been a greater distress to give up what I considered to be my duty. . . . But that did not affect my devotion to him. . . . His great love for me was at the root of his misery. . . . Near the end of his life, however, he appreciated my viewpoint. . . . He commended his sons to my care, to be brought up as I thought fit. . . . His sons had been brought up in the old atmosphere and could not change their course of life. I could not draw them to me. It was not their fault. . . . Who can erase the impressions with which he is born? It is idle to expect one's children and wards necessarily to follow the same course of evolution as oneself.

This instance to some extent serves to show what a terrible responsibility it is to be a parent.[49]

Tendulkar, *Mahatma: The Life of Mohandas Karamchand Gandhi* (Bombay: Vithalbhai K. Jhaveri & D. G. Tendulkar, March, 1952), Volume III, pp. 155–157.

[48] M. K. Gandhi, *From Yeravda Mandir* (Ahmedabad: Navajivan Publishing Company, 1937), Chapter 6, p. 25.

[49] M. K. Gandhi, *Experiments,* Part IV, Chapter 5, pp. 222–223.

*   *   *

A variety of incidents in my life have conspired to bring me in close contact with people of many creeds and many communities, and my experience with all of them warrants the statement that I have known no distinction between relatives and strangers, countrymen and foreigners, white and colored, Hindus and Indians of other faiths, whether Moslems, Parsis, Christians or Jews. . . . I cannot claim this as a special virtue as it is in my very nature, rather than a result of any effort on my part, whereas in the case of Ahimsa [nonviolence], Brahmacharya [celibacy], Aparigraha [non-possession], and other cardinal virtues, I am fully conscious of a continuous striving for their cultivation.

When I was practising [law] in Durban, my office clerks often stayed with me, and there were among them Hindus and Christians. . . . I do not recollect having ever regarded them as anything but my kith and kin. I treated them as members of my family, and had unpleasantness with my wife if ever she stood in the way of my treating them as such. . . .[50]

---

[50] *Ibid.,* Part IV, Chapter 10, p. 231.

5

THE STRUGGLE

[Among the weapons employed in the South African struggle was *Indian Opinion,* a weekly journal, which Gandhi helped found in 1903.] . . . *Indian Opinion* was published in English and Gujarati. . . . Through . . . this paper, we could very well disseminate the news of the week among the community. The English section kept those Indians informed about the movement who did not know Gujarati, and for Englishmen in India, England and South Africa, *Indian Opinion* served the purpose of a weekly newsletter. [A] struggle which relies chiefly upon internal strength cannot be wholly carried on without a newspaper, and . . . we could not perhaps have educated the local Indian community, nor kept Indians all over the world in touch with the course of events in South Africa in any other way, with the same ease and success as through *Indian Opinion*. . . .

As the community was transformed in the course of and as a result of the struggle, so was *Indian Opinion*. In the beginning, we used to accept advertisements for it. [Some] of our best men had to be spared to this. . . . Some of the good workers had to be set apart for canvassing and [collecting bills] from advertisers, not to speak of the flattery which advertisers claimed as their due. Moreover . . . if the paper was conducted not because it yielded a profit but purely with a view to service, the service should not be imposed upon the community by force but . . . only if the community wished. And the clearest proof of such a wish would be forthcoming if they became subscribers in sufficiently large numbers to make the paper self-supporting. [We] stopped advertisements in the paper. The community realized at once their proprietorship of *Indian Opinion* and their consequent responsibility for maintaining it. . . .

Just as we stopped advertisements . . . we ceased to take [private printing] jobwork in the press. . . . Compositors had now some time to spare, which was utilized in the publication of books. As . . . there was no intention of reaping profits, and as the books were printed only to help the struggle forward, they commanded good sales. . . .

[The workers'] only care now was to put their best work into the paper, so long as the community wanted it, and they were not only not ashamed of requesting any Indian to subscribe to *Indian Opinion,* but thought it even their duty to do so. A change came over the internal strength and the character of the paper and it became a force to reckon with. . . . The community had made the paper their own to such an extent that if copies did not reach Johannesburg at the expected time, I would be flooded with complaints. . . . I know of many whose first occupation after they received [it] would be to read the Gujarati section through from beginning to end. One of the company would read it, and the rest would surround him and listen. Not all who wanted to read the paper could afford to subscribe to it by themselves, and some of them would therefore club together for the purpose.[1]

. . . *Indian Opinion* was an open book to whoever wanted to gauge the strength and the weakness of the community, be he a friend, an enemy or a neutral. The workers had realized at the very outset that secrecy had no place in a movement where one could do no wrong, where there was no scope for duplicity or cunning, and where strength constituted the single guarantee of victory. The very interest of the community demanded that if the disease of weakness was to be eradicated, it must be first properly diagnosed and given due publicity. . . .[2]

[In one of the paper's early issues, Gandhi told his readers:]

. . . One thing we [the staff of *Indian Opinion*], have endeavored to observe most scrupulously: namely, never to depart from the strictest facts, and in dealing with the difficult questions that have arisen . . . we hope we have used the utmost moderation possible under the circumstances. [We] should fail in our duty if we wrote anything with a view to hurt. Facts we would always place before our readers, whether they be palatable or not, and it is by placing them constantly before the public in their nakedness that the mis-

[1] M. K. Gandhi, *Satyagraha in South Africa,* Chapter 19, pp. 220–224.
[2] *Ibid.,* Chapter 20, p. 225.

understanding now existing between the two communities in South Africa can be removed.[3]

. . . I was inundated with letters containing the outpourings of my correspondents' hearts. They were friendly, critical or bitter, according to the temper of the writer. It was a fine education for me to study, digest and answer all this correspondence. . . . It made me thoroughly understand the responsibility of a journalist, and the hold I secured in this way over the community made the future campaign workable, dignified and irresistible.[4]

[In 1904, a few months after its founding, *Indian Opinion* was in difficulties, and to cope with them at first hand, Gandhi took a trip to Durban, where the journal was published. An Englishman named Henry S. L. Polak saw him off and gave him a copy of John Ruskin's *Unto This Last*. Gandhi started reading it the moment the train left Johannesburg and read all night.]

That book marked the turning point in my life.[5]

. . . I discovered some of my deepest convictions reflected in this great book of Ruskin's and that is why it so captured me and made me transform my life. A poet is one who can call forth the good latent in the human breast. . . .

The teachings of *Unto This Last* I understood to be:

1. That the good of the individual is contained in the good of all.
2. That a lawyer's work has the same value as the barber's, inasmuch as all have the same right of earning their livelihoods from their work.
3. That a life of labor—the life of the tiller of the soil and the handicraftsman—is the life worth living.

The first of these I knew. The second I had dimly realized. The third had never occurred to me. *Unto This Last* made it as clear as

---

[3] *Indian Opinion,* January 7, 1904.

[4] M. K. Gandhi, *The Story of My Experiments With Truth,* Part IV, Chapter 13, p. 239.

[5] Statement to Andrew Freeman of the New York *Post,* October 1946, quoted in Louis Fischer, *The Life of Mahatma Gandhi,* Part I, Chapter 9, p. 69.

daylight for me that the second and the third were contained in the first. I arose with the dawn to reduce these principles to practice.[6]

It was a habit with me to forget what I did not like and to carry out in practice whatever I liked.[7]

I talked over the whole thing with Mr. [Albert] West [the British Editor], described to him the effect *Unto This Last* had produced on my mind, and proposed that *Indian Opinion* should be removed to a farm, on which everyone should labor, drawing the same living wage, and attending to the press work in their spare time. Mr. West approved . . . and three pounds was laid down as the monthly allowance per head. . . .

I do not think I took more than two days to fix up these matters with the men. . . .[8]

[Gandhi bought a farm near Phoenix, a town fourteen miles from Durban. The presses and offices of *Indian Opinion* were transferred to the farm, and the magazine's staff moved there too.

During 1904 and 1905, Gandhi, Kasturbai and their sons lived now in Johannesburg, now at Phoenix Farm. In both places, the problem of restraint and self-control preoccupied him. The year 1906 marked a crisis in Gandhi's struggle with his passions.]

. . . I was practising in Johannesburg at the time of the Zulu "Rebellion" in Natal. . . . I felt that I must offer my services to the Natal Government. [The] work set me furiously thinking in the direction of self-control. . . . It became my conviction that procreation and the consequent care of children were inconsistent with public service. I had to break up my household at Johannesburg to be able to serve during the "Rebellion." . . . During the difficult marches that had then to be performed, the idea flashed upon me that, if I wanted to devote myself to the service of the community . . . I must relinquish the desire for children and wealth and live the life of a Vanaprastha—of one retired from household cares.

The "Rebellion" did not occupy me for more than six weeks, but this brief period proved to be a very important epoch in my life. The importance of vows grew upon me more clearly than ever

[6] M. K. Gandhi, *Experiments,* Part IV, Chapter 18, p. 250.
[7] Louis Fischer, *Life of Gandhi,* p. 84.
[8] M. K. Gandhi, *Experiments,* Part IV, Chapter 19, p. 250.

before. I realized that a vow, far from closing the door to real freedom, opened it. . . . I realized that in refusing to take a vow man
was drawn into temptation and to be bound by a vow was like a
passage from libertinism to a real monogamous marriage. . . .[9]

After full discussion and mature deliberation I took the vow [of
celibacy] in 1906. I had not shared my thoughts with my wife until
then, but only consulted her at the time of taking the vow. She had
no objection.

[Let] no one believe that it was an easy thing for me. . . .

Brahmacharya means control of the senses in thought, word and
deed. . . . An aspirant after Brahmacharya will always be conscious
of his short-comings, will seek out the passions lingering in the
innermost recesses of his heart and will incessantly strive to get rid
of them. . . .[10]

[The] path of self-purification is hard and steep. [One] has to
become absolutely passion-free in thought, speech and action, to
rise above the opposing currents of love and hatred, attachment
and repulsion. I know that I have not in me as yet that triple purity
in spite of constant ceaseless striving for it. That is why the world's
praise fails to move me, indeed it very often stings me. To conquer
the subtle passions seems to me to be harder far than the physical
conquest of the world by the force of arms.[11]

[In his studies of the Bhagavad Gita, Gandhi defined the ideal
man, or the perfect Karma yogi.]

He will have no relish for sensual pleasures and will keep himself occupied with such activity as ennobles the soul. That is the
path of action. Karma yoga is the yoga [means] which will deliver
the self [soul] from the bondage of the body, and in it there is no
room for self-indulgence.

He is a devotee who is jealous of none, who is a fount of mercy,
who is without egotism, who is selfless, who treats alike cold and
heat, happiness and misery, who is ever forgiving, who is always
contented, whose resolutions are firm, who has dedicated mind
and soul to God, who causes no dread, who is not afraid of others,
who is free from exultation, sorrow and fear, who is pure, who is

[9] *Ibid.,* Part III, Chapter 7, pp. 172–173.
[10] *Ibid.,* Part III, Chapter 8, pp. 174–176.
[11] *Ibid.,* "Farewell," p. 420.

versed in action yet remains unaffected by it, who renounces all
fruit, good or bad, who treats friend and foe alike, who is
untouched by respect or disrespect, who is not puffed up by praise,
who does not go under when people speak ill of him, who loves
silence and solitude, who has a disciplined reason. Such devotion is
inconsistent with the existence at the same time of strong attachments.

As a matter of fact, he who renounces reaps a thousandfold. The
renunciation of the Gita is the acid test of faith. He who is ever
brooding over results often loses nerve in the performance of duty.
He becomes impatient and then gives vent to anger and begins to
do unworthy things, he jumps from action to action, never remaining faithful to any. He who broods over results is like a man given
to objects of senses, he is ever distracted, he says goodbye to all scru-
ples, everything is right in his estimation and he therefore resorts to
means fair and foul to attain his end.[12]

It has always been my regret that, although I started the Settlement
at Phoenix, I could stay there only for brief periods. My original
idea had been to gradually retire from practice, go and live at the
Settlement [and] earn my livelihood by manual work there. . . . I
have found by experience that man makes his plans to be often
upset by God, but, at the same time, where the ultimate goal is the
search of truth, no matter how a man's plans are frustrated, the
issue is never injurious and often better than anticipated. . . .[13]

During my professional work it was . . . my habit never to con-
ceal my ignorance from my clients or my colleagues. Wherever I
felt myself at sea I would advise my client to consult some other
counsel, or if he preferred to stick to me, I would ask him to let me
seek the assistance of senior counsel. This frankness earned me the
unbounded affection and trust of my clients. . . . This affection and
trust served me in good stead in my public work.[14]

It may be of some interest to know how the Indians used to

[12] Mahadev Desai, *The Gospel of Selfless Action, the Gita According to Gandhi*
(Ahmedabad: Navajivan Publishing House, 1946), quoted in Louis Fischer, *Life
of Gandhi,* Part I, Chapter 4, pp. 32–35.

[13] M. K. Gandhi, *Experiments,* Part IV, Chapter 21, p. 254.

[14] *Ibid.,* Part IV, Chapter 46, p. 306.

name me. . . . None, fortunately, ever insulted me by calling or regarding me as "saheb" [master]. Abdulla Sheth hit upon a fine appelation—"bhai"—i.e., brother. Others followed him and continued to address me as "bhai" until the moment I left South Africa. There was a sweet flavor about the name when it was used by the ex-indentured Indians.[15]

[My] object in practising in South Africa was service of the community. [For] this purpose, winning the confidence of the people was an indispensable condition. [When] I advised them to suffer the hardships of imprisonment for the sake of their rights, many of them cheerfully accepted the advice not so much because they had reasoned out the correctness of the course as because of their confidence in and affection for me.

. . . Hundreds of clients became friends and real co-workers in public service and their association sweetened a life that was otherwise full of difficulties and dangers.[16]

. . . Happiness, the goal to which we all are striving is reached by endeavoring to make the lives of others happy, and if by renouncing the luxuries of life we can lighten the burdens of others . . . surely the simplification of our wants is a thing greatly to be desired! And so, if instead of supposing that we must become hermits and dwellers in caves in order to practice simplicity, we set about simplifying our affairs, each according to his own convictions and opportunity, much good will result and the simple life will at once be established.[17]

[Throughout 1904, 1905 and 1906, the Transvaal Government's Asiatic Department diligently carried out all anti-Indian regulations and showed special aptitude in inventing new ones. Gandhi's writings in *Indian Opinion* criticized them.]

[The] great bulk of the Indian members of the cosmopolitan community of the Transvaal are, with the ushering in of the year 1904, to be made to leave the homes that have sheltered them, however humbly, and the businesses they have built up, and literally take up their beds and walk to a place of complete segregation,

[15] *Ibid.*, Part IV, Chapter 14, p. 242.
[16] *Ibid.*, Part IV, Chapter 46, p. 306.
[17] *Indian Opinion,* August 26, 1905.

where their existence may be forgotten, and life be made as difficult and profitless as their worst enemies might wish. Pledges and
obligations are to go for naught, professions are to be tossed care-
lessly aside, the faith of one people in another they have been
taught to regard as brothers is to be crushed and forever destroyed,
and all because the harsh voice of prejudice, the son of ignorance,
has caught the ears of our rulers, and the petty soul of the small
trader prompts the cry which may rid him of some small measure
of competition. For this the ban of excommunication is to fall upon
a people. For no crime, nor for any legitimate complaints. . . .
Homes will have to be rebuilt, businesses be reconstructed. Their
needs are to be ignored, for they will be far removed from any
European influences that might benefit them. Equally, they are to
be made impotent in respect of such usefulness as they might
yield. . . .

. . . Not so very long [ago], the doctrine of "The White Man's
Burden" was heard propounded on every hand, and was endorsed
with fervid acclamation. It was felt that power involved not only
rights . . . but serious and weighty responsibilities and duties. . . .
As it is the function of the Judge to adjudicate impartially . . . so
surely is it the business of the Ruler to rule painstakingly and with
careful regard to the needs and claims of every section of his subjects. . . . From the stronger, more was to be expected, because of
their strength. . . . They who urge that Britain conquers but for the
lust of possession might be made to stand confounded by a wise,
impartial, sympathetic rule of the weaker, more helpless and more
dependent sections of the community. [It] is to those who cultivate
the attitude of indifference that we would make the strongest
appeal. . . . The tacit contributor is not exempt from the retribu-
tion which must fall . . . for evil *is* wrought by want of thought,
and all who help in the working must partake of its harvest.

But is this monstrous injustice to be really done? Even at the
eleventh hour . . . we cannot abandon hope that the better nature,
the truer self, of our white brothers, will yet assert itself. . . .[18]

Sacrifice is the law of life. It runs through and governs every
walk of life. We can do nothing or get nothing without paying a

[18] *Indian Opinion,* December 3, 1903.

price for it. . . . If we would secure the salvation of the community
to which we belong, we must pay for it, that is, sacrifice self. . . .
True sacrifice lies in deriving the greatest pleasure from the deed,
no matter what the risk may be. Christ died on the Cross of Cal-
vary and left Christianity as a glorious heritage. . . . Joan of Arc
was burnt as a witch, to her eternal honor and to the everlasting
disgrace of her murderers—the world knows the result of her self-
sacrifice. The Americans bled for their independence.

We have given these illustrations to draw a contrast between the
very little the Indians as individuals have to sacrifice so that the
community may gain a great deal. . . . The Indians in South Africa
in general, and the Transvaal in particular, are undergoing many
troubles. Their fate . . . hangs in the balance. Their very means of
livelihood may be ruthlessly snatched. . . . They may be unceremo-
niously driven to Ghettos. What then is the self-sacrifice to be performed . . . ? Every Indian must consider the question as if it
affected him personally, put his hands into his pocket for the common good, give his time and energy. Individual differences must be
sunk in the face of common danger. Personal ease and personal
gain should be surrendered. To all this must be added patience and
self-control. The slightest deviation from the straight and narrow
path mapped out here would bring us down the precipice, not
because the cause is at all unjust or weak, but because the opposition set up against us is overwhelming.

No race or community has ever achieved anything without the
communal spirit. . . . A chain is no stronger than the weakest link
in it, and unless we are prepared to stand and work shoulder to
shoulder without flinching and without being daunted by temporary disappointments, failure would be the only fit reward, or,
rather, punishment. . . .[19]

[At the] anti-Asiatic meeting . . . the usual fallacies were dished
up with an increasing mixture of spices in order to render them
palatable. . . . For instance, one of the speakers said the Indians
lacked "the desirable qualities of residents of towns" in that they
did not leave "something of a lasting and progressive nature." . . .
To degrade a class of people with deliberation, to coop them up in

[19] *Indian Opinion,* January 21, 1904.

pens, to deprive them of the right of buying land, and then to turn round upon the very men and charge them with want of qualities desirable in citizens is a fine game. If any of these worthy speakers have traveled beyond the boundary of the district of Zoutpansberg, we might venture to direct their attention to what [the Indians] have done . . . in Cape Town, Durban and other places where they are allowed some rights. They have built business places in each of these towns which would compare favorably with any, and . . . they employed European architects, European contractors, European builders, bricklayers, carpenters, etc., and some of these buildings are tenanted also by Europeans. . . . One of the speakers said . . . "the true solution of the Asiatic question lies in the application of the maxim 'the greatest good for the greatest number.'" [We] are not blind believers in that maxim, we think it has worked untold mischief in many cases, and is yet likely to do so in the history of the world's progress. . . . The crime committed by the Indian is that he competes with [the European traders], he lowers the price of the necessaries of life, and having a fund of patience at his command, is a better seller, especially to those whose pockets are not too full, whether they be Europeans or Natives. Even then, if the Indian trader is of any disadvantage to the European traders, which we deny, he is . . . of great benefit to the largest number of the inhabitants of the Transvaal, and in proof of that [is] the very fact that he has to depend for his business on the support received from the poor whites, including the Dutch, and the Natives. . . .[20]

. . . Men, in the selfishness that blinds their reason, may think to score by injustice and oppression. . . .

Peoples are associated for their mutual advantage, and so between East and West the interaction must eventually operate to the benefit of both. . . . 'Twere as unreasonable to doubt that hidden in the murky smoke of Western materialism are immortal qualities . . . as . . . to ignore the existence in the Orient of the splendid monument of spiritual lore—the heritage of a long line of Eastern saints and sages. . . .

Branches from a common root, Oriental and Western have each

[20] *Indian Opinion*, August 13, 1904.

their mission, their place in the grand economy. . . . It rests with both to recognize that differences are not necessarily synonymous with superiority or inferiority and to patiently cultivate that spirit of self-restraint and toleration which . . . will . . . destroy the senseless rind of misunderstanding. . . .

It is worse than futile for the Oriental to pose within the cloak of Eastern dignity, to trade upon a past reputation, while at the same time greedily assimilating the very Western weaknesses he affects to despise and condemn. Let him hold fast to what is best . . . in the history of his people and . . . while retaining his self-respect, the more surely win the respect of his Western neighbors. Equally, the Western should abandon an attitude as stupidly inconsistent as that which demands from his Oriental neighbor conformity to his own ideals of propriety, while denying him every facility and encouragement.[21]

. . . Indians have been forbidden the use of the public park. . . . This matter should not be allowed to rest. [Indians] have as much right to use the park as the [City] Council itself. We hope [the Indians] will ask the question: Is there a law prohibiting Asiatics from using the park?—and pin the Council to a definite statement. If the reply is unsatisfactory, they should test the question, for we cannot conceive that in a British town, a body of ratepayers [taxpayers] can be deprived of their inherent right to use what is, after all, their own property in common with the rest of the community. This is not a question of sentiment but one of a deliberate deprivation of rights which have been paid for. . . .[22]

We are glad to see that the "Colored People" of Durban have protested against the decision to close all Government schools to colored children with the exception of those specially set apart for them. . . . We sincerely wish that Mr. Mudie [an official] could become a colored man for a time (while retaining his gentle courtesy and excellence of disposition) and be subject to the treatment accorded to colored people in this enlightened Colony. . . . Mr. Mudie seems to be unaware that colored parents have the same

[21] *Indian Opinion,* May 28, 1904.
[22] *Indian Opinion,* April 8, 1905.

affection for their children as European parents, and the same dislike to have any slight put upon them. . . .[23]

. . . It is a law of nature that the skin of races living near the equator should be black. And if we believe that there must be beauty in everything fashioned by nature, we would . . . steer clear of all narrow and one-sided conceptions of beauty. . . .[24]

. . . In my opinion, there is no place on earth and no race, which is not capable of producing the finest types of humanity, given suitable opportunities and education. . . .[25]

. . . So long as we have this contempt on the part of white races for the colored man, so long shall we have trouble. It is specially noticeable in those born here in South Africa. They are brought up to consider the native as so much dirt beneath their feet.

A lady once related to me in tones of horror and disgust her experience in a draper's shop. At the same counter a native was being served. This was too much for her dignity, and she asked the shopman if he actually served natives at the same counter with white people. The man of business frankly admitted that he did. Needless to say, this shop was avoided afterwards by one customer at least.

To answer a native's salute by anything more appreciative than a grunt is quite unnecessary, and if a "boy" does not hold out two hands to receive the "tickey" he has rightly earned, you are fully entitled to kick him for his insolence. A house boy who speaks English is considered "cheeky," but if the same boy fails to understand orders, spoken in English, then he is a stupid fool.

The native has been likened to a child, and the comparison is reasonable enough. But the average treatment of natives is not what a parent would mete out to a child. No, the native, like the child, should be taught with patience. Many a testimony I have heard, from those who have treated their native servants as intelligent beings, of the faithfulness and integrity of the trained natives, who in times of stress, have proved themselves worthy of the trust placed in them.

[23] *Indian Opinion,* September 2, 1905.
[24] M. K. Gandhi, *Satyagraha in South Africa,* Chapter 2, pp. 19–20.
[25] *Ibid.,* Chapter 2, p. 23.

Any form of government of the natives, if it is to be successful, must recognize that he is not made of wood, and is capable of progress. And if we grant that he is intelligent, he has every right to have a voice in the government of his own race.[26]

[The performance and victory of the Japanese in the Russo-Japanese War of 1904–1905 greatly impressed Gandhi.]

. . . If the progress of Japan has been unique, [its] universal self-sacrifice . . . was also unparalleled. . . . Herein is a practical lesson for any nation or individual. The measure of a nation's or an individual's self-sacrifice must ever be the measure of their growth. When, therefore, the prophets of the world preached that there was no remission of sin without shedding of blood, they uttered what was a law of nature. We, who are prone to self-indulgence, often basely misrepresent the law, giving it a coarse meaning beyond which we are incapable of looking, and fancy the text has no bearing whatsoever on self-effacement, but . . . the text we have quoted can bear only one meaning if it is also to bear fruit, namely, that the shedding of blood means shedding of our own blood, sacrificing our own little selves for the common good of all. In short, it means a realization of the unity of life. . . . From the unity of national life to the unity of all life is but a question of degree, but . . . that must be the goal of us all. . . .[27]

In spite of all the glory and the halo surrounding [the] unique siege [of Port Arthur by the Japanese], does it not suggest some very sad reflections? What could justify such bloodshed? Was not so much valor worthy of a better cause? Is man divine or brutish, when, for the sake of a strip of land, he makes himself responsible for the loss of precious lives? Is it real civilization, this awful butchery at the bidding, apparently, of two men who are called Emperors? Will this never end? These are questions more easily asked than answered. . . .

There is a moral for our countrymen to be drawn from this stupendous struggle and this beginning, let us hope, of the end. The Japanese, by sheer force of character, have brought themselves into the forefront of the nations of the world. They have shown unity, self-sacrifice, fixity of purpose, nobility of character, steel courage

[26] *Indian Opinion,* March 17, 1906.
[27] *Indian Opinion,* October 15, 1904.

and generosity to the enemy. . . . Whether here, in South Africa, or in India, we have to copy our neighbors. . . . It is right that we should insist on our rights being granted, but it is very essential that we should remove all within us that may be a hindrance to the granting thereof.[28]

. . . The rise of Japan has shewn the world that if the "white man" is to retain his supremacy, he must deserve it. Methods of oppression and repression are out of date.[29]

. . . We believe the influence of the East over the West will be due to economic and ethical causes. Who lives by the sword must perish by the sword, and if the Asiatic peoples take up the sword, they in their turn will succumb to a more powerful adversary . . .[30]

. . . I have always been loath to hide . . . the weak points of the community, or to press for its rights without having purged it of its blemishes. . . .[31]

[Accordingly, Gandhi made the following appeal in *Indian Opinion*.]

. . . We have a homely saying in India that it were better for a man to lose millions than that he should lose a good name. It follows as a corollary from the saying that once a man has acquired a bad name it is difficult for him to undo the effect and to rehabilitate himself in the popular regard. What is true of individuals is equally true of communities. The French have a name for the artistic, the English for personal bravery, the Germans for hardheadedness, the Russians for frugality, the Colonies in South Africa for gold hunger; similarly, the Indians in South Africa have rightly or wrongly got the evil reputation of being insanitary. . . . The result is that the individual members against whom such a charge could not be proved to the slightest extent, are often obliged to undergo hardships merely because they belong to the Indian community. . . . This has been very forcibly exemplified owing to the outbreak of

[28] *Indian Opinion,* January 7, 1905.
[29] *Indian Opinion,* March 25, 1905.
[30] *Indian Opinion,* March 25, 1905.
[31] M. K. Gandhi, *Experiments,* Part III, Chapter 11, p. 182.

plague. . . . Restrictions for which there would not be any warrant
if they were examined calmly and fairly, have been imposed on the
liberty of the Indians throughout South Africa. . . .

Such regulations, harsh as they undoubtedly are, ought not to
make us angry. But we should so order our conduct as to prevent a
repetition of them. . . . [We] should set about putting our houses in
order . . . literally as figuratively. The meanest of us should know
the value of sanitation and hygiene. Over-crowding should be
stamped out from our midst. We should freely let in sunshine and
air. In short, we should ingrain into our hearts the English saying,
that cleanliness is next to godliness.

And what then? We do not promise that we shall at once be
freed from the yoke of prejudice. A name once lost is not to be so
easily regained. The loss of a name is like a disease—it overtakes us
in no time, but it costs us much to remove. But why need we think
of reward in the shape of subsidence of prejudice? Is not cleanliness
its own reward? Would it not be an inestimable boon to ward off
another attack of the plague? [When] we have asserted our position as a people regarding sanitation and hygiene as part of our
being, and not merely of lip profession, the prejudice, insofar as it is
based on that charge, will go. . . . It is well for us to protest against
exaggerated charges. It is our duty to strain every nerve to prevent
legislative measures based on them. But we hold it to be equally
our duty to examine those charges critically, admit the partial truth
in them, and strive to correct the evil that may be in us. . . .[32]

[The] result of this agitation was that the Indian community learnt
to recognize more or less the necessity for keeping their houses and
environments clean. I gained the esteem of the authorities. They
saw that, although I had made it my business to ventilate grievances and press for rights, I was no less keen and insistent upon
self-purification.[33]

Courage and patience are qualities . . . one needs very badly
when . . . placed in difficult circumstances. . . .

But above all else, what is most needed in a community which

[32] *Indian Opinion,* April 30, 1904.
[33] M. K. Gandhi, *Experiments,* p. 182.

considers itself to be ill-treated at the hands of others, is the virtue of love and charity. . . . We as a people are devoted to . . . doctrines of nonresistance and of returning good for evil. . . . We then hold it to be our paramount duty not to think evil of those who we may consider are dealing unjustly by us. There is hardly any virtue in the ability to do a good turn to those who have done similarly by us. That even criminals do. But it would be some credit if a good turn could be done to an opponent. . . .[34]

. . . An infallible test of civilization is that a man claiming to be civilized should be an intelligent toiler, that he should understand the dignity of labor, and that his work should be such as to advance the interests of the community to which he belongs. . . .[35]

. . . Hitherto there has been among us a complete divorce between education and manual labor. In trying to realize the false dignity of a false education, we have forgotten the true dignity of manual labor. . . .[36]

. . . It remains for those who are endowed with more than the ordinary measure of intellect to copy the millions consciously, and use their intellect for uplifting their fellow-laborers. No longer will it then be possible for the intellectuals in their conceit to look down upon the "hewers of wood and drawers of water." For of such is the world made.[37]

. . . Let us hope that we who are learning bitter lessons in South Africa will be chastened by them and know that no creatures of God may be considered low or mean by us. We who resent the Pariah treatment in South Africa will have to wash our hands clean of this treatment of our own kith and kin in India, whom we impertinently describe as "outcasts."[38]

[Education] is one of those departments in which, while we always have a right to look to the Government to give the lead, it is possible to help ourselves. Nor is it a matter merely of money. The first thing needful is a sufficient number of self-sacrificing young men who would devote themselves to educational work as a labor

[34] *Indian Opinion,* August 20, 1903.
[35] *Indian Opinion,* March 18, 1905.
[36] *Indian Opinion,* January 20, 1910.
[37] *Indian Opinion,* January 13, 1910.
[38] *Indian Opinion,* April 23, 1910.

of love. That [is] an indispensable condition. . . . Burmese children receive, according to the Burmese notions, a full education, because the teachers are volunteers. The same rule was followed in ancient India, and even today the village schoolmaster is a poor man. . . .

. . . The duty, therefore, before young Indians in South Africa is simple and clear. The work before them is not work of a day or a few months, but . . . work of years, nor is it work which can be done without strenuous labor. They have not only to be content with poverty, but they have to train themselves for the vocation. . . . Even if one young man took it into his head to devote his lifetime to the uplifting of Indian children, he could do it. . . . [Teaching] is a department of work in which one teacher alone can be a host in himself. None need, therefore, wait for others to take up the work. And there is no calling so sacred. . . .[39]

[39] *Indian Opinion,* December 23, 1905.

[6]

VICTORY IN SOUTH AFRICA

. . . On return from the [Boer] War . . . I shuddered as I read the sections of the [Transvaal Government Ordinance] one after another. I saw nothing in it except hatred of Indians. It seemed to me that if the Ordinance was passed and the Indians meekly accepted it, that would spell absolute ruin for the Indians in South Africa. I clearly saw that this was a question of life and death for them. I further saw that even in the case of memorials [detailed written protests] and representations proving fruitless, the community must not sit with folded hands. Better die than submit to such a law. But how were we to die? What should we dare and do so there would be nothing before us except a choice of victory or death? . . .[1]

. . . Once a law is enacted, many difficulties must be encountered before it can be reversed. It is only when public opinion is highly educated that the laws in force in a country can be repealed. A constitution under which laws are modified or repealed every now and then cannot be said to be stable or well organized.[2]

[Whether] there is or there is not any law in force, the Government cannot exercise control over us without our coöperation. The existence of a law means that if we refused to accept [it], we are liable to punishment, and generally it so happens that the fear of punishment leads men to submit to the restriction. But a Satyagrahi differs from the generality of men in . . . that, if he submits to a restriction, he submits voluntarily, not because he is afraid of punishment, but because he thinks such submission is essential to the common weal. . . .[3]

[1] M. K. Gandhi, *Satyagraha in South Africa,* Chapter 11, pp. 155–156.
[2] *Ibid.,* Chapter 10, p. 140.
[3] *Ibid.,* Chapter 22, p. 247.

[Only] he who has mastered the art of obedience to law knows the art of disobedience to law. . . .[4]

The statement that I had derived my idea of Civil Disobedience from the writings of Thoreau is wrong. The resistance to authority in South Africa was well advanced before I got the essay. . . . When I saw the title of Thoreau's great essay, I began to use his phrase to explain our struggle to the English readers. But I found that even "Civil Disobedience" failed to convey the full meaning of the struggle. I therefore adopted the phrase "Civil Resistance."[5]

[The Ordinance demanded that] every Indian, man, woman or child . . . must register . . . with the Registrar of Asiatics and take out a certificate of registration.

. . . Failure to apply would be . . . an offence . . . for which the defaulter could be fined, sent to prison, or even deported. . . . The certificate must be produced before any police officer. . . . Failure . . . to produce the certificate would be . . . an offence for which the defaulter could be fined or sent to prison. Even a person walking on public thoroughfares could be required to produce his certificate. Police officers could enter private houses in order to inspect certificates. . . .[6]

[Indians stigmatized it as the "Black Act"—morally black, aimed at black, brown and yellow men. Gandhi, who was light brown, often referred to himself as "black."]

One important question before us was what agency we could use for carrying on the struggle [against the Asiatic Registration Act, passed July 31, 1907]. The Transvaal British Indian Association had a large membership. . . . The Association had resisted in the past not one obnoxious law, but quite a host of them. . . . At the same time, we must take account of external risks to which the Association would be exposed in the event of its being identified with the . . . struggle. What if the Transvaal Government declared the struggle . . . seditious and all institutions carrying it on as illegal bodies? What would, in such a case, be the position of members

[4] *Young India,* November 5, 1919.
[5] Letter to P. K. Rao, Servants of India Society, September 10, 1935, quoted in Louis Fischer, *The Life of Mahatma Gandhi,* Part I, Chapter 11, pp. 87–88.
[6] M. K. Gandhi, *Satyagraha in South Africa,* Chapter 11, pp. 156–157.

who were not [participating]? And what about the funds which were contributed at [an earlier] time . . . ?

For all these reasons the community came to the conclusion that the Satyagraha struggle should not be carried on through any of the existing organizations. They might render all help in their power and resist the Black Act in every way open to them except that of Satyagraha, for which a new body, named the "Passive Resistance Association" was started by the Satyagrahis. . . . Time fully justified the wisdom of constituting a fresh body for the work, and the . . . movement might perhaps have suffered a setback if any of the existing organizations had been mixed up with it. . . .[7]

. . . I then used the term "passive resistance" in describing it. . . . As the struggle advanced, the phrase . . . gave rise to confusion, and it appeared shameful to permit this great struggle to be known only by an English name. . . . A small prize was therefore announced in *Indian Opinion* to be awarded to the reader who invented the best designation for our struggle. . . . Shri Maganlal Gandhi [Gandhi's second cousin] suggested . . . "Sadagrah" meaning "firmness in a good cause." I liked the word but it did not fully represent the whole idea I wished it to connote. I therefore corrected it to "Satyagraha." Truth (Satya) implies Love, and Firmness (Agraha) engenders and therefore serves as a synonym for force . . . that is to say, the Force which is born of Truth and Love or Non-violence. . . .[8]

[There] is a great and fundamental difference between passive resistance and Satyagraha. If, without understanding this, those who call themselves either passive resisters or Satyagrahis believe both to be one and the same thing, there would be injustice to both. . . . The result of our using the phrase "passive resistance" in South Africa was not that people admired us by ascribing to us the bravery and the self-sacrifice of the [women] suffragists [who called themselves "passive resisters"], but we were mistaken to be a danger to person and property, which the suffragists were, and even a generous friend . . . imagined us to be weak. The power of suggestion is such that a man at last becomes what he believes him-

[7] *Ibid.*, Chapter 16, pp. 201–202.
[8] *Ibid.*, Chapter 12, pp. 172–173.

self to be. If we continue to believe ourselves and let others believe
that we are weak and helpless, and therefore offer passive resistance, our resistance would never make us strong, and at the earliest opportunity we would give up passive resistance as a weapon of
the weak. On the other hand, if we are Satyagrahis and offer Satyagraha, believing ourselves to be strong . . . we grow stronger and
stronger every day. With the increase in our strength, our Satyagraha too becomes more effective, and we would never be casting
about for an opportunity to give it up. Again, while there is no
scope for love in passive resistance, on the other hand, not only has
hatred no place in Satyagraha, but is a positive breach of its ruling
principle. While in passive resistance there is a scope for the use of
arms when a suitable occasion arrives, in Satyagraha, physical force
is forbidden, even in the most favorable circumstances. Passive
resistance is often looked upon as a preparation for the use of force,
while Satyagraha can never be utilized as such. Passive resistance
may be offered side by side with the use of arms. Satyagraha and
brute force, being each a negation of the other, can never go
together. Satyagraha may be offered to one's nearest and dearest,
passive resistance can never be offered to them, unless, of course,
they have ceased to be dear and become an object of hatred to us. In
passive resistance there is always present an idea of harassing the
other party, and there is a simultaneous readiness to undergo any
hardships entailed upon us by such activity, while in Satyagraha
there is not the remotest idea of injuring the opponent. Satyagraha
postulates the conquest of the adversary by suffering in one's own
person.[9]

[Nevertheless, Gandhi sometimes used the term "Passive Resistance" when he was discussing Civil Disobedience or Satyagraha.]

Passive Resistance . . . is the reverse of resistance by arms . . .
[for] instance, the government of the day has passed a law which is
applicable to me. I do not like it. If by using violence, I force the
government to repeal the law, I am employing what may be termed
Body-Force. If I do not obey the law, and accept the penalty for the
breach, I use Soul-Force. It involves sacrifice of self.

[If] this kind of force is used in a cause that is unjust, only the

---

[9] *Ibid.,* Chapter 13, pp. 178–179.

person using it suffers. He does not make others suffer for his mistakes. . . .[10]

. . . Real suffering bravely born melts even a heart of stone. Such is the potency of suffering . . . *there* lies the key to Satyagraha.[11]

[The] greatest and most unimpeachable evidence of this force [of Truth or Love] is to be found in the fact that, in spite of the wars of the world, it still lives on.

Thousands, indeed tens of thousands, depend for their existence on a very active working of this force. Little quarrels of millions of families in their daily lives disappear before the exercise of this force. Hundreds of nations live in peace. History does not and cannot take note of this fact. History is really a record of every interruption of the even working of the force of love or of the soul. Two brothers quarrel, one of them repents and reawakens the love . . . lying dormant in him, the two again begin to live in peace. . . . But if the two brothers . . . take up arms or go to law—which is another form of the exhibition of brute force—their doings would be immediately noticed in the press, they would be the talk of their neighbors and would probably go down in history. And what is true of families and communities is true of nations. There is no reason to believe there is one law for families and another for nations. History, then, is a record of an interruption of the course of nature. Soul-Force, being natural, is not noted in history.[12]

"The law of the survival of the fittest is the law for the evolution of the brute, but the law of self-sacrifice is the law of evolution for the man."

A kind friend has sent the above quotation from Huxley. . . . Jesus laid down the same law in much more forcible and graphic language. He said that if a man took away one's coat, one was to give up one's cloak also, or that if a man smote one on the right cheek, the left was also to be turned to him. . . . Tested, then, by this law, it seems clear that modern civilization . . . is based not

[10] M. K. Gandhi, *Hind Swaraj or Indian Home Rule* (Ahmedabad: Navajivan Publishing House, 1938), Chapter 8, pp. 57–58.

[11] M. K. Gandhi, *Satyagraha in South Africa,* Chapter 2, p. 32.

[12] M. K. Gandhi, *Hind Swaraj,* Chapter 8, pp. 56–57.

upon the human law of self-sacrifice, but upon the brutal law of the survival of the fittest (the fittest here evidently meaning physically the strongest), and that, therefore, it is inherently defective.

The basis of self-sacrifice is love. A mother loves her child and sacrifices herself for it. Jesus bade us love our enemies—a hard task! But there is no escape from it. A mother's love for her child may be selfish. The Asian prophet did not flinch from the logical consequences of the truth he gave us. To him, Love embraced the whole of humanity. Family affection and patriotism were not enough. . . . It does not require much thinking to know that, under the operation of the brute law of force, the modern world is pressed down with the weight of misery and affliction, in spite of the vast system of organized Government and mechanical contrivances to make man happy. There seems to be no relief, unless we revert to the law of Love. . . .[13]

. . . Brute force will avail against brute force only when it is proved that darkness can dispel darkness.[14]

. . . Brute force has been the ruling factor in the world for thousands of years, and mankind has been reaping its bitter harvest all along. . . . There is little hope of anything good coming out of it in the future. If light can come out of darkness, then alone can love emerge from hatred.[15]

Passive resistance is an all-sided sword. . . . It never rusts and cannot be stolen.[16]

. . . Physical force is wrongly considered to be used to protect the weak. As a matter of fact, it still further weakens the weak, it makes them dependent upon their so-called defenders or protectors. . . .[17]

[No] matter how badly they suffered, the Satyagrahis never used physical force . . . although there were occasions when they were in a position to use it effectively. [Although] the Indians had no franchise and were weak, these considerations had nothing to do with the organization of Satyagraha. This is not to say that the Indians would have taken to Satyagraha even if they had possessed arms or

[13] *Indian Opinion,* July 26, 1913.
[14] *Indian Opinion,* July 12, 1913.
[15] M. K. Gandhi, *Satyagraha in South Africa,* Chapter 24, p. 289.
[16] M. K. Gandhi, *Hind Swaraj,* Chapter 9, p. 60.
[17] *Indian Opinion,* January 15, 1910.

the franchise. Probably there would not have been any scope for Satyagraha if they had the franchise. If they had arms, the opposite party would have thought twice before antagonizing them. My point is that I can definitely assert that in planning the Indian movement, there never was the slightest thought given to the possibility or otherwise of offering armed resistance. Satyagraha is Soul-Force, pure and simple, and whenever and to whatever extent there is room for the use of arms or physical force or brute force, there and to that extent is there so much less possibility for Soul-Force. . . .[18]

. . . A Satyagrahi bids goodbye to fear. He is therefore never afraid of trusting the opponent. Even if the opponent plays him false twenty times, the Satyagrahi is ready to trust him for the twenty-first time, for an implicit trust in human nature is the very essence of his creed. . . .[19]

. . . Satyagraha is based on self-help, self-sacrifice and faith in God. . . .[20]

[We] are the makers of our own state and . . . individuals who realize the fact need not, ought not, to wait for collective action—even as a hungry man does not wait for others to commence a meal before he falls to it. The one necessary condition for action is that, like the hungry man, we must hunger after our deliverance. . . .

[We] need the same advice that was given to Martha. If we but do "the one thing needful," there is no occasion for us to be "anxious and troubled" about the many things in the shape of wanting to know what our Governors will do, or who the next Prime Minister is likely to be, or what laws affecting us are likely to be passed.[21]

. . . I believe that I have an unflinching faith in God. For many years, I have accorded intellectual assent to the proposition that death is only a big change in life and nothing more, and should be welcome whenever it arrives. I have deliberately made a supreme attempt to cast out from my heart all fear whatsoever, including the fear of death. Still, I remember occasions in my life when I have not rejoiced at the thought of approaching death as one might rejoice at the prospect of meeting a long-lost friend. Thus man often

---

[18] M. K. Gandhi, *Satyagraha in South Africa,* Chapter 13, pp. 176–177.

[19] *Ibid.,* Chapter 22, p. 246.

[20] *Ibid.,* Chapter 23, p. 282.

[21] *Indian Opinion,* May 14, 1910.

82]

remains weak, notwithstanding all his efforts to be strong, and knowledge which stops at the head and does not penetrate into the heart is of but little use in the critical times of living experience. Then again, the strength of the spirit within mostly evaporates when a person gets and accepts support from outside. A Satyagrahi must be always on his guard against such temptations.[22]

[Death] should cause no fear in us if we have lived in the fear of God, and have done nothing in violation of the voice of our conscience. Then, indeed, is death but a change for the better and, therefore, a welcome change which need not evoke any sorrow. . . . And we in South Africa, especially those who are passive resisters, must learn not only not to fear death, but must be prepared to face it and welcome it when it comes to us in the performance of our duty. . . . I wish for no better end, and I am sure no other passive resister does.[23]

Of the many accomplishments that passive resisters have to possess, tenacity is by no means the least important. They may find their ranks becoming daily thinned under a hot fire. True passive resisters must still stand their ground. They may be reviled by their own and they must cling to their faith as a child clings to its mother's breast. They may be misunderstood, and they must be content to labor under misrepresentation. They may be put to inconceivable personal inconvenience and they must suffer it patiently and cheerfully. . . . They cannot—must not—lose faith in themselves or in their mission because they may be in a minority. Indeed, all reform has been brought about by the action of minorities in all countries and under all climes. Majorities simply follow minorities. . . .[24]

. . . Experience has taught me that civility is the most difficult part of Satyagraha. Civility does not here mean the mere outward gentleness of speech cultivated for the occasion, but an inborn gentleness and desire to do the opponent good. These should show themselves in every act of a Satyagrahi.[25]

[22] M. K. Gandhi, *Satyagraha in South Africa,* Chapter 24, pp. 286–287.
[23] *Indian Opinion,* March 18, 1914.
[24] *Indian Opinion,* July 2, 1910.
[25] M. K. Gandhi, *The Story of My Experiments with Truth,* Part V, Chapter 24, p. 364.

[Though the government officials enforcing the Black Law] were so bad, I had nothing against them personally. . . .

This attitude of mine put the officials . . . perfectly at ease, and though I had to fight with their department often, and use strong language, they remained quite friendly with me. . . .

Man and his deed are two distinct things. Whereas a good deed should call forth approbation and a wicked deed disapprobation, the doer of the deed, whether good or wicked, always deserves respect or pity, as the case may be. "Hate the sin and not the sinner" is a precept which, though easy enough to understand, is rarely practiced, and that is why the poison of hatred spreads in the world.

. . . It is quite proper to resist and attack a system, but to resist and attack its author is tantamount to resisting and attacking oneself. For we are all tarred with the same brush and are children of one and the same Creator, and as such the divine powers within us are infinite. To slight a single human being is to slight those divine powers, and thus to harm not only that being, but with him, the whole world.[26]

Men of ordinary abilities also can develop morality. . . . I regard the illiteracy among my people as deplorable, and I consider it necessary to educate them, but it is not at all impossible to imbibe the Satyagraha principle in an absolutely illiterate man. This is my long-standing experience.[27]

The end of a Satyagraha campaign can be described as worthy only when it leaves the Satyagrahis stronger and more spirited than they are in the beginning.[28]

[The] fateful month of July was gradually drawing to an end, and on the last day of that month [when the Black Act went into effect], we had resolved to call a mass meeting of the Indians. . . . An attendance at public meetings of two thousand from an aggregate population of ten thousand would be considered large and satisfactory. . . . A movement of mass Satyagraha is impossible on any other condition. Where the struggle is wholly dependent upon

[26] *Ibid.,* Part IV, Chapter 9, pp. 230–231.

[27] *Young India,* November 5, 1919.

[28] M. K. Gandhi, *Experiments,* Part V, Chapter 25, p. 366.

internal strength, it cannot go on at all without mass discipline. . . . From the very first [the Satyagrahis] decided to hold public meetings only in the open, so expense was nearly avoided and none had to go back from the place of meeting disappointed for want of accommodation. All these meetings . . . were very quiet. The audiences heard everything attentively. If those who were far away from the platform could not hear a speaker, they would ask him to speak louder. [There] were no chairs at these meetings. Everyone sat on the ground. There was a very small platform designed to accommodate the chairman, the speaker and a couple of friends, and a small table and a few chairs or stools were placed upon it.

My experience has taught me that no movement ever stops or languishes for want of funds. This does not mean that any . . . movement can go on without money, but it does mean that wherever it has good men and true at its helm, it is bound to attract to itself the requisite funds. On the other hand, I have also observed that a movement takes its downward course from the time it is afflicted with a plethora of funds. When, therefore, a public institution is managed from the interest of investments, I dare not call it a sin, but I do say it is a highly improper procedure. The public should be the bank for all public institutions, which should not last a day longer than the public wish. An institution run with the interest of accumulated capital ceases to be amenable to public opinion and becomes autocratic and self-righteous. . . .[29]

. . . I have observed that voluntary workers are apt to behave as if they were not bound to render a detailed account of the business or monies with which they are entrusted because, like Caesar's wife, they are above suspicion. This is sheer nonsense, as the keeping of accounts has nothing whatever to do with trustworthiness or the reverse. Keeping accounts is an independent duty, the performance of which is essential to clean work. . . .[30]

[It] was found necessary to readminister the oath of resistance, for safety's sake, just to reinforce the awakening of the community and to probe the extent of its weakness, if any. . . .[31]

[29] M. K. Gandhi, *Satyagraha in South Africa,* Chapter 16, p. 202.
[30] *Ibid.,* Chapter 14, pp. 192–193.
[31] *Ibid.,* Chapter 16, p. 203.

[Pledges] and vows are, and should be, taken on rare occasions. . . .
Only those who take a pledge can be bound by it. [A] pledge must
not be taken with a view to produce an effect on outsiders. . . .
Everyone must search his own heart, and if the inner voice assures
him that he has the requisite strength to carry him through, then
only should he pledge himself, and then only will his pledge bear
fruit.

. . . Everyone should fully realize his responsibility, then pledge
himself only independently of others, and understand that he himself must be true to his pledge, even unto death, no matter what
others do.[32]

The first of July, 1907, arrived and saw the opening of permit
offices. The community had decided openly to picket each office,
[posting] volunteers on the roads leading thereto, and these volunteers were to warn weak-kneed Indians against the trap laid for
them there. Volunteers were provided with badges and expressly
instructed not to be impolite to any Indian taking out a permit.
They must ask him his name, but if he refused to give it, they must
not on any account be violent or rude to him. To every Indian
going to the permit office, they were to hand a printed paper detail-
ing the injuries which submission to the Black Act would involve,
and explain what was written in it. They must behave to the police,
too, with due respect. If the police abused or thrashed them, they
must suffer peacefully; if the ill-treatment by the police was insufferable, they should leave the place. If the police arrested them,
they should gladly surrender themselves. If some such incident
occurred in Johannesburg, it should be brought to my notice. At
other places, the local secretaries were to be informed, and asked
for further instructions. Each party of pickets had a captain whose
orders must be obeyed by the rest.

This was the community's first experience. . . . All who were
above the age of twelve were taken as pickets. . . . But not one was
taken who was unknown to the local workers. Over and above all
these precautions, people were informed by announcements at
every public meeting and otherwise, that if anyone desirous of taking out a permit was afraid of the pickets, he could ask the workers

[32] *Ibid.,* Chapter 12, pp. 166–167.

to detail a volunteer to escort him to the permit office and back.
Some did avail themselves of this offer.

. . . Generally speaking, there was not much molestation by the
police. When sometimes there was . . . the volunteers quietly put
up with it. They brought to bear upon their work quite an amount
of humor, in which the police too sometimes joined. They devised
various diversions . . . to beguile their time. . . .

Although the Indians who wanted to take out permits were . . .
saved from rudeness or violence from the volunteers in public, I
must admit that there arose a body of men in connection with the
movement who, without becoming volunteers, privately threatened
those [taking] out permits with violence or injury. . . . This was a
most painful development, and strong measures were adopted . . .
to stamp it out as soon as it was found out. . . . The threats left an
impression behind them and . . . far injured the cause. Those who
were threatened instantly sought Government protection and got it.
Poison was thus instilled into the community, and those who were
weak already grew weaker still. The poison thus grew more virulent, as the weak are always apt to be revengeful.

These threats created but little impression, but the force of public opinion . . . and . . . the fear of one's name being known to the
community through the presence of volunteers acted as powerful
deterrents. I do not know a single Indian who held it proper to submit to the Black Act. Those who submitted did so out of an inabil-
ity to suffer hardships or pecuniary losses [from white boycotts]
and were therefore ashamed of themselves. . . .[33]

When the Asiatic Department found that, notwithstanding all
their exertions, they could not get more than five hundred Indians
to register, they decided to arrest someone. . . . Some malevolent
Indians in Germistown suggested to the Asiatic Department that
many Indians there would take out permits if Rama Sundara was
arrested. . . . The day on which he was sentenced was celebrated
with great éclat. There was no trace of depression but . . . there was
exultation and rejoicing. Hundreds were ready to go to jail. The
officers of the Asiatic Department were disappointed. . . . They
did not get a single registrant even from Germistown. . . .

[33] *Ibid.*, Chapter 17, pp. 210–213.

But Rama Sundara turned out to be false coin. [He] bid a final goodbye to the Transvaal and to the movement. There are cunning men in every community and in every movement, and so there were in ours. . . .[34]

. . . I believe cunning is not only morally wrong but also politically inexpedient, and have therefore always discountenanced its use, even from the practical standpoint. . . .[35]

. . . The leaders of every clean movement are bound to see that they admit only clean fighters to it. But all their caution notwithstanding, undesirable elements cannot be kept out. And yet, if the leaders are fearless and true, the entry of undesirable persons into the movement without their knowing them to be so, does not ultimately harm the cause. When Rama Sundara was found out, he became a man of straw. The community forgot him, but the movement gathered fresh strength, even through him. Imprisonment suffered by him for the cause stood to our credit, the enthusiasm created by his trial came to stay, and, profiting by his example, weaklings slipped away out of the movement of their own accord. . . .

Let not the reader point the finger of scorn at Rama Sundara. All men are imperfect, and when imperfection is observed in someone in a larger measure than in others, people are apt to blame him. But that is not fair. Rama Sundara did not become weak intentionally. Man can change his temperament, can control it, but cannot eradicate it. . . . Although Rama Sundara fled away, who can tell how he might have repented of his weakness? [He] could have taken out a permit and steered clear of jail by submission to the Black Act. Further, if at all so minded, he could have become a tool of the Asiatic Department, misguided his friends, and become persona grata with the Government. Why should we not judge him charitably and say that . . . he, being ashamed of his weakness, hid his face from the community, and even did it a service?[36]

[All] truthful movements spontaneously attract to themselves all manner of pure and disinterested help. [No] other effort whatever was made during the struggle to enlist European sympathy beyond

[34] *Ibid.,* Chapter 18, pp. 215–217.
[35] *Ibid.,* Chapter 28, p. 318.
[36] *Ibid.,* Chapter 18, pp. 218–219.

the effort, if effort it can be called, involved in adherence to Truth and Truth alone. The European friends were attracted by the inherent power of the movement itself.[37]

[Some Indians took out permits under the Act, but most did not. A number of Indians were accordingly served with official notices to register or leave the Transvaal. Failing to do either, they were brought before a magistrate on January 11, 1908. Gandhi was among them.]

None of us had to offer any defence. All were to plead guilty. . . .

. . . I said I thought there should be a distinction made between my case and those that were to follow. I had just heard . . . that my compatriots . . . had been sentenced to three months' imprisonment with hard labor and had been fined a heavy amount; in lieu of payment . . . they would receive a further period of three months' hard labor. If these men had committed an offense, I had committed a greater offense. . . . The Magistrate, however . . . sentenced me to two months' simple imprisonment. . . . I was standing as an accused in the very court where I had appeared as counsel. But . . . I considered the former role as far more honorable than the latter, and did not feel the slightest hesitation in entering the prisoner's box.

. . . On the sentence being pronounced I was at once removed in custody and was then quite alone. . . . I was somewhat agitated and fell into deep thought. . . . What will happen in two months? Will I have to serve the full term? If the people courted imprisonment in large numbers, as they had promised, there would be no question of serving the full sentence. But if they failed to fill the prisons, two months would be as tedious as an age. [These thoughts] filled me with shame. How vain I was! I, who had asked the people to consider the prisons as His Majesty's hotels, the suffering . . . upon disobeying the Black Act as perfect bliss, and the sacrifice of one's all and of life itself in resisting it as supreme enjoyment! Where had all this knowledge vanished . . . ? . . . I began to laugh at my own folly. I began to think of what kind of imprisonment would be awarded to the others and whether they would be kept with me in the prison. But I was disturbed by the police officer [and] driven to Johannesburg Jail.

[37] *Ibid.,* Chapter 23, p. 282.

*   *   *

From the second or third day Satyagrahi prisoners began to arrive in large numbers. . . . The community had resolved to fill up the jail after our arrests. . . .

[Every] one of us was firm in his resolution of passing his term in jail in perfect happiness and peace. The number of Satyagrahi prisoners gradually rose to over 150. . . .[38]

. . . As the struggle advanced, there came a stage when going to jail was a perfectly easy task for some and a means of getting well-earned rest, whereas it was infinitely more difficult to remain outside, minutely to look into things, to make various arrangements, and to deal with all sorts and conditions of men.[39]

During the Satyagraha in South Africa I had altered my style of dress so as to make it more in keeping with that of the indentured laborers. . . .[40]

The Government bill [giving the Indians no choice but to register and carry identity certificates] was about to pass through the Legislature, to which a petition was presented on behalf of the Indians, but in vain. At last an "ultimatum" [letter] was sent to the Government by the Satyagrahis. The word ["ultimatum"] was not the Satyagrahis' but . . . General Smuts' [a Boer General, who became South Africa's Minister of Finance and Defence]. . . .

One reason this letter was held to be an ultimatum was that it prescribed a time limit for reply. Another . . . was that the Europeans looked upon the Indians as savages. [This fact] was sufficient reason for the Indians to write such a letter. The Indians must either confess to their being barbarians and consent to be suppressed as such, or else they must take active steps in repudiation. . . . This letter was the first of such steps. If there had not been behind [it] an iron determination to act up to it, it would have been held an impertinence, and the Indians would have proved themselves to be a thoughtless and foolish race.[41]

. . . A meeting had been called [on August 10, 1908], some two

[38] *Ibid.*, Chapter 20, pp. 230–237.
[39] *Ibid.*, Chapter 25, p. 295.
[40] M. K. Gandhi, *Experiments*, Part V, Chapter 3, p. 314.
[41] M. K. Gandhi, *Satyagraha in South Africa*, Chapter 26, pp. 304–306.

hours after the expiry of the time limit to perform the public ceremony of burning the certificates. . . .

". . . Merely burning the certificates is no crime, and will not
enable those who court imprisonment to win it," [Gandhi told the
meeting]. "By burning the certificates, we only declare our solemn
resolution never to submit to the Black Act, and divest ourselves of
the power of even showing the certificates. . . . No one need be
ashamed of getting his certificate back just now, as in doing so he
will be exhibiting a certain kind of courage. . . . We know that
some of us have fallen out of the marching army, and the burden of
those who remain has been made heavier. I would advise you to
ponder over all these considerations, and only then to take the
plunge proposed today."

The Committee had already received upwards of two thousand
certificates to be burnt. These were all . . . set ablaze. . . . The
whole assembly rose to their feet and made the place resound with
the echoes of their continuous cheers during the burning. . . . Some
of those who had still withheld their certificates brought them in
numbers to the platform. . . . When asked why he handed his certificate only at the last moments, one of these friends said he did so
as it . . . would create a greater impression. Another frankly admitted his want of courage and a feeling that the certificates might not
be burnt after all. But he could not possibly withhold the certificate
after he had seen the bonfire, and gave [the certificate] up from an
idea that the fate of all might well be his own fate too. Such frankness was a matter of frequent experience. . . .

. . . The Indians' only weapon was a faith in the righteousness
of their own cause and in God. [Thirteen] thousand unarmed Indians might appear insignificant before the well-armed. . . . As God
is the strength of the weak, it is as well that the world despises
them.[42]

[At one time, of the thirteen thousand Indians in the Transvaal,
twenty-five hundred were in jail. Some resisters served five prison
terms in quick succession, courting a new sentence the moment
they finished the old one.]

. . . The Satyagrahis could not impose a time limit upon their
Satyagraha. Whether it lasted one year or many, it was all the same

[42] *Ibid.,* Chapter 27, pp. 310–314.

to them. . . . But what about their families in the meanwhile? . . . There cannot be many in the world who would fight the good fight in spite of being compelled to condemn their nearest and dearest to the same starvation which they suffered. . . .

Till now the families of jail-going Satyagrahis were maintained by a system of monthly allowances in cash according to their need. . . . A Satyagrahi who had a family of five persons dependent upon him could not be placed on a par with another, who was a Brahmachari [Celibate] without any responsibilities. . . . There was only one solution . . . that all the families should be kept at one place and . . . become members of a sort of coöperative commonwealth. . . .

. . . Phoenix, where *Indian Opinion* was being printed . . . was three hundred miles away from Johannesburg and [it was] therefore difficult and expensive to take the families such a distance. . . . Besides, the families would not be ready to leave their homes for such a far-off place. . . .

. . . Mr. Kallenbach [a wealthy German Jewish immigrant to South Africa and friend] bought a farm of about eleven hundred acres [May 30, 1910] and gave the use of it to the Satyagrahis. . . .[43] Upon the farm there were nearly one thousand fruit-bearing trees and a small house . . . with accommodation for half-a-dozen persons. . . . We decided to build houses upon this farm and to invite the families of Satyagrahis to settle there. . . . Everything . . . from cooking to scavenging was done with our own hands. . . .

. . . The food was to be the simplest possible. The time, as well as the number of meals, was fixed. There was to be one . . . kitchen, and all were to dine in a single row. Everyone was to see to the cleaning of his own dish and other things. The common pots were to be cleaned by different parties in turn. [Neither] the women nor the men ever asked for meat. Drink, smoking, etc., were of course totally prohibited.

[We] wanted to be self-reliant . . . even in erecting buildings. . . . The structures were all of corrugated iron and therefore did not take long to raise. . . .

[The farm was named in honor of Count Leo Tolstoy, whom Gandhi admired after reading Tolstoy's *The Kingdom of God Is*

[43] *Ibid.*, Chapter 33, pp. 355–358.

Within You. They corresponded for a year, until Tolstoy's death in
1910, and Gandhi sent copies of *Indian Opinion* and his little book,
Hind Swaraj or Indian Home Rule to the Count.]

The weak became strong on Tolstoy Farm, and labor proved to
be a tonic for all.

. . . It would have been impossible to have a single settler if force
had been employed. The youngsters thoroughly enjoyed the work
on the Farm and the errands to the city. It was difficult to prevent
them from playing their pranks while engaged in work. No more
work was given to them than what they willingly and cheerfully
rendered, and I never found that the work thus done was unsatisfactory, either in quantity or in quality.

The work before us was to make the farm a busy hive of industry . . . to save money and, in the end, to make the families self-
supporting. If we achieved this . . . we could battle with the
Transvaal Government for an indefinite period. We had to spend
some money on shoes. . . . We therefore determined to learn to
make sandals. [Several] young men learnt [the method of the Trappist monks] and we commenced selling [the sandals] to friends. . . . [44]

[There] was on the Farm an ebb and flow of Satyagrahis, some
of whom would be expecting to go to prison, while others had been
released. . . .

. . . At the commencement of the struggle, Satyagrahis were
somewhat harassed by officials, and the jail authorities in some
places were unduly severe. But as the movement advanced, we
found the bitterness of the officials was softened, and in some cases
even changed to sweetness. And where there was long continued
intercourse with them, they even began to assist us. . . . [45]

[In 1913] it was realized that we would be imprisoned for long
terms. It was decided to close Tolstoy Farm. Some families
returned to their homes upon the release of the breadwinners. The
rest mostly belonged to Phoenix [Farm], which therefore was
pitched upon as the future base of operations. . . . [46]

*   *   *

[44] *Ibid.,* Chapter 34, pp. 359–366.
[45] *Ibid.,* Chapter 35, pp. 385–387.
[46] *Ibid.,* Chapter 38, p. 417.

... Mr. Justice Searle of the Cape Supreme Court gave judgment on March 14, 1913 [which] nullified in South Africa ... all marriages celebrated according to the Hindu, Moslem and Zoroastrian rites. The many married Indian women thus ceased to rank as the wives of their husbands and were degraded to the rank of concubines. ...

... Patience was impossible in the face of this insult offered to our womanhood. ... Not only could the women now be not prevented from joining the struggle, but we decided even to invite them to come into line along with the men. ...

... I knew the step of sending women to jail was fraught with serious risk. ... If afterwards they flinched at the time of actual trial or could not stand the jail, they might be led to apologize, thus not only giving me a deep shock but also causing serious damage to the movement. I decided not to broach the subject to my wife, as she could not say no to any proposal I made ... and ... I knew that in a serious matter like this the husband should leave the wife to take what step she liked on her own initiative, and should not be offended at all, even if she did not take any step whatever. The other sisters assured me they would complete their term in jail, come what might. My wife overheard my conversation ... and, addressing me, said ". . . What defect is there in me which disqualifies me for jail? I also wish to take the path to which you are inviting the others. ... If you can endure hardships and so can my boys, why cannot I? I am bound to join the struggle. . . ."[47]

The "invaders" were to go to jail for crossing the border and entering the Transvaal without permits. ...

The sisters . . . were not arrested. ... They therefore proceeded to Newcastle [the great coal-mining center of Natal state], and set about their work according to the plans [of advising the indentured Indian laborers there to strike] previously settled. Their influence spread like wildfire. ...

[The] brave Transvaal sisters . . . were sentenced to [three months'] imprisonment. . . .[48]

The women's imprisonment worked like a charm upon the

[47] *Ibid.*, Chapter 39, pp. 420–426.
[48] *Ibid.*, Chapter 40, pp. 428–429.

laborers in the mines near Newcastle, who lay down their tools and
entered the city. . . .

The strikers brought quite a host of complaints to me. . . . Leaving the question of flogging aside, there was not much room for
complaint if the collieries cut off the lights, the water supply and
other amenities [to break the strike]. . . . I therefore suggested that
the only possible course was for the laborers to leave their masters'
quarters, to fare forth, in fact, like pilgrims.

The laborers were not to be counted by tens but by hundreds.
And their number might easily swell into thousands. How was I to
house and feed this evergrowing multitude . . . ?

. . . I suggested to the laborers that they should take it that their
strike was to last for all time, and leave. . . . When they came to me,
they should bring nothing with them except their wearing apparel
and blankets. . . . They could sustain their strike and win a victory
if and only if they came out on these conditions. Those who could
not summon courage enough to take this line of action should
return to work. None should despise or harass those who thus
resumed their work. None of the laborers demurred to my conditions. From the very day that I made this announcement, there was
a continuous stream of pilgrims . . . along with their wives and
children, with bundles of clothing upon their heads.

I had no means of housing them, the sky was the only roof over
their heads. Luckily for us, the weather was favorable. . . . The
traders of Newcastle supplied cooking pots and bags of rice and dal
[peas cooked in a thick mixture as a staple]. Other places also showered rice, dal, vegetables, condiments and other things upon us. . . .

Not all were ready to go to jail, but all felt for the cause. . . .
Those who could not give anything served as volunteer workers.
Well-known and intelligent volunteers were required to look after
these obscure and uneducated men, and they were forthcoming. . . .

. . . I must take this "army" to the Transvaal and see them safely
deposited in jail. . . . The army should be divided in small batches,
each of which would cross the border separately. But I dropped
this . . . idea . . . as it would have taken too long . . . and the succes-
sive imprisonment of small batches would not produce the . . .
effect of a mass movement.

The strength of the army was about five thousand. I had not the money to pay the railway fare for such a large number. . . . And if they were taken by rail, I would be without the means of putting their morale to the test. . . . We decided that those who were disabled in their limbs should be sent by rail, and all able-bodied persons announced their readiness to go . . . on foot. . . .[49]

. . . My co-workers and I never hesitated to do sweeping, scavenging and similar work, with the result that others also took it up enthusiastically. In the absence of such sensible procedure, it is no good issuing orders to others. All would assume leadership and dictate to others, and there would be nothing done in the end. But where the leader himself becomes a servant, there are no rival claimants for leadership.[50]

. . . I wrote to the Government that we did not propose to enter the Transvaal with a view to domicile, but as an effective protest [against its anti-Indian laws] and as a pure demonstration of our distress at the loss of our self-respect. . . . The pilgrim band was composed of two thousand and thirty-seven men, one hundred and twenty-seven women and fifty-seven children.

[We] commenced the march at the appointed stroke of the hour [6:30 A.M. on November 6, 1913, two weeks and three days after the arrests of the sisters].

I was arrested thrice in four days.[51]

[When] the pilgrims reached Balfour, where three special [Government] trains were drawn up at the station to . . . deport them to Natal, [the strikers] asked for me to be called, and promised to be arrested and to board the trains [without resisting] if I advised them to. . . . This was a wrong attitude. . . . It would ill become soldiers to claim to elect their commanders or to insist upon their obeying only one of them. . . . The pilgrims were brought round [by other march leaders] and all entrained peacefully.[52]

The pilgrims were taken on . . . the special trains not for a picnic, but for baptism through fire. On the way, the Government did not care to . . . even feed them, and . . . they were prosecuted and sent to jail. . . . We expected, and even desired, as much. . . .

[49] *Ibid.,* Chapter 41, pp. 434–440.
[50] *Ibid.,* Chapter 42, pp. 447–448.
[51] *Ibid.,* Chapter 43, pp. 452–456.
[52] *Ibid.,* Chapter 45, pp. 466–469.

[News] of the strike and the arrests spread everywhere at lightning speed, and thousands of laborers unexpectedly and spontaneously came out. . . .

The Government now adopted a policy of blood and iron. . . . Mounted military policemen chased the strikers, and brought them back to their work. The slightest disturbance on the part of the laborers was answered by rifle fire. . . . But the laborers refused to be cowed down. . . .

I observed in this struggle that its end drew nearer as the distress of the fighters became more intense, and as the innocence of the distressed grew clearer. . . .[53]

. . . The Union Government had not the power to keep thousands of innocent men in jail. The Viceroy [of India] would not tolerate it, and all the world was waiting to see what General Smuts would do. . . . He had lost the power of doing justice, as he had given the Europeans in South Africa to understand that he would not . . . carry out any . . . reform. And now he felt compelled to . . . undertake . . . remedial legislation. States amenable to public opinion get out of such awkward positions by appointing a commission, which conducts only a nominal inquiry. . . . It is a general practice that the recommendations of such a commission . . . be accepted. . . .[54]

Within a short time of the issue of the report, the Government published in the official Gazette of the Union the Indians Relief Bill. . . . One part of it . . . validated in South Africa the marriages . . . held legal in India. . . . The second part abolished the annual license of three pounds. . . .[55]

[The rest of the settlement included the Government's agreement to stop indentured labor from India by 1920. Indians would not be allowed to move freely from one province to another, but Indians born in South Africa might enter Cape Colony.]

. . . The rope dancer, balancing himself upon a rope suspended at a height of twenty feet, must concentrate his attention upon the rope, and the least little error . . . means death for him. [A] Satya-

[53] *Ibid.,* Chapter 46, pp. 475–482.
[54] *Ibid.,* Chapter 47, p. 485.
[55] *Ibid.,* Chapter 50, p. 505.

grahi has to be, if possible, even more single-minded. . . . Seeing that the [restrictive] Immigration Act was [still] included [in South Africa's laws], some Indians ignorant of the principles of Satyagraha insisted upon the whole mass of the anti-Indian legislation . . . being [swept away]. I distinctly said that it would be dishonest now, having seen the opportunity, to take up a position which was not in view when Satyagraha was started. No matter how strong we were, the present struggle must close when the demands . . . were accepted. [If] we had not adhered to this principle, instead of winning, we would not only have lost all along the line, but also forfeited the sympathy which had been enlisted in our favor. . . .[56]

. . . In my humble opinion, [the settlement] is the Magna Charta of our liberty in this land . . . not because it gives us rights which we have never enjoyed . . . but because it has come to us after eight years' strenuous suffering that has involved the loss of material possessions and of precious lives. I call it our Magna Charta because it marks a change in the policy of the Government towards us, and establishes our right not only to be consulted in matters affecting us, but to have our reasonable wishes respected. . . . Above all, the settlement may well be called our Magna Charta because it has vindicated Passive Resistance as a lawful, clean weapon, and has given in Passive Resistance a new strength to the community, and I consider it an infinitely superior force to that of the vote, which history shows has often been turned against the voters themselves.[57]

. . . Experience in South Africa shows that Indians will neither deserve nor gain the respect of their European neighbors until they give unmistakable signs of their own capacity for self-respect. . . .[58]

When one considers the painful contrast between the happy ending of the Satyagraha struggle and the present condition of the Indians in South Africa, one feels for a moment as if all this suffering had gone for nothing, or is inclined to question the efficacy of Satyagraha as a solvent of the problems of mankind. . . . There is a law of nature that a thing can be retained by the same means by

---

[56] *Ibid.,* Chapter 28, pp. 318–321.
[57] *Indian Opinion,* July 29, 1914.
[58] *Indian Opinion,* November 19, 1910.

which it has been acquired. . . . The Indians in South Africa, therefore, can ensure their safety today if they can wield the weapon of
Satyagraha. There are no such miraculous properties in Satyagraha
that a thing acquired by Truth could be retained even when Truth
was given up. It would not be desirable even if it was possible. If,
therefore, the position of Indians in South Africa has now suffered
deterioration, that argues the absence of Satyagrahis among
them. . . . Individuals or bodies of individuals cannot borrow from
others qualities which they themselves do not possess. . . .[59]

[Having won the battle, Gandhi, accompanied by Mrs. Gandhi,
left South Africa forever on July 18, 1914. Both were forty-five. Just
before sailing, Gandhi sent General Smuts a gift—a pair of sandals
Gandhi had made in prison. Smuts wore them every summer at his
own farm near Pretoria, and returned them to Gandhi as a gesture
of friendship on Gandhi's seventieth birthday, in 1939. Speaking of
Gandhi's present, Smuts remarked, "I have worn these sandals for
many a summer . . . even though I may feel that I am not worthy to
stand in the shoes of so great a man. It was my fate to be the antag-
onist of a man for whom even then I had the highest respect. . . .
He never forgot the human background of the situation, never lost
his temper or succumbed to hate, and preserved his gentle humor
even in the most trying situations. His manner and spirit even then,
as well as later, contrasted markedly with the ruthless and brutal
forcefulness which is the vogue in our day. . . .[60]

While visiting British leaders in London, in 1931 Gandhi saw
Smuts, who told him apropos South Africa, "I did not give you
such a bad time as you gave me."]

I did not know that [Gandhi replied].[61]

[59] M. K. Gandhi, *Satyagraha in South Africa,* Chapter 29, pp. 338–339.
[60] Louis Fischer, *Life of Gandhi,* Part I, Chapter 15, p. 117.
[61] *Ibid.,* Part II, Chapter 32, p. 282.

PART TWO

The Mahatma

FACING THE BRITISH IN INDIA

[While Gandhi sought the support—moral and material—of Indians in India for his fight for Indians in South Africa, his interest in the beloved homeland did not dim.]

. . . More and more, as years go by, a feeling of unrest is growing in India. More and more . . . is a spirit of discontent pervading its three hundred millions. . . . And more and more, as they realize that amid the differences of creed and caste is one basic nationality, does agitation spread and take the form of definite demands for the fulfillment of the solemn assurance of the British Government that they should be given the ordinary rights of British subjects. It is impossible that national aspirations can be forever repressed, and equally impossible for India to remain a "dependency" in an Empire to which it contributes more than half the population. How often have South Africans kicked against the pricks from the Home [colonial government in London] authorities, and felt with indignation that local affairs were not properly understood. . . . Is it then surprising that the teeming millions of India should be dissatisfied with being ruled by a number of too-often self-sufficient and unsympathetic aliens ignorant of the genius of the people? Not even the "mild" Hindu can bear this forever. Is it possible for the patriotic spirits of a people with the glorious traditions of India to be content with serfdom? . . .

. . . The root of the trouble seems to be that, although there is a very great sentimental interest taken in India by the people [in Great Britain], there is, unfortunately, an equally small *practical* interest taken. Insofar as Indians are "heathens" they are interesting, insofar as they are fellow-subjects—well, the Government can look after them. But the members of the Government are too busy seeking the bubble reputation to trouble much with what will not bring place and position. . . .

It seems, then, that the hope of India lies in the British people, rather than in the British Government. . . .[1]

[No] people exists that would not think itself happier even under its own bad government than it might really be under the good governance of an alien power.

The spirit of political and international liberty is universal and, it may even be said, instinctive. No race appreciates a condition of servitude or subjection to a conquering or an alien race. If we turn our minds to the conditions which anteceded the American War of Independence, it is not difficult to understand how even the suspicion of an assumed superiority will antagonize its prospective victim to the degree of rendering coöperation almost an impossibility.

Yet it is curious how unimaginative so many Britishers are. What they recognize as a virtue in themselves is an appalling vice in others, else should we never hear of alleged sedition in Ireland, Egypt, or India. It is normal for a man to desire to be free, even if, actually, he does not merit freedom. But it is the desire itself that, in . . . time, will bring the now impossible aspiration to realization.

It cannot for one moment be alleged that a strange ruler is capable of entering into the intimate thought and feeling, the inmost life, of the ruled in the manner that is possible for those of the same or a similar nationality and tradition.[2]

The Royal Tour has given India the opportunity of shewing her loyalty to the Throne, and she has not been lacking in her demonstration. The Prince and Princess [the future King George V and Queen Mary] have seen how gay she can be, and, no doubt, imagine the land through which they passed is fairly prosperous. How much more profitable this visit would have been if, instead of merely passing through a continuous round of festivities, some of the time had been devoted to finding out the needs of India. A touch of sadness would have inevitably been added, but, perchance, there would have been awakened a bond of sympathy which would last longer and produce more good than all the glamour of the present show.[3]

[1] *Indian Opinion,* September 2, 1905.
[2] *Indian Opinion,* June 9, 1906.
[3] *Indian Opinion,* March 24, 1906.

FACING THE BRITISH IN INDIA [103

[Gandhi had commenced to connect himself with the problem of India's independence during his London sojourn, July to November, 1909. He went to lobby for the "Home" Government's influence to block further anti-Indian legislation in South Africa. He won the active support of Lord Ampthill, acting Viceroy of India in 1904, to whom he wrote, setting forth some of the tenets later to become the Mahatma's creed.]

An awakening of the National Consciousness is unmistakable. But among the majority it is in a crude shape, and there is not a corresponding spirit of self-sacrifice. Everywhere I have noticed impatience of British Rule. In some cases, the hatred of the race is virulent. In almost all cases, distrust of British statesmen is writ large on their minds. They [the statesmen] are supposed to do nothing unselfishly. Those who are against violence are so only for the time being. They do not disapprove of it, but they are too cowardly or selfish to avow their opinions publicly. Some consider that the time for violence is not yet. I have met practically no one who believes that India can ever become free without resort to violence.

I believe repression will be unavailing. At the same time, I feel that the British Rulers will not give liberally, and in time. The British people appear to be obsessed by the demon of commercial selfishness. The fault is not of men, but of the system. . . . The true remedy lies, in my humble opinion, in England's discarding modern civilization, which is ensouled by this spirit of selfishness and materialism, which is purposeless, vain, and . . . a negation of the spirit of Christianity. But this is a large order. It may then be just possible that the British Rulers in India may at least do as the Indians do, and not impose upon them . . . modern civilization. The railways, machineries and the corresponding increase of indulgent habits are the true badges of slavery of the Indian people, as they are of Europeans. I therefore have no quarrel with the rulers. I have every quarrel with their methods. . . . To me, the rise of cities like Calcutta and Bombay is a matter of sorrow rather than congratulations. India has lost in having broken up a part of her village system. Holding these views, I share the national spirit, but I totally dissent from the methods, whether of the extremists or of the moderates, for either party relies on violence ultimately. Violent method must mean acceptance of modern civilization, and therefore of the same ruinous composition we notice here. . . . I should be uninterested in the fact as to who rules. I should expect rulers to rule according to my wish, otherwise I cease to help them to rule me. . . .[4]

[On the trip back to South Africa, Gandhi wrote of his hopes for the future in his first book, *Hind Swaraj or Indian Home Rule.* The brief volume was written in Gujarati and published in installments in *Indian Opinion.* Later it was published as a book in Gujarati and English. He allowed it to be republished in India in 1921 without change, and in his introduction to still another edition in 1938 said, "After the stormy thirty years through which I have since passed, I have seen nothing to make me alter the views expounded in it."[5]]

[*Hind Swaraj or Indian Home Rule*] has had a chequered career. . . . I felt that violence was no remedy for India's ills, and that her civilization required the use of a different and higher weapon for self-protection. . . . What I wrote was so much appreciated that it was published as a booklet. It attracted some attention in India. The Bombay Government prohibited its circulation. I replied by publishing its [English] translation. I thought that . . . my English friends should know its contents.

In my opinion, it is a book which can be put into the hands of a child. It teaches the gospel of love in place of that of hate. It replaces violence with self-sacrifice. It pits soul-force against brute-force. . . .

. . . If India adopted the doctrine of love as an active part of her religion and introduced it in her politics, Swaraj [Home Rule or Self-Rule] would descend upon India from heaven. . . .[6]

. . . My countrymen impute the evils of modern civilization to the English people and, therefore, believe that the English people are bad, and not the civilization they represent. My countrymen, therefore, believe that they should adopt modern civilization and modern methods of violence to drive out the English. *Hind Swaraj*

[4] From the Westminister Palace Hotel, London, October 30, 1909, quoted in Louis Fischer, *The Life of Mahatma Gandhi,* Part I, Chapter 14, pp. 102–103.

[5] M. K. Gandhi, *Hind Swaraj or Indian Home Rule,* Chapter 1, p. 12.

[6] *Ibid.,* Introduction to 1921 edition, pp. 11–12.

has been written in order to show that they are following a suicidal policy. . . .[7]

[*Indian Home Rule* records discussions Gandhi had with Indians in London, one of them an anarchist, some of them terrorists. These interlocutors are grouped as "Reader."]

EDITOR: . . . Why do you want to drive away the English?

READER: Because India has become impoverished by their Government. They take away our money from year to year. The most important posts are reserved for themselves. We are kept in a state of slavery. They behave insolently towards us and disregard our feelings.

EDITOR: If they do not take our money away, become gentle, and give us responsible posts, would you still consider their presence to be harmful?

READER: That question is useless. It is similar to the question whether there is any harm in associating with a tiger if he changes his nature. Such a question is sheer waste of time. When a tiger changes his nature, Englishmen will change theirs. This is not possible. . . .

EDITOR: Supposing we get Self-Government similar to what the Canadians and the South Africans have, will it be good enough?

READER: That question also is useless. We may get it when we have the same powers; we shall then hoist our own flag. As is Japan, so must India be. We must own our navy, our army, and we must have our own splendor, and then will India's voice ring through the world.

EDITOR: You have well drawn the picture. In effect it means this: that we want English rule without the Englishman. You want the tiger's nature, but not the tiger; that is to say, you would make India English. And when it becomes English, it will be called not Hindustan but *Englistan*. This is not the Swaraj that I want.[8]

READER: . . . Now will you tell me something of what you have read and thought of modern civilization?

[7] *Indian Opinion,* April 2, 1910.
[8] M. K. Gandhi, *Hind Swaraj,* Chapter 4, pp. 20–21.

EDITOR: Let us first consider what state of things is described in the word "civilization." Its true test lies in the fact that people living in it make bodily welfare the object of life.... The people of Europe today live in better-built houses than they did a hundred years ago. This is considered an emblem of civilization.... Formerly, they wore skins and used spears as their weapons. Now they wear long trousers, and ... instead of spears, they carry with them revolvers containing five or more chambers. If the people of a certain country ... adopt European clothing, they are supposed to have become civilized out of savagery. Formerly, in Europe, people ploughed their lands mainly by manual labor. Now one man can plough a vast tract by means of steam engines and can thus amass great wealth.... Formerly, the fewest men wrote books that were most valuable. Now anybody writes and prints anything he likes and poisons people's minds.... Formerly, when people wanted to fight with one another, they measured between them their bodily strength; now it is possible to take away thousands of lives.... Formerly, men worked in the open air only so much as they liked. Now thousands of workmen meet together and ... work in factories or mines. Their condition is worse than that of beasts. They are obliged to work, at the risk of their lives, at most dangerous occupations, for the sake of millionaires. Formerly, men were made slaves under physical compulsion, now they are enslaved by the temptation of money and of the luxuries that money can buy.... What more need I say? All this you can ascertain.... This civilization takes note neither of morality nor of religion.... Civilization seeks to increase bodily comforts and it fails miserably even in doing so.[9]

READER: ... How can [Mohammedans, Parsis and Christians in India] be one nation? ... Hindus and Mahometans are old enemies.... We ... meet with differences at every step....[10]

EDITOR: India cannot cease to be one nation because people belonging to different religions live in it. The introduction of foreign-

[9] *Ibid.*, Chapter 6, pp. 25–26.
[10] *Ibid.*, Chapter 9, p. 34.

ers does not necessarily destroy the nation, they merge in it. . . . In reality there are as many religions as there are individuals; but those who are conscious of the spirit of nationality do not interfere with one another's religion. If they do, they are not fit to be considered a nation. . . . The Hindus, the Mahometans, the Parsis and the Christians who have made India their country are fellow-countrymen, and they will have to live in unity if only for their own interest. In no part of the world are one nationality and one religion synonymous terms; nor has it ever been so in India.

. . . Should we not remember that many Hindus and Mahometans own the same ancestors and the same blood runs through their veins? Do people become enemies because they change their religion? Is the God of the Mahometan different from the God of the Hindu)? Religions are different roads converging to the same point. What does it matter that we take different roads so long as we reach the same goal? Wherein is the cause for quarreling?[11]

READER: . . . What, then, is civilization?

EDITOR: The answer to that question is not difficult. I believe that the civilization India has evolved is not to be beaten in the world. . . . Rome went. Greece shared the same fate, the might of the Pharaohs was broken, Japan has become Westernized, of China nothing can be said, but India is still somehow or other sound at the foundation. . . . What we have tested and found true on the anvil of experience we dare not change. . . .

Civilization is that mode of conduct which points out to man the path of duty. . . . To observe morality is to attain mastery over our mind and our passions. . . . The Gujarati [Gandhi's native language] equivalent for civilization means "good conduct."

. . . We notice that the mind is a restless bird; the more it gets the more it wants, and still remains unsatisfied. The more we indulge our passions the more unbridled they become. Our ancestors, therefore, set a limit to our indulgences. They saw that happiness was largely a mental condition. A man is not

[11] *Ibid.,* Chapter 10, pp. 35–36.

necessarily happy because he is rich, or unhappy because he is poor. . . . Millions will always remain poor. Observing all this, our ancestors dissuaded us from luxuries and pleasures. We have managed with the same kind of plough as existed thousands of years ago. We have retained the same kind of cottages that we had in former times and our indigenous education remains the same as before. We have had no system of life-corroding competition. Each followed his own occupation or trade and charged a regulation wage. . . . This [ancient] nation had courts, lawyers and doctors but they were all within bounds. Everybody knew that these professions were not particularly superior; moreover, [they] did not rob people, they were considered people's dependents, not their masters. Justice was tolerably fair. The ordinary rule was to avoid courts. . . . The common people lived independently and followed their agricultural occupation. They enjoyed true Home Rule.

. . . The tendency of Indian civilization is to elevate the moral being, that of the Western civilization is to propagate immorality. . . .[12]

READER: . . . What then . . . would you suggest for freeing India?

EDITOR: . . . When we are slaves we think that the whole universe is enslaved. Because we are in an abject condition, we think that the whole of India is in that condition. . . . But if we bear in mind the above fact, we can see that if we become free, India is free. And in this thought you have a definition of Swaraj. It is Swaraj when we learn to rule ourselves. It is, therefore, in the palms of our hands. . . . But such Swaraj has to be experienced, by each one for himself. One drowning man will never save another. Slaves ourselves, it would be a mere pretention to think of freeing others. Now you will have seen that it is not necessary for us to have as our goal the expulsion of the English. If the English become Indianized we can accommodate them. If they wish to remain in India along with their civilization, there is no room for them. . . . If we keep our house in order, only those who are fit to live in it will remain. Others

---

[12] *Ibid.,* Chapter 13, pp. 43–46.

will leave of their own accord. Such things occur within the experience of all of us.[13]

READER: . . . Why should we not obtain our goal, which is good, by any means whatsoever, even by using violence?

EDITOR: . . . It is perfectly true that [the English] used brute force and that it is possible for us to do likewise, but by using similar means we can get only the same thing that they got. . . . Your reasoning is . . . saying we can get a rose through planting a noxious weed. . . . We reap exactly as we sow. . . . Fair means alone can produce fair results. . . .[14]

[Two days before Gandhi and Mrs. Gandhi reached England on their way to India from South Africa, the First World War broke out. Gandhi felt that Indians ought to do their bit for Britain. He accordingly volunteered to raise an ambulance corps headed by himself. Eighty Indians, most of them students in the United Kingdom, volunteered.]

. . . I felt that if I demanded rights as a British citizen, it was also my duty as such to participate in the defence of the British Empire. . . .[15]

Partnership in the Empire is our definite goal. We should suffer to the utmost of our ability and even lay down our lives to defend the Empire. If the Empire perishes, with it perish our cherished aspirations.

. . . To bring about [partnership in the Empire] we should have the ability to defend ourselves, that is, the ability to bear arms and to use them. . . . If we want to learn the use of arms with the greatest possible dispatch, it is our duty to enlist ourselves in the Army.[16]

. . . A votary of Ahimsa [Non-violence] remains true to his faith if the spring of all his actions is compassion. . . .

---

[13] *Ibid.,* Chapter 14, pp. 46–47.

[14] *Ibid.,* Chapter 16, pp. 51–52.

[15] M. K. Gandhi, *The Story of My Experiments with Truth,* Part III, Chapter 10, p. 179.

[16] Speech in the Kheda District, India, July, 1918, in Louis Fischer, *Life of Gandhi,* Part II, Chapter 21, p. 158.

... When two nations are fighting, the duty of a votary of Ahimsa is to stop the war. He who is not equal to that duty, he who has no power of resisting war, he who is not qualified to resist war may take part in war and yet whole-heartedly try to free himself, his nation and the world from war.

I make no distinction ... between combatants and non-combatants. [Those] who confine themselves to attending to the wounded in battle cannot be absolved from the guilt of war.[17]

In the First World War, I had just returned from South Africa. I hadn't yet found my feet. ... This did not imply any lack of faith in non-violence. But it had to develop according to circumstances, and I was not sufficiently sure of my ground.[18]

[As the best place in India for a temporary sojourn, Gandhi chose Shantiniketan, a school in Bengal maintained by Rabindranath Tagore, India's great novelist and poet laureate, who won the Nobel Prize for Literature in 1913. Tagore and Gandhi revered one another. It was Tagore, apparently, who conferred on Gandhi the title of Mahatma—"The Great Soul in beggar's garb," Tagore said.[19] Gandhi called Tagore "The Great Sentinel" and "the poet."]

True to his poetical instinct, the poet lives for the morrow and would have us do likewise. He presents to our admiring gaze the beautiful picture of the birds early in the morning singing hymns of praise as they soar into the sky. These birds have had their day's food and soared with rested wings in whose veins new blood had flowed during the previous night. I have had the pain of watching birds who for want of strength could not be coaxed even into a flutter of their wings. The human bird under the Indian sky gets up weaker than when he pretended to retire. For millions it is an eternal vigil or an eternal trance. It is an indescribably painful state which has got to be experienced to be realized. I have found it impossible to soothe suffering patients with a song. ... The hun-

[17] M. K. Gandhi, *Experiments,* Part IV, Chapter 39, pp. 291–292.

[18] Interview at Sevagram Ashram, June 4, 1942, in Louis Fischer, *A Week with Gandhi* (New York: Duell, Sloan and Pearce, 1942), p. 24.

[19] Louis Fischer, *Life of Gandhi,* Part II, Chapter 16, p. 128.

gry millions ask for one poem—invigorating food. They cannot be given it. They must earn it. And they can earn only by the sweat of their brow.[20]

[Gandhi sought his own hermitage or "ashram," and founded it May 25, 1915 at Sabarmati, across the Sabarmati River from the city of Ahmedabad. Gandhi's life now had no room for private law practice or private relations with wife and sons. Ahmedabad's textile magnates and Bombay's shipping barons supported the ashram financially. Gandhi's room was about the size of a cell, its one window had iron bars. The room opened onto a small terrace, where Gandhi slept even on the coldest nights and worked during the day.]

. . . We were in all about twenty-five men and women.

. . . Our creed was devotion to truth and our business was the search for and insistence on truth. I wanted to acquaint India with the method I had tried in South Africa and I desired to test in India the extent to which its application might be possible. So my companions and I selected the name "Satyagraha Ashram" as conveying both our goal and our method of service.[21]

[An illustrious gathering of notables attended the three-day opening ceremonies of the Hindu University Central College in Benares in February, 1916. The viceroy was there and so were numerous bejeweled maharajas, maharanis—Indian princes and princesses—and high officials, all in their dazzling panoply.

Gandhi addressed the meeting on February 4th. It broke up before he could finish.]

[If] you, the student world, to which my remarks are supposed to be addressed this evening, consider for one moment that the spiritual life for which this country is noted, and for which this country has no rival, can be transmitted through the lip, pray believe me, you are wrong. You will never be able merely through the lip to give the message that India, I hope, will one day deliver to the world. . . . [We] have now reached almost the end of our resources in speech-making, and it is not enough that our ears are

[20] *Young India,* October 13, 1921.
[21] M. K. Gandhi, *Experiments,* Part V, Chapter 9, pp. 329–330.

feasted, that our eyes are feasted, but it is necessary that our hearts have got to be touched and . . . our hands and feet have got to be moved. . . .

[It] is a matter of deep humiliation and shame for us that I am compelled this evening, under the shadow of this great college in this sacred city, to address my countrymen in a language that is foreign to me. . . . The charge against us is that we have no initiative. How can we have any if we are to devote the precious years of our lives to the mastery of a foreign tongue? . . . I have heard it said that, after all, it is English-educated India which is leading and which is doing all the things for the nation. . . . The only education we receive is English education. Surely, we must show something for it. But suppose that we have been receiving, during the past fifty years, education through our vernaculars, what should we have today? We should have today a free India, we should have our educated men, not as if they were foreigners in their own land but speaking to the heart of the nation, they would be working among the poorest of the poor, and whatever they would have gained during the past fifty years would be a heritage for the nation. . . .

The Congress [Party] has passed a resolution about self-government. . . . But I, for one, must frankly confess that I am not so much interested in what they will be able to produce as I am interested in anything that the student world is going to produce or the masses are going to produce. No paper contribution will ever make us fit for self-government. It is only our conduct that will fit us for it. And, how are we trying to govern ourselves? I want to think audibly this evening. I do not want to make a speech, and if you find me this evening speaking without reserve, pray consider that you are only sharing the thoughts of a man who allows himself to think audibly, and if you think that I seem to transgress the limits that courtesy imposes upon me, pardon me for the liberty I may be taking. I visited the Viswanath Temple last evening and as I was walking through those lanes, these were the thoughts that touched me. If a stranger dropped from above onto this great Temple and he had to consider what we as Hindus were, would he not be justified in condemning us? Is not this great temple a reflection of our own character? I speak feelingly as a Hindu. Is it right that the lanes of our sacred Temple should be as dirty as they are? . . . If even our temples are not models of roominess and cleanliness, what can our self-government be? . . .

. . . It is not comforting to think that people walk about the streets of Indian Bombay under the perpetual fear of dwellers in the storied buildings spitting upon them. I do a great deal of railway traveling. I observe the difficulty of third-class passengers. But the Railway Administration is by no means to blame for all their hard lot. We do not know the elementary laws of cleanliness. We spit anywhere on the carriage floor, irrespective of the thought that it is often used as sleeping space. We do not trouble ourselves as to how we use it; the result is indescribable filth in the compartment. The so-called better-class passengers over-awe their less fortunate brethren. Among them I have seen the student world also. Sometimes they behave no better. They can speak English and they have worn Norfolk jackets and, therefore, claim the right to force their way in and command seating accommodation. I have turned the searchlight all over, and as you have given me the privilege of speaking to you, I am laying my heart bare. Surely, we must set these things right in our progress towards self-government. . . .

. . . His Highness the Maharajah, who presided yesterday over our deliberations, spoke about the poverty of India. Other speakers laid great stress upon it. But what did we witness . . . in . . . the foundation ceremony . . . performed by the Viceroy? Certainly a most gorgeous show, an exhibition of jewellery which made a splendid feast for the eyes of the greatest jeweller who chose to come from Paris. I compare with the richly bedecked noblemen the millions of the poor. And I feel like saying to those noblemen: "There is no salvation for India unless you strip yourselves of this jewellery and hold it in trust for your countrymen in India." [Whenever] I hear of a great palace rising in any great city of India . . . I become jealous at once and I say: "Oh, it is the money that has come from the agriculturists." Over seventy-five per cent of the population are agriculturists. . . . But there cannot be much spirit of self-government about us if we take away or allow others to take away from them almost the whole of the results of their labor. Our salvation can come only through the farmer. Neither the lawyers, nor the doctors, nor the rich landlords are going to secure it.

. . . We may foam, we may fret, we may resent, but let us not forget that India of today in her impatience has produced an army of
anarchists. I myself am an anarchist, but of another type. But . . .
their anarchism has no room in India if India is to conquer the conqueror. It is a sign of fear. If we trust and fear God, we shall have
to fear no one, not Maharajahs, not Viceroys . . . not even King
George. . . . [Mrs. Annie Besant, a remarkable Englishwoman and
Indian nationalist leader who founded the institution which grew
into the Hindu University Central College: "Please stop it."] If you
consider that by my speaking as I am, I am not serving the country
and the Empire, I shall certainly stop. [Cries of "Go on."] . . . My
friends, please do not resent this interruption. If Mrs. Besant this
evening suggests that I should stop, she does so because she loves
India so well and she considers that I am erring in thinking audibly
before you, young men. But even so, I simply say this, that I want to
purge India of the atmosphere of suspicion on either side; if we are
to reach our goal, we should have an Empire which is to be based
upon mutual love and mutual trust. [There] is nothing that the students are not discussing. There is nothing that the students do not
know. I am, therefore, turning the searchlight towards ourselves. I
hold the name of my country so dear to me that I exchange these
thoughts with you, and submit to you that there is no reason for
anarchism in India. Let us frankly and openly say whatever we
want to say to our rulers and face the consequences, if what we
have to say does not please them. . . . [Many of the British] members of the Indian Civil Service are most decidedly overbearing,
they are tyrannical, at times thoughtless. . . . I grant also that, after
having lived in India for a certain number of years, some of them
become somewhat degraded. But what does that signify? They
were gentlemen before they came here, and if they have lost some
of the moral fiber, it is a reflection upon ourselves. [Cries of "No."]
Just think out for yourselves, if a man who was good yesterday has
become bad after having come in contact with me, is he responsible
that he has deteriorated or am I? The atmosphere of sycophancy
and falsity that surrounds them on their coming to India demoralizes them, as it would many of us. It is well to take the blame sometimes. If we are to receive self-government we shall have to take it.
We shall never be granted self-government. Look at the history of
the British Empire and the British nation; freedom-loving as it is, it

will not be a party to give freedom to a people who will not take it themselves. Learn your lessons, if you wish to, from the Boer War. Those who were enemies of that Empire only a few years ago, have now become friends.[22]

[At this moment many dignitaries left the platform, the commotion mounted and Gandhi had to stop. Mrs. Besant adjourned the meeting.]

. . . Ours will only then be a truly spiritual nation when we shall show more truth than gold, greater fearlessness than pomp of power and wealth, greater charity than love of self. If we will but clean our houses, our palaces and temples of the attributes of wealth, and show in them the attributes of morality, one can offer battle to any combination of hostile forces without having to carry the burden of a heavy militia. . . .[23]

---

[22] Louis Fischer, *Life of Gandhi*, Part II, Chapter 17, pp. 133–137.

[23] Speech to the Economics Society, Muir College, Allahabad, December 22, 1916, in D. G. Tendulkar, *Mahatma: The Life of Mohandas Karamchand Gandhi*, Volume I, pp. 241–242.

[8]

SEGREGATION IN INDIA

[Untouchability is segregation gone mad. In the Hindu caste, or class, system of Brahmans (the priests), Kshatriyas (soldiers), Vaisyas (merchants and farmers) and Sudras (craftsmen)—the untouchables are outcastes. An untouchable is exactly that: he must not touch a caste Hindu or anything a caste Hindu touches. Obviously, he should not enter a Hindu temple, home or shop. In villages, the untouchables live on the lowest outskirts into which dirty waters drain; in cities they inhabit the worst sections of the world's worst slums. Untouchables are confined to tasks which Hindus spurned: street cleaning, handling dead animals and men, removing refuse, etc.

To perpetuate caste, Hindus have clothed it in the religious formula of fate. The Hindus believe in reincarnation. You are a Brahman or Sudra or untouchable because of your conduct in a previous incarnation. Your misbehavior in the present life might result in caste demotion in the next. A high-caste Hindu could be born an untouchable, an untouchable could become a Brahman.

Untouchables also were called "pariahs," "suppressed classes" or "scheduled classes." Gandhi called them "Harijans—Children of God" and later named his weekly magazine after them. His fight against the system of untouchability was ferocious and lifelong.]

The question of untouchability was naturally among the subjects discussed with the Ahmedabad friends [persons who lived in Gandhi's Satyagraha Ashram]. I made it clear to them that I should take the first opportunity of admitting an untouchable candidate to the Ashram if he was otherwise worthy.[1]

---

[1] M. K. Gandhi, *The Story of My Experiments with Truth,* Part V, Chapter 9, pp. 329–330.

"Where is the untouchable who will satisfy your condition?" said a Vaisya friend self-complacently.

The Ashram had been in existence only a few months when we were put to [the] test. I received a letter. . . . "A humble and honest untouchable family is desirous of joining your Ashram. Will you accept them?"

The family consisted of Dudabhai, his wife, Danibehn, and their daughter, Lakshmi [whom Gandhi later adopted], then a mere toddling babe. Dudabhai had been a teacher in Bombay. They agreed to abide by the rules [of the Ashram] and were accepted.

But their admission created a flutter amongst the friends who had been helping the Ashram. . . .

All monetary help . . . was stopped. . . .

With the stopping of monetary help came rumors of proposed social boycott. We were prepared for all this. I had told my companions that if we were boycotted and denied the usual facilities [such as the public well, because untouchables or those who had been in contact with them would "pollute" it], we would not leave Ahmedabad. We would rather go and stay in the untouchables' quarter and live on whatever we could get by manual labor.

. . . Maganlal Gandhi one day gave me this notice: "We are out of funds. . . ."

. . . On all such occasions God has sent help at the last moment. [A rich Hindu whom Gandhi had not seen before drove up to the Ashram, handed him enough money to carry on for a year, and drove off.]

[There] was a storm in the Ashram itself. Though in South Africa untouchable friends used to come to my place and live and feed with me, my wife and other women did not seem quite to relish the admission into the Ashram of the untouchable friends. . . . The monetary difficulty had caused me no anxiety, but this internal storm was more than I could bear. . . . I pleaded with [Dudabhai] to swallow minor insults. He not only agreed but prevailed upon his wife to do likewise.

The admission of this family proved a valuable lesson to the Ashram. In the very beginning we proclaimed to the world that the Ashram would not countenance untouchability. Those who wanted to help the Ashram were thus put on their guard. . . . The fact that it is mostly the real orthodox Hindus who have met the daily growing expenses of the Ashram, is perhaps a clear indication that untouchability is shaken to its foundation. . . .[2]

Caste distinction is not observed in the Ashram because caste has nothing to do with religion in general and Hinduism in particular. It is a sin to believe anyone else is inferior or superior to ourselves. We are all equal. It is the touch of sin that pollutes us and never that of a human being. None are high and none are low for one who would devote his life to service. The distinction between high and low is a blot on Hinduism which we must obliterate.[3]

I regard untouchability as the greatest blot of Hinduism. The idea was not brought home to me by my bitter experiences during the South African struggle. It is not due to the fact that I was once an agnostic. It is equally wrong to think, as some people do, that I have taken my views from my study of Christian religious literature. These views date as far back as the time when I was neither enamoured of nor was acquainted with the Bible or the followers of the Bible.

I was hardly yet twelve when this idea had dawned on me. A scavenger named Uka, an untouchable, used to attend our house for cleaning latrines. Often I would ask my mother why it was wrong to touch him, why I was forbidden to touch him. . . . I was a very dutiful and obedient child and so far as it was consistent with respect for parents I often had tussles with them on this matter. I told my mother that she was entirely wrong in considering physical contact with Uka as sinful.[4]

Untouchability is not a sanction of religion . . . scriptures cannot transcend Reason and Truth. They are intended to purify Reason and illuminate Truth. . . . It is the spirit that giveth the light. And the spirit of the Vedas [Hindu scriptures] is purity, truth, innocence, chastity, simplicity, forgiveness, godliness and all that makes a man or woman noble and brave. There is neither nobility nor

[2] *Ibid.*, Part V, Chapter 10, pp. 329–333.

[3] Yeravda [British] Prison, August 14, 1932, in Mahadev Desai, *The Diary of Mahadev Desai* (Ahmedabad: Navajivan Publishing House, 1953), Volume I, pp. 286–287.

[4] Speech while presiding at the Suppressed [Untouchable] Classes Conference, Ahmedabad, September 13 and 14, 1921, *Young India*.

bravery in treating the great and uncomplaining scavengers of the nation as worse than dogs to be despised and spat upon. Would that God gave us the strength and the wisdom to become voluntary scavengers of the nation as the "suppressed" classes are forced to be. . . .[5]

. . . Hinduism has sinned in giving sanction to untouchability. It has degraded us, made us the pariahs of the [British] Empire. . . . What crimes for which we condemn the [British] Government as satanic, have not we been guilty of toward our untouchable brethren?

. . . It is idle to talk of Swaraj so long as we do not protect the weak and the helpless or so long as it is possible for a single Swaraj-ist to injure the feelings of any individual. Swaraj means that not a single Hindu or Moslem shall for a moment arrogantly think that he can crush with impunity meek Hindus or Moslems. Unless this condition is fulfilled we will gain Swaraj, only to lose it the next moment. We are no better than the brutes until we have purged ourselves of the sins we have committed against our weaker brethren.[6]

How is this blot on Hinduism to be removed? "Do unto others as you would that others should do unto you." I have often told English officials that if they are friends and servants of India they should come down from their pedestal, cease to be patrons . . . and believe us to be equals in the same sense they believe fellow Englishmen to be their equals. . . . I have gone a step further and asked them to repent and to change their hearts. Even so is it necessary for us Hindus to repent of the wrong we have done, to alter our behavior toward those whom we have "suppressed" by a system as devilish as we believe the English system of the government of India to be. We must not throw a few miserable schools at them, we must not adopt the air of superiority toward them. We must treat them as our blood brothers as they are in fact. We must return to them the inheritance of which we have robbed them. And this must not be the act of a few English-knowing reformers merely but it must be a conscious voluntary effort on the part of the masses. We may not wait till eternity for this much belated refor-

[5] *Young India,* January 19, 1921.
[6] *Young India,* September 13 and 14, 1921.

mation. We must aim at bringing it about within this year . . . It is a reform not to follow Swaraj but to precede it.[7]

. . . We must first cast out the beam of untouchability from our own eyes before we attempt to remove the mote from that of our "masters."[8]

. . . I do want to attain Moksha [Salvation, merging with God]. I do not want to be reborn. But if I have to be reborn, I should be born an untouchable so that I may share their sorrows, sufferings and the affronts levelled at them in order that I may endeavor to free myself and them from that miserable condition. . . .[9]

[7] *Young India,* January 19, 1921.
[8] *Young India,* October 13, 1921.
[9] Speech while presiding at the Suppressed Classes Conference, Ahmedabad, September 13 and 14, 1921, *Young India.*

CIVIL DISOBEDIENCE SUCCEEDS

I will tell you how it happened that I decided to urge the departure
of the British. It was in 1916. I was in Lucknow working for Congress [the name Indians give the Congress Party]. A peasant came
up to me looking like any other peasant of India, poor and emaci-
ated. He said, "My name is Rajkumar Shukla. I am from Champaran, and I want you to come to my district." He described the
misery of his fellow agriculturists. . . .[1] The Champaran tenant was
bound by law to plant three out of every twenty parts of his land
with indigo for his landlord. . . .

[Gandhi was unable to finish other tasks until early in 1917.]
[We] left Calcutta for Champaran looking just like fellow-
rustics. . . .

[A sympathetic lawyer named] Brajkishore Babu acquainted me
with the facts of the case. He used to be in the habit of taking up the
cases of the poor tenants. . . . Not that he did not charge fees for
these simple peasants. Lawyers labor under the belief that if they
do not charge fees they will have no wherewithal to run their
households, and will not be able to render effective help to poor
people. The figures of the fees they charged and the standard of a
barrister's fees in Bengal and Bihar staggered me.

". . . I have come to the conclusion" [said I] "that we should stop
going to law courts. . . . Where the ryots [peasants] are so crushed
and fear-stricken, law courts are useless. The real relief for them is
to be free from fear. . . ."

. . . "We shall render all the help we can," [Brajkishore Babu]
said quietly . . . "tell us what kind of help you will need."

---

[1] Interview at Sevagram Ashram, June 9, 1942, in Louis Fischer, *A Week with
Gandhi*, p. 97.

And thus we sat talking until midnight.

"I shall have little use for your legal knowledge," I said to them. "I want clerical assistance and help in interpretation. It may be necessary to face imprisonment, but much as I would love you to run that risk, you would go only so far as you feel yourselves capable of going. Even turning yourselves into clerks and giving up your profession for an indefinite period is no small thing. I find it difficult to understand the local dialect of Hindi . . . and . . . I shall want you to translate. . . . We cannot afford to pay for this work. It should all be done for love and out of a spirit of service."[2]

. . . "Such and such a number of us will do whatever you may ask. . . . The idea of accommodating oneself to imprisonment is a novel thing for us. We will try to assimilate it."[3]

. . . I decided that I would talk to thousands of peasants but, in order to get the other side of the question, I would also interview the British commissioner of the area. When I called on the commissioner he bullied me and advised me to leave immediately. . . .[4]

. . . I received a summons to take my trial . . . for disobeying the order to leave. . . .

. . . I might have legally resisted the notices. . . . Instead, I accepted them all and my conduct towards the officials was correct. . . . [They] were put at ease, and instead of harassing me they gladly availed themselves of my and my co-workers' coöperation in regulating the crowds [that had gathered around Gandhi's house]. But it was an ocular demonstration . . . that their authority was shaken. The people had for the moment lost all fear of punishment and yielded obedience to the power of love. . . .

It should be remembered that no one knew me in Champaran. The peasants were all ignorant. Champaran, being far up north of the Ganges and right at the foot of the Himalayas . . . was cut off from the rest of India. . . .

. . . No political work had yet been done amongst them. The

[2] M. K. Gandhi, *The Story of My Experiments with Truth,* Part V, Chapter 12, pp. 337–338.

[3] *Ibid.,* Part V, Chapter 13, pp. 340–341.

[4] Interview at Sevagram Ashram, June 9, 1942, in Louis Fischer, *A Week with Gandhi,* p. 98.

world outside . . . was not known to them. And yet they received me as though we had been age-long friends. . . .

That day in Champaran was an unforgettable event in my life and a red-letter day for the peasants and for me.[5]

. . . The government attorney pleaded with the magistrate to postpone the case but I asked him to go on with it. I wanted to announce publicly that I had disobeyed the order to leave. . . . I told him that I had come to collect information about local conditions and that I therefore had to disobey the British law because I was acting in obedience with a higher law, with the voice of my conscience. This was my first act of civil disobedience against the British. My desire was to establish the principle that no Englishman had the right to tell me to leave any part of my country where I had gone for a peaceful pursuit. The government begged me repeatedly to drop my plea of guilty. Finally the magistrate closed the case. Civil disobedience had won. It became the method by which India could be made free.

What I did was a very ordinary thing. I declared that the British could not order me around in my own country.[6]

[The] Collector wrote to me saying I was at liberty to conduct the . . . inquiry and that I might count on whatever help I needed from officials. . . .

[The] situation . . . was so delicate and difficult that over-energetic reports might easily damage the cause. . . . So I wrote to the editors of the principal papers requesting them not to trouble to send any reporters as I should send them whatever might be necessary for publication and keep them informed.

. . . Incorrect or misleading reports . . . were likely to incense [the planters] all the more, and their ire, instead of descending on me, would be sure to descend on the poor fear-stricken ryots and seriously hinder my search for the truth about the case.

In spite of these precautions the planters engineered a poisonous agitation against me. . . . But my extreme cautiousness and my

[5] M. K. Gandhi, *Experiments,* Part V, Chapter 14, pp. 343–344.

[6] Interview at Sevagram Ashram, June 9, 1942 in Louis Fischer, *A Week with Gandhi,* pp. 98–99.

insistence on truth, even to the minutest detail, turned the edge of their sword.[7]

Those who took down the statements [of the peasants] had to observe certain rules. Each peasant had to be closely cross-examined, and whoever failed to satisfy the test was rejected. This entailed a lot of extra time but most of the statements were thus rendered incontrovertible.

As I did not want to irritate the planters but to win them over by gentleness, I made a point of writing to and meeting such of them against whom allegations of a serious nature were made. . . . Some of the planters hated me, some were indifferent, and a few treated me with courtesy.[8]

[Gandhi's activity led to an official inquiry which] found in favor of the ryots and recommended that the planters should refund a portion of the exactions made by them . . . and that the [tithes] system should be abolished by law.[9]

It was not quite possible to carry on the work without money. . . . I had made up my mind not to accept anything from the Champaran ryots. It would be . . . misinterpreted. [Appealing] to the country at large . . . was likely to give it [a] political aspect. . . . I decided to get as much as was possible from well-to-do Biharis living outside Champaran. . . . We were not likely to require large funds, as we were bent on exercising the greatest economy in consonance with the poverty of Champaran. . . .[10]

As I gained more experience . . . I became convinced that work of a permanent nature was impossible without proper village education. . . .

In consultation with my companions, I decided to open primary schools in six villages. One of our conditions with the villagers was that they should provide the teachers with board and lodging while we would see to the other expenses. The village folk had hardly any cash in their hands but they could well afford to provide food-

[7] M. K. Gandhi, *Experiments,* Part V, Chapter 15, p. 345.
[8] *Ibid.,* Part V, Chapter 16, pp. 348–349.
[9] *Ibid.,* Part V, Chapter 19, p. 354.
[10] *Ibid.,* Part V, Chapter 16, p. 347.

stuffs. Indeed, they had already expressed their readiness to contribute grain and other raw materials.

From where to get the teachers was a great problem. . . . My
idea was never to entrust children to commonplace teachers. . . .

So I issued a public appeal for voluntary teachers. It received a
ready response. . . .

I explained to them that they were expected to teach the children
not grammar and the three R's so much as cleanliness and good
manners. . . .

The villages were insanitary, the lanes full of filth, the wells surrounded by mud and stink and the courtyards unbearably untidy.
The elder people badly needed education in cleanliness. They all
were suffering from various skin diseases. So it was decided to do
as much sanitary work as possible and to penetrate every department of their lives.

[The teachers] had express instructions not to concern themselves with grievances against planters or with politics. People who
had any complaints to make were to be referred to me. . . . The
friends carried out these instructions with wonderful fidelity. . . .[11]

[The] volunteers with their schools, sanitation work and medical relief gained the confidence and respect of the village folk and
were able to bring good influence to bear upon them.

But I must confess with regret that my hope of putting this constructive work on a permanent footing was not fulfilled. . . . As
soon as my work in Champaran was finished, work outside drew
me away. The few months' work in Champaran, however, took
such deep root that its influence in one form or another is to be
observed there even today.[12]

Whilst I was yet winding up my work [in Champaran], there
came a letter . . . about the condition of labor in Ahmedabad.
Wages were low, the [millhands] had long been agitating for an
increment and I had a desire to guide them if I could. . . .

. . . My relations with [the mill owners] were friendly, and that
made fighting with them the more difficult. I held consultations
with them and requested them to refer the dispute to arbitration,
but they refused to recognize the principle of arbitration.

[11] *Ibid.,* Part V, Chapter 17, pp. 350–351.
[12] *Ibid.,* Part V, Chapter 18, p. 353.

I had . . . to advise the laborers to go on strike. Before I did so, I . . . explained to them the conditions of a successful strike:

1. never to resort to violence.
2. never to molest [non-strikers].
3. never to depend upon alms, and
4. to remain firm no matter how long the strike continued and to earn bread during the strike by any other honest labor.

The strike went on for twenty-one days. . . .[13]

For the first two weeks, the millhands exhibited great courage and self-restraint, and daily held monster meetings. On these occasions I used to remind them of their pledge and they would shout back to me . . . that they would rather die than break their word.

But at last they began to show signs of flagging. Just as physical weakness in men manifests itself in irascibility, their attitude towards the [non-strikers] became more and more menacing as the strike seemed to weaken, and I began to fear an outbreak of rowdyism. . . . The attendance at their daily meetings began to dwindle by degrees, and despondency and despair were writ large on the faces of those who did attend. Finally, the information was brought to me that the strikers had begun to totter. I felt deeply troubled, and set to thinking furiously as to what my duty was in the circumstances. . . .

One morning—it was at a millhands' meeting—while I was still groping . . . the light came to me. . . . "Unless the strikers rally," I declared to the meeting, "and continue the strike till a settlement is reached or till they leave the mills altogether, I will not touch any food."

The laborers were thunderstruck. [They] broke out, "Not you but we shall fast. . . . Please forgive us for our lapse, we will now remain faithful to our pledge to the end."

"There is no need for you to fast," I replied. "It would be enough if you could remain true to your pledge. As you know, we are without funds and we do not want to continue our strike by living on public charity. You should therefore try to eke out a bare existence by some kind of labor so you may be able to remain unconcerned

---

[13] *Ibid.,* Part V, Chapter 20, pp. 355–356.

no matter how long the strike may continue. As for my fast, it will be broken only after the strike is settled."

. . . The hearts of the mill owners were touched, and they set about discovering some means for a settlement. [The] strike was called off after I had fasted for only three days. . . .

[To celebrate, the mill owners distributed sweets. Beggars intruded.]

The grinding poverty and starvation with which our country is afflicted is such that it drives more and more men every year into the ranks of beggars, whose desperate struggle for bread renders them insensible to all feelings of decency and self-respect. And our philanthropists, instead of providing work for them and insisting on their working . . . give them alms.[14]

. . . I must refuse to insult the naked by giving them clothes they do not need instead of giving them work which they sorely need. I will not commit the sin of becoming their patron but on learning that I had assisted in impoverishing them I would give them a privileged position and give them neither crumbs nor cast-off clothing but the best of my food and clothes and associate myself with them in work.[15]

[14] *Ibid.,* Part V, Chapter 22, pp. 358–362.
[15] *Young India,* October 13, 1921.

10

MURDER IN AN INDIAN GARDEN

[The war closed victoriously in November, 1918. With the coming of peace, India expected the restoration of civil liberties. Nationalist leaders Bal Gangadhar Tilak, known as "Lokamanya" or "Respected by the People," and Mrs. Annie Besant had been arrested during the war. Instead, a committee headed by Sir Sidney Rowlatt, who had come from England to study the administration of justice, issued a report which recommended, in effect, a continuation of the wartime rigours.]

... The recommendations of the Rowlatt Committee seemed to me ... such that no self-respecting people could submit to them.[1]

... I felt myself at a loss to discover how to offer civil disobedience against the Rowlatt Bill. ... One could disobey it only if the Government gave one the opportunity for it. Failing that, could we civilly disobey other laws? And if so, where was the line to be drawn? ...

While these cogitations were still going on, news was received that the Rowlatt Bill had been published as an Act. [On March 18, 1919, it became the law of the land.] That night I fell asleep while thinking over the question. Towards the small hours of the morning, I woke up somewhat earlier than usual. I was still in that twilight condition between sleep and consciousness, when suddenly the idea broke upon me—it was as if in a dream. ...

"[Ours] is a sacred fight" [Gandhi told his host, C. Rajagopalachari, a prominent leader of the Congress], "and it seems to me to be in the fitness of things that it should be commenced with an act of self-purification. Let all the people of India, therefore, suspend their business on [the] day [the Rowlatt Act becomes law],

---

[1] M. K. Gandhi, *The Story of My Experiments with Truth,* Part V, Chapter 29, p. 380.

and observe the day as one of fasting and prayer. [Because by religious custom] the Moslems may not fast for more than one day . . . the duration of the fast should be twenty-four hours. . . ."

. . . The people . . . had only a short notice of the hartal [business strike]. . . .

But who knows how it all came about? The whole of India from one end to the other, towns as well as villages, observed a complete hartal. . . . It was a most wonderful spectacle.[2]

[The hartal was Gandhi's first political act in India, against the British Government of India. In Delhi, the hartal provoked violence. Reports of Gandhi's arrest inflamed the already heated passions of the people. Riots occurred in Bombay. Ahmedabad citizens, too, committed acts of violence.]

A rapier run through my body could hardly have pained me more.[3]

. . . It was unbearable for me to find that the laborers amongst whom I had spent a good deal of my time, whom I had served and from whom I had expected better things, had taken part in the riots, and I felt I was a sharer in their guilt.

[I] made up my mind to suspend Satyagraha so long as people had not learnt the lesson of peace. . . .

[Friends] were unhappy over the decision. They felt that if I expected peace everywhere, and regarded it as a condition precedent to launching Satyagraha, mass Satyagraha would be an impossibility. I was sorry to disagree with them. If those amongst whom I worked and whom I expected to be prepared for non-violence and self-suffering could not be non-violent, Satyagraha was certainly impossible. I was firmly of the opinion that those who wanted to lead the people to Satyagraha ought to be able to keep the people within the limited non-violence expected of them. I hold the same opinion even today.[4]

. . . A Satyagrahi obeys the laws of society intelligently and of his own free will because he considers it to be his sacred duty to do so. It is only when a person has thus obeyed the laws . . . that he is in a position to judge as to which particular rules are good and just,

[2] *Ibid.,* Part V, Chapter 30, pp. 382–383.
[3] Louis Fischer, *The Life of Mahatma Gandhi,* Part II, Chapter 23, p. 179.
[4] M. K. Gandhi, *Experiments,* Part V, Chapter 32, pp. 390–391.

and which are unjust and iniquitous. . . . My error lay in my failure
to observe this necessary limitation. I had called on the people to
launch upon civil disobedience before they had thus qualified
themselves for it, and this mistake seemed to me of Himalayan
magnitude. . . . I realized that before a people could be fit for offering civil disobedience they should thoroughly understand its deeper
implications. That being so, before re-starting civil disobedience on
a mass scale, it would be necessary to create a band of well-tried,
pure-hearted volunteers who thoroughly understood the strict
conditions of Satyagraha. They could explain these to the people,
and by sleepless vigilance, keep them on the right path.[5]

[Whilst] this movement for the preservation of non-violence was
making steady though slow progress on the one hand, the Government's policy of lawless repression was in full career on the
other. . . .[6]

[The] press laws in force in India at that time were such that, if I
wanted to express my views untrammelled, the existing printing
presses, which were naturally run for business, would have hesitated to publish them. . . .[7]

. . . I was anxious to expound the inner meaning of Satyagraha
to the public. . . .[8]

[Gandhi therefore agreed to accept editorship of the English-
language weekly *Young India,* and its Gujarati companion, *Navajivan.*]

[These] journals helped me . . . to some extent, to remain at
peace with myself, for whilst immediate resort to civil disobedience
was out of the question, they enabled me freely to ventilate my
views and to put heart into the people. . . .[9]

. . . I am proud to think that I have numerous readers among
farmers and workers. They make India. Their poverty is India's
curse and crime. Their prosperity alone can make India a fit country to live in. . . .[10]

*   *   *

[5] *Ibid.,* Part V, Chapter 33, p. 392.
[6] *Ibid.,* Part V, Chapter 34, p. 393.
[7] *Ibid.,* p. 395.
[8] *Ibid.,* p. 394.
[9] *Ibid.,* p. 395.
[10] *Young India,* October 8, 1919.

[The two hartals in Amritsar, a city of 150,000 in the Punjab, were successful, stopping the business of the city without collision with the police and with no resort to violence. Five days later, Brigadier-General Reginald Edward Harry Dyer of the British Army arrived. He issued a proclamation on April 12, 1919 prohibiting processions and meetings. The Hunter Committee, an official board of inquiry into what happened later stated, "From an examination of the map showing the different places where the proclamation was read, it is evident that in many parts of the city the proclamation was not read."

The Hunter Report then tells the story of the massacre of April 13: "About one o'clock, General Dyer heard that the people intended to hold a big meeting about four-thirty P.M. On being asked why he did not take measures to prevent its being held, he replied: 'I went there as soon as I could. I had to think the matter out.'"

The meeting took place at Jallianwalla Bagh. Bagh means garden. "...It is a rectangular piece of unused ground...almost entirely surrounded by walls of buildings. The entrances and exits to it are few and imperfect.... At the end at which General Dyer entered there is a raised ground on each side of the entrance. A large crowd had gathered at the opposite end...and were being addressed by a man on a raised platform about one hundred and fifty yards from where General Dyer stationed his troops, [twenty-five Gurkhas—soldiers from Nepal; twenty-five Baluchis from Baluchistan armed with rifles; forty Gurkhas armed only with knives, and two armored cars).... Without giving the crowd any warning to disperse...he ordered his troops to fire and the firing continued for about ten minutes.... None [of the members of the audience] was provided with firearms, although some of them may have been carrying sticks.

"As soon as the firing commenced the crowd began to disperse.... The firing was individual and not volley firing...." The Report estimated that there were three times as many wounded as dead. This adds up to 379 dead plus 1137 wounded, or 1516 casualties with the 1650 rounds fired. The crowd, penned in the low-lying garden, was a perfect target.

"...*It was no longer a question of merely dispersing the crowd,* but one of producing a sufficient moral effect from a military point of view, not only on those who were present, but more especially throughout the Punjab. There could be no question of undue severity," stated General Dyer's dispatch to his superior, quoted in the Hunter Report, with his italics.[11]

Dyer's unnecessary massacre was the child of the British mentality then dominating India. Jallianwalla Bagh quickened India's political life and drew Gandhi into politics.]

[Earlier, Gandhi had explained.] The method of Passive Resistance is the clearest and safest because, if the cause is not true, it is the resisters, and they alone, who suffer.[12]

[Testifying before the Hunter Committee, he was asked to elaborate his principle.]

Q. [Sir Chimanlal Setalvad, an official of the Hunter Committee] Who . . . is to determine the truth?

A. [Gandhi] The individual himself would determine that.

Q. Different individuals would have different views as to Truth. Would that not lead to confusion?

A. I do not think so.

Q. Honest striving after Truth is different in every case.

A. That is why the non-violence . . . was . . . necessary. . . . Without that there would be confusion and worse.[13]

[All] terrorism is bad whether put up in a good cause or bad. [Every] cause is good in the estimation of its champion. General Dyer (and he had thousands of Englishmen and women who honestly thought with him) enacted Jallianwala Bagh for a cause which he undoubtedly believed to be good. He thought that by that one act he had saved English lives and the Empire. That it was all a figment of his imagination cannot affect the valuation of the intensity of his conviction. . . . In other words, pure motives can never justify impure or violent action. . . .[14]

---

[11] The story of the Amritsar massacre and all the quotations about it are taken from *East India . . . Report of the Committee Appointed by the Government of India to Investigate the Disturbances in the Punjab, etc.* (London: His Majesty's Stationery Office, 1920), Command 681.

[12] M. K. Gandhi, *Speeches and Writings* (Madras: Ganesh & Co., 1918), "Passive Resistance," p. 104.

[13] Hunter Committee Hearing, *Young India,* November 5, 1919.

[14] *Young India,* December 18, 1924.

11

NON-VIOLENCE

[Mahatma Gandhi always resisted politics. After his return to India he attended annual sessions of the Congress, but his public activity at such assemblies was usually limited to moving a resolution in support of the Indians in South Africa.]

I do not regard the force of numbers as necessary in a just cause, and in such a just cause every man, be he high or low, can have his remedy.[1]

... There are moments in your life when you must act even though you cannot carry your best friends with you. The still small voice within you must always be the final arbiter when there is a conflict of duty.[2]

... All may not take part in the program of self-sacrifice but all must recognize the necessity of non-violence in word or deed.[3]

[Yet in 1920 Gandhi joined the All-India Home Rule League and became its president.]

... I believe that it is possible to introduce uncompromising truth and honesty in the political life of the country. ... I would strain every nerve to make Truth and Non-violence accepted in all our national activities. Then we should cease to fear or distrust our governments and their measures. ...[4]

... It is a mockery to ask India not to hate when ... India's most sacred feelings are contemptuously brushed aside. India feels weak and helpless and so expresses her helplessness in hating the tyrant who despises her and ... compels her tender children to acknowledge his power by saluting his flag. ... Non-coöperation

---

[1] *Young India,* November 5, 1919.
[2] *Young India,* August 4, 1920.
[3] *Young India,* December 18, 1920.
[4] *Young India,* April 28, 1920.

addresses itself to the task of making the people strong and self-reliant. It is an attempt to transform hatred into pity.

A strong and self-reliant India will cease to hate . . . for she will have the power to punish . . . and therefore the power also to pity and forgive. . . . Today she can neither punish nor forgive and therefore helplessly nurses hatred.[5]

[As] party formation progresses, we suppose it would be considered quite the proper thing for party leaders to use others as tools so long as there are any to be used. Care will therefore have to be taken rather to purify our politics than for fear of being used as tools. L. Tilak [a Brahmin mathematician and scholar, one of the leaders of the nationalist movement] considers that everything is fair in politics. We have joined issue with him in that conception. . . . We consider that the political life of the country will become thoroughly corrupt if we import western tactics and methods. We believe that nothing but the strictest adherence to honesty, fair play and charity can advance the true interests of the country. . . .[6]

I do not blame the British. If we were weak in numbers as the British are we would perhaps have resorted to the same methods as they are employing. Terrorism and deception are weapons not of the strong but of the weak. The British are weak in numbers, we are weak in spite of our numbers. The result is that each is dragging the other down. It is common experience that Englishmen lose in character after residence in India and that Indians lose in courage and manliness by contact with Englishmen. This process of weakening is good neither for us two nations nor for the world.

But if we Indians take care of ourselves the English and the rest of the world would take care of themselves. Our contribution to the progress of the world must, therefore, consist in setting our own house in order.[7]

Even the most despotic government cannot stand except for the consent of the governed which . . . is often forcibly procured. . . . Immediately the subject ceases to fear the despotic force, the power is gone.[8]

---

[5] *Young India,* December 8, 1920.
[6] *Young India,* January 14, 1920.
[7] *Young India,* September 22, 1920.
[8] *Young India,* June 30, 1920.

... We must voluntarily put up with the losses and inconveniences that arise from having to withdraw our support from a government that is ruling against our will. "Possession of power and riches is a crime under an unjust government, poverty in that case is a virtue," says Thoreau. It may be that in the transition state we may make mistakes; there may be avoidable suffering. These things are preferable to national emasculation.

We must refuse to wait for the wrong to be righted till the wrong-doer has been roused to a sense of his iniquity. We must not, for fear of ourselves or others having to suffer, remain participators in it. . . .

If a father does injustice it is the duty of his children to leave the parental roof. If the headmaster of a school conducts his institution on an immoral basis the pupils must leave the school. If the chairman of a corporation is corrupt the members thereof must wash their hands clean of his corruption by withdrawing from it, even so if a government does a grave injustice the subject must withdraw coöperation wholly or partially, sufficiently to wean the ruler from wickedness. In each case conceived of by me there is an element of suffering whether mental or physical. Without such suffering it is not possible to attain freedom.[9]

. . . I know it is only my reputation as a worker and fighter which has saved me from an open charge of lunacy for having given the advice about boycott of courts and schools.

. . . It does not require much reflection to see that it is through courts that a government establishes its authority and it is through schools that it manufactures clerks and other employees. They are both healthy institutions when the government in charge of them is on the whole just. They are death-traps when the government is unjust.

. . . The lawyers are not to suspend practice and enjoy rest. They will be expected to induce their clients to boycott courts. They will improvise arbitration boards in order to settle disputes. A nation that is bent on forcing justice from an unwilling government has little time for engaging in mutual quarrels. . . .

. . . We must be specially unfit for Non-Coöperation if we are so helpless as to be unable to manage our own education to total inde-

[9] *Young India,* June 16, 1920.

pendence of the Government. Every village should manage the education of its own children. . . . If there is a real awakening the schooling need not be interrupted for a single day. The very school-masters who are now conducting Government schools, if they are good enough to resign their office, could take charge of national schools and teach our children the things they need and not make of the majority of them indifferent clerks. . . .[10]

. . . The best and the quickest way of getting rid of [the] corrod-ing and degrading Secret Service is for us to make a final effort to think everything aloud, have no privileged conversation with any soul on earth and cease to fear the spy. We must ignore his presence and treat everyone as a friend entitled to know all our thoughts and plans. I know I have achieved most satisfactory results from evolv-ing the boldest of my plans in broad daylight. I have never lost a minute's peace for having detectives by my side. The public may not know I have been shadowed throughout my stay in India. That has not only not worried me but I have even taken friendly services from these gentlemen, many have apologized for having to shadow me. As a rule what I have spoken in their presence has already been published to the world. The result is that now I do not even notice the presence of these men and I do not know that the Government is much the wiser for having watched my movements through its secret agency. . . . Removal of secrecy brings about the full disap-pearance of the Secret Service without further effort. . . .[11]

. . . A man suffering from an injustice is exposed to the tempta-tions of having his worst passions roused on the slightest pretext. By asking him to boycott British goods you inculcate the idea of punishing the wrongdoer. And punishment necessarily evokes anger.

Boycott of British goods to be effective must be taken up by the whole country at once or not at all. It is like a siege. You can carry out a siege only when you have the requisite men and instruments of destruction. One man scratching a wall with his fingernails may hurt his fingers but he will produce no effect upon the walls. [But]

[10] *Young India,* August 11, 1920.
[11] *Young India,* December 22, 1920.

one title-holder giving up his title has the supreme satisfaction of having washed his hands clean of the guilt of the donor and is unaffected by the refusal of his fellows to give up theirs. The motive of boycott being punitive lacks the inherent practicability of Non-Coöperation. The spirit of punishment is a sign of weakness. . . .[12]

I do believe that where there is a choice only between cowardice and violence, I would advise violence. Thus when my eldest son asked me what he should have done had he been present when I was almost fatally assaulted in 1908 [by an Indian extremist opposed to Gandhi's agreement with Smuts], whether he should have run away and seen me killed or whether he should have used his physical force which he could and wanted to use, and defend me, I told him it was his duty to defend me even by using violence. Hence it was that I took part in the Boer War, the so-called Zulu Rebellion and [World War I]. Hence also do I advocate training in arms for those who believe in the method of violence. I would rather have India resort to arms in order to defend her honor than that she should in a cowardly manner become or remain a helpless witness to her own dishonor.

But I believe non-violence is infinitely superior to violence, forgiveness is more manly than punishment. . . . But . . . forgiveness only when there is the power to punish. . . . A mouse hardly forgives a cat when it allows itself to be torn to pieces by her. I therefore appreciate the sentiment of those who cry out for the condign punishment of General Dyer and his ilk. They would tear him to pieces if they could. But I do not believe India to be a helpless creature. Only, I want to use India's and my strength for a better purpose.

. . . Strength does not come from physical capacity. It comes from an indomitable will. . . . We in India may in a moment realize that one hundred thousand Englishmen need not frighten three hundred million human beings. A definite forgiveness would, therefore, mean a definite recognition of our strength. . . . It matters little to me that for the moment I do not drive my point home. We feel too downtrodden not to be angry and revengeful. But I must not refrain from saying that India can gain more by waiving the right of punishment We have better work to do, a better mission to deliver to the world.[13]

. . . The Afghans have a bad Government but it is self-Government. I envy them. The Japanese learnt the art through a sea of blood. And if we today had the power to drive out the English by superior brute force we would be counted their superiors and in spite of our inexperience in debating at the Council table or in holding executive offices we would be held fit to govern ourselves. For brute force is the only test the west has hitherto recognized. The Germans were defeated not because they were necessarily in the wrong but because the allied Powers were found to possess the greater brute strength. In the end, therefore, India must either learn the art of war, which the British will not teach her, or she must follow her own way of discipline and self-sacrifice through Non-Coöperation. It is as amazing as it is humiliating that less than one hundred thousand white men would be able to rule three hundred and fifteen million Indians. They do so somewhat undoubtedly by force but more by securing our coöperation in a thousand ways and making us more and more helpless and dependent on them as time goes forward. Let us not mistake reformed councils, more law courts and even governorships for real freedom or power. They are but subtler methods of emasculation. The British cannot rule us by mere force. And so they resort to all means, honorable and dishonorable, in order to retain their hold on India. They want India's billions and they want India's manpower for their imperialistic greed. If we refuse to supply them with men and money, we achieve our goal, Swaraj [Self-Rule], equality, manliness.

For me the only training in Swaraj we need is the ability to defend ourselves against the whole world and to live our life in perfect freedom, even though it may be full of defects. Good government is no substitution for self-government. . . .[14]

. . . We must have the liberty to do evil before we learn to do good.[15]

*   *   *

[13] *Young India,* August 11, 1920.
[14] *Young India,* September 22, 1920.
[15] *Young India,* October 25, 1921.

[Gandhi toured the country incessantly, indefatigably, in torrid, humid weather, addressing mammoth mass meetings of a hundred thousand and more persons, who in those pre-microphone days, could hope to be reached only by his spirit. Gandhi would ask the people to take off their foreign clothing and put it on a heap. When all the hats, coats, shirts, trousers, underwear, socks and shoes had been heaped high, Gandhi set a match to them.]

. . . I know many will find it difficult to replace their foreign cloth all at once. Millions are too poor to buy enough khadi [homespun cloth, higher-priced because of popularity and scarcity] to replace the discarded cloth. . . . Let them be satisfied with a mere loin cloth. In our climate we hardly need more to protect our bodies during the warm months of the year. Let there be no prudery about dress. India has never insisted on full covering of the body for the males as a test of culture.

I [give this] advice under a full sense of my responsibility. In order, therefore, to set the example, I propose . . . to content myself with only a loin cloth and a chaddar [shawl] whenever found necessary for the protection of the body. I adopt the change because I have always hesitated to advise anything I may not myself be prepared to follow, also because I am anxious by leading the way to make it easy for those who cannot afford a change on discarding their foreign garments. I consider the renunciation to be also necessary for me as a sign of mourning and a bare head and a bare body is such a sign in my part of the country. . . .[16]

If I was a perfect man I own I should not feel the miseries of neighbors as I do. As a perfect man I should take note of them, prescribe a remedy and compel adoption by the force of unchallengeable truth in me. But as yet I only see as through a glass darkly and therefore have to carry conviction by slow and laborious processes, and then too not always with success. . . . I would be less human if, with all my knowledge of avoidable misery pervading the land . . . I did not feel with and for all the suffering but dumb millions of India. The hope of a steady decline in that misery sustains me. . . .[17]

. . . The millions [of peasants in India] must have a simple indus-

[16]*Young India,* September 29, 1921.
[17]*Young India,* November 17, 1921.

try to supplement agriculture. Spinning was the cottage industry years ago and if the millions are to be saved from starvation they must be enabled to reintroduce spinning in their homes and every village must repossess its own weaver.[18]

. . . Over eighty-five per cent of [India's] population have more than a quarter of their time lying idle. And therefore . . . she has steadily grown poorer because of this enforced idleness. . . . I am writing this in Puri in front of the murmuring waves. The picture of the crowd of men, women and children with their fleshless ribs . . . haunts me. If I had the power I would suspend every other activity in schools and colleges and everywhere else and popularize spinning . . . inspire every carpenter to prepare spinning wheels and ask the teachers to take these life-giving machines to every home and teach them spinning. If I had the power I would stop an ounce of cotton from being exported and would have it turned into yarn in these homes. I would dot India with depots for receiving this yarn and distributing it among weavers. Given sufficient steady and trained workers I would undertake to drive pauperism out of India during this year. . . . I am able to restrain myself from committing suicide by starvation only because I have faith in India's awakening and her ability to put herself on the way to freedom from this desolating pauperism. Without faith in such a possibility I should cease to take interest in living. . . .[19]

To a people famishing and idle the only acceptable form in which God can dare appear is work and promise of food as wages. God created man to work for his food and said that those who ate without work were thieves. Eighty per cent of India are compulsorily thieves half the year. Is it any wonder if India has become one vast prison? . . . "Why should I who have no need to work for food, spin?" may be the question asked. Because I am eating what does not belong to me. I am living on the spoliation of my countrymen. Trace the course of every pice [penny] that finds its way into your pocket and you will realize the truth of what I write. . . .[20]

. . . Even as each home cooks its own food without difficulty so may each home weave its own yarn. And just as, in spite of every

[18] *Young India,* July 21, 1920.
[19] *Young India,* April 6, 1921.
[20] *Young India,* October 13, 1921.

home having its own kitchen, restaurants continue to flourish, so will mills continue to supply our additional wants. . . .[21]

. . . I would favor the use of the most elaborate machinery if thereby India's pauperism and resulting idleness be avoided. . . .[22]

We should be ashamed of resting or having a square meal so long as there is one able-bodied man or woman without work or food.[23]

In India it must be held to be a crime to spend money on dinner and marriage parties . . . and other luxuries so long as millions of people are starving. We would not have a feast in a family if a member was about to die of starvation. If India is one family, we should have the same feeling as we would have in a private family.[24]

. . . Whatever may be true of other countries, in India . . . where more than eighty per cent of the population is agricultural and another ten per cent industrial, it is a crime to make education merely literary and to unfit boys and girls for manual work in after-life. Indeed . . . as the larger part of our time is devoted to labor for earning our bread, our children must from their infancy be taught the dignity of such labor. Our children should not be so taught as to despise labor. . . . It is a sad thing that our schoolboys look upon manual labor with disfavor, if not contempt. . . .[25]

. . . The hunt after position and status has ruined many a family and has made many depart from the path of rectitude. Who does not know what questionable things fathers of families in need of money for their children's education have considered it their duty to do. . . .[26]

[21] *Young India,* September 8, 1920.
[22] *Young India,* November 3, 1921.
[23] *Young India,* October 6, 1921.
[24] *Young India,* December 22, 1920.
[25] *Young India,* September 1, 1921.
[26] *Young India,* June 15, 1921.

12

GANDHI'S ROAD TO JAIL

[The new Viceroy, Lord Reading, had arrived in India on April 2, 1921. Shortly after his installation at New Delhi, he indicated a desire to talk with Gandhi. They had six talks. What did Reading think of Gandhi? "He came . . . in a white dhoti [loin cloth] and cap woven on a spinning wheel, with bare feet and legs, and my first impression on seeing him ushered into the room was that there was nothing to arrest attention in his appearance, and that I should have passed him by in the street without a second look at him. When he talks, the impression is different. He is direct, and expresses himself well in excellent English with a fine appreciation of the value of the words he uses. There is no hesitation about him and there is a ring of sincerity in all that he utters, save when discussing some political questions. His religious views are, I believe, genuinely held, and he is convinced to a point almost bordering on fanaticism that non-violence and love will give India its independence and enable it to withstand the British government. His religious and moral views are admirable and indeed are on a remarkably high altitude, though I must confess that I find it difficult to understand his practice of them in politics. . . . Our conversations were of the frankest; he was supremely courteous with manners of distinction. . . . He held in every way to his word in the various discussions we had."[1]

Reading had absolute power over the police and the army. The Congress Party had made Gandhi its dictator. One word from the

---

[1] From letters written to his son in May, shortly after the talks, in *Rufus Isaacs, First Marquess of Reading,* by His Son, the Marquess of Reading, 1914–1935, Volume II (London: Hutchinson & Co., Ltd., 1945), quoted in Louis Fischer, *The Life of Mahatma Gandhi,* Part II, Chapter 24, pp. 195–196.

Mahatma would have started a conflagration compared with which the 1857 Mutiny would have seemed like a minor affair.]

. . . For me patriotism is the same as humanity. I am patriotic because I am human and humane. It is not exclusive. I will not hurt England or Germany to serve India. . . . The law of a patriot is not different from that of the patriarch. And a patriot is so much the less a patriot if he is a lukewarm humanitarian. There is no conflict between private and political law. A Non-coöperator, for instance, would act exactly in the same manner toward his father or brother as he is today acting toward the [British] Government.[2]

. . . He who injures others, is jealous of others, is not fit to live in the world. For the world is at war with him and he has to live in perpetual fear of the world. . . .[3]

. . . If India makes violence her creed and I have survived I would not care to live in India. She will cease to evoke any pride in me. . . . I cling to India like a child to its mother's breast, because I feel she gives me the spiritual nourishment I need. She has the environment that responds to my highest aspiration. When that faith is gone I shall feel like an orphan without hope of ever finding a guardian.[4]

. . . If I can have nothing to do with the organized violence of the Government I can have less to do with the unorganized violence of the people. I would prefer to be crushed between the two.[5]

. . . Civil Disobedience is not a state of lawlessness and license but presupposes a law-abiding spirit combined with self-restraint.[6]

. . . Complete Civil Disobedience is rebellion without the element of violence in it. An out and out civil resister simply ignores the authority of the state. He becomes an outlaw claiming to disregard every unmoral state law. Thus, for instance, he may refuse to pay taxes. . . . In doing all this he never uses force and never resists force when it is used against him. In fact, he invites imprisonment

---

[2] *Young India,* March 16, 1921.
[3] *Young India,* October 6, 1921.
[4] *Young India,* April 6, 1921.
[5] *Young India,* November 24, 1921.
[6] *Young India,* November 17, 1921.

and other uses of force. . . . This he does because . . . he finds the bodily freedom he seemingly enjoys to be an intolerable burden. He argues to himself that a state allows personal freedom only in so far as the citizen submits to its regulations. Submission to the state law is the price a citizen pays for his personal liberty. Submission, therefore, to a state wholly or largely unjust is an immoral barter for liberty. . . . Thus considered, civil resistance is a most powerful expression of a soul's anguish and an eloquent protest against the continuance of an evil state. Is this not the history of all reform? Have not reformers, much to the disgust of their fellows, discarded even innocent symbols associated with an evil practice?[7]

. . . Our Non-coöperation is neither with the English nor with the West. Our Non-coöperation is with the system the English have established with the material civilization and its attendant greed and exploitation of the weak. Our Non-coöperation is a retirement within ourselves. Our Non-coöperation is a refusal to coöperate with the English administrators on their own terms. We say to them: "Come and coöperate and it will be well for us, for you and the world." . . . [8]

Whether you advertise the fact or not, a body not receiving the food it needs dies. Whether we advertise the fact or not the moment we cease to support the Government it dies a natural death. Personally I dislike even the resolution voting the money to be used at the discretion of the All-India Congress [Party] Committee in foreign propaganda. We want all the money we need in this country. I would far rather invest Rupees 45,000 [$9,000] in spinning wheels or establishing primary schools than in advertising our work. Every good deed is its own advertisement. . . .[9]

. . . Civil Disobedience . . . becomes a sacred duty when the state has become lawless or, which is the same thing, corrupt. And a citizen who barters with such a state shares its corruption or lawlessness.[10]

. . . In my humble opinion, rejection is as much an ideal as the

[7] *Young India,* November 10, 1921.
[8] *Young India,* October 13, 1921.
[9] *Young India,* January 19, 1921.
[10] *Young India,* January 5, 1922.

acceptance of a thing. It is as necessary to reject untruth as it is to accept truth. . . .[11]

Non-coöperation is a protest against an unwitting and unwilling participation in evil.[12]

It is not so much British guns that are responsible for our subjection as our voluntary coöperation.[13]

[A] program conceived in a religious spirit admits of no tactics or compromise with things that matter. Our present Non-coöperation refers not so much to the paralysis of a wicked government as to our being proof against wickedness. It aims therefore not at destruction but at construction. It deals with causes rather than symptoms.[14]

. . . Non-coöperation is the most potent instrument for creating world opinion in our favor. So long as we protested and coöperated, the world did not understand us. . . . The . . . question the world has undoubtedly been asking is: If things are really so bad, why do we coöperate with the Government in so pauperizing and humiliating us? Now the world understands our attitude, no matter how weakly we may enforce it in practice. The world is now curious to know what ails us. . . .[15]

. . . The dynamic force behind this great movement [of non-violence] is not vocal propaganda but the silent propaganda carried on by the sufferings of the innocent victims of a mad Government.[16]

. . . The case of non-coöperators depends for success on cultivation of public opinion and public support. They have no other force to back them. If they forfeit public opinion they have lost the voice of God for the time being.[17]

Non-coöperation is not a movement of brag, bluster or bluff. It is a test of our sincerity. It requires solid and silent self-sacrifice. It challenges our honesty and our capacity for national work. It is a movement that aims at translating ideas into action. And the more

[11] *Young India,* June 1, 1921.
[12] *Young India,* June 1, 1921.
[13] *Young India,* February 9, 1921.
[14] *Young India,* January 19, 1921.
[15] *Young India,* May 25, 1921.
[16] *Young India,* July 13, 1921.
[17] *Young India,* January 19, 1922.

we do the more we find that much more must be *done* than we had expected. . . .[18]

As larger and larger numbers of innocent men come out to welcome death their sacrifice will become the potent instrument for the salvation of all others, and there will be a minimum of suffering. Suffering cheerfully endured ceases to be suffering and is transmuted into an ineffable joy. The man who flies from suffering is the victim of endless tribulation before it has come to him and is half dead when it does come. But one who is cheerfully ready for anything and everything that comes escapes all pain, his cheerfulness acts as an anaesthetic.[19]

. . . The December [1920] Congress [the term also used for the Congress Party's annual meetings] declared its intention to acquire Swaraj within one year.

We cannot, then, do better than consecrate ourselves for greater national effort in this direction. . . . But there are . . . things in which we certainly need to make a very special effort.

Firstly, we must acquire greater mastery over ourselves and secure an atmosphere of perfect calm, peace and good will. We must ask forgiveness for every unkind word thoughtlessly uttered or unkind deed done to anyone.

Secondly, we must still further cleanse our hearts, and we Hindus and Moslems must cease to suspect one another's motives, and we should believe ourselves to be incapable of wronging one another.

Thirdly, we Hindus must call no one unclean or mean or inferior to ourselves, and must therefore cease to regard the "Pariah" class to be untouchable. We must consider it sinful to regard a fellow-being as untouchable.

These three things are matters of inward transformation and the result will be seen in our daily dealings.

The fourth is the curse of drink. . . . A supreme effort should be made . . . to induce, by respectful entreaty, the liquor-sellers to give up their licenses, and the habitual visitors to these shops to give up the habit. . . . In any case, no physical force should be used to attain

[18] *Young India,* January 12, 1921.
[19] *Young India,* October 13, 1921.

the end. A determined, peaceful campaign of persuasion must succeed.

The fifth thing is the introduction of the spinning wheel in every
home, larger production and use of khadi [homespun cloth] and
complete giving up of foreign cloth.

. . . As soon as we have rendered ourselves fit, no person on earth
can prevent our establishing Swaraj. . . .[20]

Let us not waste our resources in thinking of too many national
problems and their solutions. A patient who tries many nostrums
at a time dies. A physician who experiments on his patient with a
combination of remedies loses his reputation and passes for a
quack. Chastity in work is as essential as chastity in life. . . .[21]

. . . Let people only work programs in which they believe implicitly. Loyalty to human institutions has its well defined limits.
To be loyal to an organization must not mean subordination of
one's settled convictions. Parties may fall and parties may rise; if we
are to attain freedom our deep convictions must remain unaffected
by such passing changes.[22]

. . . We must not resort to social boycott of our opponents. It
amounts to coercion. Claiming the right of free opinion and free
action as we do, we must extend the same to others. The rule of
majority, when it becomes coercive is as intolerable as that of a
bureaucratic minority. We must patiently try to bring round the
minority to our view by gentle persuasion and argument. . . .[23]

We must . . . refrain from crying "shame, shame" to anybody,
we must not use any coercion to persuade our people to adopt our
way. We must guarantee to them the same freedom we claim for
ourselves. . . .[24]

. . . It is our exclusiveness and the easy self-satisfaction that have
certainly kept many a waverer away from us. Our motto must ever
be conversion by gentle persuasion and a constant appeal to the
head and heart. We must therefore be ever courteous and patient

[20] *Young India,* March 23, 1921.
[21] *Young India,* March 30, 1921.
[22] *Young India,* December 8, 1921.
[23] *Young India,* January 26, 1922.
[24] *Young India,* February 9, 1921.

with those who do not see eye to eye with us. We must resolutely refuse to consider our opponents as enemies of the country.[25]

[Whilst] we may attack measures and systems we may not, must not, attack men. Imperfect ourselves, we must be tender toward others and be slow to impute motives.[26]

[Gandhi preferred to try mass civil disobedience in one area, and he chose the county of Bardoli, population eighty-seven thousand, living in one hundred twenty-seven tiny villages. On February 1, 1922, he informed Lord Reading, the Viceroy, of this plan. But on February 5, eight hundred miles from Bardoli in Chauri Chaura, in the United Provinces, an Indian mob committed murder. There had been a legal procession.]

But when the procession had passed, the stragglers were interfered with and abused by the constables. [The stragglers] cried out for help. The mob returned. The constables opened fire. The little ammunition they had was exhausted and they retired to the Thana [city hall] for safety. The mob, my informant tells me, therefore set fire to the Thana. The self-imprisoned constables had to come out for dear life, and as they did so, they were hacked to pieces and the mangled remains were thrown into the raging flames.

God has been abundantly kind to me. He has warned me . . . that there is not yet in India that truthful and non-violent atmosphere which and which alone can justify mass disobedience, which can be at all described as civil which means gentle, truthful, humble, knowing, willful yet loving yet never criminal and hateful.

. . . No provocation can possibly justify the brutal murder of men who had been rendered defenceless and had virtually thrown themselves on the mercy of the mob. . . . Suppose the "non-violent" disobedience of Bardoli was permitted by God to succeed, the Government had abdicated in favor of the victors of Bardoli, who would control the unruly elements that must be expected to perpetrate inhumanity upon due provocation? Non-violent attainment of self-government presupposes a non-violent control over the violent elements in the country. Non-violent Non-coöperators can

[25] *Young India,* September 29, 1921.
[26] *Young India,* May 25, 1921.

succeed only when they have succeeded in attaining control over the hooligans of India. . . .[27]

[Gandhi was not sure he could. He accordingly suspended the civil disobedience campaign in Bardoli and canceled any defiance of the Government anywhere in India.]

Let the opponent glory in our humiliation or so-called defeat. It is better to be charged with cowardice and weakness than to be guilty of denial of our oath [of truth and non-violence]. It is a million times better to *appear* untrue before the world than to *be* untrue to ourselves.[28]

I hope . . . that whether the Government arrest me or whether they stop by direct or indirect means the publication of the three [Gandhi-edited nationalist] journals [*Young India,* Gujarati *Nava Jivan* and Hindi *Nava Jivan*] the public will remain unmoved. It is a matter of no pride or pleasure to me but one of humiliation that the Government refrain from arresting me for fear of an outbreak of universal violence and awful slaughter. . . . It would be a sad commentary upon my preaching of . . . non-violence if my incarceration was to be a signal for a storm all over the country. . . .

. . . I would regard the observance of perfect peace on my arrest as a mark of high honor paid to me by my countrymen. . . .

I do not know that my removal from their midst will not be a benefit to the people. In the first instance, the superstition about the possession of supernatural powers by me will be demolished. Secondly, the belief that people have accepted the Non-coöperation program only under my influence and that they have no independent faith in it will be disproved. Thirdly, our capacity for Swaraj will be proved by our ability to conduct our activities in spite of the withdrawal even of the originator of the current program. Fourthly and selfishly, it will give me a quiet and physical rest which perhaps I deserve.[29]

[Lord Reading ordered Gandhi's arrest, and it took place March 10, 1922 at 10:30 in the evening. Standing surrounded by a dozen or

[27] *Young India,* February 16, 1922.
[28] *Young India,* February 16, 1922.
[29] *Young India,* March 9, 1922.

more Ashramites, Gandhi offered up a prayer and joined in the singing of a hymn. Then, in a gay mood, he walked to the police car and was taken to Sabarmati prison. The next morning, Kasturbai sent clothes, goat's milk and grapes to her husband.

The charge was writing three seditious articles in *Young India*.

The first "seditious article" was "Tampering with Loyalty," which appeared September 19, 1921.]

. . . Non-coöperation, though a religious and strictly moral movement, deliberately aims at the overthrow of the Government and is therefore legally seditious in terms of the Indian Penal Code. . . .

[The] duty of the Congress [Party] and Khilafat workers is clear. We ask for no quarter, we expect none from the Government. We did not solicit the promise of immunity from prison so long as we remained nonviolent. We may not now complain if we are imprisoned for sedition. Therefore our self-respect and our pledge require us to remain calm, unperturbed and nonviolent. . . .[30]

[The government case was made easy. The second article, "A Puzzle and Its Solution," printed December 15, 1921, was even more explicit.]

. . . We are challenging the might of this Government because we consider its activity to be wholly evil. We want to overthrow the Government. We want to *compel* its submission to the people's will. We desire to show that the Government exists to serve the people, not the people the Government. . . . Whether we are one or many we must refuse to purchase freedom at the cost of our cherished convictions. . . .

It would be a thousand times better for us to be ruled by a military dictator than to have the dictatorship concealed under sham councils and assemblies. They prolong the agony and increase the expenditure. If we are so anxious to live it would be more honorable to face the truth and submit to unabashed dictation than to pretend we are slowly becoming free. There is no such thing as slow freedom. Freedom is like a birth. Till we are fully free we are slaves. All birth takes place in a moment.[31]

[30] *Young India*, September 19, 1921.
[31] *Young India*, December 15, 1921.

*   *   *

["How can there be any compromise when the British lion continues to shake his gory claws in our faces?" challenged the third seditious article, "Shaking the Manes," in *Young India* of February 23,
1922.]

. . . No empire intoxicated with the red wine of power and plun-
der of weaker races has yet lived long in this world. [It] is high time
the British people were made to realize that the fight that was commenced in 1920 is a fight to the finish, whether it lasts one month or
one year or many months or many years, and whether the representatives of Britain re-enact all the indescribable orgies of the
Mutiny days with redoubled force or whether they do not. I shall
only hope and pray that God will give India sufficient humility and
sufficient strength to remain non-violent to the end. . . .[32]

["The Great Trial," as it came to be known, was held in Ahmedabad on March 18, 1922. After the indictment was read and the
Advocate-General had stated the case against Gandhi, the judge
asked the Mahatma whether he wished to make a statement.
Gandhi had a written statement ready, which he introduced with
some extemporaneous remarks.]

. . . Non-violence is the first article of my faith [and] the last article of my creed. I had either to submit to a system which I considered had done an irreparable harm to my country or incur the risk
of the mad fury of my people bursting forth when they understood
the truth from my lips. I know my people have sometimes gone
mad. I am deeply sorry for it and I am therefore here to submit not
to a light penalty but to the highest penalty. I do not ask for
mercy. . . .

Statement

My public life began in 1893 in South Africa in troubled weather.
My first contact with British authority in that country was not of a
happy character. I discovered that as a man and an Indian I had no
rights. More correctly, I discovered that I had no rights as a man
because I was an Indian.

---

[32] *Young India,* February 23, 1922.

But I was not baffled. I thought this treatment of Indians was an excrescence upon a system that was intrinsically and mainly good. . . .

I came reluctantly to the conclusion that the British connection had made India more helpless than she ever was before, politically and economically. A disarmed India has no power of resistance against any aggressor if she wanted to engage in an armed conflict with him. . . . She has become so poor that she has little power of resisting famines. Before the British advent India spun and wove in her millions of cottages just the supplement she needed for adding to her meager agricultural resources. This cottage industry . . . has been ruined. . . . Little do town-dwellers know how the semi-starved masses of India are slowly sinking to lifelessness. . . . The law itself in this country has been used to serve the foreign exploiter. . . .

. . . I am satisfied that many Englishmen and Indian officials honestly believe they are administering one of the best systems yet devised in the world and that India is making steady though slow progress. They do not know that a subtle but effective system of terrorism and an organized display of force on the one hand and the deprivation of all powers of retaliation or self-defence on the other have emasculated the people and induced in them the habit of simulation. . . . Section 12-A under which I am happily charged is perhaps the prince among the political sections of the Indian Penal Code designed to suppress the liberty of the citizen. Affection cannot be manufactured or regulated by law. . . . I have no personal ill-will against any single administrator. . . . But I hold it to be a virtue to be disaffected towards a Government which in its totality has done more harm to India than any previous system. India is less manly under the British rule than she ever was before. . . .

In fact, I believe I have rendered a service to India and England by showing in Non-coöperation the way out of the unnatural state in which both are living. . . .[33]

[When Gandhi sat down, Mr. Justice Broomfield bowed to the prisoner and pronounced sentence. "The determination of a just sentence," the judge declared, "is perhaps as difficult a proposition

[33] *Young India*, March 23, 1922.

as a judge in this country could have to face. The law is no respecter of persons. Nevertheless, it would be impossible to ignore the fact that you are in a different category from any person I have ever tried or am likely to have to try. It would be impossible to ignore the fact that, in the eyes of millions of your countrymen, you are a great patriot and a great leader. Even those who differ from you in politics look upon you as a man of high ideals and of noble and even saintly life."

The judge then announced that Gandhi must undergo imprisonment for six years, and added that if the Government later saw fit to reduce the term "no one would be better pleased than I."

When the court was adjourned, most of the spectators in the room fell at Gandhi's feet. Many wept. Gandhi wore a benign smile as he was led away to jail.[34]

[Gandhi had no grievance. He knew when he entered Indian politics that it involved going to prison, for him and for others. That fall, the Government had begun to round up political leaders and their followers. Hundreds were arrested, including Motilal Nehru, father of Prime Minister Jawaharlal Nehru. By December, 1921, twenty thousand Indians had been jailed for Civil Disobedience and sedition. During December and January, 1922, ten thousand more were thrown into prisons for political offenses. Whenever Gandhi heard of a friend or colleague who had been arrested he telegraphed congratulations.]

. . . We have an excessive dread of prisons. I have not a shadow of a doubt that society would be much cleaner and healthier if there was less resort to law courts than there is. . . . It is not right to beggar ourselves [with legal expenses] by fighting against odds. It is hardly manful to be over-anxious about the result of political trials that involve no disgrace.[35]

. . . Imprisonments . . . are courted because we consider it to be wrong to be free under a government we hold to be wholly bad. . . .[36]

---

[34] The verbatim proceedings of Gandhi's 1922 trial are given in M. K. Gandhi, *Speeches and Writings of Mahatma Gandhi* (Madras: G. A. Natesan & Co., 1933) and in *The Great Trial of Mahatma Gandhi and Mr. Sankarlal Banker,* edited by K. P. Kesava Menon, Foreword by Mrs. Sarojini Naidu (Madras: Ganesh & Co., 1922), in Louis Fischer, *The Life of Mahatma Gandhi,* Part II, Chapter 24, pp. 201–204.

[35] *Young India,* December 3, 1919.

[36] *Young India,* November 3, 1921.

... A Government that is evil has no room for good men and women except in its prisons.[37]

What is ... the difference between those who find themselves in jails for being in the right and those who are there for being in the wrong? Both wear ... the same dress, eat the same food and are subject outwardly to the same discipline. But whilst the latter submit to discipline most unwillingly and would commit a breach of it secretly and even openly if they could, the former will willingly and to the best of their ability conform to the jail discipline and prove worthier and more serviceable to the cause than when they are outside. ...[38]

... Self-purification is the main consideration in seeking the prison. Embarrassment of the Government is a secondary consideration. It is my unalterable conviction that even though the Government may not feel embarrassed in any way whatsoever by the incarceration or even execution of an innocent, unknown but a purified person, such incarceration will be the end of that Government. Even a single lamp dispels the deepest darkness. ...[39]

... For me solitary confinement in a prison cell without any breach on my part of the code of Non-coöperation or private or public morals will be freedom. For me the whole of India is a prison even as the master's house is to his slave. A slave to be free must continuously rise against his slavery and be locked up in his master's cell for his rebellion. The cell door is the door to freedom. ...[40]

... Our discipline [in jail] must not take the form of humiliation. Discomfort must not be torture and respect must not take the form of crawling on one's belly. And therefore, on pain of being put in irons, in solitary confinement or of being shot, Non-coöperating prisoners must decline ... to stand naked before the jailer, must decline in the name of discomfort to wear stinking clothes or eat food that is unclean or indigestible and must similarly decline even

[37] Young India, September 22, 1921.
[38] Young India, December 29, 1921.
[39] Young India, February 9, 1922.
[40] Young India, June 15, 1921.

in the name of respect to open out their palms or to sit in a crouching position. . . .[41]

. . . One finds a readiness to suffer imprisonment and assaults but not loss of goods. The anomaly is at first sight difficult to understand but it is really easy to appreciate. We are so much tied down to our goods and other possessions that when no disgrace attaches to imprisonment we prefer the inconvenience to loss of property. . . . This struggle . . . can give us victory only if we become indifferent to everything through which the state can press us into subjection to its will. We must be prepared, therefore, to let our goods and our land be taken away from us and rejoice over the dispossession even as we rejoice today over imprisonments. We must rest assured that the Government will be more quickly tired of selling our chattels than it is already of taking charge of our bodies. . . . We must voluntarily, though temporarily, embrace poverty if we will banish pauperism and pariahdom from the land. The sacrifice of ease by a few of us is nothing compared to the reward which is in store for us—the restoration of the honor and prosperity of this holy land.[42]

---

[41] *Young India,* December 29, 1921.
[42] *Young India,* January 12, 1922.

13

THE POWER OF THE MIND

[When he passed through the prison gates, Gandhi left behind him a country full of perplexed politicians and an ashram full of two unhappy families—his personal family and his adopted family of secretaries, disciples, devotees and hangers-on. All of them, including Kasturbai, now called him Father, Bapu, or Bapuji, the *ji* connoting a Hindu mixture of respect and tenderness.

From young manhood, he had been sweet and kind toward everybody except his wife and sons. A tension marred his early relations with Kasturbai, but gradually it waned and he was able to relax with her too. As he aged, the passions submitted to more rigid rein, but he never quite learned to be a father to his sons.

A foreigner once asked Gandhi: "How is your family?"]

All of India is my family [Gandhi replied.][1]

[Answering the question, what did he expect of members of the Gandhi family, he said:]

I expect that all of them should devote their lives to service, practice self-control as far as possible, give up the desire of amassing riches, give up also the idea of contracting a marriage, observe brahmacharya [continence] if they are already married and obtain their livings through service. The field of service is so extensive that it can absorb any number of men and women. Is there anything more to add?[2]

[Gandhi did not count on his four sons, however. "May not an artist or a poet or a great genius," asked an interviewer, "leave a legacy of his genius to posterity through his own children?"]

---

[1] Louis Fischer, *The Life of Mahatma Gandhi,* Part II, Chapter 16, p. 129.
[2] Yeravda Prison, August 7, 1932, in Mahadev Desai, *The Diary of Mahadev Desai*, p. 278.

Certainly not [replied Gandhi]. He will have more disciples than he can ever have children.[3]

[As he was more severe with himself than with anybody else, so he was severest with his own boys. Gandhi leaned over backward to give his sons, Harilal, Manilal, Ramdas and Devadas, less than he gave other men's sons. They felt disgruntled because their father, who had a profession, denied them a professional education.]

... It has been my invariable rule to regard my boys as my friends and equals as soon as they completed their sixteen years. The tremendous changes that my outer life has undergone from time to time were bound to leave their impress on my immediate surroundings—especially on my children. Harilal, who was witness to all the changes, being old enough to understand them, was naturally influenced by the western veneer that my life at one time did have. . . . Could I have influenced him, he would have been found associated with me in my several public activities. . . . But he chose, as he had every right to do, a different and independent path. He was and still is ambitious. He wants to become rich, and that too easily. Possibly he has a grievance against me that when it was open to me to do so, I did not equip him and my other children for careers that lead to wealth and fame that wealth brings. . . .

There is much in Harilal's life that I dislike. He knows that. But I love him in spite of his faults. The bosom of a father will take him in as soon as he seeks entrance. For the present, he has shut the door against himself. . . .

... I let the world into all the domestic secrets so-called. I never make the slightest attempt to hide them, for I know that concealment can only hurt us.

... Men may be good, not necessarily their children. Men may be good in some respects, not necessarily, therefore, in all. A man who is an authority on one matter is not therefore an authority on all matters. . . .[4]

[After Harilal's wife died and Gandhi frowned on his remarriage, Harilal disintegrated completely. He took to alcohol and

[3] *Young India*, November 20, 1924.
[4] *Young India*, June 18, 1925.

women, he was often seen drunk in public. Once he wrote Gandhi suggesting that Manu, Harilal's daughter, be taken away from his sister-in-law. At the end of the long reply, Gandhi said:]

I will not still give up hope of your reformation even as I do not despair of myself. . . . And I will continue to hope while you and I are alive, and preserve this letter of yours contrary to my usual practice so that someday you may repent of having written such a foolish thing. I keep the letter not to taunt you, but to enjoy a laugh over it if ever God is so good to me. We are all liable to err. But it is our duty to correct our errors. I trust you will correct yours.[5]

[Harilal, under the influence of drink, penury and the desire for vengeance, would succumb to the offers of unscrupulous publishers and attack his father in print, signing "Abdulla," a Moslem name. He had become a Moslem.]

You must have by now heard of Harilal's acceptance of Islam. If he had no selfish purpose behind [it], I should have had nothing to say against the step. But I very much fear that there is no other motive. . . .[6]

[Harilal] must have sensation and he must have money. He has both. . . .[7]

. . . I am a believer in previous births and rebirths. All our relationships are the result of the deeds we carry from our previous births. God's laws are inscrutable and are the subject of endless search. No one will fathom them.

This is how I regard the case of my [eldest] son [Harilal]. I regard the birth of a bad son to me as the result of my evil past, whether of this life or previous. My first son was born when I was in a state of infatuation. Besides, he grew up whilst I was myself growing and whilst I knew myself very little. . . . For years he remained away from me and his upbringing was not entirely in my hands. That is why he has always been at a loose end. His grievance against me has always been that I sacrificed him and his brothers at the altar of what I wrongly believed to be the public good. My other

[5] Yeravda Prison, April 27, 1932, in Mahadev Desai, *Diary,* pp. 91–92.
[6] Letter to Mira Behn (Madeleine Slade) from Nandhi Hill, May 30, 1936, in M. K. Gandhi, *Gandhi's Letters to a Disciple* (New York: Harper & Brothers, 1950), p. 176.
[7] Letter to Rajkumari Amrit Kaur, a co-worker and disciple. June 1, 1936.

sons have laid more or less the same blame at my door but with a good deal of hesitation and they have generously forgiven me. My eldest son was the direct victim of experiments—radical changes in my life—and so he cannot forget what he regards as my blunders. Under the circumstances I believe I am myself the cause of the loss of my son and have, therefore, learnt patiently to bear it. . . . It is my firm faith that man is by nature going higher and so I have not at all lost the hope that some day he will wake up from his slumber and ignorance. Thus, he is part of my field of the experiments in nonviolence. When or whether I shall succeed, I have never bothered to know. It is enough for my satisfaction that I do not slacken my efforts in doing what I know to be my duty.[8]

[In jail, Gandhi read the Gita, the Hindu holy scripture. On first reading the Gita in 1888–89, Gandhi felt that it was "not a historical work" but an allegory. The story it tells, of a civil war between two Indian factions, was regarded by Gandhi as "the duel that perpetually went on in the hearts of mankind. . . . Physical warfare was brought in merely to make the description of the internal duel more alluring." The Gita is a dialogue between Krishna, an incarnation of God, and Arjuna, the warrior. "Krishna is the Dweller within, ever whispering to a pure heart," Gandhi wrote. Arjuna, representing higher impulses, struggles against evil. The Gita showed how to avoid the evils that accompany action; this, Gandhi asserted, is the "central teaching of the Gita." Krishna says:

Hold alike pleasure and pain, gain and loss, victory and defeat, and gird up thy loins for the fight; so doing thou shalt not incur sin.]

I regard Duryodhana and his party as the baser impulses in man, and Arjuna and his party as the higher impulses. The field of battle is our own body. . . .[9]

[Arjuna had refused to go into battle. Krishna urged him to

[8] 1940, in D. G. Tendulkar, *Mahatma: The Life of Mohandas Karamchand Gandhi,* Volume V, pp. 378–379.
[9] *Young India,* November 12, 1925.

fight, to fight and renounce the fruits of victory. This meant that
violence and renunciation were compatible. Gandhi was troubled.]

Let it be granted [he wrote in 1929, in an introduction to his
Gujarati translation of the Gita] that according to the letter of the
Gita it is possible to say that warfare is consistent with renunciation
of fruit. But after forty years' unremitting endeavor fully to enforce
the teaching of the Gita in my own life, I have, in all humility, felt
that perfect renunciation is impossible without perfect observance
of [Non-violence] in every shape and form. [Gandhi decided that
loyalty to the Gita entitled him to amend it. He often refused to be
bound by uncongenial texts, concepts and situations.

The Hindu poet Vyasa wrote a commentary on the Gita which,
Gandhi said, demonstrated to him the futility of war. Vyasa asks,
"What if the Kauravas were vanquished? And what if the Pan-
davas won? How many were left of the victors and what was their
lot?"[10]

Gandhi pressed the Gita into the service of Non-violence.]

The only tyrant I accept in this world is the "still small voice"
within me. And even though I have to face the prospect of being a
minority of one, I humbly believe I have the courage to be in such a
hopeless minority.[11]

... Constant development is the law of life, and a man who
always tries to maintain his dogmas in order to *appear* consistent
drives himself into a false position. That is why Emerson said that
foolish consistency was the hobgoblin of little minds. ...[12]

... A devotee of Truth may not do anything in deference to convention. He must always hold himself open to correction, and
whenever he discovers himself to be wrong, he must confess it at all
costs and atone for it.[13]

[On the evening of January 12, 1924, Mahatma Gandhi was hastily
carried from Yeravda Central Prison, where he had been lodged on
March 20, 1922, to Sassoon Hospital in the city of Poona. He had

[10] *Ibid.*
[11] *Young India,* March 2, 1922.
[12] *Young India,* September 20, 1928.
[13] M. K. Gandhi, *The Story of My Experiments with Truth,* Part IV, Chapter 39,
p. 293.

developed acute appendicitis. A British Army surgeon performed the appendectomy, which was successful. An abscess formed locally, however, and the patient's progress was too slow. The Government thought it wise or generous in these circumstances to release Gandhi on February 5th.

To recuperate, Gandhi went to the home of an industrialist friend who lived at Juhu, on the sea near Bombay. Indian nationalist leaders conferred with him there on the ugly situation that had arisen during the twenty-two months Gandhi spent in prison.]

... We had all kinds of news brought to us in South Africa in our jails. For two or three days during my first experience I was glad enough to receive tid-bits, but I immediately realized the utter futility of interesting myself in this illegal gratification. I could do nothing, I could send no message profitably, and I simply vexed my soul uselessly. I felt it was impossible for me to guide the movement from the jail. I therefore simply waited till I could meet those who were outside and talk to them freely, and then too ... I took only an academic interest because I felt it was not my province to judge anything. ... I well remember how the thoughts I had up to the time of my discharge from the jail on every occasion were modified immediately after discharge, and after getting first-hand information myself. Somehow or other the jail atmosphere does not allow you to have all the bearings in your mind. I would like you [Jawaharlal Nehru] to dismiss the outer world from your view altogether and ignore its existence. I know this is a most difficult task, but if you take up some serious study and some serious manual work you can do it. . . .[14]

[First, Hindu-Moslem friendship, the firm rock on which Gandhi hoped to build a united, free India, had been all but submerged in an angry tide of hostility between the two communities.]

... I regard myself as a friend of the Moslems. They are my blood brothers. Their wrongs are my wrongs. I share their sorrows and their joys. Any evil deed done by a Moslem hurts me just as much as that done by a Hindu. . . . We may not gloat over the errors of the least of our fellows.[15]

[14] Letter to Nehru from Bardoli, February 19, 1922, in Jawaharlal Nehru, *A Bunch of Old Letters* (Bombay: Asia Publishing House, 1958), p. 24.
[15] *Young India,* December 30, 1926.

... My strength lies in my asking people to do nothing that I have not tried repeatedly in my own life. I am then asking my countrymen today to adopt Non-violence as their final creed. ... Hindus and Moslems, Christians, Sikhs and Parsis must not settle their differences by ... violence. ... Again, a nation of three hundred million people should be ashamed to have to resort to force to bring to book one hundred thousand Englishmen. ... [We] need not force of arms, but force of will. ...

Acceptance of Non-violence ... will teach us to husband our strength for a better purpose, instead of dissipating it, as now, in a useless fratricidal strife. ... [16]

My Gita tells me that evil can never result from a good action. Therefore I must help the Moslems from a pure sense of duty—without making any terms with them. ... The Moslem is a fellow-sufferer in slavery. We can therefore speak to him as a friend and a comrade. ... [17]

... What can be more natural than that Hindus and Moslems born and bred in India, having the same adversities, the same hopes, should be permanent friends, brothers born of the same Mother India? The surprise is that we should fight, not that we should unite. ... [18]

[Cleanse] your hearts and have charity. Make your hearts as broad as the ocean. That is the teaching of the Koran and of the Gita. ... Why should we say [the] politics [of the enemy] are corrupt? ... So long as the world lasts, so long will there be so many differences of opinion ... I shall not hate even a traitor. ... You have no right to harbor ill-will against anyone or say a single word against him. ... A nobler prescription I cannot give you. ... [19]

... To surrender is not to confer favor. Justice that love gives is a surrender, justice that law gives is a punishment. What a lover gives transcends justice. And yet it is always less than he wishes to give because he is anxious to give more and frets that he has nothing left. ... [20]

---

[16] *Young India*, May 24, 1924.
[17] *Young India*, January 29, 1925.
[18] *Young India*, August 21, 1924.
[19] *Young India*, January 1, 1925.
[20] *Young India*, July 9, 1925.

... Before [Hindus and Moslems] dare think of freedom, they must be brave enough to love one another, to tolerate one another's religion, even prejudices and superstitions, and to trust one another. This requires faith in oneself. . . .[21]

... Love never claims, it ever gives. Love ever suffers, never resents, never revenges itself. . . .[22]

... Our ability to reach unity in diversity will be the beauty and the test of our civilization.[23]

A man is but the product of his thoughts; what he thinks, he becomes.[24]

[21] *Young India,* October 2, 1924.

[22] *Young India,* July 9, 1925.

[23] *Young India,* January 8, 1925.

[24] M. K. Gandhi, *Ethical Religion* (Madras: S. Ganesan, 1922), Chapter 6, p. 61.

14

NATIONAL INDEPENDENCE
IS NOT ENOUGH

[Gandhi, always the champion of Civil Disobedience, still—after imprisonment—believed in non-coöperation with the British Government of India. Logically, therefore, he would have pressed for a boycott of the courts, schools and government jobs and titles. But the Gandhians had grown discouraged during his absence in jail. Boycotts involved tremendous personal sacrifice which few could bear. Gandhi accordingly withdrew from Indian politics for several years. Self-Rule, he believed, depended on how good India was, not how bad the British were.]

. . . I contemplate a mental and therefore a moral opposition to immoralities. I seek entirely to blunt the edge of the tyrant's sword not by putting up against it a sharper-edged weapon, but by disappointing his expectation that I would be offering physical resistance. The resistance of the soul that I should offer instead would elude him. It would at first dazzle him and at last compel recognition . . . which . . . would not humiliate him but uplift him. It may be urged that this . . . is an ideal state. And so it is. . . .[1]

. . . My method is conversion, not coercion, it is self-suffering, not the suffering of a tyrant. I know that method to be infallible. I know that a whole people can adopt it without accepting it as its creed and without understanding its philosophy. People generally do not understand the philosophy of all their acts. My ambition is much higher than independence. Through the deliverance of India I seek to deliver the so-called weaker races of the earth from the crushing heels of Western exploitation in which England is the greatest partner. If India converts, as it can convert, Englishmen, it

[1] *Young India,* October 8, 1925.

can become the predominant partner in a world commonwealth of which England can have the privilege of becoming a partner if she chooses. . . . In no case do I want to reconcile myself to a state lower than the best for fear of consequences. It is therefore not out of expedience that I propose independence as my goal. . . . India's coming into her own will mean every nation doing likewise. . . .[2]

[A] friend begs the question when he says a revolutionary is one who "does the good and dies." That is precisely what I question. In my opinion he does the evil and dies. I do not regard killing or assassination or terrorism as good in any circumstances whatsoever. . . .

. . . If the revolutionaries succeed in attracting, not "dragging" the masses to them, they will find the murderous campaign is totally unnecessary. . . .

. . . I have not the qualifications for teaching my philosophy of life. I have barely qualifications for practising the philosophy I believe. I am but a poor struggling soul yearning to be . . . wholly truthful and wholly non-violent in thought, word and deed, but ever failing to reach the ideal. . . . I admit and assure my revolutionary friends it is a painful climb, but the pain of it is a positive pleasure for me. Each step upward makes me feel stronger and fit for the next. . . . [Revolutionary] activity is suicidal at this stage of the country's life, at any rate, if not for all time, in a country so vast, so hopelessly divided and with the masses so deeply sunk in pauperism and so fearfully terror-struck.[3]

. . . The outward freedom . . . that we shall attain, will be only in exact proportion to the inward freedom to which we may have grown at a given moment.[4]

Self-government depends entirely upon our own internal strength, upon our ability to fight against the heaviest odds. Indeed, self-government which does not require that continuous striving to attain it and to sustain it is not worth the name. I have therefore endeavored to show both in word and deed that political self-government . . . is no better than individual self-government and

[2] *Young India*, January 12, 1928.
[3] *Young India*, April 9, 1925.
[4] *Young India*, November 1, 1928.

therefore is to be attained by precisely the same means that are required for individual self-government or self-rule.[5]

The law of love governs the world. Life persists in the face of death. The universe continues in spite of destruction incessantly going on. Truth triumphs over untruth. Love conquers hate. . . .[6]

. . . Means and end are convertible terms in my philosophy of life. . . .[7]

[One] man cannot do right in one department of life whilst he is occupied in doing wrong in any other department. Life is one indivisible whole.[8]

To me political power is not an end but one of the means of enabling people to better their condition in every department of life. Political power means the capacity to regulate national life through national representatives. . . .[9]

. . . I live for India's freedom and would die for it because it is a part of Truth. Only a free India can worship the true God. I work for India's freedom because my Swadeshi [love of things belonging to India] teaches me that having been born in it and having inherited her culture I am fittest to serve her and she has a prior claim to my service. . . .[10]

I am not interested in freeing India merely from the English yoke. I am bent upon freeing India from any yoke whatsoever. . . . Hence for me the movement of swaraj is a movement of self-purification.[11]

. . . What we want, I hope, is a government not based on coercion even of a minority but on its conversion. If it is a change from white military rule to a brown, we hardly need make any fuss. . . .[12]

. . . If India succeeds in making British *Rule* impossible without matching the British bayonet with another bayonet, she will rule herself too with the same means. . . .[13]

[5] Mahadev Desai, *With Gandhi in Ceylon* (Madras: S. Ganesan, 1928), Chapter 14, p. 93.

[6] *Young India,* October 23, 1924.

[7] Congress Presidential Address, in *Young India,* December 26, 1924.

[8] *Young India,* January 27, 1927.

[9] *Young India,* July 2, 1931.

[10] *Young India,* April 3, 1924.

[11] *Young India,* June 12, 1924.

[12] *Young India,* December 19, 1929.

[13] *Young India,* April 24, 1924.

My mission is not merely brotherhood of Indian humanity. My mission is not merely freedom of India, though today it undoubtedly engrosses practically the whole of my life and the whole of my time. But through realization of freedom of India I hope to realize and carry on the mission of the brotherhood of man. . . .[14]

. . . I want India's rise so the whole world may benefit. I do not want India to rise on the ruin of other nations. If therefore India was strong and able, India would send out to the world her treasures of art and health-giving spices, but she would refuse to send out opium or intoxicating liquors although the traffic may bring much material benefit. . . .[15]

India's greatest glory will consist not in regarding Englishmen as her implacable enemies fit only to be turned out of India at the first available opportunity but in turning them into friends and partners in a new commonwealth of nations in the place of an Empire based upon exploitation of the weaker or underdeveloped nations and races of the earth. . . .[16]

My attitude towards the English is one of utter friendliness and respect. I claim to be their friend, because it is contrary to my nature to distrust a single human being or to believe that any nation on earth is incapable of redemption. I have respect for Englishmen because I recognize their bravery, their spirit of sacrifice for what they believe to be good for themselves, their cohesion and their powers of vast organization. . . . I have hope of England because I have hope of India. We will not forever remain disorganized and imitative. Beneath the present disorganization, demoralization and lack of initiative I can discover organization, moral strength and initiative forming themselves. A time is coming when England will be glad of India's friendship, and India will disdain to reject the proffered hand because it has once despoiled her. . . .[17]

. . . By a long course of prayerful discipline I have ceased for over forty years to hate anybody. I know this is a big claim. . . . But I can and do hate evil wherever it exists. I hate the system of Govern-

[14] *Young India,* April 14, 1929.
[15] *Young India,* March 12, 1925.
[16] *Young India,* January 5, 1922.
[17] *Young India,* January 29, 1925.

ment the British people have set up in India. I hate the domineering manner of Englishmen as a class in India. I hate the ruthless
exploitation of India even as I hate from the bottom of my heart the
hideous system of untouchability for which millions of Hindus
have made themselves responsible. But I do not hate the domineering Englishmen as I refuse to hate the domineering Hindus. I seek
to reform them in all the loving ways that are open to me. My Non-
coöperation has its root not in hatred, but in love. . . .

Mine is not an exclusive love. I cannot love Moslems or Hindus
and hate Englishmen. For if I love merely Hindus and Moslems
because their ways are on the whole pleasing to me, I shall soon
begin to hate them when their ways displease me, as they may well
do any moment. A love that is based on the goodness of those
whom you love is a mercenary affair. . . .[18]

. . . We all are bound by the ties of love. . . . Scientists tell us that
without the presence of the cohesive force amongst the atoms that
comprise this globe of ours it would crumble to pieces and we
would cease to exist, and even as there is cohesive force in blind
matter so much must there be in all things animate and the name
for that cohesive force among animate beings is Love. We notice it
between father and son, between brother and sister, friend and
friend. . . . Where there is love there is life, hatred leads to destruction. . . .[19]

. . . Mutual love enables Nature to persist. Man does not live by
destruction. Self-love compels regard for others. Nations cohere
because there is mutual regard among individuals composing
them. Some day we must extend the national law to the universe,
even as we have extended the family law to form nations—a larger
family.[20]

. . . Isolated independence is not the goal of the world-states. It is
voluntary interdependence. . . .[21]

Interdependence is and ought to be as much the ideal of man as
self-sufficiency. Man is a social being. Without inter-relation with
society he cannot realize his oneness with the universe or suppress

[18] *Young India,* August 6, 1925.
[19] *Young India,* October 6, 1921.
[20] *Young India,* March 2, 1922.
[21] *Young India,* July 17, 1924.

his egotism. His social interdependence enables him to test his faith and to prove himself on the touchstone of reality. If man were so placed or could so place himself as to be absolutely above all dependence on his fellow-beings he would become so proud and arrogant as to be a veritable burden and nuisance to the world. Dependence on society teaches him the lesson of humanity. . . . A man cannot become self-sufficient even in respect of all the various operations from the growing of cotton to the spinning of the yarn. He has at some stage or other to take the aid of the members of his family. And if one may take help from one's own family, why not from one's neighbors? Or otherwise what is the significance of the great saying "The world is my family"?[22]

There is no limit to extending our service to our neighbors across state-made frontiers. God never made those frontiers.[23]

The world is weary of hate, we see the fatigue overcoming the Western nations. We see that the song of hate has not benefited humanity. Let it be the privilege of India to turn a new leaf and set a lesson to the world.[24]

[At] the present moment India can teach the world little. . . . [If] India succeeds in regaining her liberty through non-violent means, she would have delivered her message to the others who are fighting for it, and what is perhaps more, she would have made the largest contribution yet known to world peace.[25]

We want freedom for our country but not at the expense or exploitation of others, not so as to degrade other countries. I do not want the freedom of India if it means the extinction of England or the disappearance of Englishmen. I want the freedom of my country so other countries may learn something from my free country, so the resources of my country might be utilized for the benefit of mankind. Just as the cult of patriotism teaches us today that the individual has to die for the family, the family has to die for the village, the village for the district, the district for the province and the province for the country, even so a country has to be free in order

[22] *Young India,* March 21, 1929.
[23] *Young India,* December 31, 1931.
[24] Mahadev Desai, *Gandhiji in Indian Villages* (Triplicane, Madras: S. Ganesan, 1927), p. 166.
[25] *Young India,* April 15, 1926.

that it may die if necessary for the benefit of the world. My love, therefore, of nationalism or my idea of nationalism is that my country may become free, that if need be the whole country may die so the human race may live. There is no room for race-hatred there. Let that be our nationalism.[26]

It is impossible for one to be an internationalist without being a nationalist. Internationalism is possible only when nationalism becomes a fact, i.e., when peoples belonging to different countries have organized themselves and are able to act as one man. It is not nationalism that is evil, it is the narrowness, selfishness, exclusiveness which is the bane of modern nations which is evil. Each wants to profit at the expense of and rise on the ruin of the other.

. . . Indian nationalism has, I hope, struck a different path. It wants to organize itself or to find full self-expression for the benefit and service of humanity at large. . . . I cannot possibly go wrong so long as I do not harm other nations in the act of serving my country.[27]

. . . Whilst Asiatic races are held under subjection and are indifferent to their own welfare, it is easy enough to treat them as they are being treated, whether in England or America or in Africa, for that matter, in their own homes, as in China and in India. But they will not long remain asleep. One can but hope, therefore, that their awakening may not lead to making confusion worse confounded and adding to the racial bitterness already existing. There is, however, no hope of avoiding the catastrophe unless the spirit of exploitation that at present dominates the nations of the West is transmuted into . . . real, helpful service, or unless the Asiatic and the African races understand that they cannot be exploited without their coöperation, to a large extent voluntary, and thus understanding, withdraw such coöperation. . . . If man, no matter what pigment he wears, will realize his status, he will discover that it is possible for him to stand erect even before a whole world in opposition.[28]

. . . Repression, if it does not cow us down, can but hasten Swaraj [Independence] for it puts us on our mettle and evokes the

[26] Mahadev Desai, *Gandhiji,* p. 170.
[27] *Young India,* June 18, 1925.
[28] *Young India,* March 18, 1926.

spirit of self-sacrifice and courage in the face of danger. Repression does for a true man or a nation what fire does for gold. . . .[29]

[A] Government that is ideal governs the least. It is no self-government that leaves nothing for the people to do. . . . The triple program [hand-spinning, Hindu-Moslem unity and removal of untouchability] is the test of our capacity for self-government. If we impute all our weaknesses to the present Government we shall never shed them.

. . . My Swaraj will be, therefore, not a result of the murder of others but a voluntary act of continuous self-sacrifice. My Swaraj will not be a bloody usurpation of rights, but the acquisition of power will be a beautiful and natural fruit of duty well and truly performed. . . . I know it will be preceded by the rise of a class of young men and women who will find full excitement in work, work and nothing but work for the nation.[30]

I shall strive for a constitution which will release India from all thralldom and patronage and give her, if need be, the right to sin.

I shall work for an India . . . in which there shall be no high class and low class of people, an India in which all communities shall live in perfect harmony. There can be no room in such an India for the curse of untouchability or the curse of intoxicating drinks and drugs. Women shall enjoy the same rights as men. Since we shall be at peace with all the rest of the world neither exploiting nor being exploited, we should have the smallest army imaginable. All interests not in conflict with the interests of the dumb millions will be scrupulously respected, whether foreign or indigenous. Personally, I hate distinction between foreign and indigenous. This is the India of my dreams. . . . I shall be satisfied with nothing else.[31]

As every country is fit to eat, to drink and to breathe, even so is every nation fit to manage its own affairs, no matter how badly.[32]

You want coöperation between nations for the salvaging of civilization. I want it too, but coöperation presupposes free nations worthy of coöperation. If I am to help in creating or restoring . . .

---

[29] *Young India,* December 26, 1924.
[30] *Young India,* August 27, 1925.
[31] *Young India,* September 10, 1931.
[32] *Young India,* October 15, 1931.

good will and resist disturbances . . . I must have the ability to do so, and I cannot . . . unless my country has come into its own. . . . For so long as India is a subject nation, not only is she a danger to peace but also England, which exploits India. Other nations may tolerate today England's imperialist policy and her exploitation of other nations, but they certainly do not appreciate it, and they would gladly help in the prevention of England's becoming a greater and greater menace. . . . Of course, you will say that India free can become a menace herself. But let us assume she will behave herself with her doctrines of non-violence if she achieves her freedom through it, and for all her bitter experiences of being a victim of exploitation.[33]

Man does not live by bread alone. Many prefer self-respect to food.[34]

[33] *Young India,* November 12, 1931.
[34] *Young India,* February 5, 1925.

15

GANDHI'S MESSAGE TO ALL MEN

. . . The more efficient a force is, the more silent and the more subtle it is. Love is the subtlest force in the world. . . .[1]

[The] force of love . . . truly comes into play only when it meets with causes of hatred. True Non-violence does not ignore or blind itself to causes of hatred, but in spite of the knowledge of their existence, operates upon the person setting those causes in motion. . . . The law of Non-violence—returning good for evil, loving one's enemy—involves a knowledge of the blemishes of the "enemy." Hence do the Scriptures say . . . "Forgiveness is an attribute of the brave."[2]

. . . I can no more preach Non-violence to a coward than I can tempt a blind man to enjoy healthy scenes. Non-violence is the summit of bravery. . . .[3]

. . . Suffering in one's own person is . . . the essence of non-violence and is the chosen substitute for violence to others. It is not because I value life low that I can countenance with joy thousands voluntarily losing their lives for Satyagraha, but because I know that it results in the long run in the least loss of life, and what is more, it ennobles those who lose their lives. . . . [Unless] Europe is to commit suicide, some nation will have to dare to disarm herself and take large risks. The level of non-violence in that nation . . . will naturally have risen so high as to command universal respect. Her judgments will be unerring, her decisions will be firm, her capacity for heroic self-sacrifice will be great, and she will want to live as much for other nations as for herself. . . .[4]

. . . They say "means are after all [just] means." I would say "means are after all everything." As the means, so the end. Violent

[1] *Young India,* December 4, 1924.
[2] *Young India,* September 29, 1927.
[3] *Young India,* May 29, 1924.
[4] *Young India,* October 8, 1925.

means will give violent Swaraj. . . . There is no wall of separation between means and end. . . . I have been endeavoring to keep the country to means that are purely peaceful and legitimate.[5]

. . . If we take care of the means we are bound to reach the end sooner or later. . . .[6]

. . . Truth is my God. Non-violence is the means of realizing Him. . . .[7]

I am not a "statesman in the garb of a saint." But since Truth is the highest wisdom, sometimes my acts appear to be consistent with the highest statesmanship. But I hope I have no policy in me save the policy of Truth and Non-violence. . . .[8]

[To] me . . . there is no way to find Truth except the way of Non-violence. . . . For I know that a man who forsakes Truth can forsake his country and his nearest and dearest ones. . . .[9]

. . . I will not sacrifice Truth and Non-violence even for the deliverance of my country or religion. . . .[10]

. . . The movement of non-violent non-coöperation has nothing in common with the historical struggles for freedom in the West. It is not based on brute force or hatred. It does not aim at destroying the tyrant. It is a movement of self-purification. It therefore seeks to convert the tyrant. . . .[11]

. . . A revolutionary murders or robs not for the good of his victims, whom he often considers to be fit only to be injured, but for the supposed good of society.[12]

. . . Conscience is the ripe fruit of strictest discipline. . . . There is no such thing, therefore, as mass conscience. . . .

. . . The introduction of conscience into our public life is welcome . . . if it has taught a few of us to stand up for human dignity and rights in the face of the heaviest odds. . . .[13]

[5] *Young India,* July 17, 1924.

[6] M. K. Gandhi, *From Yeravda Mandir* (Ahmedabad: Navajivan Press, 1937), Chapter 3, p. 13.

[7] *Young India,* January 8, 1925.

[8] *Young India,* January 20, 1927.

[9] Speech at Wardha on Hindu-Moslem riots, December, 1920, in D. G. Tendulkar, *Mahatma: The Life of Mohandas Karamchand Gandhi,* Volume II, p. 312.

[10] *Young India,* January 20, 1927.

[11] *Young India,* February 11, 1926.

[12] *Young India,* May 21, 1925.

[13] *Young India,* August 21, 1924.

... I have no secret methods. I know no diplomacy save that of truth. I have no weapon but non-violence. I may be unconsciously led astray for a while but not for all time. I have therefore well-defined limitations. ...

I am yet ignorant of what exactly Bolshevism is. I have not been able to study it. I do not know whether it is for the good of Russia in the long run. But I do know that in so far as it is based on violence and denial of God, it repels me. I do not believe in short-violent-cuts to success. Those Bolshevik friends who are bestowing their attention on me should realize that however much I may sympathize with and admire worthy motives, I am an uncompromising opponent of violent methods even to serve the noblest of causes. ... [Experience] convinces me that permanent good can never be the outcome of untruth and violence. Even if my belief is a fond delusion, it will be admitted that it is a fascinating delusion.[14]

There is no principle worth the name if it is not wholly good. I swear by non-violence because I know that it alone conduces to the highest good of mankind, not merely in the next world, but in this also. I object to violence because, when it appears to do good, the good is only temporary, the evil it does is permanent. ...[15]

... Terrorism set up by reformers may be just as bad as Government terrorism, and it is often worse because it draws a certain amount of false sympathy. ...[16]

... I invite the revolutionaries not to commit suicide and drag with them unwilling victims. India's way is not Europe's. India is not Calcutta and Bombay. India lives in her seven hundred thousand villages. If the revolutionaries are as many let them spread out into these villages and try to bring sunshine into the dark dungeons of the millions of their countrymen. That would be worthier of their ambition and love of the land than the exciting and unquenchable thirst for the blood of English officials and those who are assisting them. It is nobler to try to change their spirit than to take their lives.[17]

[A friend] says that non-violence cannot be attained by the mass of people. And yet, we find the general work of mankind is being

[14] *Young India,* December 11, 1924.
[15] *Young India,* May 21, 1925.
[16] *Young India,* December 18, 1924.
[17] *Young India,* March 12, 1925.

carried on from day to day by the mass of people acting in harmony as if by instinct. If they were instinctively violent, the world would end in no time. They remain peaceful. . . . It is when the mass mind is unnaturally influenced by wicked men that the mass of mankind commit violence. But they forget it as quickly as they commit it because they return to their peaceful nature immediately the evil influence of the directing mind has been removed.[18]

. . . I hope to demonstrate that real Swaraj [Self-Rule] will come not by the acquisition of authority by a few but by the acquisition of the capacity by all to resist authority when abused. In other words, Swaraj is to be attained by educating the masses to a sense of their capacity to regulate and control authority.[19]

. . . If we all discharge our duties, rights will not be far to seek. If leaving duties unperformed, we run after rights, they will escape us like a will o' the wisp. . . . The same teaching has been embodied by Krishna in the immortal words: "Action alone is thine. Leave thou the fruit severely alone." Action is duty, fruit is the right.

. . . He who understands the doctrine of self-help blames himself for failure. It is on this ground that I object to violence. If we blame others where we should blame ourselves, and wish for or bring about their destruction, [it] does not remove the root cause of the disease, which, on the contrary sinks all the deeper for . . . ignorance. . . .[20]

[It] is necessary for workers to become self-reliant and dare to prosecute their plans if they so desire, without hankering after the backing of . . . persons supposed to be great and influential. Let them rely upon the strength of their own conviction and the cause they seek to espouse. Mistakes there will be. Suffering, even avoidable, there must be. But nations are not easily made. . . .[21]

. . . The way of peace insures internal growth and stability. We reject it because we fancy that it involves submission to the will of the ruler who has imposed himself upon us. . . . The suffering to be undergone . . . will be nothing compared to the physical suffering and the moral loss we must incur in trying the way of war. And the

[18] *Young India,* July 8, 1926.
[19] *Young India,* January 29, 1925.
[20] *Young India,* January 8, 1925.
[21] *Young India,* May 19, 1927.

suffering in following the way of peace must benefit both. It will be like the pleasurable travail of a new birth.[22]

[He] alone is truly non-violent who remains nonviolent even though he has the ability to strike. . . . I have had in my life many an opportunity of shooting my opponents and earning the crown of martyrdom but I had not the heart to shoot any of them. For I did not want them to shoot me, however much they disliked my methods. I wanted them to convince me of my error as I was trying to convince them of theirs. "Do unto others as you would that they should do unto you."[23]

Most people do not understand the complicated machinery of the government. They do not realize every citizen silently but none the less certainly sustains the government of the day in ways of which he has no knowledge. Every citizen therefore renders himself responsible for every act of his government. And it is quite proper to support it so long as the actions of the government are bearable. But when they hurt him and his nation it becomes his duty to withdraw his support.[24]

. . . I cannot satisfy myself with false coöperation—anything inferior to twenty-four carats gold. . . . [My non-coöperation] harms no one, it is non-coöperation with evil, with an evil system, and not with the evildoer. My religion teaches me to love even an evildoer. . . .[25]

What are . . . our countrymen in South Africa to do [in the way of preventing further oppressive legislation]? There is nothing in the world like self-help. . . . Self-help in this case, as perhaps in every other, means self-suffering, self-suffering means Satyagraha. When their honor is at stake, when their rights are being taken away, when their livelihood is threatened, they have the right and it becomes their duty to offer Satyagraha. . . .

. . . We may be justly entitled to many things but Satyagraha is offered for things without which self-respect, or which is the same thing, honorable existence, is impossible.

[22] *Young India,* May 20, 1925.
[23] *Young India,* May 7, 1925.
[24] *Young India,* July 28, 1920.
[25] Speech for an "at home" given by the Indian Association, printed in *Young India,* August 25, 1925.

They must count the cost. Satyagraha cannot be offered in bravado or as a mere trial. It is therefore offered because it becomes irresistible. No price is too dear to pay for it—truth. . . .[26]

Bravery and self-sacrifice need not kill. . . .[27]

. . . Civil Disobedience means capacity for unlimited suffering without the intoxicating excitement of killing. . . .[28]

The hardest heart and the grossest ignorance must disappear before the rising sun of suffering without anger and without malice.[29]

. . . A slave is a slave because he consents to slavery. If training in physical resistance is possible, why should that in spiritual resistance be impossible? . . .[30]

The acquisition of the spirit of non-resistance is a matter of long training in self-denial and appreciation of the hidden forces within ourselves. It changes one's outlook upon life. It puts different values upon things and upsets previous calculations. And when once it is set in motion its effect . . . can overtake the whole universe. It is the greatest force because it is the highest expression of the soul. All need not possess the same measure of conscious non-resistance for its full operation. It is enough for one person only to possess it, even as one general is enough to regulate and dispose of the energy of millions of soldiers who enlist under his banner, even though they know not the why and wherefor of his dispositions. . . .[31]

Those who can suffer for one to three years will find themselves inured to suffering for thirty years.[32]

. . . Man is superior to the brute in as much as he is capable of self-restraint and sacrifice, of which the brute is incapable.[33]

. . . If every young man found himself in plenty and never knew what it was to go without . . . he may be found wanting when the trial comes. Sacrifice is joy.

[26] *Young India,* February 18, 1926.
[27] *Young India,* May 7, 1925.
[28] *Young India,* November 27, 1924.
[29] *Young India,* February 19, 1925.
[30] *Young India,* February 4, 1926.
[31] *Young India,* September 23, 1926.
[32] *Young India,* July 24, 1924.
[33] *Young India,* June 3, 1926.

... No sacrifice is worth the name unless it is a joy. Sacrifice and a long face go ill together. . . .[34]

Do you think anything on earth can be done without trouble?[35]

[With] me, the safety of the cause has not lain in numbers. . . . A general with a large army cannot march as swiftly as he would like to. He has to take note of all the different units in his army. My position is not unlike such a general's. . . . If it often means strength, it sometimes means a positive hindrance. . . . I am not without hope that I shall not be found wanting if I am left with but two human comrades or without any. . . .[36]

Strength of numbers is the delight of the timid. The valiant of spirit glory in fighting alone. . . .[37]

... I suggest the following prescription of Civil Disobedience, which even one man can offer. . . . Let a batch, or only one person . . . march on foot to the Government House . . . and walk on to the point where he or she is stopped. There let him or her stop and demand the release of detenues or his or her own arrest. To preserve intact the civil nature of this disobedience, the Satyagrahi must be wholly unarmed, and in spite of insults, kicks or worse, must meekly stand the ground and be arrested without the slightest opposition. He may carry his own food in his pocket, a bottle full of water, take his Gita, the Koran, the Bible . . . as the case may be, and his [spinning device]. If there are many such real Satyagrahis they will certainly transform the atmosphere in an immensely short time, even as one gentle shower transforms the plains of India into a beautiful green carpet in one single day.[38]

Love is the strongest force the world possesses and yet it is the humblest imaginable.[39]

... Who has not seen strong-bodied bullies surrendering helplessly to their mothers? Love conquers the brute in the son. . . .

[We] think it impossible to evoke the hidden powers of the soul. Well, I am engaged in trying to show, if I have any of these powers,

[34] *Young India,* June 25, 1925.
[35] Letter to Rajkumari Amrit Kaur, April 4, 1922.
[36] *Young India,* December 4, 1924.
[37] *Young India,* June 17, 1926.
[38] *Young India,* July 14, 1927.
[39] *Young India,* August 6, 1925.

that I am as frail a mortal as any of us and I never had anything extraordinary about me nor have any now. I claim to be a simple individual liable to err like any other fellow mortal. I own, however, that I have humility enough in me to confess my errors and to retrace my steps. I own that I have an immovable faith in God and His goodness and unconsumable passion for truth and love. But is that not what every person has latent in him? If we are to make progress, we must not repeat history but make new history. . . . If we may make new discoveries and inventions in the phenomenal world, must we declare our bankruptcy in the spiritual domain? Is it impossible to multiply the exceptions so as to make them the rule? Must man always be brute first and man after, if at all?[40]

[When] I was passing through a severe crisis of scepticism and doubt . . . I came across Tolstoy's book *The Kingdom of God Is Within You,* and was deeply impressed by it. I was at that time a believer in violence. Its reading cured me of my scepticism and made me a firm believer in [non-violence]. What has appealed to me most in Tolstoy's life is that he practised what he preached and reckoned no cost too great in his pursuit of truth. . . .

He was the greatest apostle of non-violence the present age has produced. No one in the West before him or since has written and spoken on non-violence so fully or insistently and with such penetration and insight. . . . [His] remarkable development of this doctrine puts to shame the present-day narrow and lop-sided interpretation put upon it by the votaries of Ahimsa in this land of ours. . . . True Ahimsa should mean a complete freedom from ill will and anger and hate and an overflowing love for all. For inculcating this true and higher type of Ahimsa amongst us, Tolstoy's life with its oceanlike love should serve as a beacon light and a never-failing source of inspiration. . . .[41]

Life is governed by a multitude of forces. It would be smooth sailing if one could determine the course of one's actions only by one general principle. . . . But I cannot recall a single act which could be so easily determined.

[40] *Young India,* May 6, 1926.
[41] 1928, in D. G. Tendulkar, *Mahatma,* Volume 11, pp. 418–420.

*   *   *

Let me take an illustration. I am a member of an institution which holds a few acres of land whose crops are in imminent perils from monkeys. I believe in the sacredness of all life and hence I regard it as a breach of non-violence to inflict any injury on the monkeys. But I do not hesitate to instigate and direct an attack on the monkeys in order to save the crops. . . .

Even so did I participate in three acts of War [the Boer War, the Zulu Rebellion, World War I]. I could not—it would be madness for me—to sever my connection with the society to which I belong. And on those occasions I had no thought of non-coöperating with the British Government. My position regarding that Government is totally different today and hence I should not participate voluntarily in its wars and I should risk imprisonment and even the gallows if I was forced to take up arms or otherwise take part in its military operations.

. . . I can conceive occasions when it would be my duty to vote for the military training of those who wish to take it. For I know [everyone] does not believe in non-violence to the extent I do. It is not possible to make a person or a society non-violent by compulsion.

[War] is wrong, is an unmitigated evil. I know, too, that it has got to go. I firmly believe that freedom won through bloodshed or fraud is no freedom. . . .[42]

[42] *Young India,* September 13, 1928.

[16]

GANDHI'S POLITICAL PRINCIPLES

[On September 18, 1924, Gandhi started a twenty-one day fast for Hindu-Moslem friendship.

Gandhi had been ill for months in jail. Then came the urgent appendectomy. He was fifty-five. He knew a twenty-one day fast might be fatal. He did not want to die. There were too many unfinished tasks. It gave him no pleasure to suffer.

The fast was dictated by duty to the highest cause—the universal brotherhood of man.]

... My religion teaches me that whenever there is distress which one cannot remove, one must fast and pray. ...[1]

Fasting cannot be undertaken against an opponent. Fasting can be resorted to only against one's nearest and dearest, and that solely for his or her good.[2]

... Fasting can be resorted to only against a lover, not to extort rights but to reform him, as when a son fasts for a father who drinks. ... I fasted to reform those who loved me. But I will not fast to reform General Dyer, who not only does not love me but who regards himself as my enemy. ...[3]

[Be] most careful about accusing the opponent of wickedness. ... Those whom we regard as wicked as a rule return the compliment. ... Mind is its own place, it can make hell of heaven. ...[4]

... Let us ... honor our opponents for the same honesty of purpose and patriotic motive that we claim for ourselves. ... I believe in trusting. Trust begets trust. Suspicion is foetid and only stinks.

[1] Statement issued from New Delhi, *Young India*, September 18, 1924.
[2] *Young India*, September 30, 1926.
[3] *Young India*, May 1, 1924.
[4] *Young India*, December 26, 1924.

He who trusts has never yet lost in the world. A suspicious man is lost to himself and the world. . . . Suspicion is of the brood of violence. Non-violence cannot but trust. . . .[5]

Lying is the mother of violence. A truthful man cannot long remain violent. He will perceive in the course of his search that he has no need to be violent and he will further discover that so long as there is the slightest trace of violence in him, he will fail to find the truth for which he is searching.[6]

[If] I listen to . . . Mr. Worldly-Wise, I am lost already. I do not want to foresee the future. I am concerned with taking care of the present. God has given me no control over the moment following. . . . It is true that I have often been let down. Many have deceived me and many have been found wanting. But I do not repent of my association with them. . . . The most practical, the most dignified way of going on in the world is to take people at their word, when you have no positive reason to the contrary.[7]

. . . A man who is truthful will not believe charges even against his foes. He will, however, try to understand the viewpoints of his opponents and will always keep an open mind and seek every opportunity of serving his opponents. I have endeavored to apply this law in my relations with Englishmen and Europeans in general in South Africa as well as here and not without some success. How much more then should we apply this law in our homes, in our relations, in our domestic affairs, in connection with our own kith and kin?[8]

. . . Madness answered with madness simply deepens, it never dispels it. Hinduism will be sorry stuff if it has to exist on cowardly vengeance that pursues those who can offer no effective resistance.[9]

. . . Few men are wantonly wicked. The most heinous and the most cruel crimes of which history has record have been committed under cover of religion or equally other noble motive. But . . . we are no better off for the destruction that has gone on even under

[5] *Young India,* June 4, 1925.

[6] *Young India,* May 20, 1925.

[7] *Young India,* December 26, 1924.

[8] *Young India,* September 29, 1927.

[9] Nirmal Kumar Bose, *Studies in Gandhism* (Calcutta: India Associated Publishing Company, 1947), Hindi Edition.

the highest sanction . . . religion. . . . We have no right to destroy life that we cannot create. . . .

. . . Perhaps it is as well that we are beset with danger at every point in our life, for, in spite of our knowledge of the danger and our precarious existence, our indifference to the Source of all life is excelled only by our amazing arrogance.[10]

. . . Both reason and heart refuse to reconcile themselves to torture for any crime no matter how vile the crime may be.[11]

. . . The sword is the emblem of Islam. But Islam was born in an environment where the sword was and still remains the supreme law. The message of Jesus has proved ineffective because the environment was unready to receive it. So with the message of the Prophet. The sword is too much in evidence among Mussalmans. It must be sheathed if Islam is to be what it means—peace. . . .[12]

. . . If we have no charity, and no tolerance, we shall never settle our differences amicably and must therefore always submit to the arbitrament of a third party—foreign domination. . . .[13]

. . . I came to the conclusion long ago, after prayerful search and study and discussion with as many people as I could meet, that all religions were true, and also that all had some error in them, and whilst I hold my own, I should hold others as dear as Hinduism. . . . So we can only pray, if we are Hindus, that not a Christian should become a Hindu, or if we are Moslems that not a Hindu or a Christian should become a Moslem, nor should we even secretly pray that anyone should be converted, but our inmost prayer should be that a Hindu should be a better Hindu, a Moslem a better Moslem and a Christian a better Christian. . . . I broaden my Hinduism by loving other religions as my own. . . .[14]

I disbelieve in the conversion of one person by another. My effort should never be to undermine another's faith but to make him a better follower of his own faith. This implies the belief in the truth of all religions and respect for them. . . .[15]

[10] *Young India,* July 7, 1927.
[11] *Young India,* February 26, 1925.
[12] *Young India,* December 30, 1926.
[13] *Young India,* April 17, 1924.
[14] *Young India,* January 19, 1928.
[15] Talk with Dr. John Mott, an evangelist, in 1929, in D. G. Tendulkar, *Mahatma,* Volume II, p. 450.

Let no one even for a moment entertain the fear that a reverent study of other religions is likely to weaken or shake one's faith in one's own. The Hindu system of philosophy regards all religions as containing the elements of truth in them and enjoins an attitude of respect and reverence towards them all. . . . Study and appreciation of other religions need not cause a weakening of [regard for one's own religion], it should mean extension of that regard to other religions.[16]

. . . Hinduism leaves the individual absolutely free to do what he or she likes for the sake of self-realization for which and which alone he or she is born.[17]

. . . I do not believe in the exclusive divinity of the Vedas [Hindu scriptures]. I believe the Bible [and the] Koran to be as much divinely inspired as the Vedas. . . .[18]

Religions are different roads converging to the same point. What does it matter that we take different roads so long as we reach the same goal? In reality there are as many religions as there are individuals.[19]

Mankind is one. . . . There are, of course, differences of race and status and the like, but the higher the status of a man, the greater is his responsibility.[20]

I believe that we can all become messengers of God if we cease to fear man and seek only God's Truth. I do believe I am seeking only God's Truth and have lost all fear of man.[21]

[All] religions are more or less true. All proceed from the same God but all are imperfect because they come down to us through imperfect human instrumentality. . . . [No] propaganda can be allowed which reviles other religions. . . . The best way of dealing with such propaganda is to publicly condemn it. . . .[22]

The golden rule of conduct . . . is mutual toleration, seeing that we will never all think alike and that we shall always see *Truth* in fragment and from different angles of vision. Conscience is not the

[16] *Young India,* December 6, 1928.
[17] *Young India,* October 21, 1926.
[18] *Young India,* October 6, 1921.
[19] M. K. Gandhi, *Hind Swaraj,* Chapter 2, p. 16.
[20] M. K. Gandhi, *Ethical Religion,* Chapter 6, p. 59.
[21] *Young India,* May 25, 1921.
[22] *Young India,* May 24, 1924.

same thing for all. Whilst, therefore, it is a good guide for individual conduct, imposition of that conduct upon all will be an insufferable interference with everybody else's freedom of conscience. . . . [Mutual toleration] can be inculcated among and practiced by all, irrespective of their status and training.[23]

. . . We must measure people with their own measure and see how far they come up to it. . . .[24]

. . . No doubt religion has to answer for some of the most terrible crimes in history. But that is the fault not of religion but of the ungovernable brute in man. . . .[25]

. . . True religion being the greatest thing in life and in the world, it has been exploited the most. And those who have seen the exploiters and the exploitation and missed the reality naturally get disgusted with the thing itself. But religion is after all a matter for each individual, and then too a matter of the heart, call it then by whatever name you like, that which gives one the greatest solace in the midst of the severest fire is God. . . .[26]

Rationalists are admirable beings, rationalism is a hideous monster when it claims for itself omnipotence. Attribution of omnipotence to reason is as bad a piece of idolatry as is worship of stock and stone, believing it to be God.[27]

True morality consists not in following the beaten track but in finding out the true path for ourselves and fearlessly following it.[28]

. . . Unfortunately or fortunately, we have to pass through many an ebb and flow before we settle down to real peace.[29]

. . . There is no such thing as religion overriding morality. Man, for instance, cannot be untruthful, cruel and incontinent and claim to have God on his side.[30]

*   *   *

[23] *Young India,* September 23, 1926.
[24] Letter to Mira Behn from Sholapur, February 21, 1927, in M. K. Gandhi, *Letters to a Disciple,* p. 26.
[25] *Young India,* October 14, 1926.
[26] Letter to Nehru, April 25, 1925, in Jawaharlal Nehru, *Old Letters,* p. 42.
[27] *Young India,* October 14, 1926.
[28] M. K. Gandhi, *Ethical Religion,* Chapter 2, p. 38.
[29] Letter to Mira Behn, May 2, 1927, in M. K. Gandhi, *Letters to a Disciple,* p. 33.
[30] *Young India,* November 24, 1921.

Churches, mosques and temples which cover so much hypocrisy
and humbug and shut the poorest out of them seem but a mockery
of God and His worship, when one sees the eternally renewed temple of worship under the vast blue canopy inviting every one of us
to real worship, instead of abusing His name by quarreling in the
name of religion.[31]

. . . That religion and that nation will be blotted out of the face
of the earth which pins its faith to injustice, untruth or violence.
God is Light, not darkness. God is Love, not hate. God is Truth,
not untruth. . . .[32]

[There] is not a single offense which does not, directly or indirectly,
affect many others besides the actual offender. Hence, whether an
individual is good or bad is not merely his own concern but really
the concern of the whole community, nay, of the whole world.[33]

Our desires and motives may be divided into two classes—selfish and unselfish. All selfish desires are immoral, while the desire
to improve ourselves for the sake of doing good to others is truly
moral. The highest moral law is that we should unremittingly
work for the good of mankind.[34]

I see there is an instinctive horror of killing living beings under
any circumstances whatever. For instance, an alternative has been
suggested in the shape of confining even rabid dogs in a certain
place and allowing them to die a slow death. Now my idea of compassion makes this thing impossible for me. I cannot for a moment
bear to see a dog, or for that matter any other living being, helplessly suffering the torture of a slow death. I do not kill a human
being thus circumstanced because I have more hopeful remedies. I
should kill a dog similarly situated because in its case I am without
a remedy. Should my child be attacked with rabies and there was
no helpful remedy to relieve his agony, I should consider it my duty
to take his life. Fatalism has its limits. We leave things to fate after

[31] Speech to members of the Young Men's Christian Association, Colombo,
Cevlon, in *Young India,* December 8, 1927.

[32] Congress Party Presidential Address, in *Young India,* December 26, 1924.

[33] M. K. Gandhi, *Ethical Religion,* Chapter 6, p. 57.

[34] *Ibid.,* Chapter 2, p. 39.

exhausting all the remedies. One of the remedies and the final one to relieve the agony of a tortured child is to take his life.[35]

Some days back a calf having been maimed lay in agony in the ashram. Whatever treatment and nursing was possible was given to it. The surgeon whose advice was sought . . . declared the case to be past help and past hope. . . .

. . . I felt that humanity demanded the agony should be ended by ending life itself. . . . With the clearest of convictions I got . . . a doctor kindly to administer the calf a quietus by means of a poison injection. The whole thing was over in less than two minutes.

I knew that public opinion [of the Hindus believing cattle to be sacred] would not approve of my action and that it would read nothing but himsa [violence] in it. But I know too that performance of one's duty should be independent of public opinion. I have all along held that one is bound to act according to what to one appears to be right though it may appear wrong to others. And experience has shown that that is the only correct course. That is why the poet has sung: "The pathway of love is the ordeal of fire, the shrinkers turn away from it." The pathway of ahimsa, that is, of love, one has often to tread all alone.[36]

I do not want to live at the cost of the life even of a snake. I should let him bite me to death rather than kill him. But it is likely that if God puts me to that cruel test . . . I may not have the courage to die but the beast in me may assert itself and I may seek to kill the snake in defending this perishable body. I admit that my belief has not become so incarnate in me as to warrant my stating emphatically that I have shed all fear of snakes so as to befriend them as I would like to be able to do.[37]

[Gandhi's friends argued that his retirement from politics would split the Congress Party between those who followed his work with the masses—his "Constructive Program"—and those who advocated political work in the legislative and municipal councils set up by the British Government. Gandhi was persuaded to take the presidency of the Congress Party for 1925.]

[35] *Young India,* November 18, 1926.
[36] 1928, in D. G. Tendulkar, *Mahatma,* Volume II, pp. 421–423.
[37] *Young India,* April 14, 1927.

For me, politics bereft of religion are absolute dirt, ever to be shunned. Politics concern nations and that which concerns the welfare of others must be one of the concerns of a man who is religiously inclined, in other words, a seeker after God and Truth. . . . God and Truth are convertible terms and if anyone told me that God was a God of untruth or a God of torture I would decline to worship Him. Therefore in politics also we have to establish the Kingdom of Heaven.[38]

. . . I am unable to subscribe to the methods of bribery and deceit even for gaining entrance into heaven, much less for gaining India's freedom. For heaven will not be heaven and freedom will not be freedom if either is gained through such methods.[39]

. . . I remain loyal to an institution so long as that institution conduces to my growth, to the growth of the nation. Immediately I find that the institution, instead of conducing to [this] growth, impedes it, I hold it my bounden duty to be disloyal to it. . . .

. . . What the ultimate destiny of India will be, we do not know, or we know only that . . . it will be what every one of us whose lot is cast in India wants it to be. . . . But everyone should become an optimist and then there is nothing but the brightest future for this land. . . . I want you, therefore, to approach the question in a spirit of service. . . . "Loyalty" or "disloyalty" does not matter much when a person really wants to serve.[40]

. . . There is but one God and one means. There is unity in disease, therefore there is unity in remedy. [There] is only one sovereign remedy, namely, nonviolent non-coöperation. My "followers" will therefore do well to set up their own organization of work and no talk. They must cut their way to the nation's heart through service. . . . [No one] who wants to spin or . . . promote Hindu-Moslem unity, or . . . remove untouchability requires any organization. . . .[41]

. . . Everyone who either may not see eye to eye with the Congress in all its program, or because of weakness or circumstances . . . can still work as effectively as if he were in the executive. There is

[38] *Young India,* June 18, 1925.
[39] *Young India,* May 7, 1925.
[40] *Young India,* August 13, 1925.
[41] *Young India,* July 17, 1924.

nothing, for instance, to prevent [one] from enlisting members, spinning, carrying on khaddar [hand-spinning] propaganda ... etc. Indeed, a sincere worker prefers work to the responsibility of office, and by not being on the executive [side] escapes the terrible wrangling that takes place therein.

... It is necessary ... to bring into being workers who would want no office and yet would render as effective service as the strongest official. Such men and women are the pride of a nation. They are its reserve force.[42]

... My [Congress Party] presidential address must be a thesis on hand-spinning, complete surrender by Hindus of their material ambition to the Moslems and other minorities, and ... asking Hindus to regard untouchability as a sin. If these things cannot enthuse the nation, I should be a useless President. How would it do for the Congress [Party] to have as President a man who sketched a program of putting the whole nation in pantaloons? ... We would not have him because he would not suit us. So may the case be with me.

I must not therefore allow myself to be elected. . . .[43]

... I would guide the Congress next year only if all parties [factions] wish me to. . . . I fight out of love. . . . But I must, I see, first prove my love. I thought I had proved it. . . . I am therefore retracing my steps. I ask everyone to help me. . . .[44]

Power is of two kinds. One is obtained by the fear of punishment, and the other by arts of love. Power based on love is a thousand times more effective and permanent than the one derived from fear of punishment. . . .

... I am fascinated by the law of love. It is the philosopher's stone for me. . . .[45]

After much prayer, after much heart-searching and not without fear and trembling, I have decided to [preside] at the forthcoming Congress. . . .

I have abundant faith in my cause and humanity. . . .

[42] *Young India,* July 3, 1924.
[43] *Young India,* July 17, 1924.
[44] *Young India,* September 11, 1924.
[45] *Young India,* January 8, 1925.

There is a heavy duty resting on the shoulders of Congressmen. . . . They have to show their program on their persons and in their daily conduct. They will attend the Congress as servants and not as masters demanding service. . . . They will show their faith in unity between different religious sects. . . . Hindus will show their faith in the removal of untouchability by going out of their way to be attentive to those of [the untouchables] who may attend the Congress.

. . . I have no patent remedy [for attaining self-rule]. The remedy is to be found with the delegates and visitors themselves. . . .[46]

[The masses] are as yet untouched by politics. . . . Their politics are confined to bread and salt—I dare not say butter, for millions do not know the taste of ghee or even oil. . . . It is right, however, to say that we, the politicians do represent the masses in opposition to the Government. But if we begin to use them before they are ready, we shall cease to represent them. . . . We must share their sorrows, understand their difficulties and anticipate their wants. With the pariahs [untouchables] we must be pariahs and see how we feel to clean the closets of the upper classes and have the remains of their table thrown at us. We must see how we like being in the boxes, miscalled houses, of the laborers of Bombay. We must identify ourselves with the villagers who toil under the hot sun beating down on their bent backs and see how we would like to drink water from the pool in which the villagers bathe, wash their clothes and pots and in which their cattle drink and roll. Then and not till then shall we truly represent the masses, and they will . . . respond to every call.[47]

. . . My faith in non-coöperation is as bright as ever. . . . But I cannot impose my personal faith on others . . . I can but try to convince the nation of its beauty and usefulness. . . . I may misread the mind of the Congress. When that happens, I shall cease to be any force in the Congress. . . .[48]

[When] a respectable minority objects to any rule of conduct, it would be dignified for the majority . . . to yield. . . . Numerical strength savors of violence when it acts in total disregard of any

[46] *Young India,* November 27, 1924.
[47] *Young India,* September 11, 1924.
[48] *Young India,* November 20, 1924.

strongly felt opinion of a minority. . . . No organization can run
smoothly when it is divided into camps, each growling at the other
and each determined to have its own way by hook or by crook. . . .[49]

[When] Swaraj comes different parties will work in the same
Swaraj Parliament. The Congress is intended to be a forerunner . . .
of such a Parliament.[50]

. . . What is applicable to Hindu-Moslem unity is . . . applicable
to the unity among different political groups. We must tolerate
each other, and trust to time to convert the one or the other to the
opposite belief. . . .[51]

. . . No special legislation without a change of heart can possibly
bring about organic unity. And when there is a change of heart, no
such legislation can possibly be necessary. . . .[52]

The spirit of democracy is not a mechanical thing to be adjusted by
abolition of forms. It requires change of the heart. . . . The spirit of
democracy requires the inculcation of the spirit of brotherhood. . . .[53]

. . . Democracy is not a state in which people act like sheep.
Under democracy individual liberty of opinion and action is jealousy guarded. . . .[54]

[In 1924, 1925, 1926, and 1927, the popularizing of khadi—the material woven from homespun cotton thread—possessed Gandhi's
mind. His price for accepting the Congress Party Presidency was
the wearing of khadi as a strict condition of membership in the
party. Where possible, Gandhi believed, Congress members should
spin each day.]

I would like the Congress to become . . . popular. I would therefore man it with mercantile, artisan and agricultural classes. . . . It
should be the privilege of educated classes to be behind and push
into public life those who have . . . kept aloof.[55]

[It] is impossible for us to establish a living vital connection with

[49] *Young India,* June 9, 1927.
[50] *Young India,* December 4, 1924.
[51] Congress Presidential Address, December 24, 1924, *Young India.*
[52] *Young India,* July 14, 1927.
[53] *Young India,* December 8, 1920.
[54] *Young India,* March 2, 1922.
[55] *Young India,* July 10, 1924.

the masses unless we will work for them, through them and in their midst, not as their patrons but as their servants.[56]

A starving man thinks first of satisfying his hunger before anything else. He will sell his liberty and all for the sake of getting a morsel of food. Such is the position of millions of the people of India. For them liberty, God and all such words are merely letters put together without the slightest meaning. . . . If we want to give these people a sense of freedom we shall have to provide them with work which they can easily do in their desolate homes and which would give them at least the barest living. This can only be done by the spinning wheel. And when they have become self-reliant and are able to support themselves we are in a position to talk to them about freedom, about [the] Congress [Party], etc. Those, therefore, who bring them work and means of getting a crust of bread will be their deliverers and will be also the people who will make them hunger for liberty.[57]

. . . I would like . . . to keep the Congress a mass organization. . . . The masses do not yet actively participate in or understand our method of work. Only workers in their midst can gain influence over them. . . .[58]

[To prepare for home-rule] individuals must cultivate the spirit of service, renunciation, truth, nonviolence, self-restraint, patience. . . . They must engage in constructive work [the term Gandhi gave for his three-point program: removal of untouchability, Hindu-Moslem unity and universal spinning] in order to develop these qualities. Many reforms would be effected automatically if we put in a good deal of silent work among the people.[59]

I do not believe the spiritual law works on a field of its own. On the contrary, it expresses itself only through the ordinary activities of life. It thus affects the economic, the social and the political fields.[60]

[Experience] shows we cannot be truthful and peaceful on some occasions and for some people only, if we are not so on all occasions.

[56] *Young India,* February 3, 1927.
[57] *Young India,* March 18, 1926.
[58] *Young India,* July 31, 1924.
[59] *Young India,* January 8, 1925.
[60] *Young India,* September 3, 1935.

And if we will not be considerate toward one another, we shall not be considerate to the world outside. All the prestige acquired by the Congress will be gone if we are not scrupulously clean in our dealings within or without in every detail. Pounds will take care of themselves if we could but take care of the pennies.

A true Congressman is a true servant. He ever gives, ever wants service. He is easily satisfied so long as his own comfort is concerned. He is always content to take a back seat. He is never communal or provincial. His country is his paramount consideration. He is brave to a fault because he has shed all earthly ambition, fear of Death himself. And he is generous because he is brave, forgiving because he is humble and conscious of his own failings and limitations.[61]

. . . My invitation to all to spin, if only for half an hour daily, for the sake of the starving millions of this land makes the movement at once both political and spiritual. . . .[62]

In our country manual labor is regarded as a low occupation. . . . We should spin, therefore, if only to guard against the pernicious tendency of regarding the toilers as being low in the social scale. Spinning is therefore as obligatory on the prince as on the peasant.[63]

. . . I am interested in producing the spinning atmosphere. . . . I want that atmosphere so that the idle hands I have described will be irresistibly drawn to the wheel. They will be so drawn when they see people spinning who do not need to. . . .[64]

[The spinning wheel] is not remunerative enough for individuals. . . . It is, however, enough to raise at a bound the national prosperity. . . . An increase of one rupee [about 20 cents] per head per year may mean nothing to the individual. But 5,000 rupees in a village containing [five thousand inhabitants] would mean the payment of land revenue or other dues. Thus the spinning wheel means national consciousness and a contribution by every individual to a definite constructive national work. If India can demonstrate her capacity for such an achievement by voluntary effort she

[61] *Young India,* November 19, 1925.
[62] *Young India,* November 10, 1925.
[63] *Young India,* May 20, 1926.
[64] *Young India,* April 16, 1925.

is ready for political Swaraj. Any lawful demand of a nation with a will of its own must prove irresistible. . . .[65]

. . . For me, the spinning wheel is not only a symbol of simplicity and economic freedom, but it is also a symbol of peace. For if we Hindus, Moslems, Sikhs, Christians, Parsis, Jews, unite in achieving the universalization of the wheel in India, we shall have arrived at not only real unity . . . but we shall also have acquired self-confidence and organizing ability which render violence wholly unnecessary for regaining our freedom. . . .[66]

[The] spinning movement is bringing out women from their seclusion as nothing else could have done. . . . It has given them a dignity and self-confidence which no university degree could give them. They are realizing that their active assistance is just as indispensable as that of men. . . .[67]

. . . I cannot imagine anything nobler or more national than that for, say, one hour in the day we should all do the labor the poor must do, and thus identify ourselves with them and through them, with all mankind. I cannot imagine better worship of God than that in His name I should labor for the poor even as they do.[68]

Man becomes great exactly in the degree in which he works for the welfare of his fellow-men.[69]

[Idleness], whether it be regarded as enforced or voluntary, is killing the very soul of the nation. The more I penetrate the villages, the greater is the shock delivered as I perceive the blank stare in the eyes of the villagers I meet. Having nothing else to do but to work as laborers side by side with their bullocks, they have become almost like them. It is a tragedy of the first magnitude that millions have ceased to use their hands as hands. Nature is revenging herself upon us with terrible effect for this criminal waste of the gift she has bestowed upon us human beings. . . . And it is the exquisite mechanism of the hands that among a few other things separates us from the beast. . . .

The spinning wheel alone can stop this reckless waste. It can do

[65] *Young India,* January 29, 1925.
[66] *Young India,* June 25, 1925.
[67] *Young India,* January 1, 1925.
[68] *Young India,* October 20, 1921.
[69] M. K. Gandhi, *Ethical Religion,* Chapter 8, p. 68.

that now and without any extraordinary outlay of money or intelligence. . . . With it will at once revive the ancient rustic art and the rustic song. A semi-starved nation can have neither religion nor art nor organization.[70]

[It] is not merely the wages earned by the spinners that are to be counted but it is the whole reconstruction that follows in the wake of the spinning wheel. The village weaver, the village dyer, the village washerman, the village blacksmith, the village carpenter, all and many others will then find themselves reinstated in their ancient dignity, as is already happening wherever the spinning wheel has gained a footing.[71]

. . . The plan . . . is not merely to induce the peasant to refuse to buy the cheap and nice-looking foreign fabric, but also by teaching him to utilize his spare hours in carding and spinning cotton and getting it woven by the village weavers, to dress himself in khaddar so woven and thus to save him the cost of buying foreign, and for that matter, even Indian mill-made cloth. . . .

[Enforced idleness or penury] hurt a man's soul and body just as much as intoxication. Depression is but excitement upside down and hence equally disastrous . . . and often more so, because we have not yet learnt to regard [it] as immoral or sinful. . . .[72]

[Persons] not wearing khaddar [homespun cloth] or not spinning should [not] be boycotted. On the contrary, it would be our duty to embrace them and win them ultimately to the side of khaddar by our love, certainly not by talking or thinking ill of them. . . . True boycott can be only . . . refusal to accept personal service and denying oneself the advantages of association with the person so dealt with, while being ever-ready to render him help in case of need. I would welcome that kind of boycott in the case of a person addicted to drink but not in the case of those who don't wear khaddar. . . .[73]

[The] vast majority of us . . . will find it necessary to wear khaddar on all occasions if we have to wear it on all Congress occasions. For an ardent Congressman, every occasion is a Congress occasion

---

[70] *Young India,* February 17, 1927.
[71] *Young India,* March 10, 1927.
[72] Congress Presidential Address, December 26, 1924, *Young India.*
[73] Conversation between Gandhi and Charles Freer Andrews, in *Young India,* October 31, 1924.

and he and she would be an indifferent Congressman or Congress-woman who has no Congress work during . . . twenty-four hours. [Congress members] cannot have many uniforms nor can they have money to buy yarn spun by others. They must spin themselves and thus give at least half an hour's labor to the nation. And a Congress volunteer who does not spin himself will be hard put to it to convince the candidates for Congress membership of the necessity of spinning. . . .[74]

[The suggestion to make hand-spinning the test for the vote] may be fantastical, but it is neither immoral nor harmful to the nation. Had it been workmen who had been the most influential people and not capitalists or educated men, and a property or an education test had been proposed, the powerful workmen would have ridiculed the suggestion, and might have even called it immoral. For, they could have argued, while capital or education were the possession of a few, bodily labor was common to all. . . .[75]

. . . I can only take up the wheel or speak or write about it and commend it. . . . In my loneliness, it is my only infallible friend and comforter. . . .[76]

. . . I had a long chat with [a group of nationalists from Poona]. They will not agree to spin and they will not agree to my leaving the Congress. They do not realize that I shall cease to be useful as soon as I cease to be myself. It is a wretched situation but I do not despair. . . . I know only the moment's duty. It is given to me to know no more. Why then should I worry?[77]

[74] *Young India,* November 13, 1924.
[75] *Young India,* November 27, 1924.
[76] *Young India,* September 4, 1924.
[77] Letter to Nehru, September 15, 1924, in Jawaharlal Nehru, *Old Letters,* pp. 40–41.

[17]

BELIEF AND HUMAN WELFARE

[Whilst] everything around me is ever changing, ever dying, there is underlying all that change a living power that is changeless, that holds all together, that creates, dissolves and recreates. That informing power or spirit is God. . . .

And is this power benevolent or malevolent? I see it as purely benevolent. For I can see that in the midst of death life persists, in the midst of untruth truth persists, in the midst of darkness light persists. Hence I gather that God is Life, Truth, Light. He is Love. He is the supreme Good.

. . . I shall never know God if I do not wrestle with and against evil even at the cost of life itself. . . .[1]

To me God is Truth and Love, God is ethics and morality, God is fearlessness. . . . He is all things to all men . . . He is ever forgiving for He always gives us the chance to repent. He is the greatest democrat the world knows for He leaves us "unfettered" to make our own choice between evil and good. . . .[2]

I believe in the absolute oneness of God and therefore of humanity. What though we have many bodies? We have but one soul. The rays of the sun are many through refraction. But they have the same source. I cannot, therefore, detach myself from the wickedest soul nor may I be denied identity with the most virtuous.[3]

I am endeavoring to see God through service of humanity, for I know God is neither in heaven nor down below, but in everyone.[4]

. . . If we could all give our own definitions of God there would be as many definitions as there are men and women. But behind all

[1] *Young India,* October 11, 1928.
[2] *Young India,* March 5, 1925.
[3] *Young India,* September 25, 1924.
[4] *Young India,* August 4, 1927.

that variety . . . there would be also a certain sameness. . . . For the root is one. God is that indefinable something which we all feel but which we do not know. . . . He is all things to all men. . . .[5]

. . . We have one thousand names to denote God, and if I did not feel the presence of God within me, I see so much of misery and disappointment every day that I would be a raving maniac. . . .[6]

. . . Religion is the service of the helpless. . . .

. . . The Brahman [Priest] who has understood the religion of today will certainly give Vedic [Scriptural] learning a secondary place and propagate the religion of the spinning wheel, relieve the hunger of the millions of his starving countrymen, and only then . . . lose himself in Vedic studies.

. . . If I have to make the choice between counting beads or turning the wheel, I would certainly decide in favor of the wheel, making it my rosary, so long as I found poverty and starvation stalking the land. . . .[7]

Some time ago, I was taken to a magnificent mansion called the "Marble Palace" in Calcutta. . . . The owners feed . . . in front of the palace, all the beggars who choose to go there. . . . [The] incongruity of this ragged humanity feeding whilst the majestic palace is . . . mocking at their wretched condition does not seem to strike the donors at all. . . . In Suri . . . the motor car that drove me . . . was slowly taken through the line of the beggars as they were eating. I felt humiliated, more so to think this was all done in my honor, because . . . I was "a friend of the poor." My friendship for them must be a sorry affair if I could be satisfied with a large part of humanity being reduced to beggary. Little did my friends know that my friendship for the paupers of India has made me hardhearted enough to contemplate their utter starvation with equanimity in preference to their utter reduction to beggary. . . . [If] I had the power I would stop every Sadavrata [Donation] where free meals are given. It has degraded the nation and it has encouraged laziness, idleness, hypocrisy and even crime. Such misplaced charity adds nothing to the wealth of the country . . . and gives a false sense of meritoriousness to the donor. How nice and wise it would

[5] *Young India,* March 5, 1925.
[6] *Young India,* August 6, 1925.
[7] *Young India,* August 14, 1924.

be if the donor were to open institutions where they would give
meals under healthy, clean surroundings to men and women who
would work for them.... [The] rule should be "No labor, no
meal."... I know it is easier to fling free meals in the faces of
idlers, but much more difficult to organize an institution where
honest work has to be done. [In] the initial stages ... the cost of
feeding people after taking work from them will be more than the
cost of the present free kitchens. But ... it will be cheaper in the
long run, if we do not want to increase ... the race of loafers which
is fast overrunning this land.[8]

... It is the duty of society to support the blind and the infirm,
but everyone may not take the task upon himself. The head of
Society—the State—should undertake the task and the philan-
thropically inclined should subscribe funds....[9]

If each retained possession of only what he needed, no one
would be in want and all would live in contentment.[10]

I cannot picture to myself a time when no man shall be richer
than another. But I do picture to myself a time when the rich will
spurn to enrich themselves at the expense of the poor and the poor
will cease to envy the rich. Even in a most perfect world we shall
fail to avoid inequalities but we can and must avoid strife and bitterness....[11]

[The] economic constitution of India and for that matter of the
world should be such that no one under it should suffer from want
of food and clothing.... [Everybody] should be able to get sufficient work to enable him to make the two ends meet. And this
ideal can be universally realized only if the means of production of
the elementary necessaries of life remain in the control of the
masses. These should be freely available to all as God's air and
water are or ought to be, they should not be made a vehicle of traffic for the exploitation of others. Their monopolization by any
country, nation or group of persons would be unjust. The neglect
of this simple principle is the cause of the destitution we witness

[8] *Young India,* August 13, 1925.
[9] *Young India,* November 18, 1926.
[10] M. K. Gandhi, *From Yeravda Mandir,* Chapter 9, p. 37.
[11] *Young India,* October 7, 1926.

today not only in this unhappy land but in other parts of the world too.[12]

. . . I pride myself on calling myself a scavenger, weaver, spinner, farmer . . . and do not feel ashamed that some of these things I know but indifferently. It is a pleasure to me to identify myself with the laboring classes, because without labor we can do nothing. . . . "He who eats without labor eats sin, is verily a thief" . . . is the literal meaning of a verse in the Bhagavad Gita. . . .

. . . But none of my activities are one-sided, and as my religion begins and ends with Truth and non-violence, my identification with labor does not conflict with my friendship with capital. . . .

Capital . . . and labor should supplement and help each other. They should be a great family living in unity and harmony, capital not only looking to the material welfare of the laborers but their moral welfare also, capitalists being trustees for the welfare of the laboring classes under them.[13]

. . . Throughout thirty-five years' unbroken experience of public service in several parts of the world, I have not yet understood that there is anything like spiritual or moral value apart from work and action. . . .

Come with me to Orissa, in November, to Puri, a holy place and a sanatorium, where you will find soldiers and the Governor's residence during the summer months. Within ten miles' radius . . . you will see skin and bone. . . . Talk to them of modern progress. Insult them by taking the name of God before them in vain. They will call you and me fiends if we talk about God to them. They know, if they know any God at all, a God of terror, vengeance, a pitiless tyrant. They do not know what love is. . . . They have not lost all sense of decency, but I assure you we have. We are naked in spite of our clothing, and they are clothed in spite of their nakedness. It is because of these that I wander about from place to place, I humor my people. I humor my American friends. I humored two stripling youths from Harvard. When they wanted my autograph, I said, "No autographs for Americans." We struck a bargain. "I give you my autograph and you take to khadi." . . .

[12] *Young India*, November 15, 1928.
[13] Speech to the Indian Association, in *Young India*, August 20, 1925.

But I cannot be satisfied, not till every man and woman in India is working at his or her wheel. . . . This is the one and only work which can supply the needs of the millions without disturbing them from their homes. It is a mighty task and I know that I cannot do it. . . . But I shall not lose faith in you. . . .[14]

. . . The world knows little of how much my so-called greatness depends upon the incessant drudgery and toil of silent, devoted, able and pure workers, men as well as women. . . .[15]

. . . You come in daily touch with me by doing my work as if it was your own. And this can, must and will outlast the existence of this physical body of mine. . . .[16]

. . . We really live through and in our work. We perish through our perishable bodies, if instead of using them as temporary instruments, we identify ourselves with them.[17]

. . . Let us not seek to prop virtue by imagining hellish torture after death for vice and houris hereafter as a reward for virtue in this life. If virtue has no attraction in itself, it must be a poor thing. . . . Both heaven and hell are within us. Life after Death there is, but it is not so unlike our present experiences as either to terrify us or make us delirious with joy. "He is steadfast who rises above joy and sorrow," says the Gita. The wise are unaffected either by death or life. These are but faces of the same coin.[18]

[Gandhi appealed for aid to the masses from everyone. Several times he addressed Christian missionary groups working in India.]

It is better to allow our lives to speak for us than our words. . . . Faith does not admit of telling. It has to be lived and then it becomes self-propagating.[19]

[All] are judged not according to their labels or [what they profess] but according to their actions irrespective of their professions. . . .[20]

[14] *Young India,* September 15, 1927.
[15] *Young India,* April 26, 1928.
[16] Letter to Mira Behn, May 8, 1927, in M. K. Ghandi, *Gandhi's Letters to a Disciple,* p. 34.
[17] Letter to Mira Behn, April 27, 1927, *ibid.,* p. 31.
[18] *Young India,* October 25, 1928.
[19] *Young India,* August 11, 1927.
[20] *Young India,* September 2, 1926.

... The founding of leper asylums, etc. is only one of the ways, and perhaps not the best, of serving humanity. But even such noble service loses much of its nobility when conversion is the motive behind it. That service is the noblest which is rendered for its own sake. But ... the missionaries that selflessly work away in such asylums command my respect. I am ashamed to have to confess that Hindus have become so callous as to care little for the waifs and strays of India, let alone the world.[21]

If you give me statistics that so many orphans have been reclaimed and brought to the Christian faith, I would accept them, but I do not feel convinced thereby that it is your mission. In my opinion your mission is infinitely superior to that. [Go] to the lowly cottages, not to give them something [but] to take something from them. . . .

. . . One of the greatest Christian Divines, Bishop Heber, wrote the two lines which have always left a sting with me: "Where every prospect please, and Man alone is vile." . . . I have gone from one end of the country to the other, without any prejudice, in a relentless search after truth, and I am not able to say that here in this fair land, watered by the great Ganges, the Brahmaputra and the Jumna, man is vile. He is not vile. He is as much a seeker after truth as you and I are, possibly more so. . . . You are here to find out the distress of the people of India and remove it. But I hope you are here also in a receptive mood and if there is anything that India has to give, you will not stop your ears, you will not close your eyes and steel your hearts but open up your ears, eyes and most of all, your hearts, to receive all that may be good in this land. I give you my assurance that there is a great deal of good in India. . . . I know many men who have never heard the name of Jesus Christ or have even rejected the official interpretation of Christianity *would* probably, if Jesus came in our midst today . . . be owned by him more than many of us. . . .

[If] you will refuse to see the other side, if you will refuse to understand what India is thinking, then you will deny yourselves the real privilege of service.[22]

*　　*　　*

[21] *Young India,* February 26, 1925.
[22] An address to Christian missionaries, in *Young India,* August 6, 1925.

[An American clergyman once asked Gandhi what caused him most concern.] The hardness of heart of the educated [Gandhi replied].[23]

. . . If you [students] spend your next vacation in some far-off village in the interior you . . . will find the people cheerless and fear-stricken. You will find houses in ruins. You will look in vain for any sanitary or hygienic conditions. You will find the cattle in a miserable way, and yet you will see idleness stalking there. The people will tell you of the spinning wheel's having been in their homes long ago. . . . They have no hope left in them. They live, for they cannot die at will. They will spin only if *you* spin. Even if a hundred out of a population of three hundred in a village spin, you assure them of an additional income of 1,800 rupees [$360] a year. You can lay the foundation of solid reform on this income in every village. . . . "I am alone, how can I reach seven hundred thousand villages?" This is the argument pride whispers to us. Start with the faith that if you fix yourself up in one single village and succeed, the rest will follow. . . .

. . . The education is not "national" that takes no count of the starving millions of India, and that devises no means for their relief. . . .[24]

. . . Students have to react upon the dumb millions. They have to learn to think not in terms of a province or a town or a class or a caste, but in terms of a continent and of the millions who include untouchables, drunkards, hooligans and even prostitutes, for whose existence in our midst every one of us is responsible. . . .[25]

Our self-sacrifice must . . . be in terms of the requirements of the country. . . .

. . . We dare not support able-bodied members of the family— men or women—who will not work. We may not contribute a single pice towards the expenses of conforming to meaningless or superstitious customs, such as caste-dinners or towards forming expensive marriage connections. Every marriage and every death brings an unnecessary cruel burden upon the head of the family. . . .

. . . When it is difficult for millions to make even the two ends

[23] Louis Fischer, *The Life of Mahatma Gandhi,* Part II, Chapter 27, p. 226.
[24] *Young India,* June 17, 1926.
[25] *Young India,* June 9, 1927.

meet, when millions are dying of starvation, it is monstrous to think of giving our relatives a costly education. Expansion of the mind will come from hard experience, not necessarily in the college or the schoolroom. . . . The golden rule to apply in all such cases is resolutely to refuse to have what millions cannot. This ability to refuse will not descend upon us all of a sudden. The first thing is to cultivate the mental attitude that we will not have possessions or facilities denied to millions, and the next immediate thing is to rearrange our lives as fast as possible in accordance with our mentality.

. . . Progress towards self-rule will be in exact proportion to the increase in the number of workers who will dare to sacrifice their all for the cause of the poor.[26]

If America has to model her schools and colleges so as to enable students to earn their scholastic expenses, how much more necessary it must be for our schools and colleges? Is it not far better that we find work for poor students than that we pauperize them by providing free studentships? It is impossible to exaggerate the harm we do to India's youth by filling their minds with the false notion that it is ungentlemanly to labor with one's hands and feet for one's livelihood or schooling. . . . No one likes to be reminded in after-life that he had to depend upon charity for his education. . . .[27]

I value education in the different sciences. Our children cannot have too much of chemistry and physics. . . .

. . . I do regard spinning and weaving as the necessary part of any national system of education. I do not aim at taking the whole of the children's time for this purpose. Like a skilled physician I tend, and concentrate my attention on, the diseased limb knowing that is the best way of looking after the others. I would develop in the child his hands, his brain and his soul. The hands have atrophied. . . .[28]

. . . An academic grasp without practice behind it is like an embalmed corpse, perhaps lovely to look at but nothing to inspire or ennoble. . . .[29]

[26] *Young India,* June 24, 1926.
[27] *Young India,* August 2, 1928.
[28] *Young India,* March 12, 1925.
[29] *Young India,* September 1, 1921.

... [The British Government schools] have made us what we were intended to become—clerks and interpreters. . . .[30]

... The worst thing that can happen to boys in school is to have to render blind obedience to everything the teacher says. On the contrary, if teachers are to stimulate the reasoning faculty of boys and girls under their care, they would continuously tax their reason and make them think for themselves. . . .

... Pupils should . . . learn something about the deep poverty of the masses. They should have an ocular demonstration of some villages that are crumbling down to pieces. They should know the population of India. They should know the extent of this peninsula and they should know what it is that all the many millions can do to add to their scanty resources. They should learn to identify themselves with the poor and the downtrodden in the land. They should be taught to deny themselves, so far as possible, things the poorest cannot have. . . .[31]

[Please do] not look to my life, but take me even as a finger-post, a lamp-post on the road that indicates the way but cannot walk the way itself. I cannot present my life as an example. . . . Whomsoever you follow, howsoever great he might be, see to it that you follow the spirit of the master and not imitate him mechanically. . . . Let each follow . . . according to his individual development. . . .

... Higher education stands for unity, for catholicity, for toleration and wide outlook. The culture a university imparts should make you find the points of contact, and avoid those of conflict. If you could see the inner springs of actions and not the outward manifestations thereof, you would find a wonderful unity. . . . Leave the outward expression, the doctrine, the dogma and the form and behold the unity and oneness of spirit. . . . Then there will be no need to divide this universe of ours between heaven and hell, no need to divide fellow-beings into virtuous and vicious, the eternally saved and the eternally damned. Love shall inform your actions and pervade your life.[32]

[30] *Young India,* June 1, 1921.
[31] *Young India,* June 24, 1926.
[32] *Young India,* February 9, 1928.

[18]

SEX, SANITATION, AND SEGREGATION

[Gandhi's year as President of the Congress Party ended in December 1925. He then took a vow of a year's "political silence." In the silent year there were fifty-two silent Mondays when Gandhi did not speak. On those days, he would listen to an interviewer and occasionally tear off a corner of a piece of paper and pencil a few words in reply. Since this was not the best way to conduct a conversation, the weekly day of silence gave him some privacy.]

. . . It has often occurred to me that a seeker after truth has to be silent. I know the wonderful efficacy of silence. I visited a Trappist monastery in South Africa. A beautiful place it was. Most of the inmates of that place were under a vow of silence. I enquired of the Father the motive of it, and he said the motive is apparent. We are frail human beings. We do not know very often what we say. If we want to listen to the still small voice that is always speaking within us, it will not be heard if we continually speak. I understood that precious lesson. . . .[1]

[The silences] happened when I was being torn to pieces. I was working very hard, traveling in hot trains incessantly, speaking at many meetings, and being approached in trains and elsewhere by thousands of people who asked questions, made pleas, and wished to pray with me. I wanted to rest for one day a week. So I instituted the day of silence. Later of course I clothed it with all kinds of virtues and gave it a spiritual cloak. But the motivation was really nothing more than that I wanted to have a day off.

Silence is very relaxing. It is not relaxing in itself. But when you can talk and don't, it gives you great relief—and there is time for thought.[2]

---

[1] *Young India,* August 6, 1925.
[2] Interview, June 6, 1942, in Louis Fischer, *A Week with Gandhi*, p. 42.

Experience has taught me that silence is a part of the spiritual discipline of a votary of truth. Proneness to exaggerate, to suppress or modify the truth wittingly or unwittingly is a natural weakness of man and silence is necessary in order to surmount it. A man of few words will rarely be thoughtless in his speech, he will measure every word.[3]

Silence of the sewn-up lips is no silence. One may achieve the same result by chopping off one's tongue but that too would not be silence. He is silent who having the capacity to speak utters no idle word.[4]

[Apart from the fifty-two Mondays, the "silent" year was in no sense silent. He did not travel, he addressed no mass meetings, but he talked, wrote, received visitors and maintained a correspondence from the ashram at Ahmedabad with thousands of persons in India and other countries.

Taking advantage of relative leisure in the "silent year," Gandhi read Havelock Ellis, Forel, Paul Bureau's *Toward Moral Bankruptcy* and other European authorities on family and sex. Gandhi always advocated birth control. The method he favored, however, was self-control. In many articles that came from his pen or pencil in "silent" 1926 and often thereafter, Gandhi consistently opposed the use of contraceptives—they were a Western vice.]

. . . It is dinned into one's ears that the gratification of the sex urge is a solemn obligation like the obligation of discharging debts . . . and not to do so would involve the penalty of intellectual decay. This sex urge has been isolated from the desire for progeny and it is said by the protagonists of the use of contraceptives that conception is an accident to be prevented except when the parties desire to have children. I venture to suggest this is a most dangerous doctrine to preach anywhere, much more so in a country like India. . . . Marriage loses its sanctity when its purpose and highest use is conceived to be the satisfaction of the animal passion without contemplating the natural result of such satisfaction.[5]

[3] M. K. Gandhi, *The Mind of Mahatma Gandhi,* compiled by R. K. Prabhu and U. R. Rao (London: Oxford University Press, 1945), Chapter 6, p. 32.
[4] *Harijan,* June 24, 1933.
[5] *Harijan,* March 28, 1936.

*   *   *

There can be no two opinions about the necessity of birth-control. But the only method handed down from ages past is self-control or Brahmacharya. . . . The union is meant not for pleasure but for bringing forth progeny. And union is a crime when the desire for progeny is absent.

Artificial methods . . . make a man and woman reckless. . . . It is wrong and immoral to seek to escape the consequences of one's acts. It is good for the person who over-eats to have an ache and then fast. It is bad for him to indulge his appetite and then escape the consequences by taking tonics or other medicine. . . .[6]

In my opinion, sexual union to be legitimate is permissible only when both parties desire it. I do not recognize the right of either party to compel satisfaction. . . .

. . . I cannot help saying that the desire not to have more children is not enough reason for refusing satisfaction. It appears almost cowardly to reject one's wife's advances merely for fear of having to support children. . . .[7]

It is better to enjoy through the body than to be enjoying the thought of it. It is good to disapprove of sensual desires as soon as they arise in the mind and try to keep them down but if for want of physical enjoyment the mind wallows in thoughts of enjoyment then it is legitimate to satisfy the hunger of the body. About this I have no doubt.[8]

As long as you derive inner help and comfort from anything, you should keep it. If you were to give it up in a mood of self-sacrifice or out of a stern sense of duty, you would continue to want it back, and that unsatisfied want would make trouble for you. Only give up a thing when you want some other condition so much that the thing no longer has any attraction for you, or when it seems to interfere with that which is more greatly desired.[9]

[Recognize] the limitations of your body and insist on having the

---

[6] *Young India,* March 12, 1925.

[7] *Young India,* April 26, 1928.

[8] Hindi *Navajivan,* May 9, 1929.

[9] *Vishna-Bharati Quarterly,* New Series II, Part II, quoted in Numal Kumar Bose, *Studies in Gandhism,* Hindi edition.

things it may need for its upkeep, even as a trustee would be bound to secure the well-being of his ward. Be sure that you do not pamper the body. . . . [10]

. . . Though the external may have its use . . . I have all my life thought of growth from within. External appliances are perfectly useless if there is no internal reaction. When a body is perfect within, it becomes impervious to external adverse influences and is independent of external help. . . . If, therefore, we would all work to bring about internal perfection we need not take up any other activity at all. . . . [11]

I have learnt through bitter experience . . . to conserve my anger and as heat conserved is transmuted into energy even so our anger controlled can be transmuted into a power which can move the world. [12]

. . . I am prepared to recognize the limitations of human nature for the very simple reason that I recognize my own. . . . But . . . I do not deceive myself by refusing to distinguish between what I ought to do and what I fail to do. . . . Many things are impossible and yet are the only things right. A reformer's business is to make the impossible possible by giving an ocular demonstration of the possibility in his own conduct. . . . [13]

A man or woman completely practicing Brahmacharya [Chastity] is absolutely free from passion. Such a one therefore lives nigh unto God, is Godlike.

. . . I have gained control over the body. I can be master of myself during my waking hours. I have fairly succeeded in learning to control my tongue. But I have yet to cover many stages in the control of my thoughts. . . .

[In] the hours of sleep, control over the thoughts is much less. When asleep the mind would be swayed by all sorts of thoughts, by unexpected dreams, and by desire for things done and enjoyed by the flesh before. . . .

[10] Letter to Mira Behn, February 4, 1929, in M. K. Gandhi, *Gandhi's Letters to a Disciple,* pp. 50–51.
[11] *Young India,* September 4, 1924.
[12] *Young India,* September 15, 1920.
[13] *Young India,* February 5, 1925.

[He] who has not mastered his palate cannot master the carnal desire. It is very difficult, I know, to master the palate. But mastery of the palate means automatic mastery of the other senses. One of the rules . . . is to abjure completely or, as much as possible, all condiments. A more difficult rule to cultivate is the feeling that the food we eat is to sustain the body, never to satisfy the palate. We take air not for the pleasure of it but to breathe. . . .[14]

If I were sexually attracted towards women, I have courage enough, even at this time of life, to become a polygamist. I do not believe in free love—secret or open. Free open love I have looked upon as a dog's love. Secret love is besides cowardly.[15]

[In] non-violent conduct, whether individual or universal, there is an indissoluble connection between private personal life and public. You may be as generous and charitable as you like in judging men but you cannot overlook private deflections from the right conduct.[16]

. . . Why should one *know* the taste of what one does not need or wish to take? Do you know this is the reasoning that has been applied to justify every form of vice? It is the million times told story of the forbidden apple. . . .[17]

. . . I do not subscribe to the superstition that everything is good because it is ancient. I do not believe either that anything is good because it is Indian. . . . [Opium] and such other intoxicants and narcotics stupefy a man's soul and reduce him to a level lower than that of beasts. Trade in them is demonstrably sinful. Indian States should close all liquor shops . . . I trust the day is not distant when there will be not a single liquor shop in our peninsula.[18]

[It] betrays want of imagination and lack of sympathy with the people if [a] minister believes that as a prohibitionist he has nothing more to do but to declare prohibition and prosecute those who will break his laws. [There] is a larger and more constructive side to prohibition. People drink because of the conditions to which they

[14] *Young India,* June 5, 1924.
[15] *Harijan,* November 4, 1939.
[16] Nirmal Kumar Bose, *Studies in Gandhism,* Hindi Edition.
[17] Letter to Mira Behn, January 10, 1927, in M. K. Gandhi, *Letters to a Disciple,* pp. 22–23.
[18] *Young India,* January 8, 1925.

are reduced. It is the factory laborers and others that drink. They
are forlorn, uncared for, and they take to drink. They are no more
vicious by nature than teetotallers are saints by nature. The majority of people are controlled by their environment. Any minister
who is sincerely anxious to make prohibition a success will have to
develop the zeal and qualities of a reformer. . . . He will have to
convert every drink shop into a refreshment shop and concert
room combined. Poor laborers will want some place where they can
congregate and get wholesome, cheap, refreshing, non-intoxicating
drinks, and if they can have some good music at the same time, it
would prove as a tonic to them and draw them. . . . Whereas total
prohibition in the West is most difficult of accomplishment, I hold
it is the easiest of accomplishment in this country. When an evil
like drink in the West attains the status of respectability, it is the
most difficult to deal with. With us drink is still, thank God, sufficiently disrespectable and confined not to the general body of the
people but to a minority of the poorer classes.[19]

[Millions] of Indians are teetotallers by religion and by habit.
Millions therefore cannot possibly be interested in keeping up the
nefarious liquor traffic. . . .[20]

[Times without number, Gandhi attacked the institution of child
marriage as "a fruitful source of life, adding to the population."]
. . . Any tradition, however ancient, if inconsistent with morality
is fit to be banished from the land. . . . [The] institution of child
widowhood and child marriage may be considered to be an ancient
tradition, and even so, many an ancient horrible belief and superstitious practice. I would sweep them out of existence if I had the
power.[21]

It is irreligion, not religion, to give religious sanction to a brutal
custom. . . .
This custom of child marriage is both a moral as well as a physical evil. . . . Fight for Swaraj means not mere political awakening

[19] *Young India,* September 8, 1927.
[20] *Young India,* March 3, 1927.
[21] *Young India,* September 22, 1927.

but an all round awakening—social, educational, moral, economic and political.

Legislation is being promoted to raise the age of consent. It may be good for bringing a minority to book. But it is not legislation that will cure a popular evil, it is enlightened public opinion that can do it. . . .[22]

. . . I would . . . postpone marriage till a boy or girl is well advanced [over sixteen and nearer twenty], and is capable of shouldering the burden. . . . The way to do it is for those who feel the necessity of reform to initiate it themselves and advocate it among their neighbors. . . .[23]

[Just as Moslems, Christians and even untouchables borrowed the institution of caste from the Hindus, so the Hindus in places succumbed to Islam's purdah or segregation of women. Gandhi questioned this "institution" also.]

[Why] is there all this morbid anxiety about female purity? Have women any say in the matter of male purity? We hear nothing of women's anxiety about men's chastity. Why should men arrogate to themselves the right to regulate female purity? It cannot be superimposed from without. It is a matter of evolution from within and therefore of individual self-effort.[24]

Of all the evils for which man has made himself responsible, none is so degrading, so shocking or so brutal as his abuse of the better half of humanity—to me, the female sex, not the weaker sex. It is the nobler of the two for it is even today the embodiment of sacrifice, silent suffering, humility, faith and knowledge.[25]

. . . I [have] met a large number of these unfortunate sisters [prostitutes]. . . . It is a matter of bitter shame and sorrow, of deep humiliation that a number of women have to sell their chastity for man's lust. Man the law-giver will have to pay a dreadful penalty for the degradation he has imposed upon the so-called weaker sex. When

[22] *Young India,* August 26, 1926.
[23] *Young India,* July 2, 1925.
[24] *Young India,* November 25, 1926.
[25] *Young India,* September 15, 1921.

woman, freed from man's snares, rises to the full height and rebels against man's legislation and institutions designed by him, her rebellion, no doubt nonviolent, will be none the less effective. . . . The pity of it is that the vast majority of the men who visit these pestilential haunts are married men and therefore commit a double sin. They sin against their wives to whom they have sworn allegiance, and they sin against the sisters whose purity they are bound to guard with as much jealousy as that of their own blood sisters. It is an evil which cannot last for a single day, if we men of India realize our own dignity.[26]

[Man] cannot be made good by law. . . . I would certainly stop women of ill-fame from acting as actresses, I would prevent people from drinking and smoking, I would certainly prevent all the degrading advertisements that disfigure even reputable journals and newspapers. . . . But to regulate these things by law . . . would be a remedy probably worse than the disease. . . . There is no law against using kitchens as closets or drawing rooms as stables. But public opinion, that is, public taste will not tolerate such a combination. The evolution of public opinion is at times a tardy process but it is the only effective one.[27]

[Gandhi emerged from the year of silence with views unchanged. His program was still Hindu-Moslem unity, the removal of untouchability and the promotion of homespun. Indeed, Gandhi's program in its simplest terms remained the same for decades. The nation needed to be strengthened from within, Gandhi felt; otherwise, resolutions in favor of independence were empty words and vain gestures.]

[Katherine Mayo's book *Mother India*] is the report of a drain inspector sent out with the one purpose of opening and examining the drains of the country to be reported upon. . . . If Miss Mayo had confessed that she had gone to India merely to open out and examine the drains of India, there would perhaps be little to complain about her compilation. But she says, in effect, with a certain amount of triumph "the drains are India." . . .

[26] *Young India,* April 16, 1925.
[27] *Young India,* July 9, 1925.

. . . Her case is to perpetuate white domination in India on the plea of India's unfitness to rule herself.

The irony of it all is that she has inscribed this book "To the peoples of India." She has certainly not written it as a reformer, and out of love. If I am mistaken in my estimate, let her come back to India. Let her subject herself to cross-examination, and if her statements escape unhurt through the fire of cross-examination, let her live in our midst and reform our lives. . . .

. . . Whilst I consider the book to be unfit to be placed before Americans and Englishmen (for it can do no good to them), it is a book that every Indian can read with some degree of profit. We may repudiate the charge as it has been framed by her, but we may not repudiate the substance underlying the many allegations she has made. It is a good thing to see ourselves as others see us. . . .

. . . Overdrawn her pictures of our insanitation, child-marriages, etc. undoubtedly are. But let them serve as a spur to much greater effort than we have hitherto put forth in order to rid society of all cause of reproach. Whilst we may be thankful for anything good that foreign visitors may be able honestly to say of us, if we curb our anger, we shall learn, as I have certainly learnt, more from our critics than from our patrons. . . .[28]

. . . It is we ourselves with our inertia, apathy and social abuse that more than England or anybody else block our way to freedom. And if we cleanse ourselves of our shortcomings and faults no power on earth can even for a moment withhold Swaraj from us. . . .[29]

. . . I do not believe that the killing of even every Englishman can do the slightest good to India. The millions will be just as badly off as they are today. . . . The responsibility is more ours than that of the English for the present state of things. The English will be powerless to do evil if we will but be good. Hence my incessant emphasis on reform from within.[30]

. . . The one thing which we can and must learn from the West is

[28] *Young India,* September 15, 1927.
[29] 1928, in D. G. Tendulkar, *Mahatma, The Life of Mohandas Karamchand Gandhi,* Volume II, pp. 418–420.
[30] *Young India,* May 21, 1925.

the science of municipal sanitation. . . . Our narrow and tortuous lanes, our congested, ill-ventilated houses, our criminal neglect of sources of drinking water require remedying. . . . It is a superstition to consider that vast sums of money are required for . . . sanitary reform. We must modify Western methods of sanitation to suit our requirements. And as my patriotism is inclusive and admits of no enmity or ill-will, I do not hesitate, in spite of my horror of Western materialism, to take from the West what is beneficial for me. And as I know Englishmen to be resourceful, I gratefully seek their assistance in such matter. . . . Dirt, as the English say, is "matter misplaced."[31]

. . . I [once] shared my dreams and visions [of an ideal city of Ahmedabad] with Dr. Hariprasad whom I often met. I used to tell him of the citizen service I had done in South Africa—service which I am thankful was true service inasmuch as it was silent and of which most of you know nothing—and I concerted measures for improving the sanitation and health of the city. We had intended to form a committee of servants who would visit every nook and corner of the city in order to give the citizens object lessons in cleaning closets and streets, and in general conservancy by doing the work ourselves. We had also intended to plan and suggest measures for the expansion of the city by opening suburbs and inviting citizens to go and settle there rather than live in congested areas. Such things we knew could not be done satisfactorily by fresh taxation. We therefore thought of going with the beggar's bowl to the rich citizens and asking them to donate land in the heart of the city for opening little gardens for the children to play in. We had intended too to think out schemes . . . to afford the fullest facility for the education of every child. . . . It was also our intention to ensure a supply of pure and cheap milk by municipalizing all the city dairies. . . . But . . . a huge hurricane blew over the country in the shape of the Rowlatt Bills . . . I may only say that my heart weeps to see the misery, the squalor and the dirt in the streets of Ahmedabad as I pass through them. How can starvation and dirt be allowed to exist in a city of such riches and rich traditions?[32]

[31] *Young India,* December 26, 1924.
[32] *Young India,* August 28, 1924.

[The] highest form of Municipal life . . . has yet to be evolved by us in India. . . . It will not be till we have men whose ambition will be more than fully satisfied if they can keep the gutters and closets of their cities scrupulously clean and supply the purest milk at the cheapest rates and rid them of drunkenness and prostitution.[33]

[If] the people had really developed a sense of civic responsibility three-fourths of the municipal work could be done without the Government's assistance or patronage. . . . [In] a small place like Ahmedabad [they need] no elaborate machinery to light their streets, to clean their latrines and their roads, and to manage their schools, and there could be no question of police if the citizens were all good and pure, or if they had a citizen guard for guarding peaceful citizens against thieves, loafers or hooligans. Those men who are real servants of the people would become municipal councillors for the sake of service and not for the sake of gaining fame or engaging in intrigues and finding employment for their needy friends or relatives. What is wanted, therefore, is zealous education of the people on the part of workers, not merely by means of speeches, but through silent social service rendered without the slightest expectation of reward, even in the shape of thanks, but, on the contrary, with every expectation of receiving the execration and worse of a public enraged over every attempt to make it give up its superstitious or insanitary habits. . . .[34]

. . . There are many things which municipalities can remedy if they will only treat the cities under their care as if they were their own houses. . . .

. . . It is high time we developed a healthy sense of civic duty. In this matter we have much to learn from the West. People of the West are builders of big cities. They know the value of fresh air, clean water and clean surroundings. . . .[35]

. . . The Devil succeeds only by receiving help from his fellows. He always takes advantage of the weakest spots in our natures in order to gain mastery over us. Even so does the Government retain its control over us through our weaknesses or vices. And if we would

[33] *Young India,* July 16, 1925.
[34] *Young India,* July 21, 1921.
[35] *Young India,* February 3, 1927.

render ourselves proof against its machinations we must remove our weaknesses. It is for that reason that I have called Non-coöperation a process of purification. As soon as that process is completed this Government must fall to pieces for want of the necessary environment just as mosquitoes cease to haunt a place whose cesspools are filled up and dried.

Has not a just Nemesis overtaken us for the crime of untouchability? Have we not reaped as we have sown? . . . We have segregated the "pariah" and we are in turn segregated in the British Colonies. . . .

. . . The slave owner is always more hurt than the slave. We shall be unfit to gain Swaraj so long as we would keep in bondage a fifth of the population of Hindustan. Have we not made the "pariah" crawl on his belly? Have we not segregated him? And if it is religion so to treat the "pariah" it is the religion of the white race to segregate us. And if it is no argument for the white race to say we are satisfied with the badge of our inferiority, it is less for us to say the "pariah" is satisfied with his. Our slavery is complete when we begin to hug it.[36]

. . . I am unconcerned with the question of what place untouchables will have in any political constitution that may be drawn up. Every one of the artificial props that may be set up in the constitution will be broken to bits if we Hindus do not wish to play the game. . . . This removal of untouchability is not to be brought about by any legal enactment. It will be brought about only when the Hindu conscience is roused to action and of its own accord *removes* the shame. . . .[37]

. . . Governments cannot afford to lead in matters of reform. By their very nature Governments are but interpreters and executors of the expressed will of the people whom they govern, and even a most autocratic Government will find itself unable to impose a reform which its people cannot assimilate. . . .[38]

It is a tragedy that religion for us means today nothing more than restrictions on food and drink, nothing more than adherence

[36] *Young India,* November 24, 1920.
[37] *Young India,* June 30, 1927.
[38] *Young India,* October 20, 1927.

to a sense of superiority and inferiority. . . . Birth and observance of forms cannot determine one's superiority and inferiority. Character is the only determining factor. God did not create men with the badge of superiority or inferiority; no scripture which labels a human being as inferior or untouchable because of his or her birth can command our allegiance, it is a denial of God and Truth, which is God.[39]

. . . It is a blasphemy to say that God set apart any portion of humanity as untouchable. . . .[40]

Untouchability poisons Hinduism as a drop of arsenic poisons milk.

Knowing the quality of milk and the use of milk, and knowing the quality of arsenic, we should be impatient with the man sitting near a pitcher of milk and trying to remove arsenic grain by grain, and we should throw the whole pitcher overboard. . . . I feel therefore that patience in a matter of this character is not a virtue. It is impossible to restrain ourselves. Patience with evil is really trifling with evil and with ourselves. . . .[41]

. . . I would far rather that Hinduism died than that untouchability lived.[42]

We can do nothing without Hindu-Moslem unity and without killing the snake of untouchability. Untouchability is a corroding poison that is eating into the vitals of Hindu society. . . . No man of God can consider another man as inferior to himself. He must consider every man as his blood brother. It is the cardinal principle of every religion.[43]

[As] I know that God is found more often in the lowliest of His creatures than in the high and mighty, I am struggling to reach the status of these. . . . Hence my passion for the service of the suppressed classes [untouchables]. And as I cannot render this service

[39] Speech to a women's meeting, Harijan tour, August 2, 1934, in D. G. Tendulkar, *Mahatma,* Volume III, p. 343.
[40] Congress Presidential Address, *Young India,* December 26, 1924.
[41] *Young India,* October 20, 1927.
[42] Speech at last meeting of Minorities [Untouchables] Committee, November 13, 1931, Mahadev Desai, *The Diary of Mahadev Desai,* Volume I, Appendix 1, p. 322.
[43] *Young India,* February 23, 1921.

without entering politics, I find myself in them. Thus I am no master, I am but a struggling, erring, humble servant of India and, therethrough, of humanity.[44]

... That belief in untouchability can co-exist with learning in the same person, adds no status to untouchability but makes one despair of mere learning's being an aid to character or sanity.[45]

[It] is not enough for you to hold the belief passively that untouchability is a crime. He who is a passive spectator of crime is really, and in law, an active participator in it.... [46]

... The breaking of heads will not serve the purpose. Orthodoxy will stiffen its back and suck nourishment out of the blood of its martyrs. For if the orthodox are injured, sympathy will irresistibly be drawn towards them though their cause is wrong.... And even if force succeeded, it would merely mean mechanical use of a single public road [by untouchables, forbidden to use it] and not change of opinion.

What, however, the Hindu Reformers want is the conversion of the orthodox people who have made of untouchability a religion. This they will do only by suffering.... Satyagraha is utter self-effacement, greatest humiliation, greatest patience and brightest faith. It is its own reward.[47]

... The silent loving suffering of one single pure Hindu ... will be enough to melt the heart of millions of Hindus, but the sufferings of thousands of non-Hindus in behalf of the untouchables will leave the Hindus unmoved. Their blind eyes will not be opened by outside interference, however well-intentioned and generous it may be, for it will not bring home to them the sense of guilt.... All reform to be sincere and lasting must come from within.[48]

You [Untouchables] should realize that you are cleaning Hindu society. You have therefore to purify your lives. You should cultivate the habits of cleanliness so that no one may point his finger at you. Use alkali ash or earth if you cannot afford to use soap to keep

[44] *Young India,* September 11, 1924.
[45] *Young India,* July 29, 1926.
[46] *Young India,* October 20, 1927.
[47] *Young India,* February 26, 1925.
[48] *Young India,* May 1, 1924.

yourselves clean. Some of you are given to drinking and gambling which you must get rid of. . . . You must not ask the Hindus to emancipate you as a matter of favor. Hindus must do so, if they want, in their own interests. You should, therefore, make them feel ashamed by your own purity and cleanliness. . . .[49]

The following is almost a verbatim report of the quiet talk I gave to the inmates of the Satyagraha Ashram at Vykom. The Ashram has at the present moment over fifty volunteers who stand or squat in front of the four barricades which are put up to guard the four entrances to the Vykom temple [from untouchables]. . . . I reproduce the talk as being of general interest and applicable to all Satyagrahis.

[The] success of the movement depends more on yourself than on outside support. If there is nothing in you, or if there is not much in you, any amount of enthusiasm brought about by a passing visit like mine will be of no avail. . . .

. . . I would ask you to forget the political aspect of the program. Political consequences of this struggle there are, but you are not to concern yourself with them. If you do, you will miss the true result and also miss the political consequences, and when the real heat of the struggle is touched you will be found wanting. . . . We are endeavoring to rid Hinduism of its greatest blot. The prejudice we have to fight against is an age-long prejudice. . . . If you think the struggle is to end with opening the roads in Vykom to the unapproachables, you are mistaken. The road must be opened. It has got to be opened. But that will be the beginning of the end. The end is to get all such roads . . . opened . . . and not only that, but we expect our efforts may result in amelioration of the general condition of the untouchables. . . . That will require tremendous sacrifice. For our aim is not to do things by violence to opponents. . . . The question is whether you are capable of every suffering that may be imposed upon you or may be your lot in the journey towards the goal. Even whilst you are suffering, you may have no bitterness—no trace of it—against your opponents. [It] is not a mechanical act at all. . . . I want you to feel like loving your oppo-

---

[49] Speech at Suppressed [Untouchables] Classes Conference, Ahmedabad, *Young India,* September 13 and 14, 1921.

nents, and the way to do it is to give them the same credit for honesty of purpose which you would claim for yourself. I know that it
is a difficult task. I confess that it was a difficult task for me yesterday whilst I was talking to those friends who insisted on their right
to exclude the unapproachables from the temple roads. [Immedi-
ately] we begin to think of things as our opponents think of them
we shall be able to do them full justice. I know this requires a
detached state of mind, and it is a state very difficult to reach. Nevertheless, for a Satyagrahi it is absolutely essential. Three-fourths
of the miseries and misunderstandings in the world will disappear
if we step into the shoes of our adversaries and understand their
standpoint. We will then agree with our adversaries quickly or
think of them charitably. In our case there is no question of our
agreeing with them quickly as our ideals are radically different.
But we may be charitable to them and believe that they actually
mean what they say. . . . Our business, therefore, is to show them
that they are in the wrong, and we should do so by our suffering. I
have found that mere appeal to reason does not answer where prejudices are age-long and based on supposed religious authority.
Reason has to be strengthened by suffering, and suffering opens
the eyes of understanding. . . . I know that it is a difficult and slow
process. But if you believe in the efficacy of Satyagraha, you will
rejoice in this slow torture and suffering, and you will not feel the
discomfort of your position as you go and sit in the boiling sun
from day to day. . . .

I regard you as soldiers in this campaign. . . . If we are to become
a powerful nation you must obey all directions that may be given to
you from time to time. This is the only way in which either political
or religious life can be built up. You must have determined for
yourselves certain principles and you must have joined the struggle
in obedience to these principles. . . . Every piece of work in connection with the struggle is just as important as any other piece,
and therefore the work of sanitation in the Ashram is just as
important as spinning away at the barricades. And if in this place
the work of cleaning the closets and compound is more distasteful
than spinning, it should be considered far more important and
profitable. . . .

I know all this will sound hard and difficult for you. [It] will be wrong on my part if I deceive you or myself in believing that this is an easy thing.

Much corruption has crept into our religion. We have become lazy as a nation. . . . Selfishness dominates our action. . . . We are uncharitable to one another. And if I did not draw your attention to the things I have, it would not be possible to rid ourselves of all these evils. Satyagraha is a relentless search for truth, and a determination to reach truth. I can only hope you will realize the import of what you are doing. And if you do, your path will be easy—easy because you will take delight in difficulties and you will laugh in hope when everybody is in despair. . . .[50]

[50] *Young India,* March 19, 1925.

THE LIBERTY MARCH

[Traveling incessantly through the country making propaganda for khadi, Hindu-Moslem amity and desegregation of untouchables, meeting crowds numbering hundreds of thousands, the Mahatma broke down and became ill.]

Well, my cart has stuck in the mire. Tomorrow it might break down beyond hope of repair. What then? [The Gita] proclaims that everyone that is born must die, and everyone that dies must be born again. Everyone comes, repays part of his obligation and goes his way.[1]

[As soon as he recuperated, however, he returned to his favorite pursuit: traveling in tightly packed third-class railway cars from region to region and village to village bringing his philosophy to the poor. In December, 1928, en route to the annual Congress Party convention in Calcutta, he was asked about his attitude toward a political war of independence.]

I would decline to take part in it. [He was then asked for his view of a national militia.] I would support the formation of a national militia under [self-rule] if only because I realize that people cannot be made nonviolent by compulsion. Today I am teaching the people how to meet a national crisis by non-violent means.[2]

[Violence filled the air of India. The intellectuals in the Congress Party and their followers were growing impatient. They wanted action to oust the British.]

If India attains what will be to me so-called freedom by violent means she will cease to be the country of my pride.[3]

---

[1] Letter to women of Sabarmati Ashram, quoted in Louis Fischer, *The Life of Mahatma Gandhi,* Part II, Chapter 27, p. 247.

[2] *Ibid.,* Part II, Chapter 28, p. 257.

[3] *Young India,* May 9, 1929.

[Prophetically he pictured the ideal: freedom should come non-violently] through a gentlemanly understanding with Great Britain.

But then, it will not be an imperialistic haughty Britain maneuvering for world supremacy but a Britain humbly trying to serve the common end of humanity.[4]

[The younger leaders of the Congress Party, among them Jawaharlal Nehru and Subhas Chandra Bose, were asking for complete independence within a year and for action to attain it. The Congress Party convention instructed its members and friends to withdraw from all legislatures set up by the British Government in India. It sanctioned the non-payment of taxes and a massive Civil Disobedience movement. It accepted Gandhi's condition that he was to determine the nature, scope and timing of the movement. The poet Rabindranath Tagore came to see Gandhi at Sabarmati Ashram on January 18, 1930, and inquired what Gandhi proposed to do.]

I am furiously thinking night and day, and I do not see any light coming out of the surrounding darkness.[5]

[Gandhi was waiting to hear his "Inner Voice."]

The "Inner Voice" may mean a message from God or from the Devil, for both are wrestling in the human breast. Acts determine the nature of the Voice.[6]

[Finally he knew. He had heard the Inner Voice, and on March 2, 1930, he wrote an unprecedented letter to the British Viceroy, Lord Irwin, later Lord Halifax.]

Dear Friend, Before embarking on Civil Disobedience and taking the risk I have dreaded to take all these years, I would fain approach you and find a way out.

My personal faith is absolutely clear. I cannot intentionally hurt anything that lives, much less human beings, even though they may do the greatest wrong to me and mine. Whilst, therefore, I hold the British rule to be a curse, I do not intend harm to a single Englishman or to any legitimate interest he may have in India. . . . And why do I regard the British rule as a curse?

[4] *Ibid.*
[5] Louis Fischer, *The Life of Mahatma Gandhi,* Part II, Chapter 31, p. 264.
[6] *Ibid.,* p. 264.

It has impoverished the dumb millions by a system of progressive exploitation and by a ruinous expensive military and Civil administration which the country can never afford.

It has reduced us politically to serfdom. It has sapped the foundations of our culture. And by the policy of cruel disarmament, it has degraded us spiritually. . . .

I fear . . . there never has been any intention of granting . . . Dominion Status to India in the immediate future. . . .

[The] whole revenue system has to be so revised as to make the peasant's good its primary concern. But the British system seems to be designed to crush the very life out of him. Even the salt he must use to live is so taxed as to make the burden fall heaviest on him, if only because of the heartless impartiality of its incidence. The tax shows itself still more burdensome on the poor man when it is remembered that salt is the one thing he must eat more than the rich man. . . . The drink and drug revenue, too, is derived from the poor. It saps the foundations both of their health and morals.

The iniquities sampled above are maintained in order to carry on a foreign administration, demonstrably the most expensive in the world. . . . I have too great a regard for you as a man to wish to hurt your feelings. I know that you do not need the salary you get. Probably the whole of your salary goes for charity. But a system that provides for such an arrangement deserves to be summarily scrapped. What is true of the Viceregal salary is true generally of the whole administration. . . . Nothing but organized non-violence can check the organized violence of the British government. . . .

This non-violence will be expressed through civil disobedience, for the moment confined to the inmates of the Satyagraha [Sabarmati] Ashram, but ultimately designed to cover all those who choose to join the movement. . . .

My ambition is no less than to convert the British people through non-violence, and thus make them see the wrong they have done to India. I do not seek to harm your people. I want to serve them even as I want to serve my own. . . .

If the [Indian] people join me as I expect they will, the sufferings they will undergo, unless the British nation sooner retraces its steps, will be enough to melt the stoniest hearts.

[If] my letter makes no appeal to your heart, on the eleventh day of this month, I shall proceed with such co-workers of the Ashram as I can take, to disregard the provisions of the Salt Laws. . . . It is, I know, open to you to frustrate my design by arresting me. I hope that there will be tens of thousands ready, in a disciplined manner, to take up the work after me. . . .

This letter is not in any way intended as a threat but is a simple and sacred duty peremptory on a civil resister. . . . Your sincere friend, M. K. Gandhi.[7]

[Lord Irwin did not reply. His secretary sent a four-line acknowledgment saying, "His Excellency . . . regrets to learn that you contemplate a course of action which is clearly bound to involve violation of the law and danger to the public peace."[8]

On March 12th, prayers having been sung, Gandhi and seventy-eight male and female members of the ashram, whose identities were published in *Young India* for the benefit of the police, left Sabarmati for Dandi, due south of Ahmedabad. Following winding dirt roads from village to village, Gandhi and his seventy-eight disciples walked two hundred miles in twenty-four days.] We are marching in the name of God, [Gandhi said].

[He had no trouble in walking.] Less than twelve miles a day in two stages with not much luggage, [he said]. Child's play. [Several became fatigued and footsore, and had to ride in a bullock cart. A horse was available for Gandhi throughout the march but he never used it.] The modern generation is delicate, weak, and much pampered, [Gandhi commented. He was sixty-one. He spun every day for an hour and kept a diary and required each ashramite to do likewise.

The entire night of April 5th, the ashramites prayed, and early in the morning they accompanied Gandhi to the sea. He dipped into the water, returned to the beach, and there picked up some salt left by the waves. Mrs. Sarojini Naidu, standing by his side cried, "Hail, Deliverer." Gandhi had broken the British law which made it a punishable crime to possess salt not obtained from the British government salt monopoly. Gandhi, who had not used salt for six years, called it a] nefarious monopoly. [Salt, he said, is as essential as air and water, and in India all the more essential to the hard-working, perspiring poor man and his beasts because of the tropical heat.

[7] *Ibid.,* p. 266.
[8] *Ibid.,* p. 267.

The act performed, Gandhi withdrew from the scene. India had its cue. Gandhi had communicated with it by lifting up some grains of salt.

All India began making salt illegally. The biography of *Viscount Halifax,* by Alan Campbell Johnson, records that sixty thousand political offenders were arrested. Finally Gandhi was arrested. From jail he wrote to Miss Slade, the Englishwoman who had become a disciple and co-worker.]

I have been quite happy and making up for arrears in sleep.[9]

[To the children of the ashram he wrote a special note.]

Little birds, ordinary birds cannot fly without wings. With wings, of course, all can fly. But if you, without wings, will learn how to fly, then all your troubles will indeed be at an end. And I will teach you.

See, I have no wings, yet I come flying to you every day in thought. Look, here is little Vimala, here is Hari and here is Dharmakumar. And you can also come flying to me in thought. . . .

Send me a letter signed by all, and those who do not know how to sign may make a cross.

Bapu's blessings.[10]

[Just before his arrest, Gandhi had drafted a letter to the Viceroy announcing his intention to raid the Dharasana Salt Works with some companions. Mrs. Sarojini Naidu, the poet, led twenty-five hundred volunteers to the site one hundred and fifty miles north of Bombay. Webb Miller, the well-known correspondent of the United Press, was on the scene and described the proceedings. When a picked group of the marchers approached, police officers ordered them to retreat. They continued to advance. "Suddenly," Webb Miller reported, "at a word of command, scores of native policemen rushed upon the advancing marchers and rained blows on their heads with their steel-shod lathis. Not one of the marchers even raised an arm to fend off the blows. They went down like nine-pins. . . . The waiting crowd of marchers groaned and sucked in their breath in sympathetic pain at every blow. Those struck

[9] *Ibid.,* p. 272.
[10] *Ibid.,* p. 273.

down fell sprawling, unconscious or writhing with fractured skulls or broken shoulders. . . . The survivors, without breaking ranks, silently and doggedly march on until struck down." When the first column was laid low, another advanced. Then another.

"By eleven (in the morning)," Miller continued, "the heat had reached 116 and the activities of the Gandhi volunteers subsided." Miller went to a temporary hospital and counted three hundred and twenty injured, many of them unconscious, others in agony from body and head blows. Two men had died. The same scenes were repeated for several days.

Rabindranath Tagore wrote in the *Manchester Guardian* of May 17, 1930, "Those who live in England, far away from the East, have now got to realize that Europe has completely lost her former moral prestige in Asia. She is no longer regarded as the champion throughout the world of fair dealing, and the exponent of high principle, but as the upholder of Western race supremacy and the exploiter of those outside her own borders.

"For Europe, this is, in actual fact, a great moral defeat that has happened. Even though Asia is still physically weak and unable to protect herself from aggression where her vital interests are menaced, nevertheless she can now afford to look down on Europe where before she looked up."[11] He attributed the achievement in India to Mahatma Gandhi.

The Salt March made it clear to many Englishmen that they could not rule India against the wishes of the Indians, and it made it clear to Indians that they had it in their power to make orderly British rule in their country impossible.

January 26, 1931, had been fixed by the Congress Party as the day of Independence, for on that day a Declaration of Independence had been issued by the Congress Party. On January 26, Lord Irwin released Gandhi from jail. This was taken by Gandhi and others as a gesture of friendship and conciliation. On February 16 Gandhi, the ex-prisoner, kept an appointment with the Viceroy in his palace. Winston Churchill remarked that he was revolted by "the nauseating and humiliating spectacle of this one-time Inner Temple lawyer now seditious fakir, striding half-naked up the

[11] *Ibid.,* pp. 274–277.

steps of the Viceroy's palace, there to negotiate and to parley on equal terms with the representative of the King-Emperor."[12]

Gandhi returned for many more interviews with the Viceroy. At the end of the conferences, the Irwin-Gandhi Pact was signed on March 5, 1931. On that day Gandhi addressed Indian and American journalists.]

I am aware that I must have, though quite unconsciously, given him cause for irritation. I must also have tried his patience, but I cannot recall an occasion when he allowed himself to be betrayed into irritation or impatience. [The settlement was] provisional . . . conditional . . . a truce. India cannot be satisfied with anything less [than complete independence]. The Congress [Party] does not consider India to be a sickly child requiring nursing, outside help and other props.[13]

[In effect Gandhi had been recognized by the British Government as a power with which it had to negotiate.

Gandhi sailed for England from Bombay on August 29 to negotiate with the British Government at the Second Round Table Conference. The day after his arrival in England, the Columbia Broadcasting System arranged for a radio address to the United States. Gandhi refused to prepare a script and spoke extemporaneously. In the studio, he eyed the microphone and said] Do I have to speak into that? [He was already on the air.]

. . . We [in India] feel that the law that governs brute creation is not the law that should guide the human race. That law is inconsistent with human dignity.

I, personally, would wait, if need be, for ages rather than seek to attain the freedom of my country through bloody means. I feel in the innermost recesses of my heart, after a political experience extending over an unbroken period of close upon thirty-five years, that the world is sick unto death of blood-spilling. The world is seeking a way out, and I flatter myself with the belief that perhaps it will be the privilege of the ancient land of India to show the way out to the hungering world.

[12] *Ibid.,* Part II, Chapter 32, p. 277.
[13] *Ibid.,* pp. 278–279.

I have, therefore, no hesitation whatsoever in inviting all the great nations of the earth to give their hearty coöperation to India in her mighty struggle. . . .

. . . It is my certain conviction that no man loses his freedom except through his own weakness. I am painfully conscious of our own weaknesses. We represent in India all the principal religions of the earth, and it is a matter of deep humiliation to confess that we are a house divided against itself, that we Hindus and Moslems are flying at one another. It is a matter of still deeper humiliation to me that we Hindus regard several millions of our own kith and kin as too degraded even for our touch. I refer to the so-called "untouchables."

These are no small weaknesses in a nation struggling to be free. . . . [14]

[During the broadcast a note was passed to Gandhi warning him his time was almost up and New York would cut him off in three minutes. Unperturbed, Gandhi delved into the economics of British rule and closed with a plea:]

. . . May I not, then, on behalf of the semi-starved millions, appeal to the conscience of the world to come to the rescue of a people dying to regain its liberty?[15]

[The CBS producer signaled him to stop.] Well, that's over, [Gandhi said. He was still on the air. His voice was clear and the reception perfect.

During his stay in England Gandhi visited Lancashire, the center of the British textile industry, whose products he had urged Indians to boycott. He had said:]

. . . My very English efficient nurse whom I loved to call "tyrant" because she insisted in all loving ways on my taking more food and more sleep than I did, with a smile round her lips . . . gently remarked . . . "As I was shading you with my umbrella I could not help smiling that you, a fierce boycotter of everything British, probably owed your life to the skill of a British surgeon handling British surgical instruments, administering British drugs,

[14] Haridas T. Muzumdar, *Gandhi Versus the Empire* (New York: Universal Publishing Company, 1932), Chapter 15, pp. 167–168.
[15] *Ibid.,* p. 170.

and to the ministrations of a British nurse. Do you know . . . the umbrella that shaded you was of British make?" [Gandhi replied:] ". . . Do you know that I do not boycott anything merely because it is British? I simply boycott all foreign cloth because the dumping down of foreign cloth in India has reduced millions of my people to pauperism." . . .[16]

[The boycott of British textiles had caused widespread unemployment in Lancashire. Nevertheless, Gandhi visited Lancashire during his stay in England. After a meeting that Gandhi addressed, one man said, "I am one of the unemployed, but if I was in India I would say the same thing that Mr. Gandhi is saying." There is a telling photograph, taken outside the Greenfield Mill at Darwen, Lancashire, showing Gandhi, wrapped in white cotton from neck to knee, overcome with coyness and squeezed in amidst cotton factory workers, most of them women, one of them holding his hand, and all of them cheering the Mahatma and smiling. He made friends among those whom he hurt.

In London, Gandhi stayed in an East End settlement house called Kingsley Hall, five miles from the center of the city and from St. James's Palace where the Round Table Conference sat. He enjoyed living among his own kind, the poor people, he said.]

In that settlement, which represents the poor people of the East End of London, I have become one of them. They have accepted me as a member, and as a favored member of their family. . . . I have come in touch with so many Englishmen. It has been a priceless privilege to me. They have listened to what must have often appeared to them to be unpleasant, although it was true. [They] have never shown the slightest impatience or irritation. It is impossible for me to forget these things. . . . I consider that it was well worth my paying this visit to England in order to find this human affection.

[Although] in Lancashire, the Lancashire people had perhaps some reason for becoming irritated against me, I found no irritation and no resentment. . . . The operatives, men and women, hugged me. They treated me as one of their own. I shall never forget that.

[16] *Young India,* May 15, 1924.

... All this hospitality, all this kindness, will never be effaced from my memory, no matter what befalls my unhappy land. . . .[17]

[Questioned by a reporter about his dress, Gandhi said] You people wear plus-fours, mine are minus fours.[18]

[Gandhi went to Buckingham Palace to have tea with King George V and Queen Mary. On the eve of the event, all England was agog over what he would wear. He wore a loincloth, sandals, a shawl and his dangling watch. Later someone asked Gandhi whether he had had enough on.] The King, [Gandhi replied] had enough on for both of us.[19]

[In a letter to a child at the ashram who asked him to describe London, Gandhi wrote:] London is a very big city. It has many chimneys which blacken everything. Nothing there will stay white. The sun is rarely visible. But the English people are more industrious than we are. And roads in England are very clean.[20]

[England was not yet parting with power in India. That was the crucial fact. But Gandhi was not giving up, as he told the Conference.]

[Of] course, the [British] Government may not tolerate, no Government has tolerated, open rebellion. No Government may tolerate Civil Disobedience . . . I shall hope against hope, I shall strain every nerve to achieve an honorable settlement for my country, if I can do so without having to put the millions of my countrymen and countrywomen, and even children, through this ordeal of fire. [But] if a further ordeal of fire has to be our lot, I shall approach that with the greatest joy and with the greatest consolation that I wag doing what I felt to be right, the country was doing what it felt to be right, and the country will have the additional satisfaction of knowing that it was not at least taking lives, it was giving lives—it was not making the British people directly suffer, it was suffering. . . . I do know that you will suffer, but I want you to suffer

---

[17] Speech delivered at the plenary session of the Round Table Conference, London, 1931, C. Rajagopalachari and J. C. Kumarappa, Editors, *The Nation's Voice* (Ahmedabad: Navajivan Publishing House, 1932), Chapter 11, p. 88.

[18] Louis Fischer, *Life of Gandhi,* Part II, Chapter 32, p. 280.

[19] *Ibid.,* p. 280.

[20] While in Yeravda Prison, May 30, 1932, in Mahadev Desai, *The Diary of Mahadev Desai*, Volume I, p. 140.

because I want to touch your hearts, and when your hearts have been touched, then will come the psychological moment for negotiation. . . .[21]

[The Round Table Conference was fruitless and Gandhi returned to India by way of Paris, Switzerland, where he met Romain Rolland, and Rome, where he visited the daughter of Count Leo Tolstoy and went to see Mussolini.]

Somehow or other I dread a visit to Europe and America. Not that I distrust the peoples of these great continents any more than I distrust my own but I distrust myself. I have no desire to go to the West in search of health or for sightseeing. I have no desire to deliver public speeches. I detest being lionized. . . . If God ever sent me to the West, I should go there to penetrate the hearts of the masses, to have quiet talks with the youth of the West and have the privilege of meeting kindred spirits—lovers of peace at any price save that of truth.

. . . I believe my message to be universal but as yet I feel that I can best deliver it through my work in my own country. . . .

. . . Owing to my distrust of myself over a general visit, I wanted to make my visit to [Romain Rolland, author of *Jean Christophe,* a literary masterpiece of the twentieth century] that wise man of the West, the primary cause of my journey to Europe. . . .[22]

[Gandhi later described his visit with Mussolini.]

He has the eyes of a cat, they moved about in every direction as if in constant rotation. The visitor would totally succumb before the awe of his gaze like a rat running directly into the mouth of a cat out of mere fright. I was not to be dazed like that but I noticed that he had so arranged things about him that a visitor would easily get stricken with terror. The walls of the passage through which one has to pass to reach him are all overstudded with various types of swords and other weapons. He keeps no arms on his person.[23]

["Was he not a remarkable personality?" asked a visitor of Gandhi's.]

[21] Speech delivered at the plenary session of the Round Table Conference, London, 1931, C. Rajagopalachari and J. C. Kumarappa, *The Nation's Voice,* Chapter 11, pp. 78–79.
[22] D. G. Tendulkar, *Mahatma: The Life of Mohandas Karamchand Gandhi,* Volume II, p. 417.
[23] Louis Fischer, *Life of Gandhi,* Part II, Chapter 33, pp. 294–295.

THE LIBERTY MARCH

Yes, but a cruel man. A regime based on such cruelty cannot last long.[24]

[There] is no state run by Nero or Mussolini which has not good points about it, but we have to reject the whole once we decide to non-coöperate with the system. "There are in our country grand public roads and palatial institutions," said I to myself, "but they are part of a system which crushes the nation. I should not have anything to do with them. They are like the fabled snake with a brilliant jewel on its head, but which has fangs full of poison." . . .[25]

[When Gandhi returned to Bombay on December 28, 1931, he reported to the Indian people about his stay abroad.]

I have come back empty-handed, but I have not compromised the honor of my country.[26]

I am not conscious of a single experience throughout my three months' stay in England and Europe that made me feel that after all East is East and West is West. On the contrary, I have been convinced more than ever that human nature is much the same, no matter under what clime it flourishes, and that if you approached people with trust and affection you would have ten-fold trust and thousand-fold affection returned to you.[27]

[24] Visit with Major Mehta, a jail official, in Yeravda Prison, May 26, 1932, Mahadev Desai, *Diary,* p. 130.
[25] *Young India,* December 31, 1931.
[26] Louis Fischer, *Life of Gandhi,* Part II, Chapter 33, p. 297.
[27] *Ibid.,* Part II, Chapter 34, pp. 298–299.

[20]

HOW TO ENJOY JAIL

[On January 4 Gandhi was arrested and lodged in Yeravda Jail. Since he worshiped God in prison he called it his "mandir"—temple—and there wrote a book entitled *From Yeravda Mandir*. His thoughts turned to questions of religion, God and prayer. Mahadev Desai, Gandhi's secretary who had also been arrested and imprisoned at Yeravda, noted that Gandhi leaned "on a wooden board. Very often he keeps it close to the wall and not at an angle. I remarked that if it was kept at an angle it would not fall down from time to time and would be more comfortable."]

Perhaps, but the proper thing to do is to keep it straight so that the backbone and waist remain straight in their turn and do not bend. It is a general principle that if you keep one thing straight it will tend to straighten everything else and crookedness at one point will make for crookedness at many other points.[1]

Instead of thinking of improving the world let us concentrate on self-improvement. We can scarcely find out if the world is on the right or the wrong path. But if we take the straight and narrow path we shall find all taking it too or discover the method of inducing them to take it. . . .[2]

. . . If the world is on fire we cannot extinguish it by our impatience. In fact it is not for us to extinguish it at all. Do you know that when there is a big blaze the firemen do not waste any water on it at all. They only try to save the neighborhood. . . . When we have done our individual duty that is as good as having extinguished the whole of the fire. In appearance it is still burning but

[1] Entry for May 31, 1932, in Mahadev Desai, *The Diary of Mahadev Desai*, p. 142.
[2] Entry for August 7, 1932, *ibid.*, p. 276.

we may rest assured that it has been put out. This is all I have found as a result of my quest of truth. . . . We can only insist upon what is possible. It is no use pining after the air of the mountains on the moon, as it is beyond our reach. The same is true of our duty. . . .[3]

. . . We tend to become what we worship. . . .[4]

[Gandhi's stay in prison stimulated his thinking about himself and about jails.]

. . . Jail for us is no jail at all. . . .[5]

[We] have no strangers. All strangers are friends, including criminals, as also jailors. We have here [in Yeravda prison] learned to recognize friends among animals. We have a cat who is a revelation. And if we had vision enough, we should appreciate the language of trees and plants and value their friendship.[6]

. . . If a dying man has his heart in the world he is unhappy himself and the cause of unhappiness in others, the same is the case with a prisoner in jail, who should cease to think of the outside world, for imprisonment means civil death. . . . This prescription of mine is no new discovery. Bunyan could not have written *The Pilgrim's Progress* and Lokamanya Tilak his commentary on the Gita if in prison they had continued to worry about the outside world.[7]

. . . Self-control is the best thing for a prisoner and his friends and dear ones. But self-control to be self-control must brace one up. It becomes mechanical or superimposed when it unnerves or saddens one. . . .[8]

[Train] yourself to . . . *feel happy*. In a manner everybody trains himself to do without things when he cannot get them. A follower of the Gita dharma [duty] trains himself to do without things *with happiness* . . . for happiness of the Gita is not the opposite of unhap-

[3] Letter written by Gandhi to Chhaganlal Joshi, August 20, 1932, *ibid.*, pp. 296–297.

[4] Gandhi's reply to a co-worker's letter, June 13, 1932, *ibid.*, p. 160.

[5] Remark in conversation with fellow-prisoners, March 15, 1932, *ibid.*, p. 12.

[6] Letter to Mira Behn, August 31, 1932, in M. K. Gandhi, *Gandhi's Letters to a Disciple,* p. 117.

[7] Letter to fellow-prisoners, August 15, 1932, in Mahadev Desai, *Diary,* p. 288.

[8] Letter to Mira Behn, February 4, 1932, in M. K. Gandhi, *Letters to a Disciple,* p. 97.

piness. It is superior to that state. The devotee of the Gita is neither happy nor unhappy. And when that state is reached, there is no pain, no pleasure, no victory, no defeat, no deprivation, no possession. Prison life is a life of privilege if we learn to practise the Gita teaching. . . .[9]

[Describing life in prison with Gandhi, Desai noted in his diary, "We take honey and lime juice after prayers at 4 A.M. Boiling water is poured upon [it], we then wait for a few minutes until the beverage is fit to drink. Since yesterday Bapu has begun to cover his tumbler with a piece of cloth."]

Mahadev, do you know why I cover my tumbler? There are many minute germs in the air which might fall into the tumbler if it is uncovered, and the piece of cloth keeps them out.

[Sardar Vallabhbhai Patel, Gandhi's co-prisoner, who was a Congress Party leader and later headed the provisional government of Independent India, commented, "We cannot observe Ahimsa [Non-Violence] to such an extent." "Bapu laughed," Desai wrote. "Bapu" or "Father" was the affectionate title given to Gandhi by his followers. Everyone called him Bapu.]

We may not observe Ahimsa but we must see that our food and drink are free from dirt.[10]

We must make the best possible use of the invaluable leisure in jail. Perhaps the best of uses would be to cultivate the power of independent thought. We are often thoughtless and therefore like only to read books or, worse still, to talk. . . . As a matter of fact, there is an art of thinking just as there is an art of reading. We should be able to think the right thought at the right time and not indulge in thinking useless thoughts as well as in reading useless books. . . . It is my experience during every incarceration that it affords us a fine opportunity of thinking . . . to some purpose. . . .[11]

. . . My own reading is quite odd. I am doing some Urdu at present. I am also trying to get some idea of currency and exchange, as

---

[9] Letter to Mira Behn, March 4, 1933, *ibid.,* p. 142.

[10] Entry for March 22, 1932, Mahadev Desai, *Diary,* p. 21.

[11] Entry for June 10, 1932, *ibid.,* p. 156.

ignorance of it would be inexcusable. There is the desire to render service at the back of these studies. The same desire impels me to deepen my knowledge of Tamil as well as Bengali and Marathi. If we have to stay in jail for a pretty long time, I may recommence the study of all these languages. . . .[12]

[Never] write a bad hand whether there is hurry or not. This lesson everyone should learn from my misfortune. Bad writing and bad everything is truly [violence]. We have a rare opportunity of learning the virtue of patience in prison life.[13]

. . . The word "criminal" should be taboo from our dictionary. Or we are all criminals. "Those of you that are without sin cast the first stone." And no one was found to dare cast the stone at the sinning harlot. As a jailer once said, all are criminals in secret. . . . Let them therefore be good companions. I know this is easier said than done. And that is exactly what the Gita and as a matter of fact all religions enjoin upon us to do.[14]

. . . There is need for reform in the administration of prisons. A prison should be a house of correction and not punishment. [Why] should a forger have fetters on his legs in prison? The fetters will not improve his character. . . .[15]

. . . The more we punish, the more persistent crimes become. They may change color but the substance is the same. The way to serve the adversary's soul is to appeal to the soul. It defies destruction, but it is amenable to appeals tuned to the required pitch. Souls must react upon souls. And since non-violence is essentially a quality of the soul, the only effective appeal to the soul must lie through non-violence. And do we not arrogate to ourselves infallibility when we seek to punish our adversaries? Let us remember that they regard us to be as harmful . . . as we regard them. . . .[16]

*   *   *

[12] Letter to a disciple who asked his advice about what to read, *ibid.,* p. 208.

[13] Letter to Mira Behn, November 3, 1932, in M. K. Gandhi, *Letters to a Disciple,* p. 126.

[14] Letter to Mira Behn, October 19, 1932, in M. K. Gandhi, *Bapu's Letters to Mira* (Ahmedabad: Navajivan Publishing House, 1949), p. 124.

[15] Entry for June 17, 1932, in Mahadev Desai, *Diary,* p. 170.

[16] *Young India,* April 30, 1925.

... I would draw the distinction between killing and detention ...
I think there is a difference not merely in quantity but also in quality. I can recall the punishment of detention. I can make reparation
to the man upon whom I inflict corporal punishment. But once a
man is killed, the punishment is beyond recall or reparation. God
alone can take life because He alone gives it.[17]

---

[17] *Young India,* October 8, 1925.

21

FAST AGAINST INDIAN PREJUDICE

[While Gandhi was in Yeravda Jail he decided to fast as a protest against Hindu mistreatment of India's sixty million untouchables, whom he called "Harijans"—Children of God. He announced that unless there was an improvement in the Hindu attitude toward untouchables he would fast unto death.]

. . . The Harijan movement is too big for mere intellectual effort. There is nothing so bad in the world. And yet I cannot leave religion and therefore Hinduism. My life would be a burden to me if Hinduism failed me. I love Christianity, Islam and many other faiths through Hinduism. . . . But then I cannot tolerate it with untouchability. . . .[1]

[Gandhi began his fast on September 20. He awoke at 2:30 A.M., made his ablutions and wrote a letter to Tagore.]

. . . I enter the fiery gates at noon. If you can bless the effort I want it. You have been a true friend because you have been a candid friend often speaking your thoughts aloud. . . . Though it can now only be during my fast, I will yet prize your criticism, if your heart condemns my action. I am not too proud to make an open confession of my blunder, whatever the cost of the confession, if I find myself in error. If your heart approves of the action I want your blessing. It will sustain me. . . .[2]

[Just as Gandhi posted this letter he received a telegram from Tagore: "It is worth sacrificing precious life for the sake of India's unity and her social integrity . . . I fervently hope that we will not

---

[1] Letter to Nehru from Yeravda Central Prison, May 2, 1933, in Jawaharlal Nehru, *A Bunch of Old Letters,* p. 110.

[2] Louis Fischer, *The Life of Mahatma Gandhi,* Part II, Chapter 34, p. 310.

callously allow such national tragedy to reach its extreme length Stop Our sorrowing hearts will follow your sublime penance with reverence and love."[3]

Gandhi thanked Tagore for his] loving and magnificent wire. It will sustain me in the midst of the storm I am about to enter.[4]

What my word in person cannot do my fast may. . . .[5]

. . . Under certain circumstances [fasting] is the one weapon which God has given us for use in times of utter helplessness. We do not know its use or fancy that it begins and ends with mere deprivation of physical food. . . . Absence of food is an indispensable but not the largest part of it. The largest part is the prayer—communion with God. It more than adequately replaces physical food.[6]

[There] is no inherent merit in mortification of the flesh.[7]

[As Gandhi's fast continued and he grew physically weaker, fear spread throughout India that he might die.]

It is a wrong thing to rehearse a calamity (an event believed by us to be a calamity, though in fact it may be a blessing) and to reproduce in advance the feelings one would have. It is enough that we hold ourselves prepared for the worst. . . .[8]

I am not aching for martyrdom but if it comes in my way in the prosecution of what I consider to be the supreme duty in defence of the faith I hold . . . I shall have earned it.[9]

[It] is not always a fact that the pain of death is greater for men than the pain of living. It is we ourselves who have made of death a fearful thing. . . .[10]

[People] die only to be born again. Sorrow therefore is entirely uncalled for. . . .[11]

[3] *Ibid.,* p. 310.

[4] *Ibid.,* p. 311.

[5] Nirmal Kumar Bose, *Studies in Gandhism,* Hindi edition.

[6] Letter to Mira Behn from Yeravda, May 8, 1933, in M. K. Gandhi, *Gandhi's Letters to a Disciple,* p. 149.

[7] *Harijan,* November 2, 1935.

[8] Letter to Mira Behn, December 29–30, 1932, in M. K. Gandhi, *Letters to a Disciple,* p. 131.

[9] *Harijan,* June 29, 1934.

[10] Letter to a friend, May 12, 1932, in Mahadev Desai, *The Diary of Mahadev Desai,* p. 110.

[11] Letter to a friend, March 21, 1932, *ibid.,* p. 21.

... It is nature's kindness that we do not remember past births. Where is the good either of knowing in detail the numberless births we have gone through? Life would be a burden if we carried such a tremendous load of memories. A wise man deliberately forgets many things, even as a lawyer forgets the cases and their details as soon as they are disposed of. . . .[12]

... It is well if we live and it is equally well if we die. . . . Somehow or other we refuse to welcome death as we welcome birth. We refuse to believe in the evidence of our senses, that we could not possibly have any attachment for the body without the soul, and we have no evidence whatsoever that the soul perishes with the body.[13]

... The idea that death is not a fearful event has been cherished by me for many a year, so that I recover soon enough from the shock of the deaths even of near and dear ones.[14]

... Both birth and death are great mysteries. If death is not a prelude to another life, the intermediate period is a cruel mockery. We must learn the art of never grieving over death, no matter when and to whom it comes. I suppose that we shall do so when we have really learnt to be utterly indifferent to our own [deaths], and the indifference will come when we are every moment conscious of having done the task to which we are called. . . .[15]

... It is better to leave a body one has outgrown. To wish to see dearest ones as long as possible in the flesh is a selfish desire, and it comes out of weakness or want of faith in the survival of the soul after the dissolution of the body. . . . True love consists in transferring itself from the body to the dweller within and then necessarily realizing the oneness of all life inhabiting numberless bodies. . . .[16]

[The day before the fast started, twelve temples in Allahabad were made accessible to Harijans for the first time. On the first day of the fast some of the most sacred temples throughout the country

[12] Letter to Mira Behn, January 25, 1931, in M. K. Gandhi, *Letters to a Disciple,* p. 87.
[13] Letter to Mira Behn, May 4, 1933, *ibid.,* p. 148.
[14] Letter to X, June 16, 1932, in Mahadev Desai, *Diary,* pp. 167–168.
[15] Letter to Mira Behn, May 18, 1936, in M. K. Gandhi, *Letters to a Disciple,* p. 172.
[16] Letter to Mira Behn, July 6, 1931, *ibid.,* p. 89.

opened their doors to untouchables. Every subsequent day scores of holy places lowered the bars against Harijans.

Mrs. Swarup Rani Nehru, Jawaharlal's very orthodox mother, let it be known that she had accepted food from the hand of an untouchable. Thousands of prominent Hindu women followed her example. At the strictly Hindu Benares University, Principal Dhruva, with numerous Brahmans, dined publicly with street cleaners, cobblers and scavengers. Similar meals were arranged in hundreds of other places.

In villages, small towns and big cities, congregations, organizations, citizens' unions, etc., adopted resolutions promising to stop discriminating against untouchables. Copies of these resolutions formed a man-high heap in Gandhi's prison yard.

Villages and small towns allowed untouchables to use water wells. Hindu pupils shared benches formerly reserved for untouchables. Roads and streets were opened to Harijans.

A spirit of reform, penance and self-purification swept the land. During the six fast days most Hindus refrained from going to cinemas, theaters or restaurants. Weddings were postponed.

As he lay on his cot in prison, Gandhi negotiated with representatives of Hindus and untouchables. Convinced that he had achieved at least some improvement in the lot of the Harijans, he bowed to the entreaties of his friends and agreed to break off the fast.

The fast could not kill the curse of untouchability, which was more than three thousand years old. Access to a temple is not access to a good job. The Harijans remained the dregs of Indian society. Nor did segregation end when Gandhi slowly drank his orange juice. But after the fast untouchability forfeited its public approval. The belief in it was destroyed. A practice full of mystic overtones and undercurrents, deeply imbedded in a complicated religion, was recognized as morally illegitimate. A taboo hallowed by custom, tradition and ritual lost its potency. It had been socially improper to consort with Harijans. In many circles now it became socially improper not to consort with them. To practice untouchability branded one a bigot, a reactionary. Before long, marriages were taking place between Harijans and Hindus; Gandhi made a point of attending some.

Five days after the end of the fast Gandhi's weight had gone up to ninety-nine and three-quarter pounds, and he was spinning and working for many hours.]

The fast was really nothing compared with the miseries that the outcasts have undergone for ages. And so I continue to hum "God is great and merciful."[17] [He remained in prison.]

[17] Letter to Mira Behn, in Louis Fischer, *Life of Gandhi,* Part II, Chapter 34, pp. 320–321.

22

BLUEPRINT FOR A BETTER LIFE

[In February, 1933, Gandhi, still in prison, had started the Harijan Sevak Sangh, a society to help Harijans, and *Harijan,* a new weekly which replaced *Young India,* suspended by the Government.]

. . . The fight against Sanatanists [orthodox Hindus who believe the doctrine of untouchability] is becoming more and more interesting, if also increasingly difficult. The one good thing is that they have been awakened from a long lethargy. The abuses they are hurling at me are wonderfully refreshing. I am all that is bad and corrupt on this earth. But the storm will subside. For I apply the sovereign remedy of ahimsa, nonretaliation. The more I ignore the abuses, the fiercer they are becoming. But it is the death dance of the moth round a lamp. . . .[1]

. . . *Harijan* is a views-paper as distinguished from a newspaper. People buy and read it not for amusement but for instruction and [for] regulating their daily conduct. They literally take their weekly lessons in Non-violence. . . .[2]

[On May 8, Gandhi undertook a three weeks' fast for self-purification and to impress the ashram with the importance of service rather than indulgence—the presence of an attractive American woman visitor had caused some backsliding. The first day of the fast the Government released him. It seemed certain after the physical agony of the seven days of the "Epic Fast" against untouchability that twenty-one days without food would kill him. And Britain did not want a dead Gandhi within prison walls.

He completed the fast and survived.

[1] Letter to Nehru, February 15, 1933, in Jawaharlal Nehru, *A Bunch of Old Letters,* p. 109.
[2] *Harijan,* July 19, 1942.

Throughout his remaining years Gandhi continued to evolve ideas for a better material and spiritual life. These ideas were relevant then and remain relevant for India.]

... Every man has an equal right to the necessaries of life even as birds and beasts have. ...[3]

I hate privilege and monopoly. Whatever cannot be shared with the masses is taboo to me.[4]

[Economic equality] is the master key to non-violent Independence. Working for economic equality means abolishing the eternal conflict between capital and labor. It means the levelling down of the few rich in whose hands is concentrated the bulk of the nation's wealth ... and the levelling up of the semi-starved millions. ... A non-violent system of government is clearly an impossibility so long as the wide gulf between the rich and the hungry millions persists. The contrast between the palaces of New Delhi and the miserable hovels of the poor laboring class nearby cannot last one day in a free India, in which the poor will enjoy the same power as the richest in the land. A violent and bloody revolution is a certainty one day unless there is a voluntary abdication of riches and the power that riches give, and a sharing of them for the common good.[5]

All have not the same capacity. It is in the nature of things, impossible. ... I would allow a man of intellect to earn more, I would not cramp his talent. ...[6]

I want to bring about an equalization of status. The working classes have all these centuries been isolated and relegated to a lower status. ... I want to allow no differentiation between the son of a weaver, of an agriculturist and of a school master.[7]

Complete renunciation of one's possessions is a thing which very few even among ordinary folk are capable of. All that can legitimately be expected of the wealthy class is that they should hold

---

[3] *Young India,* March 26, 1931.

[4] *Harijan,* November 2, 1934.

[5] M. K. Gandhi, *Constructive Program: Its Meaning and Place* (Ahmedabad: Navajivan Publishing House, 1945), second edition, Chapter 13, pp. 20–22.

[6] *Young India,* November 26, 1931.

[7] *Harijan,* January 15, 1938.

their riches and talents in trust and use them for the service of the
society. To insist on more would be to kill the goose that laid the
golden eggs.[8]

... Regard human labor [as] more even than money and you
have an untapped and inexhaustible source of income which ever
increases with use. ...[9]

... Swaraj as conceived of by me does not mean the end of ...
capital. Accumulated capital means ruling power. I am for the
establishment of right relations between capital and labor ... I do
not wish for the supremacy of the one over the other. I do not think
there is any natural antagonism between them. The rich and the
poor will always be with us. ...[10]

I do not believe the capitalists and the landlords are all exploiters
by an inherent necessity or there is a basic or irreconcilable antagonism between their interests and those of the masses. All exploitation
is based on the coöperation, willing or forced, of the exploited. ...[11]

[Destruction] of the capitalist must mean destruction in the end
of the worker, and no human being is so bad as to be beyond
redemption, no human being is so perfect as to warrant his destroying him whom he wrongly considers to be wholly evil.[12]

There is in English a very potent word, and you have it in
French also, all the languages of the world have it—it is "No," and
the secret we have hit upon is that when Capital wants Labor to say
"Yes," Labor roars out "No," if it means "No." And immediately
Labor comes to recognize that it has got its choice of saying "Yes"
when it wants to ... and "No" when it wants to. ... Labor is free
of Capital and Capital has to woo Labor. And it would not matter
in the slightest degree that Capital has guns and even poison gas at
its disposal. Capital would still be perfectly helpless if Labor would
assert its dignity by making good its "No." Labor does not need to

[8] Prayer speech to village work trainees, April 11, 1945. Pyarelal, *Mahatma
Gandhi: The Last Phase* (Ahmedabad: Navajivan Publishing House, 1956), Volume I, Chapter 3, p. 66.

[9] Letter to the British Governor of Bengal, December 8, 1945, M. K. Gandhi,
Gandhiji's Correspondence with the Government, 1944–1947 (Ahmedabad: Navajivan Publishing House, 1959), p. 109.

[10] *Young India,* January 8, 1925.

[11] *The Amrita Bazar Patrika,* August 3, 1934.

[12] *Young India,* March 26, 1931.

retaliate but . . . stand defiant, receiving the bullets and poison gas, and still insist upon its "No." . . . [A] laborer who courts death and has the courage to die without even carrying arms, with no weapon of self-defence, shows a courage of a much higher degree than a man who is armed from top to toe.[13]

. . . Prophets and supermen are born only once in an age. But if even a single individual realizes the ideal of [Non-violence] in its fullness, he covers and redeems the whole society. Once Jesus had blazed the trail, his twelve disciples could carry on his mission without his presence. It needed the perseverance and genius of so many generations of scientists to discover the laws of electricity but today everybody, even children, use electric power in their daily life. Similarly, it will not always need a perfect being to administer an ideal State, once it has come into being. What is needed is a thorough social awakening to begin with. The rest will follow. . . .[14]

Industrialism is, I am afraid, going to be a curse for mankind. Exploitation of one nation by another cannot go on for all time. Industrialism depends entirely on your capacity to exploit, on foreign markets' being open to you and on the absence of competition. . . . And why should I think of industrializing India to exploit other nations? Don't you see the tragedy of the situation—that we can find work for our three hundred millions unemployed but England can find none for its three millions and is faced with a problem that baffles the greatest intellects of England. The future of industrialism is dark. . . . And if the future of industrialism is dark for the West, would it not be darker still for India?[15]

. . . I have no quarrel with steamships or telegraphs. They may stay, if they can, without the support of industrialism and all it connotes. They are not an end. [But] we must not suffer exploitation for the sake of steamships and telegraphs. . . .

. . . To change to industrialism is to court disaster. The present

[13] M. K. Gandhi, *India's Case for Swaraj,* compiled and edited by Waman P. Kabadi (Bombay: Yeshanand & Co., 2nd ed., 1932), p. 393.
[14] In conversation with village workers, 1942, Pyarelal, *The Last Phase,* Volume II, Chapter 21, p. 633.
[15] *Young India,* November 12, 1931.

distress is undoubtedly insufferable. Pauperism must go. But industrialism is no remedy. The evil does not lie in the use of bullock carts. It lies in our selfishness and want of consideration for our neighbors. If we have no love for our neighbors, no change, however revolutionary, can do us any good. And if we love our neighbors, the paupers of India, for their sakes, we shall use what they make for us [homespun cloth], for their sakes we who should know shall not engage in an immoral traffic with the West in the shape of buying the foreign fineries and taking them to the villages.

[The] one great change to make is to discard foreign cloth and reinstate the ancient cottage industry of handspinning. We must thus restore our ancient and healthgiving industry if we would resist industrialism.

I do not fight shy of capital. I fight capitalism. The West teaches one to avoid concentration of capital, to avoid a racial war in another and deadlier form. Capital and Labor need not be antagonistic to each other. I cannot picture to myself a time when no man shall be richer than another. But I do picture to myself a time when the rich will spurn to enrich themselves at the expense of the poor and the poor will cease to envy the rich. Even in a most perfect world, we shall fail to avoid inequalities, but we can and must avoid strife and bitterness. . . .[16]

India's destiny lies not along the bloody way of the West, of which she shows signs of tiredness but along the bloodless way of peace that comes from a simple and godly life. *India is in danger of losing her soul.* She cannot lose it and live. She must not, therefore, lazily and helplessly say, "I cannot escape the onrush from the West." She must be strong enough to resist it for her own sake and that of the world.[17]

. . . I make bold to say that the Europeans themselves will have to remodel their outlook if they are not to perish under the weight of the comforts to which they are becoming slaves.

It may be that my reading is wrong, but I know that for India to run after the Golden Fleece is to court certain death. Let us engrave on our hearts the motto of a Western philosopher, "plain

[16] *Young India,* October 7, 1926.
[17] *Young India,* October 7, 1931.

living and high thinking." Today it is certain that the millions cannot have high living and we the few who profess to do the thinking
for the masses run the risk, in a vain search after high living, of
missing high thinking.[18]

[Those] from the West should not consciously or unconsciously
lay violent hands upon the manners, customs and habits of the
[East] insofar as they are not repugnant to fundamental ethics and
morality.... Tolerate what is good in them and do not hastily,
with your preconceived notions, judge them.... In spite of your
belief in the greatness of Western civilization and in spite of your
pride in all your achievements, I plead with you for humility and
ask you to leave some little room for doubt.... Let us each one live
our life and if ours is the right life, where is the cause for hurry [to
change it]? ...[19]

There is a growing body of enlightened opinion which distrusts
[Western] civilization, which has insatiable material ambition at
one end, and consequent war at the other. But whether good or
bad, why must India become industrial in the Western sense?

The Western civilization is urban. Small countries like England
or Italy may afford to urbanize their systems. A big country like
America with a very sparse population, perhaps cannot do otherwise. But one would think that a big country, with a teeming population [of] an ancient rural tradition which has hitherto answered
its purpose, need not, must not, copy the Western model. What is
good for one nation situated in one condition is not necessarily
good enough for another, differently situated. One man's food is
often another man's poison. Physical geography of a country has a
predominant share in determining its culture. A fur coat may be a
necessity for the dweller in the polar regions, it will smother those
living in the equatorial regions.[20]

... The distinguishing characteristic of modern civilization is
an infinite multiplicity of human wants.... The modern or Western insatiableness arises really from want of a living faith in a
future state, and therefore also in Divinity. The restraint of ancient

[18] *Young India,* April 4, 1931.
[19] Speech to Young Men's Christian Association, Columbo, Ceylon, in *Young
India,* December 8, 1927.
[20] *Young India,* July 25, 1929.

or Eastern civilization arises from a belief, often in spite of ourselves, in a future state and the existence of A Divine Power. . . .[21]

If we are to make progress we must not repeat history but make new history. . . .[22]

[Though mankind] is not all of the same age, the same height, the same skin and the same intellect, these inequalities are temporary and superficial, the soul that is hidden beneath this earthly crust is one and the same for all men and women belonging to all climes. [There] is a real and substantial unity in all the variety that we see around us. The word "inequality" has a bad odor about it, and it has led to arrogance and inhumanities, both in the East and the West. What is true about men is also true about nations, which are but groups of men. . . .

[There] is no such thing as a literal complete revival of ancient tradition possible, even if it were desirable. . . . And I am humble enough to admit that there is much we can profitably assimilate from the West. Wisdom is no monopoly of one continent or one race. My resistance to Western civilization is really a resistance to its indiscriminate and thoughtless imitation based on the assumption that Asiatics are fit only to copy everything that comes from the West. I do believe that if India has patience enough to go through the fire of suffering and to resist any unlawful encroachment upon its own civilization, which imperfect though it undoubtedly is, has hitherto stood the ravages of time, she can make a lasting contribution to the peace and solid progress of the world.[23]

. . . There is nothing to prevent me from profiting by the light that may come out of the West. Only I must take care that I am not overpowered by the glamor of the West. I must not mistake the glamor for true light.[24]

. . . The political domination of England is bad enough. The cultural is infinitely worse. For whilst we resent and therefore endeavor to resist the political domination, we hug the cultural, not

[21] *Young India,* June 2, 1927.
[22] *Young India,* May 6, 1926.
[23] *Young India,* August 11, 1927.
[24] *Harijan,* January 13, 1940.

realizing in our infatuation that when the cultural domination is complete the political will defy resistance. . . .[25]

Mere withdrawal of the English is not independence. It means the consciousness in the average villager that he is the maker of his own destiny, he is his own legislator through his chosen representative.[26]

India became impoverished when our cities became foreign markets and began to drain the villages dry by dumping cheap and shoddy goods from foreign lands.[27]

When I succeed in ridding the villages of their poverty, I have won [Independence].[28]

I would say if the village perishes India will perish too. India will be no more India. . . . The revival of the village is possible only when it is no more exploited. Industrialization on a mass scale will necessarily lead to passive or active exploitation of the villagers as the problems of competition and marketing come in. Therefore we have to concentrate on the village being self-contained, manufacturing mainly for use. Provided this character of the village industry is maintained there would be no objection to villagers using even the modern machines and tools they can make and can afford to use. Only they should not be used as a means of exploitation of others.[29]

What I object to is the "craze" for machinery, not machinery as such. The craze is for what they call labor-saving machinery. Men go on "saving labor" till thousands are without work and thrown on the open streets to die of starvation. I want to save time and labor not for a fraction of mankind but for all, I want the concentration of wealth not in the hands of a few but in the hands of all. Today machinery merely helps a few to ride on the backs of millions. The impetus behind it all is not the philanthropy to save labor but greed. It is against this constitution of things that I am fighting with all my might.

[25] *Young India*, July 9, 1925.

[26] *Young India*, February 13, 1930.

[27] *Harijan*, February 27, 1937.

[28] Louis Fischer, *Mahatma Gandhi: His Life and Message for the World* (New York: New American Library, 1954), Chapter 14, p. 351.

[29] *Harijan*, August 29, 1936.

. . . The supreme consideration is man. The machine should not tend to make atrophied the limbs of man. For instance, I would make intelligent exceptions. Take the case of the Singer Sewing Machine. It is one of the few useful things ever invented and there is a romance about the device itself. Singer saw his wife laboring over the tedious process of sewing and seaming with her own hands and simply out of his love for her he devised the sewing machine in order to save her from unnecessary labor. He, however, saved not only her labor but also the labor of everyone who could purchase a sewing machine.

. . . This mad rush for wealth must cease, and the laborer must be assured not only of a living wage but of a daily task that is not a mere drudgery. The machine will, under these conditions, be as much a help to the man working it as to the State or the man who owns it. . . . The sewing machine had love at its back. . . . The saving of labor of the individual should be the object and the honest humanitarian consideration, and not greed the motive. Replace greed by love and everything will come right.[30]

Pandit Nehru wants industrialization because he thinks that if it is socialized, it would be free from the evils of capitalism. My own view is that the evils are inherent in industrialism, and no amount of socialization can eradicate them.[31]

As a moderately intelligent man, I know man cannot live without industry. Therefore, I cannot be opposed to industrialization. But I have a great concern about introducing machine industry. The machine produces too much too fast, and brings with it a sort of economic system which I cannot grasp. I do not want to accept something when I see its evil effects, which out-weigh whatever good it brings with it. I want the dumb millions of our land to be healthy and happy, and I want them to grow spiritually. As yet, for this purpose we do not need the machine. There are many, too many, idle hands. But as we grow in understanding, if we feel the need of machines, we certainly will have them. We want industry, let us become industrious. Let us become more self-dependent, then we will not follow the other people's lead so much. We shall introduce machines if and when we need them. Once we have

[30] *Young India,* November 13, 1924.
[31] *Harijan,* September 29, 1940.

shaped our life on [Nonviolence], we shall know how to control the machine.[32]

. . . Your "mass production" is . . . production by the fewest possible number through the aid of highly complicated machinery. . . . My machinery must be of the most elementary type, which I can put in the homes of the millions.[33]

There is a difference between the civilization of the East—the civilization of India—and that of the West. It is not generally realized wherein the difference lies. Our geography is different, our history is different, our ways of living are different. Our continent, though vast, is a speck of the globe, but it is the most thickly populated, barring China. Well, now, the economics and civilization of a country where the pressure of population on land is greatest are and must be different from those of a country where the pressure is least. Sparsely populated, America may have need of machinery. India may not need it at all. Where there are millions and millions of units of idle labor, it is no use thinking of labor-saving devices. . . .

Not that there is not enough land. . . . It is absurd to say India is overpopulated and the surplus population must die. . . . Only we have got to be industrious and make two blades of grass grow where one grows today.

The remedy is to identify ourselves with the poor villager and to help him make the land yield its plenty, help him produce what we need and confine ourselves to use what he produces, live as he lives and persuade him to take to more rational ways of diet and living.[34]

Let not capitalists and other entrenched personages range themselves against the poor villagers and prevent them from bettering their hard lot by dignified labor.[35]

["What would happen in a free India?" asked Louis Fischer of Gandhi, visiting him for a week in June, 1942. "What is your program for the improvement of the lot of the peasantry?"]

[32] *Community Service News,* September-October, 1946.
[33] *Harijan,* November 2, 1934.
[34] *Harijan,* November 5, 1935.
[35] *Harijan,* October 27, 1946.

The peasants would take the land. We would not have to tell them to take it. They would take it.

["Would the landlords be compensated?" Fischer asked.]

No. That would be fiscally impossible. You see, [Gandhi smiled] our gratitude to our millionaire friends [who supported Gandhi's ashrams and works] does not prevent us from saying such things. The village would become a self-governing unit living its own life.

["But there would of course be a national government," Fischer said.]

No.

["But surely you need a national administration to direct the railroads, the telegraphs and so on."]

I would not shed a tear if there were no railroads in India.

["But that would bring suffering to the peasant, he needs city goods and he must sell his produce in other parts of the country and abroad. The village needs electricity and irrigation. No single village could build a hydro-electric power station or an irrigation system like the Sukkhar barrage in Sind."]

And that has been a big disappointment [Gandhi interjected]. It has put the whole province in debt.

["I know, but it has brought much new land under cultivation, and it is a boon to the people."]

I realize [Gandhi said shaking his head] that despite my views there will be a central government administration. However, I do not believe in the accepted Western form of democracy with its universal voting for parliamentary representatives.

["What would you have India do?"]

There are seven hundred thousand villages in India. Each would be organized according to the will of its citizens, all of them voting. Then there would be seven hundred thousand votes and not four hundred million. Each village, in other words, would have one vote. The villages would elect their district administrations, and the district administrations would elect the provincial admin-istrations, and these in turn would elect a president who would be the national chief executive.

["That is very much like the Soviet system."]

I did not know that [Gandhi admitted]. I don't mind.[36]

---

[36] Louis Fischer, *A Week with Gandhi*, pp. 55–56.

An ideal Indian village will be so constructed as to lend itself to perfect sanitation. It will have cottages with sufficient light and ventilation built of material obtainable within a radius of five miles of it. The cottages will have courtyards enabling householders to plant vegetables for domestic use and to house their cattle. The village lanes and streets will be free of all avoidable dust. It will have wells according to its needs and accessible to all. It will have houses of worship for all, also a common meeting place, a village common for grazing its cattle, a coöperative dairy, primary and secondary schools in which industrial education will be the central fact, and it will have panchayats [village councils of five persons elected by the people] for settling disputes. It will produce its own grains, vegetables and fruit, and its own [homespun material]. This is roughly my idea of a model village. . . . Given . . . coöperation among the people, almost the whole of the program other than model cottages can be worked out at an expenditure within the means of the villagers . . . without Government assistance. . . . The greatest tragedy is the hopeless unwillingness of the villagers to better their lot.[37]

. . . There will be a compulsory service of village guards who will be selected by rotation from the register maintained by the village. . . . Since there will be no system of punishments in the accepted sense, this panchayat will be the legislature, judiciary and executive combined to operate for its year of office. . . . Here there is perfect democracy based upon individual freedom. The individual is the architect of his own government. . . . He and his village are able to defy the might of a world. For the law governing every villager is that he will suffer death in the defence of his and his village's honor.[38]

We have long been accustomed to think that power comes only through legislative assemblies. I have regarded this belief as a grave error brought about by inertia or hypnotism. A superficial study of British history has made us think that all power percolates to the people from parliaments. The truth is that power resides in the people, and it is entrusted for the time being to those whom they may choose as their representatives. Parliaments have no power or

[37] *Harijan,* January 9, 1937.
[38] *Harijan,* July 26, 1942.

even existence independently of the people. . . . Civil Disobedience is the storehouse of power. Imagine a whole people unwilling to conform to the laws of the legislature, and prepared to suffer the consequences of non-compliance! They will bring the whole legislative and executive machinery to a standstill. The police and the military are of use to coerce minorities, however powerful they may be. But no police or military coercion can bend the resolute will of a people who are out for suffering to the uttermost.[39]

. . . Simple homes from which there is nothing to take away require no policing, the palaces of the rich must have strong guards to protect them. . . . So must huge factories. Rurally organized India will run less risk of foreign invasion than urbanized India, well-equipped with military, naval and air forces.[40]

[If] India is to attain true freedom, and through India the whole world also, then sooner or later the fact must be recognized that people will have to live in villages, not in towns, in huts, not in palaces. [The millions] of people will never be able to live at peace with each other in towns and palaces. They will then have no recourse but to resort to both violence and untruth.

[Without] truth and non-violence there can be nothing but destruction for humanity. We can realize truth and non-violence only in the simplicity of village life . . . I must not fear if the world today is going the wrong way. It may be that India too will go that way and like the proverbial moth, burn itself eventually in the flame round which it dances more and more fiercely. But it is my bounden duty up to my last breath to try to protect India and through India, the entire world from such a doom.[41]

[Gandhi believed the only method of achieving independence was work—welfare work—among the people, which he called "constructive work" or "constructive program."]

[For] such an indefinable thing as Swaraj [Self-Rule] people must have previous training in doing things of [national] interest. Such work must throw together the people and their leaders, whom they would trust implicitly. Trust begotten in the pursuit of

---

[39] M. K. Gandhi, *Constructive Program,* Chapter 1, pp. 8–9.
[40] *Harijan,* December 30, 1939.
[41] Letter to Nehru, October, 1945, in *Bhoodan,* March 26, 1960.

continuous constructive work becomes a tremendous asset at the critical moment. . . . Individual Civil Disobedience among an unprepared people and by leaders not known to or trusted by them is of no avail, and mass Civil Disobedience is an impossibility. . . .[42]

[The] Constructive Program is the truthful and non-violent way of winning Poorna Swaraj [Complete Independence]. . . .

Civil Disobedience, mass or individual, is an aid to Constructive effort and is a full substitute for armed revolt. Training is necessary as well for Civil Disobedience as for armed revolt. Only the ways are different. . . . Training for military revolt means learning the use of arms, ending perhaps in the atomic bomb. For Civil Disobedience it means the Constructive Program.

. . . Political pacts, we know, have been and can be [broken], but personal friendship with individuals cannot be. . . . Such friendships, selfless and genuine, must be the basis for political pacts. . . . [The] men composing the Government are not to be regarded as enemies. To regard them as such will be contrary to the non-violent spirit. Part we must, but as friends.

[The Constructive Program] should prove as absorbing as politics, so called, and platform oratory, and certainly more important and useful.[43]

[It] is necessary to know the place of Civil Disobedience in a nation-wide non-violent effort.

It has three definite functions:

1. It can be effectively offered for the redress of a local wrong.
2. It can be offered without regard to effect, though aimed at a particular wrong or evil, by way of self-immolation in order to rouse local consciousness or conscience. . . .
3. . . . Civil Disobedience can never be directed for a general cause, such as for Independence. The issue must be definite and capable of being clearly understood and within the power of the opponent to yield. . . .

[When] Civil Disobedience is itself devised for the attainment of Independence, previous preparation is necessary, and it has to

---

[42] *Young India,* January 9, 1930.
[43] M. K. Gandhi, *Constructive Program,* Foreword to 1945 edition, p. iii.

be backed by the visible and conscious effort of those who are engaged in the battle. Civil Disobedience is thus a stimulation for the fighters and a challenge to the opponent. . . . Civil Disobedience in terms of Independence without the coöperation of the millions by way of constructive effort is mere bravado and worse than useless.[44]

[Gandhi intended the members of the Congress Party, who took the lead in the independence movement, to carry on the Constructive Program.]

. . . In our country there has been a divorce between labor and intelligence. The result has been stagnation. . . .

[One] ought to learn how to handle and make simple tools. Imagine the unifying and educative effect of the whole nation simultaneously taking part in the processes up to spinning! Consider the levelling effect of the bond of common labor between the rich and the poor.[45]

[Home-spun cloth] to me is the symbol of the unity of Indian humanity, of its economic freedom and equality, and therefore, ultimately, in the poetic expression of Jawaharlal Nehru, "the livery of India's freedom."[46]

Divorce between intelligence and labor has resulted in criminal neglect of the villages. And so, instead of having graceful hamlets dotting the land, we have dung-heaps. The approach to many villages is not a refreshing experience. . . .[47]

. . . Village economy cannot be complete without the essential village industries such as hand-grinding, hand-pounding, soap-making, paper-making, match-making, tanning, oil-pressing, etc. Congressmen can interest themselves in these and, if they are villagers or will settle down in the village, they will give these industries a new life and a new dress. All should make it a point of honor to use only village articles whenever and wherever available. Given the demand, there is no doubt that most of our wants can be sup-

[44] *Ibid.,* Chapter 18, pp. 28–29.
[45] *Ibid.,* Chapter 4, p. 11.
[46] *Ibid.,* p. 12.
[47] *Ibid.,* Chapter 6, p. 15.

plied from our villages. When we have become village-minded, we will not want imitations of the West or machine-made products, but we will develop a true national taste in keeping with the vision of a new India, in which pauperism, starvation and idleness will be unknown.[48]

. . . If India was pulsating with new life, if we were all in earnest about winning independence in the quickest manner possible by truthful and non-violent means, there would not be a leper or beggar in India uncared for and unaccounted for. . . .[49]

[So] far as the Harijans [Children of God—Gandhi's name for the untouchables] are concerned, every Hindu should make common cause with them and befriend them in their awful isolation—such isolation as perhaps the world has never seen in the monstrous immensity one witnesses in India. I know from experience how difficult the task is. But it is part of the task of building the edifice of [Home-rule]. . . .[50]

. . . If we are to reach our goal through non-violent effort, we may not leave to the future government the fate of thousands of men and women who are laboring under the curse of intoxicants and narcotics.

Medical men can make a most effective contribution toward the removal of this evil. They have to discover ways of weaning the drunkard and the opium addict from the curse.

Women and students have a special opportunity in advancing this reform. By many acts of loving service they can acquire on addicts a hold which will compel them to listen to the appeal to give up the evil habit.

Congress [Party] committees can open recreation booths where the tired laborer will rest his limbs, get healthy and cheap refreshments, and find suitable games. All this work is fascinating and uplifting. The non-violent approach to [Self-Rule] is a novel approach. In it old values give place to new. In the violent way such reforms may find no place. Believers in that way, in their impatience and, shall I say, ignorance, put off such things to the day of deliverance.

[48] *Ibid.,* Chapter 5, pp. 14–15.
[49] *Ibid.,* Chapter 17, p. 25.
[50] *Ibid.,* Chapter 2, p. 10.

They forget that lasting and healthy deliverance comes from within—from self-purification. . . .[51]

. . . Congressmen who want to build up the structure of [Self-Rule] from its very foundation dare not neglect the children. Foreign rule has unconsciously, though none the less surely, begun with the children in the field of education. Primary education is a farce designed without regard to the wants of the India of the villages, and for that matter, even of the cities. Basic education links the children, whether of the cities or the villages, to all that is best and lasting in India. It develops both the body and the mind, and keeps the child rooted to the soil with a glorious vision of the future in the realization of which he or she begins to take his or her share from the very commencement of his or her career in school. . . .[52]

[Adult education] has been woefully neglected by Congressmen. Where they have not neglected it, they have been satisfied with teaching illiterates to read and write. If I had charge of adult education, I should begin with opening the minds of the adult pupils to the greatness and vastness of their country. The villager's India is contained in his village. . . . We have no notion of the ignorance prevailing in the villages. The villagers know nothing of foreign rule and its evils. What little knowledge they have picked up fills them with the awe the foreigner inspires. The result is the dread and hatred of the foreigner and his rule. They do not know how to get rid of it. They do not know that the foreigner's presence is due to their own weaknesses and their ignorance of the power they possess to rid themselves of the foreign rule. My adult education means, therefore, first, true political education of the adult by word of mouth. . . . Side by side with the education by mouth will be the literary education. . . .[53]

. . . Congressmen have not felt the call to see that women became equal partners in the fight for [Self-Rule]. They have not realized that woman must be the true helpmate of man in the mission of service. Woman has been suppressed under custom and law, for which man was responsible, and in the shaping of which she had

[51] *Ibid.,* Chapter 3, pp. 10–11.
[52] *Ibid.,* Chapter 7, pp. 15–16.
[53] *Ibid.,* Chapter 8, pp. 16–17.

no hand. . . . But as every right in a non-violent society proceeds from the previous performance of a duty, it follows that rules of social conduct must be framed by mutual coöperation and consultation. They can never be imposed from outside. Men have not realized this truth in its fullness in their behavior toward women. They have considered themselves to be lords and masters . . . instead of . . . friends and co-workers. . . .

. . . Wives should not be dolls and objects of indulgence, but should be treated as honored comrades in common service. To this end, those who have not received a liberal education should receive such instruction as is possible from their husbands. . . .[54]

This is . . . the outcome of conversations I had with some co-workers in Sevagram. . . .

. . . Many people do many things, big and small, without connecting them with Non-violence or Independence. They have then their limited value, as expected. The same man appearing as a civilian may be of no consequence, but appearing in his capacity as General he is a big personage, holding the lives of millions at his mercy. Similarly, the [spinning wheel] in the hands of a poor widow brings a paltry [penny] to her, in the hands of a Jawaharlal it is an instrument of India's freedom. It is the office which gives the [spinning wheel] its dignity. It is the office assigned to the Constructive Program which gives it an irresistible prestige and power.

Such at least is my view. It may be that of a mad man. If it makes no appeal to the Congressman, I must be rejected. For my handling of Civil Disobedience without the Constructive Program will be like a paralyzed hand attempting to lift a spoon.[55]

[54] *Ibid.*, Chapter 9, pp. 17–18.
[55] *Ibid.*, "Conclusion," p. 29.

23

GANDHI ON SOCIALISM AND COMMUNISM

[Gandhi's hostility to violence and untruth, his objection to the omnipotent State, which embodies both, and his economic ideas made him anti-Communist.]

I do not believe . . . that an individual may gain spiritually and those who surround him suffer. . . . I believe in the essential unity of man and . . . of all that lives. Therefore, I believe that if one man gains . . . the whole world gains with him, and if one man fall, the whole world falls to that extent. I do not help opponents without at the same time helping myself and my co-workers. . . .[1]

Bolshevism is the necessary result of modern materialistic civilization. Its insensate worship of matter has given rise to a school which has been brought up to look upon materialistic advancement as the goal of life and which has lost touch with the final things in life. . . . I prophesy that if we disobey the law of the final supremacy of spirit over matter, of liberty and love over brute force, in a few years' time we shall have Bolshevism rampant in this land which was once so holy.[2]

Whilst I have the greatest admiration for the self-denial and spirit of sacrifice of our [Communist] friends, I have never concealed the sharp difference between their method and mine. They frankly believe in violence and all that is in its bosom. . . .

. . . Their one aim is material progress. . . . I want freedom for full expression of my personality. I must be free to build a staircase to Sirius if I want to. . . .[3]

. . . I look upon an increase of the power of the State with the

[1] *Young India,* December 4, 1924.
[2] Louis Fischer, *Mahatma Gandhi: His Life and Message for the World,* Chapter 15, p. 88.
[3] Discussion with Louis Fischer, July, 1946, recorded by Pyarelal, in K. G. Mashruwala, *Gandhi and Marx* (Ahmedabad: Navajivan Publishing House, 1951), Appendix III, p. 109.

greatest fear because, although while apparently doing good by minimizing exploitation, it does the greatest harm to mankind by destroying individuality which lies at the root of all progress. . . .[4]

I do not believe in the doctrine of the greatest good for the greatest number. It means in its nakedness that in order to achieve the supposed good of fifty-one per cent the interest of forty-nine per cent may be, or rather should be, sacrificed. It is a heartless doctrine and has done harm to humanity. The only real, dignified, human doctrine is the greatest good of all, and this can be achieved only by uttermost self-sacrifice.[5]

No action which is not voluntary can be called moral. So long as we act like machines there can be no question of morality. If we want to call an action moral it should have been done consciously and as a matter of duty. Any action that is dictated by fear or by coercion of any kind ceases to be moral.[6]

Democracy and violence can go ill together. The States that are today nominally democratic have either to become frankly totalitarian or, if they are to become truly democratic, they must become courageously nonviolent. It is a blasphemy to say non-violence can be practiced only by individuals and never by nations which are composed of individuals.[7]

I am too conscious of the imperfections of the species to which I belong to be irritated against any member thereof. My remedy is to deal with the wrong wherever I see it, not to hurt the wrong-doer, even as I would not like to be hurt for the wrongs I continually do.[8]

The Communists seem to make trouble-shooting their profession. I have friends among them. Some of them are like sons to me. But it seems they do not make any distinction between fair and foul, truth and falsehood. They deny the charge. But their reported acts seem to sustain it. Moreover, they take their instructions from Rus-

[4] Interview with Nirmal Kumar Bose, 1934, in D. G. Tendulkar, *Mahatma: The Life of Mohandas Karamchand Gandhi,* Volume IV, p. 15.
[5] Letter to an Indian friend, July 4, 1932, in Mahadev Desai, *The Diary of Mahadev Desai*, p. 149.
[6] M. K. Gandhi, *Ethical Religion,* Chapter 3, p. 43.
[7] *Harijan,* November 12, 1938.
[8] *Young India,* March 12, 1930.

sia, whom they regard as their spiritual home . . . I cannot countenance this dependence on an outside power. . . .[9]

[The] means to me are just as important as the goal, and in a
sense more important in that we have some control over them,
whereas we have none over the goal if we lose control over the
means.[10]

Nothing . . . should be done secretly. This is an open rebellion. . . .
A free man would not engage in a secret movement.[11]

[On one of Gandhi's silent Mondays, a group of fifteen "Socialist"
students visited him. Gandhi jotted down replies to their questions
on slips of paper, his practice on days of silence.]

Now tell me how many of you have servants in your homes?
[They said a servant in each home.] And you call yourselves Socialists while you make others slave for you! It is a queer kind of Socialism which, I must say, I cannot understand. If you will listen to me,
I will say, do not involve yourselves in any ism. Study every ism.
Ponder and assimilate what you have read and try to practice yourself what appeals to you out of it. But for heaven's sake, do not set
out to establish any ism. The first step in the practice of Socialism is
to learn to use your hands and feet. It is the only sure way to eradicate violence and exploitation from society. We have no right to talk
of Socialism so long as there is hunger and unemployment and the
distinction between high and low amongst us and around us.[12]

Socialism is a beautiful word and so far as I am aware in Socialism all the members of society are equal—none low, none high. In
the individual's body the head is not high because it is [at] the
top . . . nor are the soles of the feet low because they touch the
earth. Even as members of the individual's body are equal so are
the members of society. . . .

In [Socialism] the prince and the peasant, the wealthy and the
poor, the employer and the employee are all on the same level. . . .

In order to reach this state we may not look on things philosoph-

[9] *Harijan,* October 6, 1946.
[10] Letter to Nehru, August 17, 1934, in Jawaharlal Nehru, *A Bunch of Old Letters,* p. 118.
[11] Speech to a session of the Congress Party, August 8, 1942, in M. K. Gandhi,
Gandhiji's Correspondence with the Government, 1942–1944, p. 147.
[12] Pyarelal, *Mahatma Gandhi: The Last Phase,* Volume II, Chapter 6, p. 133.

ically and say we need not make a move until all are converted to Socialism. . . .

Socialism begins with the first convert. . . .

This Socialism is as pure as crystal. It therefore requires crystal-like means to achieve it. Impure means result in an impure end. Hence the prince and the peasant will not be equalled by cutting off the prince's head nor can the process of cutting off equalize the employer and the employed. One cannot reach truth by untruth-fulness. Truthful conduct alone can reach truth. . . . Harbor impurity of mind or body and you have untruth and violence in you.[13]

[13] *Harijan,* July, 1947.

[24   ]

GANDHI ABOUT HIMSELF

. . . I have never yet copy-righted any of my writings. . . . I dare not be exclusive. . . .[1]

. . . I own no property and yet I feel that I am perhaps the richest man in the world. For I have never been in want either for myself or for my public concerns. God has always and invariably responded in time. . . . It is open to the world, therefore, to laugh at my dispossessing myself of all property. For me the dispossession has been a positive gain. I would like people to compete with me in my contentment. It is the richest treasure I own. . . .[2]

. . . The life I am living is certainly very easy and very comfortable, if ease and comfort are a mental state. I have all I need without the slightest care of having to keep any personal treasures. Mine is a life full of joy in the midst of incessant work. In not wanting to think of what tomorrow will bring for me I feel as free as a bird. . . .[3]

I am a poor mendicant. My earthly possessions consist of six spinning wheels, prison dishes, a can of goat's milk, six homespun loincloths and towels, and my reputation which cannot be worth much.[4]

I do not want to foresee the future. I am concerned with taking care of the present. God has given me no control over the moment following.[5]

[1] *Young India,* March 25, 1926.
[2] *Young India,* April 30, 1925.
[3] *Young India,* October 1, 1925.
[4] Remark to a customs official at Marseilles, September 11, 1931, in D. G. Tendulkar, *Mahatma: The Life of Mohandas Karamchand Gandhi,* Volume III, p. 142.
[5] *Young India,* December 26, 1924.

Having flung aside the sword, there is nothing except the cup of love which I can offer to those who oppose me. It is by offering that cup that I expect to draw them close to me. I cannot think of permanent enmity between man and man, and believing as I do in the theory of rebirth, I live in the hope that if not in this birth, in some other birth, I shall be able to hug all humanity in friendly embrace.[6]

[Prayer] has saved my life. . . . I had my share of the bitterest public and private experiences. They threw me into temporary despair. If I was able to get rid of that despair it was because of prayer. It has not been a part of my life as truth has been. It came out of sheer necessity as I found myself in a plight where I could not possibly be happy without it. And as time went on my faith in God increased and more irresistible became the yearning for prayer. Life seemed to be dull and vacant without it. . . . In spite of despair staring me in the face on the political horizon, I have never lost my peace. . . . That peace comes from prayer. . . . I am indifferent as to the form. Everyone is a law unto himself in that respect. . . . Let everyone try and find that as a result of daily prayer he adds something new to his life.[7]

I am in the world feeling my way to light "amid the encircling gloom." I often err and miscalculate. . . . My trust is solely in God. And I trust men only because I trust God. . . .[8]

. . . It is to me a matter of perennial satisfaction that I retain generally the affection and the trust of those whose principles and policies I oppose. . . .[9]

Differences of opinion should never mean hostility. If they did, my wife and I should be sworn enemies of one another. I do not know two persons in the world who had no difference of opinion and as I am a follower of the Gita I have always attempted to regard those who differ from me with the same affection as I have for my nearest and dearest.[10]

---

[6] *Young India,* April 2, 1931.

[7] At a prayer meeting on board ship to London, 1931, in D. G. Tendulkar, *Mahatma,* Volume III, pp. 139–140.

[8] *Young India,* December 4, 1924.

[9] *Young India,* March 17, 1927.

[10] *Young India,* March 17, 1927.

. . . I have no desire to carry a single soul with me if I cannot appeal to his or her reason.[11]

. . . I do not claim to lead or have any party, if only for the reason that I seem to be constantly changing and shifting my ground. . . . I must respond to varying conditions and yet remain changeless within. I have no desire to drag anybody. My appeal is continuously to the head and heart combined. . . .[12]

. . . The highest honor that my friends can do me is to enforce in their own lives the program I stand for or resist me to their utmost if they do not believe in it. Blind adoration in the age of action is perfectly valueless, is often embarrassing and equally, often painful.[13]

In the majority of cases addresses [compliments] presented to me contain adjectives which I am ill able to carry. . . . They unnecessarily humiliate me for I have to confess I do not deserve them. When they are deserved their use is superfluous. They cannot add to the strength of the qualities possessed by me. They may, if I am not on my guard, easily turn my head. The good a man does is more often than not better left unsaid. Imitation is the sincerest flattery.[14]

When I think of my littleness and my limitations . . . and of the expectations raised about me . . . I become dazed for the moment but I come to myself as soon as I realize these expectations are a tribute not to me, a curious mixture of Jekyll and Hyde, but to the incarnation, however imperfect but comparatively great in me, of the two priceless qualities of truth and non-violence.[15]

Truth to me is infinitely dearer than the "mahatmaship" which is purely a burden. It is my knowledge of my limitations and my nothingness which has so far saved me from the oppressiveness of "mahatmaship." . . .[16]

The Mahatma I must leave to his fate. Though a non-coöperator I shall gladly subscribe to a bill to make it criminal for anybody to call me Mahatma and to touch my feet. . . .[17]

[11] *Young India,* July 14, 1920.
[12] *Young India,* August 20, 1925.
[13] *Young India,* July 12, 1924.
[14] *Young India,* May 21, 1925.
[15] *Young India,* October 8, 1925.
[16] Statement in 1928 in D. G. Tendulkar, *Mahatma,* Volume II, pp. 43–44.
[17] *Young India,* March 17, 1927.

* * *

My soul refuses to be satisfied so long as it is a helpless witness of a single wrong or a single misery. But it is not possible for me, a weak, frail, miserable being, to mend every wrong or to hold myself free of blame for all the wrong I see. The spirit in me pulls one way, the flesh in me pulls in the opposite direction. . . . I cannot attain freedom [from the two forces of spirit and flesh] by a mechanical refusal to act, but only by intelligent action in a detached manner. . . .[18]

. . . Let good news as well as bad pass over you like water over a duck's back. When we hear any, our duty is merely to find out whether any action is necessary, and if it is, to do as an instrument in the hands of Nature without being affected by or attached to the result. . . .[19]

. . . If you work with detachment, you will refuse to be rushed and you will refuse to let anything get on your nerves. . . . You know the story of King Janak [of Hindu scripture]. He was Duty personified. His capital was in flames. He knew it. But some busybody reported it to him. His answer was, "What care I whether my capital is reduced to ashes or remains intact!" He had done all he could to save it. His going to the scene of operations and fussing would have distracted the attention of the fire-brigade and others, and made matters worse. [He] had done his part and was therefore quiet and at ease. So may—must—we be, if we have done our best, whether our work flourishes or perishes.[20]

. . . Time and again in my life, contrary to all wise counsels, I have allowed myself to be guided by the inner voice—often with spectacular success. But success and failure are of no account. [They] are God's concern, not mine.[21]

. . . On the lonesome way of God on which I have set out I need no earthly companions. Let those who will, therefore, denounce me if I am the impostor they imagine me to be though they may not

[18] *Young India,* November 17, 1921.

[19] Letter to Mira Behn, December 13, 1930, in M. K. Gandhi, *Gandhi's Letters to a Disciple,* p. 79.

[20] Letter to Mira Behn, October 19, 1930, *ibid.,* p. 75.

[21] Manu Gandhi, *Eklo Jane Re* (Ahmedabad: Navajivan Publishing House, 1954), p. 181.

say so in so many words. It might disillusion the millions who persist in regarding me as a Mahatma. I must confess the prospect of being so debunked greatly pleases me.[22]

. . . There is a state in life when a man does not need . . . to proclaim his thoughts, much less to show them by outward action. Mere thoughts act. They attain that power. Then it can be said of him that his seeming inaction constitutes his action. . . . My striving is in that direction.[23]

. . . I regard it as self-delusion, if not worse, when a person says he is wearing himself away in service. . . . The body is like a machine requiring to be well-kept for full service. . . . I have not felt ashamed to take the required rest. . . . Rest properly and in due time taken is like the proverbial timely stitch.[24]

You need not worry about my health. . . . I am taking the rest that is possible. B.P. [blood-pressure] is under control. Jumpy, I fear, it will remain unless I lead the forest life and cease all outward activity. But this would be wrong. I must discover the art of living long though full of activity to the end. . . .[25]

. . . In my pursuit after Truth I have discarded many ideas and learnt many new things. Old as I am in age I have no feeling that I have ceased to grow inwardly or that my growth will stop with the dissolution of the flesh. . . .[26]

. . . I am not a perfect being. Why should you see eye to eye with me in my errors? That would be blind faith. Your faith in me should enable you to detect my true error much quicker than a fault-finder. . . . Therefore, you should not paralyze your thought by suppressing your doubts and torturing yourself that you do not agree with my view in particular things. You should . . . pursue the discussion . . . till you have the clearest possible grasp of all my ideals about it.[27]

[22] Conversation with disciples, February 25, 1947, in Pyarelal, *Mahatma Gandhi: The Last Phase,* Volume I, Chapter 23, p. 586.

[23] *Harijan,* October 26, 1947.

[24] Letter to Mira Behn, September 28, 1930, in M. K. Gandhi, *Letters to a Disciple,* pp. 74–75.

[25] Letter to Mira Behn, January 20, 1939, *ibid.,* p. 190.

[26] *Harijan,* April 29, 1933.

[27] Letter to Mira Behn, April 27, 1933, in M. K. Gandhi, *Letters to a Disciple,* p. 145.

I have never made a fetish of consistency. I am a votary of Truth and I must say what I feel and think at a given moment on the question without regard to what I may have said before on it. . . . As my vision get clearer my views must grow clearer with daily practice. . . .[28]

[When] doubts haunt me, when disappointments stare me in the face, and when I see not one ray of light on the horizon, I turn to the Bhagavad Gita and find a verse to comfort me, and I immediately begin to smile in the midst of overwhelming sorrow. My life has been full of external tragedies, and if they have not left any visible and indelible effect on me, I owe it to the teaching of the Bhagavad Gita.[29]

[A new arrival at Gandhi's Ashram in Sevagram was a widow with her nine-year-old son. The boy agreed to attend the Ashram school, but only if Gandhi would visit his hostel first. Gandhi came on a surprise visit, planning to stay only five minutes but remaining forty-five, examining everything.]

The torn bed-sheets should have been patched up or doubled and turned into a quilt, I did much blanket quilting whilst I was in prison in the Transvaal. Such blankets are warm and lasting. . . . Torn rags . . . should be washed and tidily kept. They can be used for patching torn clothes. . . . And, why should not those who have more than their requirement in winter clothing be taught to part with their superfluous clothing to those who are insufficiently provided? . . .

All these may appear to you to be trifles but all big things are made up of trifles. My entire life has been built on trifles. To the extent to which we have neglected to inculcate the importance of little things on our boys, we have failed, or rather . . . I have failed. . . .

If you tell me that in this way you cannot do justice to more than one or two boys, I will say, "Then have one or two only and no more." By undertaking more than we can properly manage, we introduce into our soul the taint of untruth.[30]

I teach the children under my care not by being angry with

[28] *Harijan,* September 28, 1934.
[29] *Young India,* August 6, 1925.
[30] Pyarelal, *Last Phase,* Volume I, Chapter 6, p. 141.

them, but I teach them, if at all, by loving them, by allowing for their ignorance, and by playing with them. . . .[31]

I can truthfully say I am slow to see the blemishes of fellow beings, being myself full of them and therefore being in need of their charity. I have learnt not to judge any one harshly and to make allowances for defects that I may detect.[32]

Somehow I am able to draw the noblest in mankind and that is what enables me to maintain my faith in God and human nature.[33]

When I was a little child there used to be two blind performers in Rajkot. One of them was a musician. When he played on his instrument, his fingers swept the strings with an unerring instinct and everybody listened spellbound to his playing. Similarly there are chords in every human heart. If we only knew how to strike the right chord, we would bring out the music.[34]

. . . My work will be finished if I succeed in carrying conviction to the human family that every man or woman, however weak in body, is the guardian of his or her self-respect and liberty. This defence avails though the whole world may be against the individual resister.[35]

. . . I am an irrepressible optimist, because I believe in myself. That sounds very arrogant, doesn't it? But I say it from the depths of my humility. . . . I am an optimist because I expect many things from myself. I have not got them, I know, as I am not yet a perfect being. . . . I want to attain that perfection by service.[36]

Whenever I see an erring man, I say to myself I have also erred, when I see a lustful man I say to myself so was I once, and in this way I feel kinship with everyone in the world and feel that I cannot be happy without the humblest of us being happy.[37]

. . . We must feel one with all. And I have discovered that we never give without receiving consciously or unconsciously. There is

[31] *Young India,* October 21, 1926.
[32] *Harijan,* March 11, 1939.
[33] *Harijan,* April 15, 1939.
[34] *Harijan,* May 27, 1939.
[35] Statement made August 5, 1944, on the second anniversary of the "Quit India" movement, in D. G. Tendulkar, *Mahatma,* Volume VI, p. 336.
[36] Address to Anglo-Indians, in *Young India,* August 13, 1925.
[37] *Young India,* February 10, 1927.

a reserve which I want us all to have. But that reserve must be a fruit of self-denial, not sensitiveness. . . .[38]

Whenever you are in doubt, or when the self becomes too much with you, apply the following test. Recall the face of the poorest and the weakest man whom you may have seen, and ask yourself if the step you contemplate is going to be of any use to *him*. Will he gain anything by it? Will it restore him? . . . Then you will find your doubts and . . . self melting away.[39]

Q. [Gandhi] Do you want compliments?

A. [Louis Fischer: Don't we all?]

[Gandhi] Yes, but sometimes we have to pay too dearly for them.[40]

The purpose of life is undoubtedly to know oneself. We cannot do it unless we learn to identify ourselves with all that lives. The sum-total of that life is God. . . . The instrument of this knowledge is boundless, selfless service.[41]

This is enough for the man who is true to himself: Do not undertake anything beyond your capacity and at the same time do not harbor the wish to do less than you can. One who takes up tasks beyond his powers is proud and attached, on the other hand one who does less than he can is a thief. If we keep a time-table we can save ourselves from this last-mentioned sin indulged in even unconsciously. . . .[42]

[Learning Bengali, Gandhi drew squares on his notebook for the writing exercises.]

That is how my teacher used to teach us to draw characters of the alphabet. It is an excellent method. People think one ceases to be a student when his school days are over. With me it is the other way about. I hold that so long as I live, I must have a student's inquiring mind and thirst for learning.[43]

[38] Letter to Mira Behn, January 3, 1927, in M. K. Gandhi, *Letters to a Disciple,* p. 22.

[39] Pyarelal, *Last Phase,* Volume I, Chapter 3, p. 65.

[40] Talk with Louis Fischer, June 5, 1942, in Louis Fischer, *A Week with Gandhi*, p. 39.

[41] Letter to an English friend, Muriel Lester, June 21, 1932, in Mahadev Desai, *The Diary of Mahadev Desai,* p. 184.

[42] Letter to Narandas Gandhi, July 10, 1932, *ibid.,* p. 221.

[43] Manu Gandhi's Diary, February 2, 1947.

[Sometimes] Art lies in not interfering with Nature's unevenness and irregular curves and lines. Fancy hammering the earth into a perfect sphere! Perhaps then we should cease to be. . . .[44]

. . . My room may have blank walls and I may even dispense with the roof so I may gaze out upon the starry heavens overhead that stretch in an unending expanse of beauty. What conscious art of man can give me the panoramic scenes that open out before me when I look up to the sky above with all its shining stars? This, however, does not mean I refuse to accept the value of productions of Art . . . but only that I personally feel how inadequate these are compared with the eternal symbols of beauty in Nature. . . .[45]

. . . When we look at the sky we have a conception of infinity, cleanliness, orderliness and grandeur which is purifying for us. Man may land on planets and stars and find life there is much the same as on earth But their beauty radiates ineffable peace from a distance. . . .[46]

If I had no sense of humor I should long ago have committed suicide.[47]

It is not that I am incapable of anger, for instance, but I succeed on almost all occasions to keep my feelings under control. . . . Such a struggle leaves one stronger. . . . The more I work at this law the more I feel the delight in my life, the delight in the scheme of the universe. It gives me a peace and a meaning of the mysteries of Nature that I have no power to describe.

It takes a fairly strenuous course of training to attain to a mental state of non-violence. In daily life it has to be a course of discipline, though one may not like it, for instance, the life of a soldier. But . . . unless there is hearty coöperation of the mind, a mere outward observance will be simply a mask, harmful both to the man himself and others. The perfect state is reached only when mind and body and speech are in proper coördination. But it is always a case of intense mental struggle.[48]

[44] Letter to Rajkumari Amrit Kaur, February 24, 1936.
[45] *Young India,* November 13, 1924.
[46] Letter to a disciple from Yeravda Jail, July 24, 1932, in Mahadev Desai, *Diary,* p. 252.
[47] *Young India,* August 18, 1921.
[48] *Young India,* October 1, 1931.

. . . The sexual sense is the hardest to overcome in my case. It has been an incessant struggle. It is for me a miracle how I have survived it. The one I am engaged in may be, ought to be, the final struggle.[49]

My darkest hour was when I was in Bombay a few months ago. It was the hour of my temptation. Whilst I was asleep I suddenly felt as though I wanted to see a woman. Well a man who had tried to rise superior to the instinct for nearly forty years was bound to be intensely pained when he had this frightful experience. I ultimately conquered the feeling, but I was face to face with the blackest moment of my life and if I had succumbed to it, it would have meant my absolute undoing. . . .[50]

[In a letter of encouragement to Dr. P. C. Roy, Gandhi describes himself.]

It is nonsense for you to talk of old age so long as you outrun young men in the race for service and in the midst of anxious times fill rooms with your laughter and inspire youth with hope when they are on the brink of despair.[51]

[To another friend, Rajkumari Amrit Kaur, he offered caution.]

I don't like this persistent sadness about you. It is so inconsistent with faith in God, faith in human nature, faith in unbreakable friendship. However, enough of argument. The sadness will go in time. . . .[52]

. . . There is nothing that wastes the body like worry, and one who has any faith in God should be ashamed to worry about anything whatsoever. It is a difficult rule, no doubt, for the simple reason that faith in God with the majority of mankind is either an intellectual belief or a blind belief, a kind of superstitious fear of something indefinable. . . .[53]

. . . What is the value of "working for our own schemes" when they might be reduced to naught in the twinkling of an eye, or

[49] Letter to Rajkumari Amrit Kaur, May 7, 1938.
[50] *Harijan,* December 26, 1936.
[51] Yeravda Jail, May 22, 1932, in Mahadev Desai, *Diary,* p. 124.
[52] Letter to Rajkumari Amrit Kaur, July 21, 1939.
[53] *Young India,* September 1, 1927.

when we may be equally swiftly and unawares taken away from them? But we may feel strong as a rock if we could truthfully say, "We work for God and His schemes." Then all is as clear as daylight. Then nothing perishes. . . . Death and destruction have *then* . . . no reality about them. For death or destruction is then but a change. An artist destroys his picture for creating a better one. A watchmaker throws away a bad spring to put in a new and useful one.[54]

My imperfections and failures are as much a blessing from God as my successes and my talents. . . . Why should He have chosen me, an imperfect instrument, for such a mighty experiment? I think He deliberately did so. He had to serve the poor dumb ignorant millions. A perfect man might have been their despair. When they found that one with their failings was marching on towards Ahimsa [the practice of love] they too had confidence in their own capacity. . . .[55]

Man often becomes what he believes himself to be. If I keep on saying to myself that I *cannot* do a certain thing, it is possible that I may end by really becoming incapable of doing it. On the contrary, if I have the belief that I *can* do it, I shall surely acquire the capacity to do it, even if I may not have it at the beginning.[56]

There is no such thing as "Gandhism" and I do not want to leave any sect after me. I do not claim to have originated any new principle or doctrine. I have simply tried in my own way to apply the eternal truths to our daily life and problems. . . . The opinions I have formed and the conclusions I have arrived at are not final, I may change them tomorrow. . . . All I have done is to try experiments in [Truth and Non-violence] on as vast a scale as I could. . . . I have sometimes erred and learnt by my errors. . . . By instinct I have been truthful but not non-violent. . . . [It] was in the course of my pursuit of truth that I discovered non-violence. . . .

Well, all my philosophy, if it may be called by that pretentious name, is contained in what I have said. But you will not call it "Gandhism," there is no "ism" about it. And no elaborate literature or propaganda is needed about it. . . . Those who believe in the

---

[54] *Young India,* September 23, 1926.
[55] *Harijan,* July 21, 1940.
[56] *Harijan,* September 1, 1940.

simple truths I have laid down can propagate them only by living them. . . .[57]

If I can say so without arrogance and with due humility, my message and methods are, indeed, in their essentials for the whole world and it gives me keen satisfaction to know they have already received a wonderful response in the hearts of a large and daily growing number of men and women in the West.[58]

[57] D. G. Tendulkar, *Mahatma,* Volume IV, pp. 66–67.
[58] *Young India,* September 17, 1925.

GANDHI'S ADVICE
TO NEGROES

[Gandhi usually asked his American visitors about the treatment of Negroes in the United States. American Negroes were among his visitors and correspondents.]

A civilization is to be judged by its treatment of minorities.[1]

[A group of American Negroes sent Gandhi a telegram of encouragement, to which he replied in *Young India:*]

Theirs is perhaps a task more difficult than ours. But they have some very fine workers among them. Many students of history consider that the future is with them. They have a fine physique. They have a glorious imagination. They are as simple as they are brave. Monsieur Finot has shown by his scientific researches that there is in them no inherent inferiority. . . . All they need is opportunity. I know that if they have caught the spirit of the Indian movement [the spirit of non-violence] their progress must be rapid.[2]

[It] may be through the Negroes that the unadulterated message of Non-violence will be delivered to the world.

[Discussing Non-violence with Gandhi, Dr. Howard Thurman, a Negro minister and writer, asked him, "How are we to train individuals or communities in this difficult art?"]

There is no royal road, except through living the creed in your life. . . . If for mastering of the physical sciences you have to devote a whole lifetime, how many lifetimes may be needed for mastering the greatest spiritual force that mankind has known? But why

---

[1] Louis Fischer, *The Life of Mahatma Gandhi,* Part II, Chapter 43, p. 425.
[2] *Young India,* August 21, 1924.

GANDHI'S ADVICE TO NEGROES

worry even if it means several lifetimes? For, if this is the only permanent thing in life, if this is the only thing that counts, then whatever effort you bestow on mastering it is well-spent. . . .[3]

If you feel humiliated [by a bully, for example] you will be justified in slapping [him] in the face or taking whatever action you
might deem necessary to vindicate your self-respect. The use of
force, in the circumstance, would be the natural consequence if you
are not a coward. But if you have assimilated the non-violent spirit,
there should be no feeling of humiliation in you. Your non-violent
behavior should then either make the bully feel ashamed of himself
and prevent the insult, or make you proof against it, so that the
insult would remain . . . in the bully's mouth and not touch you
at all.

. . . Non-violence . . . is not a mechanical thing. You do not
become non-violent by merely saying, "I shall not use force." It
must be felt in the heart. . . . When there is that feeling it will
express itself through some action. It may be a sign, a glance, even
silence. But, such as it is, it will melt the heart of the wrong-doer
and check the wrong.[4]

. . . Supposing I was a Negro and my sister was ravished by a
white or lynched by a whole community, what would be my
duty?—I ask myself. And the answer comes to me: I must not wish
ill to these but neither must I coöperate with them. It may be that
ordinarily I depend on the lynching community for my livelihood.
I refuse to coöperate with them, refuse even to touch the food that
comes from them and I refuse to coöperate with even my brother
Negroes who tolerate the wrong. . . .[5]

[Persecution of the Indians and Negroes in South Africa by the
whites never ceased to arouse Gandhi's indignation.]

. . . South Africa has many wise men and women. . . . It will be
a tragedy for the world if they do not rise superior to their debilitat-
ing surroundings and give a proper lead to their country on this

[3] *Harijan,* March 14, 1936.
[4] *Harijan,* March 9, 1940.
[5] Talk with Dr. Howard Thurman in 1936, in D. G. Tendulkar, *Mahatma: The
Life of Mohandas Karamchand Gandhi,* Volume IV, p. 61.

vexed and vexing problem of White supremacy. Is it not by this time a played out game?[6]

The real "White Man's Burden" is not insolently to dominate colored or black people under the guise of protection, it is to desist from the hypocrisy which is eating into them. It is time white men learnt to treat every human being as their equal. There is no mystery about whiteness of the skin. It has repeatedly been proved than given equal opportunity, a man, be he of any color or country, is fully equal to any other.

Therefore, white men throughout the world . . . should act upon their fellow-men in South Africa . . . "Do unto others as you would that they should do unto you." Or, do they take in vain the name of Him who said this? Have they banished from their hearts the great colored Asiatic who gave to the world the above message? Do they forget that the greatest of the teachers of mankind were all Asiatics and did not possess a white face? These, if they descended on earth and went to South Africa, will all have to live in the segregated areas and be classed as Asiatics and colored people unfit by law to be equals of Whites.

Is a civilization worth the name which requires for its existence the very doubtful prop of racial legislation and lynch law? . . .[7]

Those who agree that racial inequality must be removed and yet do nothing to fight the evil are impotent. I cannot have anything to say to such people. After all, the underdogs will have to earn their own salvation.[8]

. . . If you think of the vast size of Africa, the distance and natural obstacles separating its various parts, the scattered condition of its people and the terrible divisions among them, the task might well appear to be hopeless. But there is a charm which can overcome all these handicaps.

The moment the slave resolves that he will no longer be a slave, his fetters fall. He frees himself and shows the way to others. Free-

[6] Prayer speech, November 17, 1947, M. K. Gandhi, *Delhi Diary* (Ahmedabad: Navajivan Publishing House, 1948), Chapter 67, p. 178.

[7] *Harijan,* June 30, 1946.

[8] Interview on All-India Radio, October 23, 1947. Government of India Information Service, Washington, D.C., Bulletin No. 3531.

dom and slavery are mental states. Therefore, the first thing is to say to yourself: "I shall no longer accept the role of a slave. I shall not obey orders as such but shall disobey them when they are in conflict with my conscience." The so-called master may lash you and try to force you to serve him. You will say: "No, I will not serve you for your money or under a threat." This may mean suffering. Your readiness to suffer will light the torch of freedom which can never be put out.[9]

[9] Talk with university-educated Negro soldiers from West Africa in *Harijan,* February 24, 1946.

[26]

LOVE VERSUS WAR AND DICTATORS

[Gandhi's correspondence with children gave him much joy, and he attended to it with the same devotion and care that he showed all his work. A little girl once wrote him: "We are working to prevent war and making posters. God bless you." Gandhi gave this reply:]

I was delighted to have your sweet notes with funny drawings made by you. . . . Yes, it is little children like you who will stop all war. This means that you never quarrel with other boys and girls or among yourselves. You cannot stop big wars if you carry on little wars yourselves. . . . May God bless you all. My kisses to you all if you will let me kiss you. . . .[1]

. . . It is a trite saying that one half the world knows not how the other lives. Who can say what sores might be healed, what hurts solved, were the doings of each half of the world's inhabitants understood and appreciated by the other?[2]

War with all its glorification of brute force is essentially a degrading thing. It demoralizes those who are trained for it. It brutalizes men of naturally gentle character. It outrages every beautiful canon of morality. Its path of glory is foul with the passions of lust, and red with the blood of murder. This is not the pathway to our goal. The grandest aid to development of strong, pure, beautiful character which is our aim, is the endurance of suffering. Self-restraint, unselfishness, patience, gentleness, these are the flowers

[1] Entry for August 24, 1932, in Mahadev Desai, *The Diary of Mahadev Desai,* pp. 308–309.
[2] *Indian Opinion,* June 2, 1906.

which spring beneath the feet of those who accept but refuse to impose suffering. . . .[3]

A pacifism which can see the cruelties only of occasional military warfare and is blind to the continuous cruelties of our social system is worthless. Unless our pacifism finds expression in the broad human movement which is seeking not merely the end of war but our equally non-pacifist civilization as a whole, it will be of little account in the onward march of mankind. The spirit of life will sweep on, quite uninfluenced by it.[4]

Immediately the spirit of exploitation is gone armaments will be felt as a positively unbearable burden. Real disarmament cannot come unless the nations of the world cease to exploit one another.[5]

A society which anticipates and provides for meeting violence with violence will either lead a precarious life or create big cities and magazines for defence purposes. It is not unreasonable to presume from the state of Europe that its cities, its monster factories and huge armaments are so intimately interrelated that the one cannot exist without the other.[6]

Even if Hitler was so minded, he could not devastate seven hundred thousand non-violent villages. He would himself become non-violent in the process.[7]

[As Gandhi watched the darkness advance during the 1930's across China, Abyssinia, Spain, Czechoslovakia and above all, Germany, his zeal for pure pacifism grew. He saw the Second World War approaching.]

. . . I have the unquenchable faith that, of all the countries in the world, India is the one country which can learn the art of non-violence, that if the test were applied even now, there would be found, perhaps, thousands of men and women who would be willing to die without harboring malice against their persecutors. I have harangued crowds and told them repeatedly that they might

---

[3] *Indian Opinion,* February 12, 1910.
[4] *Young India,* November 18, 1926.
[5] *Harijan,* November 12, 1938.
[6] *Harijan,* January 13, 1940.
[7] *Harijan,* November 4, 1939.

have to suffer much, including death by shooting. Did not thousands of men and women brave hardships during the salt campaign equal to any that soldiers are called upon to bear? No different capacity is required from what has been already evinced, if India has to contend against an invader. Only it will have to be on vaster scale.

One thing ought not to be forgotten. India unarmed would not require to be destroyed through poison gas or bombardment. . . . Free India can have no enemy. And if her people have learnt the art of saying resolutely "No" and acting up to it, I daresay no one would want to invade her. Our economy would be modelled as to prove no temptation for the exploiter.

. . . The world is looking for something new and unique from India. . . .

. . . For India to enter into the race for armaments is to court suicide. With the loss of India to non-violence the last hope of the world will be gone. . . .[8]

. . . I believe that Independent India can discharge her duty towards a groaning world only by adopting a simple but ennobled life by developing her thousands of cottages and living at peace with the world.

Whether such plain living is possible for an isolated nation, however large geographically and numerically in the face of a world armed to the teeth, and in the midst of pomp and circumstance, is a question open to the doubt of a skeptic. The answer is straight and simple. If plain life is worth living, then the attempt is worth making, even though only an individual or a group makes the effort.[9]

Several letters have been received by me asking me to declare my views about the Arab-Jew question in Palestine and the persecution of the Jews in Germany. It is not without hesitation that I venture to offer my views on this very difficult question.

My sympathies are all with the Jews. I have known them intimately in South Africa. Some of them became lifelong compan-

[8] *Harijan,* October 14, 1939.
[9] *Harijan,* September 1, 1946.

ions. Through these friends I came to learn much of their age-long persecution. They have been the untouchables of Christianity. The parallel between their treatment by Christians and the treatment of untouchables by Hindus is very close. Religious sanction has been invoked in both cases for the justification of the inhuman treatment meted out to them. . . .

But my sympathy does not blind me to the requirements of justice. The cry for a national home for the Jews does not make much appeal to me. . . . Why should they not, like other peoples of the earth, make that country their home where they are born and where they earn their livelihood?

The nobler course would be to insist on a just treatment of the Jews wherever they are born and bred. The Jews born in France are French in precisely the same sense that Christians born in France are French. If the Jews have no home but Palestine, will they relish the idea of being forced to leave the other parts of the world in which they are settled? . . .

But the German persecution of the Jews seems to have no parallel in history. . . .

Germany is showing to the world how efficiently violence can be worked when it is not hampered by any hypocrisy or weakness masquerading as humanitarianism. It is also showing how hideous, terrible and terrifying it looks in its nakedness.

Can the Jews resist this organized and shameless persecution? Is there a way to preserve their self-respect, and not to feel helpless, neglected and forlorn? I submit there is. . . . If I were a Jew and were born in Germany and earned my livelihood there, I would claim Germany as my home even as the tallest gentile German might, and challenge him to shoot me or cast me in the dungeon; I would refuse to be expelled or to submit to discriminating treatment. And for doing this I should not wait for the fellow-Jews to join me in civil resistance, but would have confidence that in the end the rest were bound to follow my example. If one Jew or all the Jews were to accept the prescription here offered, he or they cannot be worse off than now. And suffering voluntarily undergone will bring them an inner strength and joy which no number of resolutions of sympathy passed in the world outside Germany can. . . .

. . . I am convinced that, if someone with courage and vision can arise among them to lead them in non-violent action, the winter of their despair can in the twinkling of an eye be turned into the summer of hope. And what has today become a degrading manhunt can be turned into a calm and determined stand offered by unarmed men and women possessing the strength of suffering given to them by Jehovah. It will be then a truly religious resistance offered against the Godless fury of dehumanized man. The German Jews will score a lasting victory over the German gentiles in the sense that they will have converted the latter to an appreciation of human dignity. They will have rendered service to fellow-Germans and proved their title to be the real Germans as against those who are today dragging, however unknowingly, the German name into the mire.

And now a word to the Jews in Palestine. I have no doubt that they are going about things in the wrong way. The Palestine of the Biblical conception is not a geographical tract. It is in their hearts. But if they must look to the Palestine of geography as their national home, it is wrong to enter it under the shadow of the British gun. A religious act cannot be performed with the aid of the bayonet or the bomb. They can settle in Palestine only by the goodwill of the Arabs. They should seek to convert the Arab heart. They can offer Satyagraha in front of the Arabs and offer themselves to be shot or thrown into the Dead Sea without raising a little finger against them. They will find the world opinion in their favor in their religious aspiration. There are hundreds of ways of reasoning with the Arabs, if they will only discard the help of the British bayonet. As it is, they are co-sharers with the British in despoiling a people who have done no wrong to them.

. . . Every country is their home, including Palestine, not by aggression but by loving service. . . .[10]

. . . If [the Jewish people] were to adopt the matchless weapon of non-violence, whose use their best prophets have taught and which Jesus the Jew who gladly wore the crown of thorns bequeathed to a groaning world, their case would be the world's, and I have no doubt that among the many things the Jews have given to the world, this would be the best and the brightest. It is twice blessed.

[10] *Harijan,* November 26, 1938.

It will make them happy and rich in the true sense of the word, and it will be a soothing balm to the aching world.[11]

. . . I happen to have a Jewish friend [Herman Kallenbach, who purchased the farm for Gandhi's first ashram in South Africa] living with me. He has an intellectual belief in non-violence. But he says he cannot pray for Hitler. He is so full of anger over the German atrocities that he cannot speak of them with restraint. I do not quarrel with him over his anger. He wants to be non-violent, but the sufferings of his fellow-Jews are too much for him to bear. What is true of him is true of thousands of Jews who have no thought even of "loving the enemy." With them, as with millions, "revenge is sweet, to forgive is divine."[12]

It is no non-violence if we love merely those that love us. It is non-violence only when we love those that hate us. I know how difficult it is to follow this grand law of love. But are not all great and good things difficult to do? . . .[13]

. . . Human nature will find itself only when it fully realizes that to be human it has to cease to be beastly or brutal. . . .[14]

A violent man's activity is most visible, while it lasts. But it is always transitory. . . . Hitler . . . Mussolini . . . and Stalin . . . are able to show the immediate effectiveness of violence. . . . But the effects of Buddha's non-violent action persist and are likely to grow with age. And the more it is practiced, the more effective and inexhaustible it becomes, and ultimately the whole world stands agape and exclaims, "A miracle has happened." All miracles are due to the silent and effective working of invisible force. Non-violence is the most invisible and the most effective.[15]

Belief in non-violence is based on the assumption that human nature in the essence is one and therefore unfailingly responds to the advances of love. . . .

How can non-violence combat aerial warfare, seeing that there are no personal contacts? The reply to this is that behind the death-

[11] *Harijan,* July 21, 1946.
[12] *Harijan,* February 18, 1939.
[13] Letter to a friend, December 31, 1934, in Nirmal Kumar Bose, *Selections from Gandhi,* p. 18.
[14] *Harijan,* October 8, 1938.
[15] *Harijan,* March 20, 1937.

dealing bomb there is the human hand that releases it, and behind that still is the human heart that sets the hand in motion. And at the back of the policy of terrorism is the assumption that terrorism if applied in a sufficient measure will produce the desired result, namely, bend the adversary to the tyrant's will. But supposing a people make up their mind that they will never do the tyrant's will, nor retaliate with the tyrant's own methods, the tyrant will not find it worth his while to go on with his terrorism. . . .[16]

. . . If some other country resorts to methods which I consider to be inhuman, I may not follow them. . . . The caliphs [heads of Islam] issued definite instructions to the armies of Islam that they should not destroy the utility services, they should not harass the aged and women and children, and I do not know that the arms of Islam suffered any disaster because the armies obeyed these instructions.[17]

. . . I see neither bravery nor sacrifice in destroying life or property for offence or defence. I would far rather leave, if I must, my crops and homestead for the enemy to use than destroy them for the sake of preventing their use by him. There is reason, sacrifice and even bravery in so leaving my homestead and crops if I do so not out of fear, but because I refuse to regard anyone as my enemy. . . .[18]

[One who believes in violence will wish God "to save the King, scatter his enemies, frustrate their knavish tricks"—as in the British national anthem.] If God is the Incarnation of Mercy, He is not likely to listen to such prayer but it cannot but affect the minds of those who sing it, and in times of war it simply kindles their hatred and anger to white heat. [But the soldier of non-violence] may give the supposed enemy a sense of right, and bless him. His prayer for himself will always be that the spring of compassion in him may ever be flowing, and that he may ever grow in moral strength so that he may face death fearlessly.[19]

. . . We have to live and move and have our being in [non-violence], even as Hitler does in [violence]. . . . Hitler is awake all

[16] *Harijan,* December 24, 1938.
[17] *Harijan,* May 24, 1942.
[18] *Harijan,* March 22, 1942.
[19] *Harijan,* October 13, 1940.

the twenty-four hours of the day in perfecting his [practices]. He wins because he pays the price.[20]

[Dictators] have up to now always found ready response to the violence they have used. Within their experience, they have not come across organized non-violent resistance on an appreciable scale, if at all. Therefore, it is not only highly likely, but . . . inevitable, that they would recognize the superiority of non-violent resistance over any display of violence that they may be capable of putting forth.

. . . Supposing a people make up their mind they will never do the tyrant's will, nor retaliate with the tyrant's own methods, the tyrant will not find it worth his while to go on with his terrorism. If sufficient food is given to the tyrant, a time will come when he will have more than his surfeit. If all the mice in the world held conference together and resolved that they would no more fear the cat but all run into her mouth, the mice would live.[21]

[While their country was being invaded, non-violent resisters] would offer themselves unarmed as fodder for the aggressor's cannon. . . . The unexpected spectacle of endless rows upon rows of men and women simply dying rather than surrender to the will of an aggressor must ultimately melt him and his soldiery.[22]

Who enjoys the freedom [afterward] when whole divisions of armed soldiers rush into a hailstorm of bullets to be mown down? But in the case of non-violence, everybody seems to start with the assumption that the non-violent method must be set down as a failure unless he himself at least lives to enjoy the success thereof. This is both illogical and invidious. In Satyagraha [Soul-Force] more than in armed warfare, it may be said that we find life by losing it.[23]

. . . We are discussing a final substitute for armed conflict called war, in naked terms, mass murder.[24]

The science of war leads one to dictatorship pure and simple. The science of non-violence alone can lead on to pure democracy.[25]

[20] *Harijan,* July 21, 1940.
[21] *Harijan,* December 24, 1938.
[22] *Harijan,* April 13, 1940.
[23] *Harijan,* July 28, 1940.
[24] *Harijan,* May 12, 1946.
[25] *Harijan,* October 15, 1938.

... Where a whole nation is militarized the way of military life becomes part and parcel of its civilization.[26]

I believe all war to be wholly wrong. But if we scrutinize the motives of two warring parties, we may find one to be in the right and the other in the wrong. For instance, if A wishes to seize B's country, B is obviously the wronged one. Both fight with arms. I do not believe in violent warfare but all the same B, whose cause is just, deserves my moral help and blessings.[27]

My resistance to war does not carry me to the point of thwarting those who wish to take part in it. I reason with them. I put before them the better way and leave them to make the choice.[28]

The present war is the saturation point in violence. It spells to my mind also its doom. Daily I have testimony of the fact that [non-violence] was never before appreciated by mankind as it is today. . . .[29]

["How would you meet the atom bomb . . . with non-violence?" Margaret Bourke-White, on assignment for *Life* magazine, asked Gandhi on January 30, 1948, a few hours before he was assassinated.]

I will not go underground. I will not go into shelter. I will come out in the open and let the pilot see I have not a trace of ill-will against him. The pilot will not see our faces from his great height, I know. But the longing in our hearts—that he will not come to harm—would reach up to him and his eyes would be opened. If those thousands who were done to death in Hiroshima, if they had died with that prayerful action . . . their sacrifice would not have gone in vain.[30]

[Non-violence] is the only thing the atom bomb cannot destroy. I did not move a muscle when I first heard that an atom bomb had wiped out Hiroshima. On the contrary, I said to myself, "Unless the world adopts non-violence, it will spell certain suicide for mankind."[31]

[26] *Harijan,* March 1, 1942.
[27] *Harijan,* August 18, 1940.
[28] *Harijan,* January 18, 1942.
[29] *Harijan,* August 11, 1940.
[30] Pyarelal, *Mahatma Gandhi: The Last Phase,* Volume II, Chapter 25, pp. 808–809.
[31] *Ibid.,* p. 808.

There have been cataclysmic changes in the world. Do I still adhere to my faith in Truth and Non-violence? Has not the atom bomb exploded that faith? Not only has it not done so but it has clearly demonstrated to me that the twins constitute the mightiest force in the world. Before them, the atom bomb is of no effect. The opposing forces are wholly different in kind, the one moral and spiritual, the other physical and material. The one is infinitely superior to the other, which by its very nature has an end. The force of the spirit is ever progressive and endless. Its full expression makes it unconquerable in the world. . . . What is more, that force resides in everybody, man, woman and child, irrespective of the color of the skin. Only in many it lies dormant, but it is capable of being awakened by judicious training.[32]

It has been suggested by American friends that the atom bomb will bring in Ahimsa [Non-violence] as nothing else can. It will, if it is meant that its destructive power will so disgust the world that it will turn away from violence for the time being. This is very like a man glutting himself with dainties to the point of nausea and turning away from them, only to return with redoubled zeal after the effect of nausea is well over. Precisely in the same manner will the world return to violence with renewed zeal after the effect of disgust is worn out.

So far as I can see, the atomic bomb has deadened the finest feeling that has sustained mankind for ages. There used to be the so-called laws of war which made it tolerable. Now we know the naked truth. War knows no law except that of might. The atom bomb brought an empty victory to the allied armies but it resulted for the time being in destroying the soul of Japan. What has happened to the soul of the destroying nation is yet too early to see. . . . I assume that Japan's greed was the more unworthy [ambition]. But the greater unworthiness conferred no right on the less unworthy of destroying without mercy men, women and children of Japan in a particular area.

The moral to be legitimately drawn from the supreme tragedy of the bomb is that it will not be destroyed by counter-bombs even as violence cannot be by counter-violence. Mankind has to get out of violence only through non-violence. Hatred can be overcome only

[32] *Harijan*, February 10, 1946.

by love. Counter-hatred only increases the surface as well as the depth of hatred. . . .[33]

We have to make truth and non-violence not matters for mere individual practice but for practice by groups and communities and nations. That at any rate is my dream. . . .[34]

[Before] general disarmament . . . commences . . . some nation will have to dare to disarm herself and take large risks. The level of non-violence in that nation, if that event happily comes to pass, will naturally have risen so high as to command universal respect. Her judgments will be unerring, her decisions firm, her capacity for heroic self-sacrifice will be great, and she will want to live as much for other nations as for herself.[35]

[33] *Harijan,* July 7, 1946.
[34] *Harijan,* March 2, 1940.
[35] *Young India,* October 8, 1925.

27

"QUIT INDIA"

[The day the Second World War started, England took India into the war by proclamation without consulting any Indians. India resented this additional proof of foreign control.

The day after the war's beginning, Gandhi pledged publicly that he would not embarrass the British government. He would also lend moral support to England and her allies. Even one who disapproves of war should distinguish between aggressor and defender.

"Should the thought of consequences that might accrue to the enemy as a result of your non-violence at all constrain you?" Gandhi was asked by an American visitor, Dr. Benjamin Mays, President of Morehouse College, in 1937.]

Certainly. You may have to suspend your movement. . . .[1]

. . . I am and have always been a friend of the British. Therefore I could never use the weapon of Civil Disobedience during the war unless there was a very grave reason, as for instance the thwarting of India's natural right to freedom.

[If] I wanted to do it, I could start Civil Disobedience today on the strength of my supposed influence with the masses. But I would be doing so merely to embarrass the British Government. This cannot be my object. . . . It is my conviction that we cannot improve the food situation and alleviate the suffering of the people unless power and responsibility are transferred from the British into Indian hands. Without such a transfer, the attempt of Congressmen and others to alleviate the people's sufferings are most likely to lead to conflicts with the Government.[2]

---

[1] *Harijan,* March 20, 1937.
[2] Interview with Stuart Gelder, a journalist, July 4, 1944, in M. K. Gandhi, *Gandhiji's Correspondence with the Government, 1944–1947,* Appendix I, pp. 283–284.

Q. [Louis Fischer] It seems to me that the British cannot possibly withdraw altogether. That would mean making a present of India to Japan. . . . You do not mean, do you, that they must also withdraw their armies?

A. [Gandhi] No, Britain and America and other countries too can keep their armies here and use Indian territory as a base for military operations. I do not wish Japan to win the war. I do not want the Axis to win. But I am sure that Britain cannot win unless the Indian people become free. Britain is weaker and Britain is morally indefensible while she rules India. I do not wish to humiliate England.[3]

. . . I see no reason why the presence of [British troops in India] should, in any shape or form, affect the feeling of real freedom. Did the French feel differently when during the last war the English troops were operating in France? When my master of yesterday becomes my equal and lives in my house on my own terms, surely his presence cannot detract from my freedom. Nay, I may profit by his presence which I have permitted.[4]

[Thousands of Indian refugees were straggling out of Burma to escape the conquering Japanese. Japan was next door to India. England apparently lacked the strength to protect India from invasion. Gandhi wrote an open letter "To the Japanese."]

I must confess at the outset that though I have no ill will against you, I intensely dislike your attack upon China. From your lofty height you have descended to imperial ambition. You will fail to realize that ambition and may become the authors of the dismemberment of Asia, thus unwittingly preventing World Federation and brotherhood without which there can be no hope for humanity.

Ever since I was a lad of eighteen studying in London, over fifty years ago, I learnt, through the writings of the late Sir Edwin Arnold, to prize the many excellent qualities of your nation. I was thrilled when in South Africa I learnt of your brilliant victory over Russian arms. After my return to India from South Africa in 1915,

[3] Talk with Louis Fischer, June 5, 1942, in Louis Fischer, *A Week with Gandhi*, pp. 31–32.
[4] *Harijan,* July 19, 1942.

I came in close touch with Japanese monks who lived as members of our Ashram from time to time. One of them became a valuable member of the Ashram in Sevagram, and his application to duty, his dignified bearing, his unfailing devotion to daily worship, affability, unruffledness under varying circumstances, and his natural smile which was positive evidence of his inner peace had endeared him to all of us. And now that owing to your declaration of war against Great Britain he has been taken away from us, we miss him as a dear co-worker. He has left behind him as a memory his daily prayer and his little drum, to the accompaniment of which we open our morning and evening prayers.

If I were a free man, and if you allowed me to come to your country, frail though I am, I would not mind risking my health, maybe my life, to come to your country to plead with you to desist from the wrong you are doing to China and the world, and therefore to yourself.

But I enjoy no such freedom. And we are in the unique position of having to resist an imperialism that we detest no less than yours and Nazism. Our resistance to it does not mean harm to the British people. We seek to convert them. Ours is an unarmed revolt against British rule. . . .

To Britain and the Allies we have appealed in the name of justice, in proof of their professions, and in their own self-interest. To you I appeal in the name of humanity. It is a marvel to me that you do not see that ruthless warfare is nobody's monopoly. If not the Allies, some other power will certainly improve upon your method and beat you with your own weapon. Even if you win you will leave no legacy to your people of which they would feel proud. They cannot take pride in a recital of cruel deeds, however skillfully achieved.

Even if you win it will not prove that you were in the right; it will prove only that your power of destruction was greater. . . .

Our appeal to Britain is coupled with the offer of Free India's willingness to let the Allies retain their troops in India. The offer is made in order to prove that we do not in any way mean to harm the Allied cause, and in order to prevent you from being misled into feeling that you have but to step into the country that Britain has vacated. Needless to repeat that if you cherish any such idea and will carry it out, we will not fail in resisting you with all the might that our country can muster. I address this appeal to you in the hope that our movement may even influence you and your partners in the right direction, and deflect you and them from the course which is bound to end in your moral ruin and the reduction of human beings to robots.

The hope of your response to my appeal is much fainter than that of response from Britain. I know that the British are not devoid of a sense of justice, and they know me. I do not know you enough to be able to judge. All I have read tells me that you listen to no appeal but to the sword. How I wish that you are cruelly misrepresented, and that I shall touch the right chord in your heart! Anyway, I have an undying faith in the responsiveness of human nature. On the strength of that faith I have conceived the impending movement in India, and it is that faith which has prompted this appeal to you.[5]

It is folly to suppose that aggressors can ever be benefactors. The Japanese may free India from the British yoke, but only to put in their own instead. I have always maintained that we should not seek any other Power's help to free India from the British. . . .[6]

[Our] attitude is that of complete non-coöperation with the Japanese army; therefore, we may not help them in any way, nor may we profit by any dealings with them. [We] cannot sell anything to them. If people are not able to face the Japanese army, they will do as armed soldiers do—retire when they are overwhelmed. . . . If, however, the people have not the courage to resist the Japanese unto death, and not the courage and capacity to evacuate the portion invaded by the Japanese, they will do the best they can in the light of instructions. One thing they should never do—to yield willing submission to the Japanese. That will be a cowardly act, and unworthy of freedom-loving people. . . .[7]

[5] This article appeared in *Harijan* and was reprinted in the London *Tribune*, October 23, 1942.

[6] *Harijan,* April 26, 1942.

[7] Letter to Mira Behn, May 31, 1942, in M. K. Gandhi, *Gandhi's Letters to a Disciple,* pp. 213–214.

*   *   *

[What] may have been enough to affect the old occupant would be wholly different from what would be required to keep off the invader. Thus we can disown the authority of the British rulers by refusing taxes, and in a variety of [other] ways. These would be inapplicable to withstand the Japanese onslaught. Therefore, whilst we may be ready to face the Japanese, we may not ask the Britishers to give up their position of vantage merely on the unwarranted supposition that we would succeed by mere non-violent effort in keeping off the Japanese.

Lastly, whilst we must guard ourselves in our own way, our non-violence must preclude us from imposing on the British a strain which must break them. That would be a denial of our whole history for the past twenty-two years.[8]

Non-violence cannot be taught to a person who fears to die and has no power of resistance. A helpless mouse is not non-violent because he is always eaten by pussy. He would gladly eat the murderess if he could but he ever tries to flee. . . . We do not call him a coward because he is made by nature to behave no better than he does. But a man who when faced by danger behaves like a mouse is rightly called a coward. He harbors violence and hatred in his heart and would kill his enemy if he could without hurting himself. . . . Bravery is foreign to his nature. Before he can understand non-violence he has to be taught to stand his ground and even suffer death in the attempt to defend himself. . . . Whilst I may not actually help anyone to retaliate I must not let a coward seek shelter behind non-violence so-called. Not knowing the stuff of which non-violence is made, many have honestly believed that running away from danger every time was a virtue compared to offering resistance, especially when it was fraught with danger to one's life. As a teacher of non-violence I must . . . guard against such an unmanly belief.[9]

Fearlessness connotes freedom from all external fear—fear of disease, bodily injury and death, of dispossession, of losing one's nearest and dearest, of losing reputation or giving offence, and so on. . . .[10]

[8] *Harijan,* July 5, 1942.
[9] *Harijan,* July 20, 1935.
[10] M. K. Gandhi, *From Yeravda Mandir,* Chapter 7, p. 27.

In truth we fear death most, and hence we ultimately submit to superior brute force. . . . Some will resort to bribery, some will crawl on their bellies or submit to other forms of humiliation, and some women will even give their bodies rather than die. Whether we crawl on our bellies or whether a woman yields to the lust of man is symbolic of the same love of life which makes us stoop to anything. Therefore, only he who loses his life shall save it. . . . To enjoy life one should give up the lure of life. . . .[11]

The art of dying follows as a corollary from the art of living.[12]

. . . How can one be compelled to accept slavery? I simply refuse to do the master's bidding. He may torture me, break my bones to atoms, and even kill me. He will then have my dead body, not my obedience. Ultimately, therefore, it is I who am the victor . . . for he has failed in getting me to do what he wanted done.[13]

. . . The nation as a whole has never been and never been claimed to be, non-violent. . . . And what is decisive is that India has not yet demonstrated the non-violence of the strong, such as would be required to withstand a powerful army of invasion. If we had developed that strength, we would have acquired our freedom long ago. . . .[14]

. . . My love of the British is equal to that of my own people. I claim no merit for it, for I have equal love for all mankind without exception. It demands no reciprocity. I own no enemy on earth. That is my creed.[15]

. . . The news about the destruction in England is heart-rending. The Houses of Parliament, the Abbey, the Cathedral seemed to be immortal. . . .[16]

[Winston Churchill was Prime Minister of Great Britain and stirring England to gallant resistance. He had, through the years, made numerous statements against Indian independence. On

[11] *Harijan,* March 1, 1942.

[12] *Harijan,* April 7, 1946.

[13] *Harijan,* June 7, 1942.

[14] *Harijan,* July 19, 1942.

[15] *Bombay Statesman,* August 8, 1942.

[16] Letter to Mira Behn, May 22, 1941, in M. K. Gandhi, *Letters to a Disciple,* p. 205.

November 10, 1942, he issued his famous dictum: "I have not become the King's First Minister in order to preside at the liquidation of the British Empire." Gandhi wrote him a letter.]

You are reported to have the desire to crush the "naked fakir," as you are said to have described me. I have been long trying to be a fakir and that, naked—a more difficult task. I therefore regard the expression as a compliment, though unintended. I approach you then as such, and ask you to trust and use me for the sake of your people and mine and through them those of the world. Your sincere friend. . . .[17]

. . . Perhaps the chief difficulty [in gaining the confidence of the British officials in India] is the opinion reported to have been held by Mr. Churchill. . . . He is said to want to "crush" me, "the naked fakir." The body can be crushed, never the spirit. . . .

[Nothing] dismays or disappoints me. If I represent the truth . . . I know that the wall of distortion and suspicion will topple. . . .[18]

[The American public was disturbed by the low war morale of the Indian people; having been a colony of Britain the United States understood India's aspirations. In London, U.S. Ambassador John G. Winant tried unsuccessfully to dissuade Prime Minister Churchill from stating publicly that the Atlantic Charter's self-government clause did not apply to India. Face to face at the White House and in transatlantic telephone conversations, Roosevelt had discussed India with Churchill and urged him to make an acceptable offer to the Indian people.

Robert E. Sherwood, in his book *Roosevelt and Hopkins,* stated that "Hopkins said a long time later that he did not think that any suggestions from the President to the Prime Minister in the entire war were so wrathfully received as those relating to the solution of the Indian problem. . . ."

Gandhi felt that unless England purged herself by freeing India the war could not be won and the peace could not be won.]

[17] July 17, 1944, in M. K. Gandhi, *Correspondence with the Government, 1944–1947,* p. 11.
[18] Letter to Miss Agatha Harrison, a friend in London, July 13, 1944, *ibid.,* p. 34.

[The] whole of India is a vast prison. The Viceroy is the irresponsible superintendent of the prison with numerous jailers and warders under him. The four hundred millions of India are not the only prisoners. There are others similarly situated in the other parts of the earth under other superintendents.

A jailer is as much a prisoner as his prisoner. There is no doubt a difference. From my point of view he is worse. . . .[19]

. . . A country under alien subjection can have only one political goal, namely, its freedom from that subjection. . . .

. . . The cry of "Quit India" has arisen from a realization of the fact that if India is to shoulder the burden of representing or fighting for the cause of mankind, she must have the glow of freedom now. Has a freezing man ever been warmed by the promise of the warmth of the sunshine coming at some future date?[20]

. . . If the British wish to document their right to win the war and make the world better, they must purify themselves by surrendering power in India. Your President talks about the Four Freedoms. Do they include the freedom to be free? We are asked to fight for democracy in Germany, Italy and Japan. How can we when we haven't got it ourselves?[21]

. . . I cannot work for Allied victory without trust. If they trust us, a settlement will be easy to achieve. Freedom for India will bring hope to Asiatic and other exploited nations. Today there is no hope for the Negroes. But Indian freedom will fill them with hope.[22]

. . . The moment we are free we are transformed into a nation prizing its liberty and defending it with all its might, and therefore helping the Allied cause.[23]

. . . British rule in India in any shape or form must end. Hitherto the rulers have said, "We would gladly retire if we knew to whom

[19] March 7, 1945, Foreword to M. K. Gandhi, *Correspondence with the Government, 1942–1944,* p. xiii.
[20] Letter to Lord Samuel from Detention Camp, May 15, 1943, *ibid.,* p. 100.
[21] Interview with Louis Fischer, June 6, 1942, Louis Fischer, *A Week with Gandhi,* pp. 58–59.
[22] Interview with Stuart Gelder, July 4, 1944, in M. K. Gandhi, *Correspondence with the Government, 1944–1947,* Appendix I, p. 285.
[23] *Harijan,* June 14, 1942.

we should hand over the reins." My answer now is, "Leave India to God. If that is too much, then leave her to anarchy." . . .[24]

[Hatred] injures the hater, never the hated. . . . If we are strong the British become powerless. I am therefore trying to wean the people from their hatred by asking them to develop the strength of mind to invite the British to withdraw. . . . With the British withdrawal the incentive to welcome the Japanese goes. [The] millions of India can resist the Japanese, even without the possession of arms, modern and ancient, if they are properly organized. . . . The British presence invites the Japanese, it promotes communal disunion and other discords, and what is perhaps the worst of all, deepens the hatred born of impotence. Orderly British withdrawal will turn the hatred into affection. . . .[25]

. . . Do the British get from India all they want? What they get today is from an India which they hold in bondage. Think what a difference it would make if India were to participate in the war as a free ally. That freedom, if it is to come, must come today. . . .

. . . How is this mass of humanity to be set aflame in the cause of world deliverance unless and until it has touched and felt freedom? Today there is no life left in them. It has been crushed out of them. If luster has to be restored to their eyes, freedom has to come not tomorrow but today. . . .[26]

. . . America and Britain are very great nations but their greatness will count as dust before the bar of dumb humanity, whether African or Asiatic. They and they alone have the power to undo the wrong. They have no right to talk of human liberty and all else unless they have washed their hands clean of the pollution. The necessary wash will be their surest insurance of success for they will have the good wishes—unexpressed but no less certain—of millions of dumb Asiatics and Africans. Then but not till then, will they be fighting for a new order. This is the reality. . . .[27]

. . . Whether Britain wins or loses, imperialism has to die. It is

[24] *Harijan,* May 24, 1942.
[25] *Harijan,* May 31, 1942.
[26] Speech to the Congress Party, August 8, 1942, M. K. Gandhi, *Correspondence with the Government, 1942–1944,* p. 142.
[27] Talk with Louis Fischer, June 6, 1942, Louis Fischer, *A Week with Gandhi,* pp. 63–64.

certainly of no use now to the British people, whatever it may have been in the past. . . .[28]

. . . The freedom of India means everything for us, but it means also much for the world. For freedom won through non-violence will mean the inauguration of a new order in the world.

There is no hope for mankind in any other way.[29]

[Several hundred Congress Party leaders assembled August 7, 1942. Shortly after midnight of August 8, Gandhi addressed the delegates.]

. . . Every one of you should, from this very moment, consider yourself a free man or woman and even act as if you are free and no longer under the heel of this Imperialism. This is no make-believe. You have to cultivate the spirit of freedom before it comes physically. The chains of a slave are broken the moment he considers himself a free man. He will then tell his master: "I have been your slave all these days but I am no longer that now. You may kill me, but if you do not and if you release me from the bondage, I will ask for nothing more from you. For henceforth, instead of depending upon you, I shall depend upon God for food and clothing. God has given me the urge for freedom and therefore I deem myself to be a free man." . . .[30]

[The delegates went home to sleep. Gandhi, Nehru and scores of others were awakened by the police a few hours later—before sunrise—and carried off to prison. Gandhi was sent into a palace of the Aga Khan at Yeravda. The next day, Kasturbai got herself arrested by announcing that she would address a meeting in Bombay at which Gandhi had been scheduled to speak.

Gandhi spent much time in prison teaching his wife Indian geography and other subjects. He had little success in his persistent efforts to improve her reading and writing of Gujarati. She was seventy-four.

[28] *Harijan,* July 19, 1942.
[29] Introduction to "Draft: Instructions for the Guidance of Civil Resisters," August 7, 1942, M. K. Gandhi, *Correspondence with the Government, 1942–1944,* Addenda IV, p. 356.
[30] *Ibid.,* Number 51, pp. 83–84.

Kasturbai had been ailing, and in December, 1943, she became seriously ill with chronic bronchitis. The Government gave permission for her sons and grandsons to visit her. Ba especially asked for her first-born, Harilal, who had been estranged from his parents.

On February 22, her head resting in Gandhi's lap, she died. At the funeral Gandhi offered a prayer borrowed from Hindu, Parsi, Moslem and Christian scriptures. Devadas lit the pyre. The ashes were buried beside those of Mahadev Desai, Gandhi's secretary, adviser and chronicler for twenty-four years, who had died in prison beside Gandhi a short time before.

When Gandhi returned from the cremation, he sat on his bed in silence and then, from time to time, as the thoughts came, he spoke.]

I cannot imagine life without Ba. . . . Her passing has left a vacuum which never will be filled. . . . We lived together for sixty-two years. . . . And she passed away in my lap. Could it be better? I am happy beyond all measure.[31]

. . . Though for her sake I have welcomed her death as bringing freedom from living agony, I feel the loss more than I had thought I should. We were a couple outside the ordinary. [Continence, after the age of thirty-seven] knit us together as never before. We ceased to be two different entities. . . . The result was that she became truly my *better* half.[32]

. . . I learnt the lesson on non-violence from my wife, when I tried to bend her to my will. Her determined resistance to my will on the one hand, and her quiet submission to the suffering my stupidity involved on the other, ultimately made me ashamed of myself and cured me of my stupidity in thinking that I was born to rule over her, and in the end she became my teacher in non-violence. . . .[33]

[Six weeks after Kasturbai's passing, Gandhi suffered a severe attack of benign tertian malaria, during which he was delirious. At first he thought he could cure it with a fruit-juice diet and fasting.

[31] Louis Fischer, *The Life of Mahatma Gandhi,* Part II, Chapter 39, p. 394.
[32] Letter to the British Viceroy, Lord Wavell, from prison, *ibid.,* p. 394.
[33] *Harijan,* December 24, 1938.

After two days he relented and took quinine, and in two days the fever disappeared.

On May 3, 1944, Gandhi's physicians issued a bulletin saying his anemia was worse and his blood pressure low. Agitation for his release swept India. At 8 A.M. May 6, Gandhi and his associates were released. This was Gandhi's last time in jail. Altogether he spent 2,089 days in Indian and 249 days in South African prisons.]

28

INDEPENDENCE AND SORROW

[The nearer England came to victory the clearer it became that political changes in India could not be delayed.

By 1945, India was too restive to hold, and Britain had suffered too heavily in the war to contemplate the colossal expenditure of men and treasure that would have been required to suppress another non-violent conflict with Gandhi or a violent contest if he lost control.

On July 26, the Labor Party defeated the Conservatives—Clement R. Attlee replaced Winston Churchill as Prime Minister.

On August 14, Japan's surrender was accepted by the Allied Powers. The British Labor Government immediately announced that it sought "an early realization of self-government in India."

Prime Minister Attlee announced that a British Cabinet mission consisting of Lord Pethick-Lawrence, the Secretary of State for India; Sir Stafford Cripps, President of the Board of Trade; and Albert V. Alexander, First Lord of the Admiralty, were coming to India to settle the terms of liberation. Gandhi went to Delhi to meet the British ministers and stayed in the untouchables' slums where Cripps, Pethick-Lawrence and Alexander, as well as many Indians, visited him regularly.

After weeks of study, the Cabinet mission issued a statement: "We were greatly impressed by the very genuine and acute anxiety of the Moslems lest they should find themselves subjected to a perpetual Hindu-majority rule. This has become so strong and widespread amongst the Moslems that it cannot be allayed by mere paper safe-guards. If there is to be internal peace in India it must be secured by measures which will insure to the Moslems a control in all matters vital to their culture, religion and economic and other interests."[1]

---

[1] Louis Fischer, *The Life of Mahatma Gandhi,* Part III, Chapter 42, p. 417.

The division of India—part for the Moslems, part for the Hindus—the mission said, would weaken the country's defenses and violently tear in two its communications and transport systems. "Finally there is the geographical fact that the two halves to the proposed [Moslem] Pakistan State are separated by some seven hundred miles and the communications between them both in war and peace would be dependent on the goodwill of Hindustan. . . ."[2]

Gandhi regarded the vivisection of India as] blasphemy.

[The demand for Pakistan] as put forth by the Moslem League is un-Islamic and I have not hesitated to call it sinful. Islam stands for unity and the brotherhood of mankind, not for disrupting the oneness of the human family. Therefore, those who want to divide India into possibly warring groups are enemies alike of India and Islam. They may cut me to pieces but they cannot make me subscribe to something which I consider to be wrong.[3]

A friend from Eastern Pakistan asks how can I declare myself an inhabitant of undivided India when it is cut into two, and when to be of one part excludes you from the other? Whatever the legal pundits may say, they cannot dominate the mind of man. Who can prevent the friend from declaring himself as a citizen of the world even though legally he is not, and though he may be, as he will be, prevented from entering many States under their laws? Legal status should not worry a man who has not reduced himself to the state of a machine as many of us have. So long as the moral condition is sound, there is no warrant for anxiety. What every one of us has to guard against is the harboring of ill-will against a State or its people. . . .[4]

In actual life, it is impossible to separate us into two nations. We are not two nations. Every Moslem will have a Hindu name if he goes back far enough in his family history. Every Moslem is merely a Hindu who has accepted Islam. That does not create nationality. . . . We in India have a common culture. In the North, Hindi and Urdu are understood by both Hindus and Moslems. In Madras, Hindus and Moslems speak Tamil, and in Bengal, they

[2] *Ibid.,* p. 418.

[3] *Harijan,* October 6, 1946.

[4] Prayer speech, December 15, 1947, in M. K. Gandhi, *Delhi Diary,* Chapter 95, p. 259.

both speak Bengali and neither Hindi nor Urdu. When communal riots take place, they are always provoked by incidents over cows and by religious processions. That means that it is our superstitions that create the trouble and not our separate nationalities.[5]

... We must not cease to aspire, in spite of [the] wild talk, to befriend all Moslems and hold them fast as prisoners of our love.[6]

[If] India is divided she will be lost forever. Therefore ... if India is to remain undivided, Hindus and Moslems must live together in brotherly love, not in hostile camps organized either for defensive action or retaliation. ...[7]

[On August 12, 1946, Lord Wavell, the British Viceroy, commissioned Nehru to form the government. Nehru went to see Mohamed Ali Jinnah, the President of the Moslem League, and offered him a choice of places in the Government for the League. Jinnah refused.

On September 2, Nehru became Prime Minister of India. Jinnah proclaimed September 2 a day of mourning and instructed Moslems to display black flags. The Moslem League announced that it would abstain from the national Constituent Assembly.

The Moslem League had declared August 16 "Direct Action Day." Savage riots lasting four days broke out in Calcutta. "Official estimates," wrote Lord Pethick-Lawrence, "placed the casualties at some five thousand killed and fifteen thousand wounded, and unofficial figures were higher still."[8]

Every day Gandhi preached against the uninterrupted violence between the two communities.]

... Fratricide will not abate by intimidation and violence. ... If through deliberate courage the Hindus had died to a man, that would have been the deliverance of Hinduism and India, and purification for Islam in this land. As it was, a third party [the British] had to intervene. ... Neither the Moslems nor the Hindus ... have gained by the intervention. ...[9]

[5] Conversation with Louis Fischer, June 6, 1942, in Louis Fischer, *A Week with Gandhi,* pp. 45–46.

[6] *Harijan,* October 6, 1946.

[7] Remark to Pyarelal, a co-worker and disciple, in Noakhali, 1947, in Pyarelal, *Mahatma Gandhi: The Last Phase,* Volume I, Chapter 11, p. 405.

[8] Louis Fischer, *Life of Gandhi,* Part III, Chapter 44, p. 443.

[9] *Harijan,* September 8, 1946.

. . . Hindus and Moslems [must] realize that if India is to be an independent nation, one or both must deliberately cease to look to British authority for protection. . . . Whoever wants to drink the ozone of freedom must steel himself against seeking military or police aid. He or they must ever rely upon their own strong arms or what is infinitely better, their strong mind and will, which are independent of arms, their own or others'.[10]

. . . A nation that desires alien troops for its safety, internal or external, or has them imposed upon it, can never be described as independent in any sense of the term. It is an effete nation unfit for self-government. The acid test is that it should be able to stand alone, erect and unbending. During the interim period [while power is being transferred from British hands] we must learn to hop unaided if we are to walk when we are free. We must cease from now to be spoon-fed.

That . . . things are not happening as we would wish is to be accounted as our weakness . . . not the cussedness of the British Government or their people. Whatever we get will be our deserts, not a gift from across the seas. . . .[11]

[The] thirteen-months' stay of British power and British arms are really a hindrance rather than a help because everybody looks for help to the great military machine they have brought into being. . . .[12]

. . . This ancient method of progressing by making mistakes and correcting them is the proper way. Keep a child in cotton wool and you stunt it or kill it. If you will let it develop into a robust man, you will expose his body to all weathers, teaching him how to defy them. Precisely in the same manner, a government worth the name has to show the nation how to face deficits, bad weather and other handicaps of life through its own collective effort instead of its being helped to live effortlessly any how.[13]

I would love to attempt an answer to a question which has been addressed to me from more than one quarter of the globe. It is:

[10] *Harijan,* September 15, 1946.

[11] *Harijan,* June 2, 1946.

[12] Press conference, May 5, 1947, reported by the Associated Press in *Information Cables,* Government of India Information Service, Washington, D.C.

[13] Prayer speech, December 8, 1947, in M. K. Gandhi, *Delhi Diary,* Chapter 88, p. 242.

How can you account to the growing violence among your own people on the part of political parties for the furtherance of political ends? . . . Does your message of non-violence still hold good for the world? . . .

In reply I must confess my bankruptcy, not that of non-violence. . . .

One more question has been and is being asked: If you are certain that India is going the wrong way, why do you associate with the wrongdoers? Why do you not plough your own lovely furrow and have faith that if you are right, your erstwhile friends and followers will seek you out? . . . All I can say is that my faith is as strong as ever. It is quite possible that my technique is faulty. . . . Millions like me may fail to prove the truth in their own lives, that would be their failure, never of the eternal law.[14]

Hope for the future I have never lost and never will. . . . The failure of my technique of non-violence causes no loss of faith in non-violence itself. . . .[15]

There was a time when people listened to me because I showed them how to give fight to the British without arms when they had no arms and the British Government was fully equipped and organized for an armed fight. But today I am told that my non-violence can be of no avail against the [Hindu-Moslem riots] and, therefore, people should arm themselves for self-defence. If this is true, it has to be admitted that our thirty years of non-violent practice was an utter waste of time. We should have from the beginning trained ourselves in the use of arms.

But I do not agree that our thirty years' probation in non-violence has been utterly wasted. It was due to our non-violence, defective though it was, that we were able to bear up under the heaviest repression, and the message of independence penetrated every nook and corner of India. But as our non-violence was the non-violence of the weak, the leaven did not spread. Had we adopted non-violence as the weapon of the strong, because we realize that it was more effective than any other weapon, in fact, the mightiest force in the world, we would have made use of its full potency and not have

[14] Written message for the prayer meeting, June 15, 1947, in D. G. Tendulkar, *Mahatma,* Volume VIII, pp. 22–23.
[15] *Harijan,* November 23, 1947.

discarded it as soon as the fight against the British was over, or we were in a position to wield conventional weapons. . . . If we had the atom bomb, we would have used it against the British.[16]

[Widespread Moslem attacks on Hindus had taken place during October, 1946, in the distant Noakhali and Tippera rural areas of East Bengal. These seemed to alarm the Mahatma more than urban disturbances. Hitherto, interreligious amity had prevailed in India's villages. Gandhi decided to go to Noakhali.]

I find myself in the midst of exaggeration and falsity. I am unable to discover the truth. There's terrible mutual distrust. Oldest friendships have snapped. . . .

My suggestion to the [Moslem] League Ministers is that they should give us one honest and brave Moslem to accompany one equally honest and brave Hindu for each affected village. They should guarantee, at the cost of their lives if need be, the safety of returning Hindu refugees. I am sorry to have to confess that without some such thing it seems to me difficult to induce them to return to their villages. From all accounts received by me, life is not as yet smooth and safe for the minority community in the villages. They, therefore, prefer to live as exiles from their own homes, crops, plantations and surroundings and live on inadequate and ill-balanced doles.[17]

. . . I have no watertight divisions such as religious, political and others. Let us not lose ourselves in the forest of words. Is the tangle to be solved violently or non-violently—that is the question. . . .[18]

[But worse woes were in store. In the neighboring province of Bihar, with a population of thirty-one million Hindus and five million Moslems, the events in Noakhali and Tipper had incensed the majority community. October 25 was declared "Noakhali Day." Thousands of Hindus paraded the streets and country lanes shout-

---

[16] Prayer speech, June 16, 1947, in Pyarelal, *Last Phase,* Volume II, Chapter 14, pp. 326–327.

[17] Interview reported by the Associated Press in the *Bombay Chronicle,* November 22, 1946.

[18] Discussion with disciples just before leaving for Noakhali, in Pyarelal, *Last Phase,* Volume I, Chapter 14, p. 387.

ing "Blood for blood." In the next week, "the number of persons officially verified as killed by rioters," wrote the Delhi correspondent of the London *Times,* was four thousand, five hundred and eighty. Gandhi later put the total at more than ten thousand. The victims were preponderantly Moslem.

Gandhi went to Noakhali to teach the Noakhali Hindus to be brave by being brave with them. He lived in forty-nine villages, rising at four in the morning, walking three or four miles on bare feet to a village, staying there one or two or three days talking and praying with the inhabitants, and then trekking on to the next village. Arriving in a place, he would go to a peasant's hut, preferably a Moslem's hut, and ask to be taken in with his companions. If rebuffed, he would try the next hut. He subsisted on local fruits and vegetables and goat's milk if he could get it. This was his life from November 7, 1946 to March 2, 1947. He had just passed his seventy-seventh birthday.

Gandhi's task in Noakhali consisted in restoring inner calm so that the refugee Hindus could return and feel safe and so that the Moslems would not attack them again.

Gandhi might have sent a message from Delhi or preached a sermon. But he was a man of action. He believed that the difference between what we do and what we could do would suffice to solve most of the world's problems.

The division of India caused the violent deaths of hundreds of thousand of Indians. It caused fifteen million refugees to wander from their homes into distant uncertainty. It provoked the war in Kashmir.

Gandhi saw that no Pakistan was possible unless the Congress Party accepted it, for they could not split India and antagonize the majority in order to please Jinnah and the minority. Nobody listened to Gandhi. The Congress Party leaders were afraid to delay independence.]

This day, 26th January, is Independence Day. This observance was quite appropriate when we were fighting for Independence we had not seen nor handled. Now! We have handled it and we seem to be disillusioned. At least I am, even if you are not.

What are we celebrating today? Surely not our disillusionment. We are entitled to celebrate the hope that the worst is over and that we are on the road to showing the lowliest of the villagers that it means his freedom from serfdom and that he is no longer a serf born to serve the cities and towns of India but that he is destined to exploit the city dwellers for the advertisement of the finished fruits of well-thought-out labors, that he is the salt of the Indian earth, that it means also equality of all classes and creeds, never the domination and superiority of the major community over a minor, however insignificant it may be in number or influence. Let us not defer the hope and make the heart sick. Yet what are the strikes and a variety of lawlessness but a deferring of the hope? These are symptoms of our sickness and weakness. . . . I wonder if we can remain free from the fever of power politics, or the bid for power which afflicts the political world, the East and West. [Let] us permit ourselves to hope that though geographically and politically India is divided into two, at heart we shall ever be friends and brothers helping and respecting one another and be one for the outside world.[19]

[Out of the part of the Punjab assigned to Pakistan, moving in the direction of New Delhi, came millions of Hindus and Sikhs fleeing the knives and clubs of Moslems. Out of the Indian Union, moving toward Pakistan, came millions of Moslems fearing the daggers and lathis of Hindus and Sikhs. Police and even the military were animated by the same passions as the aggressors and often helped them to loot and kill.

The Nehru government set up camps outside Delhi to catch the migrants before they entered the city. Gandhi visited several. He went as often as he could to both Hindu and Moslem camps. He preached self-help.]

[Government] control gives rise to fraud, suppression of truth, intensification of the black market and artificial scarcity. Above all, it unmans the people and deprives them of initiative, it undoes the teaching of self-help they have been learning for a generation. It makes them spoon-fed. This is a tragedy next only, if indeed not equal to, the fratricide on a vast scale and the insane exchange of population resulting in unnecessary deaths, starvation and want of

[19] Prayer speech, January 26, 1948, in M. K. Gandhi, *Delhi Diary,* Chapter 136, pp. 380–381.

proper residence and clothing, more poignant for the coming of inclement weather. . . .[20]

[President Truman advised] the American people that they should eat less bread and thus save the much-needed grain for starving Europe. He added that Americans would not lose in health by the recommended act of self-denial. I tender my congratulations to President Truman on this philanthropic gesture. I must decline . . . the suggestion that at the back of this philanthropy there is a sordid motive of deriving a pecuniary advantage for America. A man must be judged by his action, not the motive prompting it. . . . If many must die of starvation, let us at least earn the credit of having done our best in the way of self-help, which ennobles a nation.[21]

I have not the least doubt that this tragedy can be turned to good account by the correct behavior of the sufferers. . . . In this consummation, I have no doubt that all specially qualified men and women such as doctors, lawyers . . . nurses, traders and bankers should make common cause with the others and lead a coördinated camp life in perfect coöperation, feeling not like helpless dependents on charity, but resourceful, independent men and women making light of their sufferings, a life fully of promise for the future and worthy of imitation by the people amongst whom the camp life is lived. Then, when the professional people have been inured to corporate, unselfish life and when they can be spared from these camps, they would branch out into villages . . . shedding the fragrance of their presence wherever they may happen to be.[22]

. . . I have never recognized the necessity of the military. But that is not to say that nothing good can come out of it. It gives valuable lessons in discipline, corporate existence, sanitation, and an exact time-table containing provision for every useful activity. There is almost pin-drop silence in such camps. . . . I would like our refugee camps to approach that ideal. Then there is no inconvenience, rain or no rain.

[20] Prayer speech, November 3, 1947, *ibid.,* Chapter 53, p. 134.
[21] *Ibid.,* Chapter 25, p. 68.
[22] *Harijan,* December 7, 1947.

These camps become quite inexpensive provided all work, including the building up of this canvas city, is done by the refugees who are their own sweepers, cleaners, road-makers, trench-diggers, cooks, washermen. No work is too low for them. Every variety of work connected with the camp is equally dignified. Careful and enlightened supervision can bring about the desirable and necessary revolution in social life. Then indeed the present calamity would be turned into a blessing in disguise. Then no refugee will become a burden wherever he goes. He will never think of himself alone, but will always think of the whole of his fellow sufferers and never want for himself what his fellows cannot have. This is not to be done by brooding but by prompt action. . . .[23]

The citizens of Delhi and the refugees have a heavy task in front of them. Let them seek occasions for meeting together as often as possible in perfect mutual trust. It was a soul-stirring sight for me to meet Moslem sisters in large numbers yesterday. . . . They were in purdah [heavy veiling of the face], most of them. . . . I suggested that they would not have the purdah before their fathers or brothers. Why should they think me less? And off went the purdah without exception. This is not the first time that the purdah has disappeared before me. I mention the incident to illustrate what genuine love, as I claim mine to be, is able to do. The Hindu and Sikh women should go to the Moslem sisters and establish friendship with them. They should invite them on ceremonial occasions and be invited. Moslem girls and boys should be attracted to common schools, not communal. They should mix in sports. . . . Delhi is poorer for the disappearance of the exquisite workmanship of the Moslems. It is a miserable and miserly thing for the Hindus and Sikhs to wish to take away from them their means of livelihood. . . . In this great country of ours there is room for all. . . . The condition of keeping me in your midst is that all the communities in India live at peace with one another, not by force of arms but that of love, than which there is no better cement to be found in the world.[24]

---

[23] Prayer speech, October 13, 1947, M. K. Gandhi, *Delhi Diary,* Chapter 35, p. 84.

[24] Prayer speech, January 19, 1948, *ibid.,* Chapter 129, pp. 360–361.

*   *   *

[One] will lose nothing by believing. Disbelief is a treacherous mate. Let him beware. For my part, I am unrepentant. I have trusted all my life with my eyes open. I propose to trust [my] Moslem friends too till they prove themselves untrue. Trust begets trust. It gives you strength to combat treachery. . . .[25]

[Like] the brave men and women that we ought to be under hard-earned freedom, we should trust even those whom we may suspect as our enemies. Brave people disdain distrust. . . .[26]

You must not lose faith in humanity. If a few drops are dirty, the ocean does not become dirty.[27]

[October 2, 1947, was the Mahatma's seventy-eighth birthday. Sheaves of telegrams were delivered from abroad and all parts of India.]

Where do congratulations come in? Would it not be more appropriate to send condolences? There is nothing but anguish in my heart. Time was whatever I said the masses followed. Today, mine is a lone voice in India.

Many friends had hoped that I would live to be 125, but I have lost all desire to live long—let alone to 125. I could not live while hatred and killing fill the atmosphere.[28]

[As a Hindu, Gandhi was sternest with Hindus.]

. . . We should never make the mistake of thinking that we never make any mistakes. The bitterest critic is bitter because he has some grudge, fancied or real, against us. We shall set him right if we are patient with him, and whenever the occasion arises, show him his error or correct our own, when we are to be found in error. . . . Undoubtedly, balance is to be preserved. Discrimination is ever necessary. Deliberately mischievous statements have to be ignored. . . .

. . . Nature has so made us that we do not see our backs, it is

---

[25] Prayer speech, December 15, 1947, *ibid.,* Chapter 95, p. 258.

[26] Prayer speech, January 16, 1948, *ibid.,* Chapter 126, pp. 350–351.

[27] Letter to Rajkumari Amrit Kaur, August 29, 1947.

[28] *New York Herald-Tribune,* October 3, 1947.

reserved for others to see them. Hence it is wise to profit by what they see.[29]

... The misdeeds of Hindus in the Union [of India] have to be proclaimed by Hindus from the housetops, if those of the Moslems in Pakistan are to be arrested or stopped.[30]

[The killings in Delhi had ceased. Gandhi's presence in the city had produced its effect. But he was still in "agony." With his fingertips, he sensed the danger of a new wave of riots.

On January 13, 1948, Mahatma Gandhi commenced his last fast. It engraved an image of goodness on India's brain.

The fast, Gandhi declared on the first day, was directed to the conscience of all—to the Hindus and Moslems in the India Union and to the Moslems of Pakistan.]

Each of us should turn the searchlight inward and purify his or her heart as much as possible. ... You should think how best to improve yourselves and work for the good of the country. ... No one can escape death. Then why be afraid of it? In fact, death is a friend who brings deliverance from suffering.[31]

I do not want to die ... of a creeping paralysis of my faculties— a defeated man. An assassin's bullet may put an end to my life. I would welcome it. But I would love, above all, to fade out doing my duty with my last breath.[32]

I believe in the message of truth delivered by all the religious teachers of the world. And it is my constant prayer that I may never have a feeling of anger against my traducers, that even if I fall victim to an assassin's bullet I may deliver up my soul with the remembrance of God upon my lips. I shall be content to be written down an impostor if my lips utter a word of anger or abuse against my assailant at the last moment.[33]

[29] Prayer speech, December 1, 1947, in M. K. Gandhi, *Delhi Diary,* Chapter 81, pp. 222–224.

[30] *Harijan,* December 21, 1947.

[31] All-India Radio broadcast, January 16, 1948, in Louis Fischer, *Life of Gandhi,* Part III, Chapter 49, p. 497.

[32] Conversation with a friend, February, 1947, Pyarelal, *Last Phase,* Volume I, Chapter 22, p. 562.

[33] Speech in New Delhi, 1947, *ibid.,* Volume II, Chapter 5, p. 101.

Have I that non-violence of the brave in me? My death alone will show that. If someone killed me and I died with prayer for the assassin on my lips and God's remembrance and consciousness of His living presence in the sanctuary of my heart, then alone would I be said to have had the non-violence of the brave.[34]

If anybody tried to take out my body in a procession after I died, I would certainly tell them—if my corpse could speak—to spare me and cremate me where I had died.[35]

After I am gone no single person will be able completely to represent me. But a little bit of me will live in many of you. If each puts the cause first and himself last the vacuum will to a large extent be filled.[36]

[His disciple and friend, Rajkumari Amrit Kaur, who was later to become Minister of Health in Independent India, asked Gandhi in January, 1948, "Were there any noises [threats] in your prayer meeting today, Bapu?" This was Gandhi's reply.]

No. . . . If I am to die by the bullet of a madman I must do so smiling. There must be no anger within me. God must be in my heart and on my lips. And you promise me one thing. Should such a thing happen you are not to shed one tear.[37]

Supposing that there is a wave of self-purification throughout India, Pakistan will become pak [peace]. It will be a State in which past wrongs will have been forgotten. . . . Then and not till then shall I repent that I ever called it a sin. . . . I want to live to see that Pakistan not on paper, not in the orations of Pakistani orators, but in the daily life of every Pakistani Moslem. Then the inhabitants of the Union [of India] will forget that there ever was any enmity between them and if I am not mistaken, the Union will proudly copy Pakistan, and if I am alive I shall ask her to excel Pakistan in well-doing. . . .

. . . I remember to have read, I forget whether in the Delhi Fort

[34] Prayer speech in New Delhi, June 16, 1947, *ibid.,* Volume II, Chapter 14, p. 127.

[35] Comment after hearing a Moslem friend had died, 1947, *ibid.,* Volume II, Chapter 17, p. 417.

[36] *Ibid.,* Volume II, Chapter 24, p. 782.

[37] Conversation with friends, January 28, 1948, D. G. Tendulkar, *Mahatma,* Volume VIII, p. 345.

or the Agra Fort, when I visited them in 1896, a verse on one of the gates, which when translated reads: "If there is paradise on earth, it is here, it is here, it is here." That Fort with all its magnificence at its best, was no paradise in my estimation. But I should love to see that verse with justice inscribed on the gates of Pakistan at all the entrances. In such paradise, whether it is in the Union [of India] or Pakistan, there will be neither paupers nor beggars, nor high nor low, neither millionaire employers nor half-starved employees, nor intoxicating drinks nor drugs. There will be the same respect for women as vouchsafed to men, and the chastity and purity of men and women will be jealously guarded. Where every woman, except one's wife, will be treated by men of all religions as mother, sister or daughter, according to her age. Where there will be no untoucha-bility and where there will be equal respect for all faiths. They will be all proudly, joyously and voluntarily bread laborers. I hope everyone who listens to me or reads these lines will forgive me if stretched on my bed and basking in the sun, inhaling life-giving sunshine I allow myself to indulge in this ecstasy. . . .[38]

[Ever since 11 A.M. on January 13, when Gandhi commenced to fast, committees representing numerous communities, organiza-tions and refugee groups in Delhi had been meeting in the house of Dr. Rajendra Prasad, the new Congress President, in an effort to establish real peace. It was not a matter of obtaining signatures to a document. They must make concrete pledges which they knew their followers would carry out. If the pledges were broken, Gandhi could ascertain the fact and then he would fast irrevocably to death.

At last, on the morning of January 18, the pledge was drafted and signed and over a hundred delegates repaired from Prasad's home to Birla House.

There Gandhi agreed and slowly drank eight ounces of orange juice.]

. . . In the name of God we have indulged in lies, massacres of people, without caring whether they were innocent or guilty, men or women, children or infants. We have indulged in abductions, forcible conversions, and we have done all this shamelessly. I am

---

[38] January 14, 1948, M. K. Gandhi, *Delhi Diary,* Chapter 124, pp. 340–342.

not aware if anybody has done these things in the name of Truth.
With that same name on my lips I have broken the fast. . . .
Telegrams after telegrams have come from Pakistan and the
Indian Union to do [so]. I could not resist the counsel of all these
friends. I could not disbelieve their pledge that come what may,
there would be complete friendship between the Hindus, Moslems,
Sikhs, Christians, Parsis and Jews, a friendship not to be broken.
To break that friendship would be to break the nation.

. . . The spirit of [my] vow is sincere friendship between the
Hindus, Moslems and Sikhs of the Union and a similar friendship in Pakistan. . . . If there is darkness in the Union, it would be
folly to expect light in Pakistan. But if the night in the Union is dis-
pelled beyond the shadow of a doubt, it cannot be otherwise in
Pakistan. . . .[39]

. . . Our concern is the act itself, not the result of the action. . . .[40]

---

[39] January 18, 1948, *ibid.*, Chapter 128, pp. 356–357.
[40] Letter to Mira Behn, January 16, 1948, M. K. Gandhi, *Letters to a Disciple,*
p. 228.

29

LAST VICTORY

[The first day after the fast, Gandhi was carried to prayers in a chair. The second day, he again had to be carried to prayers. At question time, a man urged Gandhi to proclaim himself a reincarnation of God.] Sit down and be quiet, [Gandhi replied with a tired smile.[1]

While Gandhi was speaking, the noise of an explosion was heard. People congratulated him for remaining unruffled. The next day, he made this comment.]

I would deserve praise only if I fell as a result of such an explosion and yet retained a smile on my face and no malice against the doer. No one should look down on the misguided youth who had thrown the bomb. He probably looks upon me as an enemy of Hinduism.[2]

[When the grenade failed to reach its target, another conspirator to kill Gandhi came to Delhi.

His name was Nathuram Vinayak Godse. He was thirty-five and the editor and publisher of a Hindu Mahasabha weekly in Poona. Godse was also a high-degree Brahman.

"I sat brooding intensely on the atrocities perpetrated on Hinduism and its dark and deadly future if left to face Islam outside and Gandhi inside," Godse said, "and . . . I decided all of a sudden to take the extreme step. . . ." Godse was bitter that Gandhi made no demands on the Moslems, although he did not hate Gandhi.

Gandhi's prayer meeting on Sunday, January 25, 1948, had an unusually heavy attendance. Gandhi was pleased. It gladdened his

---

[1] Louis Fischer, *The Life of Mahatma Gandhi,* Part III, Chapter 50, p. 539.
[2] *Ibid.,* p. 539.

heart, he said, to be told by Hindu and Moslem friends that Delhi had experienced "a reunion of hearts."

Nathuram Godse was in the front row of the congregation, his hand in his pocket gripping a small pistol.

"I actually wished him well and bowed to him in reverence."

In response to Godse's obeisance and the reverential bows of other members of the congregation, Gandhi touched his palms together, smiled and blessed them. At that moment Godse pulled the trigger. Gandhi fell, and died with a murmur.]

Oh, God.[3]

[The news was conveyed to the country by Prime Minister Nehru by radio.

"The light has gone out of our lives and there is darkness everywhere and I do not quite know what to tell you and how to say it. Our beloved leader, Bapu as we call him, the father of our nation, is no more. Perhaps I am wrong to say that. Nevertheless, we will not see him again as we have seen him these many years. We will not run to him for advice and seek solace from him, and that is a terrible blow not to me only but to millions and millions in this country. And it is difficult to soften the blow by any advice that I or anyone else can give you.

"The light has gone out, I said, and yet I was wrong. For the light that shone in this country was no ordinary light. The light that has illumined this country for these many years will illumine this country for many more years, and a thousand years later that light will still be seen in this country, and the world will see it and it will give solace to innumerable hearts. . . ."[4]

"Mahatma Gandhi was the spokesman for the conscience of all mankind," General George C. Marshall, United States Secretary of State, said.

Albert Einstein declared, "Generations to come, it may be, will scarce believe that such a one as this ever in flesh and blood walked upon this earth."]

[3] *Ibid.,* pp. 504–505.
[4] Government of India, Ministry of Information and Broadcasting, *Homage to Mahatma Gandhi* (New Delhi: Ministry of Information and Broadcasting, 1948), pp. 9–10.

SUGGESTIONS FOR
FURTHER READING

GANDHI, MOHANDAS KARAMCHAND. *An Autobiography: The Story of My Experiments with Truth.* Mahadev Desai, tr. Ahmedabad, India: Navajivan Publishing House, 1927; current ed. with foreword by Sisela Bok, Boston: Beacon Press, 1957, 1993. Gandhi's account of his early life, published serially in *Young India;* stops with 1920. Coverage of the years in South Africa is so sparse as to make little sense without *Satyagraha in South Africa.*

———. *Satyagraha in South Africa.* Valji Govindji Desai, tr. Ahmedabad: Navajivan, 1928; rev. ed. 1950; reprints include: Greenleaf Books, 1979. An invaluable account of Gandhi's development of the "matchless weapon" he called *satyagraha.*

Anthologies & Collections

GANDHI, MOHANDAS KARAMCHAND. *All Men Are Brothers: Life and Thoughts of Mahatma Gandhi as Told in His Own Words.* Krishna Kripalani, ed. UNESCO, 1958; several reprints available. An excellent and very readable anthology; the first chapter is an autobiographical summary drawn from many sources.

———. *Hind Swaraj and Other Writings.* Anthony J. Parel, ed. Cambridge Texts in Modern Politics. Cambridge University Press, 1997. *Hind Swaraj* (1st ed., 1910) is Gandhi's essential summary of the principles on which his movement was based. It and other important pamphlets by Gandhi are available in separate editions as well (see *Resources,* below).

———. *Life and Works of Mahatma Gandhi* ("Multimedia Gandhi"). Publications Division, Govt. of India [1999]. CD-ROM with Gandhi's collected works, including a comprehensive index, together with film and audio clips, hundreds of photos, and reference material. Available through GandhiServe and other sources (see *Resources,* below).

———. *The Mind of Mahatma Gandhi.* R. K. Prabhu and U. R. Rao, eds. Ahmedabad: Navajivan, 1945; 2nd ed. 1967. Several reprints available, including one by Greenleaf Books, 1988.

———. *Selected Works.* Shriman Narayan, ed. 6 vols. Ahmedabad: Navajivan, 1968. A handy set that includes the *Autobiography* and *Satyagraha in South Africa* with other basic works like *Hind Swaraj*.

————. *Vows and Observances*. Berkeley, Calif.: Berkeley Hills Press, 1999 (3rd ed. Navajivan, 1945, as *From Yeravda Mandir: Ashram Observances*). Good summaries of Gandhi's principal practices and their rationale.

Historical Background

WOLPERT, STANLEY. *A New History of India*. Oxford: Oxford University Press, 1977, 1982.

Biographical

EASWARAN, EKNATH. *Gandhi the Man: The Story of His Transformation*. 3rd ed. Tomales, Calif: Nilgiri Press, 1997 (1st ed., 1972). A personal overview focusing on Gandhi's transformation and the sources of his spirituality.

FISCHER, LOUIS. *Gandhi: His Life and Message for the World*. New York: Harper, 1950; New American Library, 1954. A particularly good starting point for studying Gandhi: brief, readable, and straightforward. Fischer makes good use of several long, personal interviews with Gandhi.

————. *The Life of Mahatma Gandhi*. New York: Harper, 1950; HarperCollins, 1983. Fischer's fuller biography.

NANDA, B. R. *Mahatma Gandhi: A Biography*. Delhi: Oxford University Press, 1958. A balanced, authoritative biography by a respected scholar.

PYARELAL [Pyarelal Nair]. *Mahatma Gandhi: Last Phase, 1946–1498*. 2 vols. Navajivan, 1956–1958. Pyarelal was Gandhi's personal secretary after Mahadev Desai's death; this work covers Gandhi's last years in detail, when Pyarelal was at Gandhi's side.

————. *Mahatma Gandhi—The Early Phase*. 4 vols. Navajivan [1965–]. Especially good for the years in South Africa.

SHEEAN, VINCENT. *Lead, Kindly Light*. New York: Random House, 1949. A thoughtful, personal assessment of Gandhi's life and contribution to civilization by an American writer who was with Gandhi at the end of his life.

TENDULKAR, D. G. *Mahatma: Life of Mohandas Karamchand Gandhi*. 8 vols. Publications Division, Govt. of India, 1951–1954. The other extreme from Fischer's short biography. Tendulkar includes a great deal of source material, much of it from Gandhi himself, and often covers events in detail day by day, giving the reader a sense of being present as the story unfolds.

The Bhagavad Gita

The Gospel of Selfless Action, or, The Gita According to Gandhi. Ahmed-abad: Navajivan, 1946. Reprints include: *The Bhagavad Gita According to Gandhi.* John Strohmeier, ed. Introduction by Michael Nagler. Berkeley, Calif: Berkeley Hills Books, 2000. Gandhi's translation of the Bhagavad Gita with an excellent introduction and additional notes by Mahadev Desai, which make the work available to a much wider and more critical audience.

The Bhagavad Gita. Translated and with an introduction by Eknath Easwaran. Vintage Spiritual Classics. New York: Vintage Books, 2000. (Original ed.: Nilgiri Press, 1985)

Resources

Navajivan Trust (Navajivan Publishing House), Ahmedabad 380 014, Gujarat, India. Founded by Gandhi in 1929, Navajivan is the orga-nization to which he assigned all his writings. Online at http://navajivantrust.org.

GandhiServe Foundation (Peter Rühe), Rathausstrasse 51a, 12105 Berlin, Germany. A vast resource for all things related to Gandhi, with solid connections in India and a global sales presence. Online at http://www.gandhiserve.com.

Greenleaf Books (Andrew Harvey), South Acworth, NH 03607, USA. A well-established resource for material on Gandhi and related topics, located on a small farm practicing Gandhian principles.

South Asia Books (Gerald Barrier), P.O. Box 502, Columbia, MO 65205, USA. Another knowledgeable and extensive resource for books by and about Gandhi, as well as India and South Asia generally. Online at http://www.southasiabooks.com.

Many of the books by Gandhi recommended above are available in full text on the Internet. GandhiServe (http://www.gandhiserve.com) main-tains a reliable page of links.

INDEX

Abdulla (Harilal Gandhi), 158
Action, 26, 62–63, 82–83
Afghans, 138
Africa, 282–283 (*See also* South Africa; *specific cities*)
Agra Fort, 320
Agriculturists, 113
Ahimsa, 14, 49, 58, 73, 109–110, 180, 238, 246, 278, 293 (*See also* Love; Non-violence)
Ahmedabad, Ind., 111, 116–117, 125–127, 151, 216–217
Ahmedabad strike, 125–127
Alexander, Albert V., 307
Allied powers, 138, 296, 297–298, 302–304
All-India Home Rule League, 133
Ambulance Corps, 49–50, 109
America, 102, 205, 251, 296, 303
Americans, 201, 234, 280–283, 293, 301, 315
Ampthill, Lord, 103
Amritsar, Ind., 131–132
Anarchists (*See* Revolution)
Aparigraha (*See* Gandhi on his non-possession)
Appeal to Every Briton in South Africa (Gandhi), 39
Arabs, 288
Arjuna, 159–160
Arnold, Sir Edwin, 296–297
Arrests, 86–87, 95, 122–123, 149–150, 179, 228, 236, 304 (*See also* Jail)

Art, 196, 276
Ashrams, 111, 116–119, 149–150, 156, 221–223, 225–227, 246, 273, 297 (*See also* Phoenix Farm)
Asians/Asia, 68, 170, 229, 252, 282, 296, 302–304
Atheism, 14
Atlantic Charter, 301–302
Atomic bomb, 259, 292–293
Attlee, Clement R., 307
Axis Powers, 296 (*See also* Allied Powers)

Babu, Brajkishore, 121–122
Bardoli massacres, 148–149
Beggars, 127, 199–201, 261, 320 (*See also* Poverty)
Bell (*Standard Elocutionist*), 23
Benares University, 111, 244
Besant, Annie, 114, 115, 128
Bhagavad Gita, 26, 54–55, 62–63, 159–160, 162, 201, 202, 224, 237–238, 269–270, 273
Bible, 37, 118, 287
Bihar, Ind., 312–313
Birth control, 209
Blind, the, 200
Body, as a possession, 56
Boer War, 49–50, 52–54, 114
Bolshevism, 175 (*See also* Revolution)
Bombay Government, 104
Books, 238–239
Bose, Subhas Chandra, 225
Bourke-White, Margaret, 292

Boycotts, 135–137, 147, 164,
    196–197, 231–232
Brahmacharya, 57, 210 (*See also*
    Celibacy)
British Conservative Party, 307
British Empire, 40, 49, 101, 108–109,
    114–115, 119, 218 (*See also*
    Imperialism)
British Government, 101–102, 119,
    128–129, 130–132, 142–143,
    145, 149–150, 153–154,
    164–165, 181, 206, 217–218,
    225–227, 230, 233, 259, 295 (*See
    also* British rule)
British Labor Party, 307
British national anthem, 49, 290
British people, 101–102, 103–105,
    151, 167, 168–170, 232–234
British rule, 49, 65, 101–104,
    105–109, 114–115, 119, 121,
    123, 134, 138, 144, 151–153,
    162, 164–165, 166, 167–168,
    176, 206, 215–216, 224–225,
    225–228, 252–253, 262,
    296–300, 302–304,
    309–310 (*See also* British
    Government)
British Secret Service, 136
Broomfield, Justice, 152–153
Buddha, 52, 289
Bunyan, John, 238
Bureau, Paul, 208
Business, 33 (*See also* Capitalists)

Cabinet Mission, 307–308
Calcutta, Ind., 103, 199
Canadians, 105
Capital punishment, 240
Capitalists, 201, 247–249, 250, 255
Caste system, 4, 18–20, 116, 118–119,
    146, 204, 213 (*See also*
    Untouchability)
Celibacy, 53, 62, 210, 305
Chamberlain, Joseph, 39, 52–53
Champaran campaign, 121–127
Chauri Chaura, Ind., 148
Child marriage, 8–10, 212–213

Children, 27, 41, 61, 92, 124–125,
    205–206, 216, 228, 262,
    273–274, 284
China, 107, 170, 296–297
Christ, 36, 66, 79–80, 184, 203, 249,
    282
Christian literature, 118
Christianity, 36, 103, 184, 203,
    286–287
Christians, 107, 162, 195
Churches, 187
Churchill, Winston S., 229, 300–301,
    307
Cities, 103, 175, 216–217
Civil Disobedience, 76–80, 121–127,
    129–130, 143–146, 225–226,
    258–260, 295 (*See also* Non-
    cooperation; Non-violence)
"Civil Disobedience" (Thoreau),
    75–76
Civil Resistance (*See* Civil
    Disobedience; Non-
    cooperation)
Civilization, 72–73 (*See also*
    Westernization)
Cleanliness (*See* Sanitation)
Colonialism (*See* Imperialism)
Columbia Broadcasting System,
    230–231
Commissions, 96
Communism, 264–266 (*See also*
    Totalitarianism)
Community spirit, 66–67
Compliments, 270, 275
Confession, 13
Congress Party (*See* Indian National
    Congress)
Congressmen, 191, 193–194,
    196–197, 260–263 (*See also*
    Public workers)
Constitutions, 75
Constructive Program, 125, 171,
    188, 193–194, 215, 258–263 (*See
    also* Village system)
Criminals , 73, 239
Cripps, Sir Stafford, 307
Cunning, 59, 87

Davi, Mavji "Joshiji," 17–18
Death, 81–82, 198, 202, 204, 243,
    278, 291, 299–300, 305, 318–319
Delhi Fort, 319–320
Democracy, 280
Desai, Mahadev, 236, 238, 305
Dharasana Salt Works, 228–229
Dhruva (Principal, Benares
    University), 244
Diet, 211 (See also Gandhi on his
    vegetarianism)
Direct Action Day, 309
Disarmament, 285, 294
Doctors, 108, 113, 261
Drinking, 146, 171, 196, 211–212,
    217, 220–221, 261
Drugs, 171, 211, 261
Dudabhai Family, 117
Duplicity, 59
Durban, S.A., 31, 57
Duryodhana, 159
Duty, 63, 73, 82, 197, 236, 271
Dyer, Reginald E. H., 131–132,
    182

East End, London, 232–233
Education, 73–74, 112, 124–125,
    135–136, 141, 204–206,
    238–239, 261–263 (See also
    Gandhi on his education)
Egypt, 102
Einstein, Dr. Albert, 323
Ellis, Havelock, 208
End and means (See Means)
Enemies, 49, 80 (See also Opponents)
England, 103, 170, 233
English language, 33, 112
English people (See British people)
Englishman (newspaper), 42
Equality, 39–40
Escombe, Harry, 44, 45–46
Europe, 106, 173, 234 (See also
    Westernization)
Evolution, 79–80

Families, 183
Farmers, 108, 113, 121, 130, 141, 192

Fasting, 126–127, 182, 241–246,
    318–320
Finot, Monsieur, 280
Fischer, Louis, 255–256, 295–296
Force, 78–79, 80–81 (See also
    Violence)
Foreigners, 106–107
Forel, 208
France, 296
From Yeravda Mandir (Gandhi), 236
Funds, 84, 193–194
Funerals (See Death)

Gambling, 220–221
Gandhi, Devadas (son), 156–157
Gandhi, Harilal (son), 19, 27, 46,
    156–159
Gandhi, Karamchand "Kaba"
    (father), 5, 13–16
Gandhi, Kasturbai (wife)
    celibacy agreement with, 62, 305
    death, 305
    jailing, 93–94, 304
    non-possession, 54–55
    quarrels, 9, 51, 57, 269
    separations, 9–10, 19, 30, 53
    studies, 16, 27, 304
    wedding, 8–9
Gandhi, Laxmidas (brother), 28–29,
    56
Gandhi, Maganlal (cousin), 77
Gandhi, Manilal (son), 30, 46,
    156–157
Gandhi, Putlibai (mother), 5–6,
    16–17, 27, 118
Gandhi, Tulsidas (uncle), 4–5
Gandhi, Uttamchand "Ota"
    (grandfather), 4–5
Gandhi on his
    arrests, 95, 122–123, 149–150 (See
    also Arrests; Gandhi on his
    jailings; Jail)
    autograph, 201
    birthday, 317
    caste, 4, 18–20
    celibacy, 62, 210, 305
    character, 23

Gandhi on his (*cont.*)
  childhood, 6–8
  children, 54–55 (*See also*
    Children)
  Congress Party presidency,
    190–197
  dancing lessons, 22–23, 25
  dress, 21–23, 47–48, 89, 139, 232
  education, 7–8, 10, 17, 22–23,
    25–26, 238–239, 272–273
  English, 10, 23
  family, 17, 25, 55–56, 156–159 (*See
    also* Gandhi on his children)
  fasts, 126–127, 182, 241–246,
    318–320
  fears, 6–7, 11, 81–82, 188
  followers, 189–190, 270, 272, 278
  fund handling, 25–26, 47–48
  health, 10–11, 272 (*See also*
    Gandhi's health)
  humility, 179–180
  humor, 270, 276
  jailings, 88–89, 149–150, 161, 228,
    237–240, 273 (*See also* Arrests;
    Gandhi on his arrests)
  law practice, 28, 34, 63–64
  life, 3–4, 206, 275
  life insurance, 54
  limitations, 3
  livelihood (*See* Gandhi on his law
    practice)
  lynching, 44–46
  manual labor, 63, 95, 201
  marriage, 8–10, 27, 30 (*See also*
    Gandhi, Kasturbai)
  mercy killing, 187–188
  music lessons, 22–23
  nationalism, 169–170
  newspapers, 130 (*See also* Harijan;
    Indian Opinion; Navajivan)
  non-cooperation, 122–124, 177,
    181 (*See also* Civil Disobedi-
    ence; Non-cooperation)
  non-possession, 54–57, 61–62, 268
  non-secrecy, 4, 19, 136, 175
  non-violence, 44–46, 57, 151,
    164–166, 311 (*See also* Non-
    violence)

nursing
  brother-in-law, 42
  father, 15–16
opinions, 278–279
opponents, 183, 264, 265–266, 269
patriotism, 169
political work, 3–4, 87, 270
politics, 182–197, 255–256,
  266–267, 270
possessions, 54–57, 61–62, 268
practices, 61–62
principles, 181, 182–197
public work, 63
rebirth, 4, 120
religion, 81, 177, 182, 189, 195,
  199, 201, 241, 269
reputation, 269
sainthood, 174
salvation, 3–4, 36, 120
self-reliance, 271–272
self-respect, 29–30, 31–32
shyness, 6–7, 10, 24–25, 28
silences, 24–25, 207–208, 214
sorrows, 273
spinning, 140, 197, 199, 201 (*See
  also* Spinning)
teaching, 27, 33, 273–274
temper, 48, 210, 276
temple-going, 14
thoughts, 24–25
titles, 3–4, 64, 270–272
train eviction, 31–32, 33
travels, 234–235
trustfulness, 182–183
vegetarianism, 11–13, 21,
  23–24
walks, 10–11, 25
war work, 181
work, 63, 202, 219–220, 234, 269,
  271, 274
writings, 268
Gandhi's health, 160–161, 182,
  305–306, 322
Gandhi's Mahatma title, 3–4, 110,
  270–272
Gandhi's silent year, 207–208,
  214
Gandhism, 278–279

George V, 102, 114, 233
Germans/Germany, 138, 286–289
God, 3–4, 36–37, 53, 55, 63, 81, 90,
    114, 119, 140, 145, 148, 151, 158,
    160, 174, 180, 183, 185–187,
    193, 198–199, 200–201,
    219–220, 225, 240, 242,
    251–252, 269, 271, 274,
    277–278, 290, 304
Godse, Nathuram Vinayak,
    322–323
Government House, 179
Great Trial, 151–153
Greece, 107
Green Pamphlet, 40–41

Halifax, Lord (*See* Irwin, Lord)
Happiness, 56, 64
Harijan, 246
Harijan Sevak Sangh Society, 246
Harijans, 116 (*See also*
    Untouchability)
Hariprasad, Dr., 216
Hartals (*See* Strikes)
Hate, 77–78, 82–83, 104, 169,
    293–294, 303
Heber, Bishop, 203
Hind Swaraj or Indian Home Rule
    (Gandhi), 92, 104–105
Hindu scriptures, 36–37, 118–119,
    159–160, 162, 173, 198–199,
    271, 273 (*See also Bhagavad
    Gita*)
Hindu University Central College,
    111–115
Hinduism, 36–37, 118–119, 183–185,
    198–199, 218–221, 221–223, 241
Hindu-Moslem friendship, 146,
    161–163, 171, 182, 184–185,
    192, 219–220, 231, 308–309,
    317–318, 320–321 (*See also*
    Religious unity)
Hindus, 106–107, 119–120, 161–163,
    168–169, 195, 203, 218–221,
    231, 261, 287, 312–316, 318
Hiroshima, 292–293
History, 79–80
Hitler, Adolf, 285, 289–291

Home Government (*See* Indian
    Self-rule)
Homespun cloth, 139, 192, 196–197,
    232, 250, 260 (*See also*
    Spinning)
Houses of Parliament, 300
Hunter Committee, 131–132
Huxley, Sir Thomas, 79
Hygiene (*See* Sanitation)

Ideal man, 62–63
Imperialism, 71, 164–165, 170–172,
    303–304
Independence, 101–102, 137–138,
    164–169, 171–172, 181, 189, 193–
    194, 215–216, 225, 229–231, 247,
    253, 259–261, 263, 296, 300, 302–
    304 (*See also* Indian Self-rule)
Independence Day, 313
Indian army, 105, 109–110, 115, 137,
    152, 171, 181, 224, 258–259, 286
Indian civilization, 104
Indian constitution, 218
Indian Declaration of
    Independence, 229
Indian Franchise, An Appeal, 39
Indian Home Rule (Gandhi), 92,
    104–105
Indian Mutiny, 151
Indian National Congress, 112, 133,
    142, 144, 146–147, 150,
    188–194, 196–197, 207,
    224–225, 229, 260, 304, 313
Indian Opinion, 58–61, 104
Indian Penal Code, 150, 152
Indian princes, 52, 113
Indian Self-rule, 101–102, 104–105,
    108–109, 112–114, 119–120,
    133, 138, 146–148, 165–166,
    169, 171–172, 176, 193–194,
    212, 218, 248, 258–260,
    261–263, 286, 310 (*See also*
    Independence)
Indian Socialists, 266–267
Indian Union, 318–321
Indifference, 65–66
Indigo farmers (*See* Champaran
    campaign)

Individual effort (*See* Self-reliance)
Industrialization (*See* Machinery)
Inns of Court, London, 23
Intellectuals, 73, 247 (*See also*
    Education)
Ireland, 102
Irwin, Lord, 225–230
Irwin-Gandhi Pact, 230
Islam, 184, 290, 308 (*See also*
    Moslems)

Jail, 64, 88–89, 93–96, 149–150,
    153–156, 159–161, 173, 228,
    237–240, 273, 302, 306
Jallianwalla Bagh, 131–132
Japanese/Japan, 70, 105, 107, 138,
    292–293, 296–299
Jean Christophe (Rolland), 234
Jews, 195, 286–289
Jinnah, Mohamed Ali, 309
Joan of Arc, 66
Johnson, Alan Campbell, 228
Juhu, Ind., 161
Justice, 43

Kallenbach, Herman, 91, 289
Kasmir, Ind., 312
Kaur, Rajkumari Amrit, 277–278,
    319
Khadi (*See* Homespun cloth)
Khilafat workers, 150
Killing animals, 14, 52, 181
Kingdom of God Is Within You
    (Tolstoy), 36, 91–92, 180
Kingsley Hall, London, 232
Koran, 37, 162
Krishna, 159–160, 176
Krishnashanker (teacher), 10

Labor, 63, 73, 92, 95, 110–111,
    140–141, 148, 194–196,
    201–202, 204–205, 247–250,
    254, 260, 266, 271, 273, 275,
    316
Labor strikes, 93–96, 125–127 (*See
    also* Strikes)
Lancashire, Eng., 231–233
Land reform, 255–256

Landlords, 113
Law courts, 108, 121, 138
Laws, 75–76, 79–80, 81, 143, 152,
    212–213, 218 (*See also* Non-
    cooperation)
Lawyers, 37, 60, 108, 113, 121–122
Leaders, 87
Leadership, 95
Lepers, 203, 261
London, Eng., 17–19, 21–26, 103,
    105–109, 230–234
Love, 13–14, 49, 72–73, 77–78,
    79–80, 104, 162–163, 166, 168,
    173, 179–180, 188, 190, 198,
    201, 243, 264, 278, 289, 293
Love-force (*See* Non-cooperation)
Loyalty, 189

Machinery, 103, 106, 141, 249–250,
    253–255, 260–261
Majorities, 67, 82
Manchester Guardian, 229
Manual labor (*See* Labor)
Manu's Laws, 14
Maritzburg Station, S.A., 31–33
Marriage, 8–10, 27, 30, 93–94, 96,
    212–213
Marriage ceremonies, 8–9, 204
Marshall, Gen. George C., 323
Mary (Queen), 102, 233
Materialism, 103, 106, 114, 264–265
Mayo, Katherine, 162, 214–215
Mays, Dr. Benjamin, 295
Means, 63, 98, 103, 109, 132, 166,
    169, 173–174, 189, 261, 266–267
Mehtab, Sheik, 12–13
Miller, Webb, 228–229
Minorities, 82, 133, 280
Morality, 14, 83, 211, 265 (*See also*
    Religion)
Moslem League, 309, 312
Moslem State (*See* Pakistan)
Moslems, 106–107, 119, 128–129,
    161–163, 184, 189, 195, 231,
    307–308, 312–316, 318 (*See also*
    Islam)
Mosques, 187
Mother India (Mayo), 214–215

Mott, Dr. John R., 32
Mudie (Durban official), 68–69
Municipalities (*See* Cities)
Mussolini, Benito, 234–235

Naidu, Mrs. Sarojini, 227, 228
Nature, 69, 276
Navajivan, 130
Nazism, 297
Negroes, 170–171, 280–283
Nehru, Jawaharlal, 161, 225, 254,
    260, 263, 309, 314, 323
Nehru, Motilal, 153
Nehru, Mrs. Swarup Rani, 244
New Delhi, Ind., 318
Newcastle strikers, 93–96
Newspapers, 43, 58–61, 104, 130,
    246
Noakhali, Ind., 312
Non-cooperation, 66, 70–71, 76–
    98, 104–105, 133–136, 138,
    149, 150, 152, 154, 164,
    170–171, 174, 177–181,
    189, 191, 218, 221–223,
    224–225, 233–235, 248, 263,
    282–283, 284–288, 290–
    291, 295, 298, 308 (*See also*
    Civil Disobedience; Non-
    violence)
Non-cooperators, 73, 77–79, 80–84,
    85–86, 89–96, 129–130,
    154–155, 176–179, 274
Non-violence, 44–46, 57, 82–83,
    90–91, 97–98, 129–130,
    132–141, 148–149, 151, 160,
    162, 164–166, 173–178,
    179–181, 201, 211, 220–223,
    220–226, 230–231, 239, 247,
    249–287, 258–261, 264–265,
    276, 280–281, 285–286,
    288–294, 297, 299–300, 304,
    305, 311 (*See also* Ahimsa; Civil
    Disobedience; Non-
    cooperation)

Oath of Resistance, 84–85
Officials, 119, 122–123
Old age, 277

Opponents, 73, 81, 83, 148, 221–222,
    236–237, 239, 259–260, 264,
    274, 290
Oppression, 66–67, 71
Orissa, Ind., 201
Outcasts (*See* Untouchables)

Pacifism, 285 (*See also* Non-violence)
Pakistan
    formation, 308–309, 319–320
    massacres, 309–314, 317
    refugees, 314–316
    religious unity, 308–309, 317–318,
        320–321
Palestine, 286–288
Pariahs (*See* Untouchables)
Parsis, 106–107, 162, 195 (*See also*
    Religious unity)
Passive resistance, 76–80, 132 (*See
    also* Civil Disobedience; Non-
    cooperation; Non-violence)
Patel, Sardar Vallabhbhai, 238
Patience, 219
Patriotism, 80, 143, 169, 216
Pethick-Lawrence, Lord, 307,
    309
Phoenix Farm, 61, 63, 91, 92
Physical training, 10–11, 27
Pickets, 85–87 (*See also* Strikes)
Pilgrim's Progress (Bunyan), 238
Plea for Vegetarianism (Salt), 23–24
Pledges (*See* Vows)
Polak, Henry S. L., 60
Political parties, 148
Political workers (*See* Public
    workers)
Politics, 133–134, 166, 175, 191–195,
    221–222
Poona nationalists, 197
Possessions, 54–56, 155, 200, 205,
    247–248
Poverty, 54, 56, 74, 113–114, 127,
    130, 135, 155, 206, 253 (*See also*
    Beggars)
Prasad, Dr. Rajendra, 320
Prayer, 269, 290
Prejudice, 32–33, 39–40, 48, 65–70,
    72, 75, 170

Prestige, 52
Prison (*See* Jail)
Prohibition (*See* Drinking)
Propaganda (*See* Public opinion)
Prostitution, 204, 213–214, 217
Public opinion, 43, 75, 82, 86–88, 97,
    145, 214, 217
Public workers, 33–34, 50–51,
    53–54, 61, 190, 216 (*See also*
    Congressmen)
Publicity (*See* Secrecy)
Punjab, Ind., 314
Purdah, 316
Puri, Ind., 201
"Puzzle and Its Solution" (Gandhi),
    150

Race, 68–69
Rajagopalachari, C., 128
Reading, Lord, 142, 148–150
Rebirth, 158
Reform, 83, 193, 210–211, 216,
    218–219, 220, 236–237
Refugee camps, 314–316
Reincarnation (*See* Rebirth)
Religion, 4, 57, 106–107, 183–187,
    196, 199, 206, 212, 218–221,
    251–252, 264–265 (*See also*
    Morality)
Religious unity, 106–107, 162–163,
    192, 195 (*See also* Hindu-
    Moslem friendship)
Revolution, 114–115, 175
Revolutionaries, 165
Rolland, Romain, 234
Rome, 107
Roosevelt, Franklin D., 302
Roosevelt and Hopkins (Sherwood),
    301–302
Round Table Conference, 230–234,
    235
Rowlatt, Sidney, 128
Rowlatt Bills, 128, 216
Roy, Dr. P. C., 277
Ruskin, John, 60–61
Russia, 175, 265–266
Russo-Japanese War, 70

Sabarmati, Ind., 111
Sabarmati Ashram (*See* Satyagraha
    Ashram)
Sabarmati prison, 149–150
Salt March, 226–228, 285–286
Salt (*Plea for Vegetarianism*), 23–24
Salt tax, 226
Sanitation, 33, 35, 41, 72, 112–113,
    216–217, 222, 230, 257, 316
Satyagraha (*See* Civil Disobedience;
    Non-violence)
Satyagraha Ashram, 111, 116–119,
    149–150, 156, 225, 226–227, 246
Satyagraha Campaign (*See* South
    Africa Indian Movement)
Satyagrahis (*See* Non-cooperators;
    Non-violence)
Saunders (*The Englishman*), 42
Schools (*See* Education)
Searle, Justice, 93
Secrecy, 59, 157, 266 (*See also* British
    Secret Service)
Segregation, 218 (*See also*
    Untouchability)
Self-reliance, 81, 133, 176–177, 188,
    274, 315
Self-respect, 97, 172, 209–210
Self-rule (*See* Indian self-rule)
Service, 42, 189, 192–193, 194, 217
    (*See also* Public Workers;
    Labor)
Setalvad, Sir Chimanlal, 132
Sevagram Ashram, 273, 297
Sex urge, 15–16, 208–209, 211, 277
    (*See also* Celibacy)
"Shaking the Manes" (Gandhi), 151
Sherwood, Robert E., 301–302
Sheth, Dada Abdulla, 31, 37, 64
Sheth, Tyeb, 37
Shukla, Rajkumar, 121
Sikhs, 162, 195 (*See also* Religious
    unity)
Silence, 24–25, 207–208, 214
Singer sewing machine, 254
Sinha, Dr. Sachchidananda, 22
Slavery, 178, 282–283, 304
Smuts, Jan Christian, 89, 96, 98

Social movements, 87–88 (*See also* Civil Disobedience; Non-cooperation; Non-violence)

Socialism, 266–267

South Africa, 110, 117, 151, 216, 281–282

South Africa Indian Movement
Black Acts, 64–69, 75–77, 86–88, 90
community self-improvement, 35, 59–60, 71–74
conditions now, 98
European public opinion, 87–88
identity certificates, 76, 89–90, 97
marriages invalidated, 93–94, 96
Natal Indian Congress, 34–35, 38–39
native South Africans, 69–70
non-cooperation, 76–78, 80–98
permits, 85–88, 93
Protest March, 94–96
Relief Bill, 96–98
secrecy, 59
traders, 67
Transvaal British Indian Association, 76
Transvaal Government, 64, 76, 92, 95
Transvaal Indian Ordinance, 75–77, 96–97
Union Government, 96
white South Africans, 69–70, 101, 105

Spinning, 139–141, 144, 147, 171, 190, 192–197, 199, 201–202, 204, 205, 222, 250, 260, 263 (*See also* Homespun cloth)

St. Paul's Cathedral, 300

Standard Elocutionist (Bell), 23

Story of My Experiments with Truth (Gandhi), 3

Strikes, 93–96, 125–127, 129, 131

Students, 113, 114, 204–206

Suburbs, 216

Sukkhar barrage, 256

Sundara, Rama, 87

Swami, Becharji, 16–17

Swaraj (*See* Independence; Indian Self-rule)

Tagore, Rabindranath, 110, 225, 229, 241–242

"Tampering with Loyalty" (Gandhi), 150

Taxes, 216

Temperament, 87

Temple of Kali, 52

Temples, 112–113, 187, 221, 243–244

Thoreau, Henry David, 76, 135

Three-point program (*See* Constructive Program)

Thurman, Dr. Howard, 280

Tilak, Bal Gangadhar (Lokamanya), 128, 134, 237

Tippera, Ind., 312–313

Tolstoy, Leo, 36, 91–92, 180

Tolstoy Farm, 61, 63, 91–92

Totalitarianism, 234–235, 289–292 (*See also* Communism)

Toward Moral Bankruptcy (Bureau), 208

Trappists, 207

Triple program (*See* Constructive Program)

Truman, Harry S., 315

Trust, 63, 81, 114, 148, 182–183, 269, 302, 316

Truth, 4, 14–15, 33, 98, 132, 160, 166, 174–175, 178, 183, 185–186, 189, 198, 201, 208, 222, 236–237, 258, 267, 272–273, 293–294

Truth-force (*See* Non-cooperation)

Uka, 118

Unity, 70, 101 (*See also* Religious unity)

Unto This Last (Ruskin), 60–61

Untouchability, 36–37, 116–120, 168, 171, 190, 218–221, 231, 241, 243–244, 246, 287

Untouchables, 41, 73–74, 116–120, 146, 191, 261

Vedas (*See* Hindu scriptures)
Village system, 103, 108, 124–125, 175, 191, 194–197, 204, 206, 253, 255–258, 260–262, 285–286
Violence, 71, 79, 103–104, 132, 137, 143, 175, 183–184, 220, 221–222, 224–225, 239, 261–262, 267, 284, 287–288, 290, 292, 293 (*See also* Non-violence)
Viscount Halifax (Johnson), 228 (*See also* Irwin, Lord)
Volunteers, 41, 84–86, 94, 122, 125
Vote, 80–81, 97, 256–258
Vows, 61–62, 84–85
Vyasa (poet), 160
Vykom Ashram, 221–223

War, 79, 110, 181, 284–286, 289–294
Wavell, Lord F. M. Archibald P., 309
Wealth, 52

West, Albert, 61
Westernization, 67–68, 71, 103–109, 134, 216, 249–253, 254–255, 260–261
Westminster Abbey, 300
White Man's Burden, 65, 282
White supremacy, 71
Winant, John G., 301
Women, 195, 201, 213–214, 261–263, 316
Women's rights, 171
Work (*See* Labor)
World Federation, 296
World War I, 109–110, 137
World War II, 284–304, 307
Worry, 277
Writing, 59–60

Yeravda Central Prison, 153–156, 159–160, 236–246, 304–306
Young India, 130, 150–151, 246, 280

Zulu rebellion, 61

Louis Fischer (1896–1970) was born and educated in Philadelphia. He was sent to Berlin by the New York *Post* in 1921, and during the next twenty-five years he covered many of the most important events in Europe and Asia. He spent several years in Russia and was in India in 1942, 1946, 1948, 1950, 1952, 1954, and 1958; he was an authority on both countries as well as on the Middle East. Outside of Europe and India, his travels took him to every part of the world, including Pakistan, Burma, Siam, Indo-China, Hong Kong, the Philippines, Japan, and Alaska, interviewing and watching virtually every important world leader at work. He was the house guest of Mahatma Gandhi in 1942 and 1946. He knew Roosevelt, Churchill, Stalin, Tito, and Nehru. Fischer edited *The Essential Gandhi* while at the Woodrow Wilson School of Public and International Affairs at Princeton University.

Eknath Easwaran (1911–1999) was director of the Blue Mountain Center of Meditation, which he founded in 1961 in Berkeley, California, after coming to the United States on the Fulbright exchange program as a professor of English literature in 1959. He is the author of many books on the practice of the spiritual life, including *Meditation* (1978), *Gandhi the Man* (1972), and *Take Your Time: Finding Balance in a Hurried World* (1994). This preface was drawn from his many writings and lectures on Mahatma Gandhi.

John F. Thornton is a literary agent, former book editor, and the coeditor, with Katharine Washburn, of *Dumbing Down* (1996) and *Tongues of Angels, Tongues of Men: A Book of Sermons* (1999). He lives in New York City.

Susan B. Varenne is a New York City high-school teacher with a strong avocational interest in and wide experience of spiritual literature (M.A., The University of Chicago Divinity School; Ph.D., Columbia University).